JOHN STAINER

A LIFE IN MUSIC

Music in Britain, 1600–1900

ISSN 1752-1904

Series Editors:
RACHEL COWGILL & PETER HOLMAN
(Leeds University Centre for English Music)

This series provides a forum for the best new work in this area; it takes a deliberately inclusive approach, covering immigrants and emigrants as well as native musicians. Contributions on all aspects of seventeenth-, eighteenth- and nineteenth-century British music studies are welcomed, particularly those placing music in its social and historical contexts, and addressing Britain's musical links with Europe and the rest of the globe.

Proposals or queries should be sent in the first instance to Dr Rachel Cowgill, Professor Peter Holman or Boydell & Brewer at the addresses shown below. All submissions will receive prompt and informed consideration.

Dr Rachel Cowgill, School of Music, University of Leeds, Leeds, LS2 9JT
email: r.e.cowgill@leeds.ac.uk

Professor Peter Holman, School of Music, University of Leeds, Leeds, LS2 9JT
email: p.k.holman@leeds.ac.uk

Boydell & Brewer, PO Box 9, Woodbridge, Suffolk, IP12 3DF
email: editorial@boydell.co.uk

ALREADY PUBLISHED

Lectures on Musical Life
William Sterndale Bennett
edited by Nicholas Temperly, with Yunchung Yang

Portrait of Sir John Stainer by Hubert von Herkomer (1896)

JOHN STAINER

A LIFE IN MUSIC

Jeremy Dibble

THE BOYDELL PRESS

First published 2007
The Boydell Press, Woodbridge

ISBN 978 184383 297 3

The Boydell Press is an imprint of Boydell & Brewer Ltd
PO Box 9, Woodbridge, Suffolk IP12 3DF, UK
and of Boydell & Brewer Inc.
668 Mt Hope Avenue, Rochester, NY 14620, USA
website: www.boydellandbrewer.com

A catalogue record of this publication is available
from the British Library

This publication is printed on acid-free paper

Designed and typeset in Adobe Minion Pro by
David Roberts, Pershore, Worcestershire

Printed in Great Britain by
Antony Rowe Ltd, Chippenham, Wiltshire

For my friend, John Rippin,
an inspirational teacher
and musician

❧ Contents

List of Illustrations

Frontispiece Portrait of Sir John Stainer by Hubert von Herkomer (1896) (by permission of the Chapter of St Paul's Cathedral)

PLATES
(between pp.338 & 339)

Abbreviations

GB-Bco	Birmingham, Royal College of Organists
GB-Bp	Birmingham Public Libraries
GB-BRu	University of Bristol Library, Bristol
GB-CA	Canterbury Cathedral Library
GB-En	National Library of Scotland, Edinburgh
GB-HEr	Hertfordshire Record Office, Hertford
GB-Lam	Royal Academy of Music, London
GB-Lbl	British Library, London
GB-Lsa	Royal Society of Arts, London
GB-Lcm	Royal College of Music, London
GB-LEbc	Brotherton Library, University of Leeds, Leeds
GB-Lgl	Guildhall Library, London
GB-Llp	Lambeth Palace Library, London
GB-Lma	London Metropolitan Archive
GB-Lna	National Archive, Kew, London
GB-Lsp	St Paul's Cathedral Library, London
GB-Lu	London University Library, London
GB-Lwa	Westminster Abbey Library, London
GB-NWr	Norfolk Public Record Office
GB-Ob	Bodleian Library, Oxford
GB-Obac	Balliol College Library, Oxford
GB-Oexc	Exeter College Library, Oxford
GB-Okc	Keble College Library, Oxford
GB-Omc	Magdalen College Library, Oxford
GB-Ooc	Oriel College Library, Oxford
GB-Owoc	Worcester College Library, Oxford
GB-ShP	Shulbrede Priory
GB-WO	Worcester Cathedral Library, Worcester
US-NYpl	New York Public Library
US-NYpm	Pierpont Morgan Library, New York

JRS	John Ranald Stainer
MN	Michael Newsom
RN	Roger Norris

FASHION is only the fringe of the robe of art, the hem of the garment of that mighty power which moves among the struggling mass of mankind, teaching them to value and cultivate those higher qualities and tastes which call forth into life and light a hidden store of tenderness, sympathy and brotherhood. The gentle and refining influence of art can, indeed, make a man something even better than a reasonable or clever being – namely a loveable being … And of all the branches of art, not one is more capable of realising this lofty aim than that which hovers round the cradle, is the handmaid of worship, the pleasure of the home, and hymns its farewell over our grave – Music.

John Stainer, 'The Influence of Fashion
on the Art of Music', 1899

Preface

ANY study of the Victorian musical world and the later nineteenth century sooner or later brings one into contact with John Stainer. A towering figure in the field of Anglican church music and in the nation's 'organ' world, he was also deeply influential in pedagogy, scholarship, the country's institutional development of musical training and the musical lives of London and Oxford. Born three years after Queen Victoria came to the throne (and during the year of her marriage to Prince Albert), he died prematurely at 60, his life spanning her entire reign. In this respect he was the archetypal Victorian composer, embodying many of those central values associated with the era – the supreme position of the cathedral organist, the pre-eminence of the organ loft as the musical *locus* of training and the role of church music as a compositional aspiration.

He died a much-respected man for his contribution to the musical life of the nation – the dinner thrown for him on his retirement from St Paul's in 1888 has rarely if ever been equalled – yet in the Edwardian age, and especially after World War I, he suffered the ignominy of almost total neglect and excoriation from a generation who wanted to turn its back on the composer of *The Crucifixion* and 'High Victorianism' as aberrations of an artistically infertile era and a period of musical values which, as Ernest Walker commented in 1907, were characterised by 'a tide of sentimentalism', 'cheaply sugary harmony' and 'palsied part-writing',[1] and 'whose normal attitude involved the sacrifice by the musician of some of his musicianship in the supposed interest of religion'.[2]

The somewhat inconsistent and often inaccurate appraisals of Fellowes,[3] the loosely dismissive comments of W. M. Atkins, who considered most of Stainer's church music 'deservedly forgotten',[4] the largely damning assessment of

---

[1] E. Walker, *A History of Music in England* (Oxford: Clarendon Press, 1907), 308.

[2] E. Walker, 'A Generation of Music', in *Free Thought and the Musician and Other Essays* (London: Oxford University Press, 1946), 75.

[3] E. Fellowes, *English Cathedral Music from Edward VI to Edward VII* (London: Methuen & Co., 1941), *Memoirs of an Amateur Musician* (London: Methuen & Co., 1946).

[4] W. M. Atkins, 'The Age of Reform: 1831–1934', in *A History of St Paul's Cathedral and the Men Associated with it*, ed. W. R. Matthews & W. M. Atkins (London: Phoenix House, 1957), 273.

Long,[5] Howes' exclusion of his work as a composer in favour of his scholarship,[6] or Caldwell's tepid remarks[7] have done little to help Stainer's cause, yet none of these seemed willing to measure Stainer's music against the musical aesthetic of the times, nor attempt to analyse more closely those essential stylistic features which, with our perspective of a century or more, reveal a potent conduit that links the genius of S. S. Wesley with the late nineteenth-century flowering of Parry, Stanford and even Elgar. Only in Temperley's pioneering *The Music of the English Parish Church* and Gatens's *Victorian Cathedral Music in Theory and Practice* are more balanced and penetrating evaluations of Stainer offered.

More importantly, a study of Stainer in the round, which includes not just his anthems and services but his remarkable madrigals, his songs, his works for soli, chorus and orchestra (which includes not only *The Daughter of Jairus* and *St Mary Magdalen* but also the much earlier *Gideon*), his published writings and his papers (whether for the Church Congress, Musical Association or at Oxford) provides a much more holistically informative context for the nature of his musical language, the scope of his composition and the stylistic confines in which he chose to work.

Moreover, given Stainer's choice, driven by an unshakeable Christian faith, to work within the confines of church music, we not only need to view him as a reformer, especially at St Paul's, but as someone who steadfastly resisted the pressures of widespread nineteenth-century Puritan zealotry to return ecclesiastical music to its 'sixteenth-century home', to plainchant, or to a more Protestant ethic of participation where the notion of the trained choir as intercessor was regarded as alien or unnecessary. In this respect Stainer's church music, be it in the form of anthems, services or hymnody, steered an important course between the restrained idiom of the 'church style' and the Romanticism of his own time in which the discipline of a classical axis (Goss, Attwood and ultimately Mozart) was heavily infused by an emotional and eclectic receptivity for Spohr, Mendelssohn, Schubert, Schumann, Gounod and John Bacchus Dykes, as well as a healthy admiration for Brahms and Wagner.

It is therefore vital to recover Stainer's status as a composer which for so long has been relegated far below those scholarly achievements (for which he has nevertheless rightly been credited), and it is also important within the broader equation of the man's personality and *Weltanschauung* to understand the unusual chemistry of his conflicting imperatives – the conservatism of his High Church religion and the

[5] K. R. Long, *The Music of the English Church* (London: Hodder & Stoughton, 1971).

[6] F. Howes, *The English Musical Renaissance* (London: Secker & Warburg, 1966), 288.

[7] J. Caldwell, *The Oxford History of English Music*, vol. 2: *From 1715 to the Present Day* (Oxford: Oxford University Press, 1999), 308.

conscience of a Gladstonian democratic Liberalism – which produced *The Cruci-fixion*, an edifying 'High Victorian' meditation specifically designed for *parish* resources, yet governed by a perspective of musical excellence on the part of the composer. It was precisely these factors that produced the miniature masterpieces of 'How beautiful upon the mountain', 'God so loved the world' and the hymns 'Love divine' and 'Cross of Jesus', compositions which breathe Stainer's fastidious personality and heartfelt conviction.

ACKNOWLEDGEMENTS

There are many people whom I must thank for their assistance in the completion of this book.

First of all I must thank several of Stainer's many descendants: John Ranald Stainer for letting me scrutinise so many of his grandfather's surviving manu-scripts, letters and other papers; Michael Newsom for allowing me to study his col-lection of letters, manuscripts and photographs; Juliet Dusinberre for her advice; Gareth Stainer for showing me Stainer's presentation batons; Duncan Stainer, Alastair Sampson and David Pennant.

To Jo Wisdom I owe much for his extensive knowledge of the St Paul's Cathe-dral Library – without his guidance I would not have come upon so much crucial documentation new to this study – and to the holdings in the Guildhall Library. The help of Robin Darwall-Smith, both in guiding me around the archives of the Macfarlane Library in Magdalen College and the larger context of Oxford academia in the nineteenth century, was vital. I must also thank Peter Horton, Celia Clarke and Paul Collen of the Royal College of Music, Bridget Palmer of the Royal Academy, Andrew McCrae of the Royal College of Organists, Peter Ward Jones of the Bodleian Library and Kenneth Dunn of the National Library of Scot-land for their help in locating archival materials for me and to the librarians of the British Library, Balliol, Exeter, Keble, Oriel and Worcester Colleges in Oxford as well as Barry Orford at Pusey House. To other libraries I must extend my thanks: to the Norfolk Record Office for access to their archive of Arthur Mann; to Lam-beth Palace Library; to the Royal Society of Arts; to the National Archive at Kew; to Birmingham Central Libraries; to the Pierpont Morgan Library, New York for access to the Sullivan archive; to the libraries of Westminster Abbey, Canterbury Cathedral and Worcester Cathedral and to the staff of the Special Collections of Durham University.

I would also like to take the opportunity to acknowledge the financial assistance of the Arts and Humanities Research Council for making available funds for travel and accommodation (without which the completion of this study would have been more elongated) and Durham University for their award of the Sir Derman

Christopherson Fellowship which provided me with substantial study leave to research the book. I am also grateful to the Dean's Fund of Durham University for making additional funds available to me for publication of this book, and to the Ouseley Trust for their financial assistance.

To my friends, who have taken a special interest in the production, I must make particular mention: to Timothy Storey, whose fascinating study of St Paul's Cathedral Choir provided me with the impetus to embark upon this book in the first place; to Simon King, who gave me much advice and information about the St Paul's choir library; to my colleague Fabrice Fitch for his advice connected with Stainer's early music scholarship; to John Rippin, who engendered a respect in Stainer's music from my years as a schoolboy; to Simon Fleming for bringing a number of Stainer archives to my attention; to Roger Norris for letting me see, and quote from, Stainer letters in his possession; to Giles Brightwell for assisting me with a number of research enquiries in London; to Lucia Gri for help in obtaining information about Stainer's death in Italy; to Patrick Zuk for his assistance with the musical examples; to John Harper and Nicholas Temperley for advice; and to my old friend Anthony Purkiss for the loan of accommodation during my research in Norfolk. I must extend huge thanks to Laura Ponsonby, Ian and Kate Russell at Shulbrede Priory for access to Parry's diaries and letters; their hospitality has always been remarkable.

Completion of this book could not have taken place without the unstinting accommodation offered to me by mother, Pamela Dibble, and, of course, there has always been the indefatigable support of my wife, Alison.

JEREMY DIBBLE
Durham 2006

I ❧ 1840–1857

A Musical Youth:
St Paul's Cathedral (1)

I very much appreciate the kind tone of your letter. I must think over the matter of the biographical notice. My life has been so varied and cast in so many spheres of work that its story would almost make a book. At one time I began to collect notes for an autobiography but my scheme was nipped in the bud by pressing work. I intended to include a lot of illustrations of ceremonies, places, with a few <u>funny</u> sketches illustrating true stories. Your article would just spoil my autobiography – unless you became my Boswell(!) and carried it on.[1]

JOHN Stainer's letter to Frederick George Edwards, organist, writer and editor of the *Musical Times* since 1897, was written in response to one of numerous invitations Edwards had extended, and would continue to extend, to eminent men in Britain's expanding musical profession for a series of leading biographical articles. These commenced in 1898 and concluded five years later in 1903. Stainer's first reaction to Edwards' suggestion of an article had been entirely negative: 'as regards your kind proposal to introduce <u>me</u> into the Mus. Times, I hope you will not be offended if I ask to be excused. Find younger men! it will give them a leg up into the stirrup! Best thanks all the same, for thinking of me.'[2] Yet the subject of biography, indeed autobiography, had been on Stainer's mind prior to Edwards' suggestion for an article, and that he, still only fifty-eight years old, was duly aware of the extraordinary variety of work that had absorbed his life from the age of seven and of the part that he had played in the rapidly burgeoning environment of Britain's musical life. But it seems that Stainer, who by 1898 was close to retirement and desirous of the need to withdraw from the public gaze, required time to dwell on the prospect of a more fulsome biographical intrusion. Edwards' hope, therefore, of a more rapid publication, adjacent to those of Stainer's younger distinguished colleagues – notably Frederick Bridge, Sir Hubert Parry and Charles Villiers Stanford (who were by now all pillars of Britain's musical institutions) – was to be frustrated. Instead, Stainer bided his time, and, with the help of his older children, John Frederick Randall, Edward and Charles Lewis, who had already begun to explore their ancestors in 1890, he attempted to order his thoughts and

---

[1] Letter from Stainer to F. G. Edwards, 19 October 1898, *GB-Lbl* Egerton 3092.
[2] Letter from Stainer to F. G. Edwards, 30 July 1897, *GB-Lbl* Egerton 3092.

memories, a process which is clear from the detailed correspondence that ensued with Edwards. But Stainer was not to be persuaded. In November 1899 his wish to remain a private citizen was reiterated: 'You are very kind, but I must stick to my obstinacy. I really want to sink into private life as soon as I have produced a few things long ago promised to friends'[3] and a *post scriptum* to a letter of December 1900 continued to disappoint Edwards' continued appeals: 'No thank you! I wish to avoid the biographical pages of the M.T. while in the flesh.'[4] Yet Edwards would not be put off, and so implored Stainer to consider the matter during his holiday to France and Italy in early 1901. Writing from Dover, Stainer was to show no weakening of his resolution, but his choice of words was to be eerily prophetic: 'I think you must tell Mr John Paterson that if he will be so good as to wait till I am dead, you will give him a few facts about my life from authentic sources in the Mus. Times within a black border!'[5] On 31 March 1901, to the consternation of his family, friends, and colleagues, John Stainer was unexpectedly and abruptly taken ill and died of heart failure at the Hotel de Londres in Verona. After years of postponement and waiting, Edwards finally found his chance to publish his Stainer article, but this time, within its black border, it served not only as a biographical tribute but as an obituary to his friend and mentor.[6]

There is, nevertheless, some incipient evidence that Stainer quietly pursued the notion of an autobiography. His allusion to 'a few <u>funny</u> sketches illustrating true stories' in his letter of 19 October 1898 appears to have led to the purchase of a sketchbook in Italy, which resulted in one pencil illustration, 'early efforts', portraying the young Stainer when he was tall enough to reach the keys of his father's house organ at their home at No. 2 Broadway, Southwark.[7] From subsequent notes in the form of further pictorial titles, this was clearly intended to be the first of a series of personal sketches which was abruptly curtailed by his unexpected death.[8] How much further Stainer would have taken these sketches to form an autobiographical account of substance is a matter of conjecture. Yet, what is clear from his comments to Edwards, is that, modesty and reticence aside, he sensed that his life

---

[3] Letter from Stainer to F. G. Edwards, 6 November 1899 *GB-Lbl*.

[4] Letter from Stainer to F. G. Edwards, 1 December 1900 *GB-Lbl*.

[5] Letter from Stainer to F. G. Edwards, 28 January 1901 *GB-Lbl*.

[6] See F. G. Edwards, 'John Stainer', *Musical Times* 39 (May 1901), 296–309.

[7] Ibid., 299.

[8] The sketchbook contained the following list of potential illustrations: 'First steps', 'After a successful solo', 'Pursuit of art under difficulties', 'The book closet', 'Praise ye, &c', and 'C. Lockey and the solo' allude to his youthful experiences at St Paul's Cathedral and St Michael's College, Tenbury; and a second section under the heading 'Oxford' with the headings 'The gentleman's tired', 'Corfe's Knocker', 'After the Dead March', and 'A walk with the V.[ice] P.[resident]' surely refers to his time at Magdalen College, Oxford.

had been one of significant achievement and that his 'story' was worth the telling. A twenty-first-century perspective does indeed confirm that Stainer's contribution to the British musical profession and to musical life in general was substantial and lasting, but, more than that, it also provides us with an example of a native musician, who, by dint of his sheer talent, rose from humble beginnings to public exaltation during a period of British history underpinned by political reform and societal change.

John Stainer was born on 6 June 1840 at No. 2 Broadway in Southwark,[9] Surrey (or 'The Borough' as it is often called), renowned, as witnessed by Shakespeare and Dickens, for its many historic inns ('The George', of Elizabethan vintage, and an important eighteenth-century coaching inn which acted as a terminus for traffic and mail from south-eastern England, still survives) and its famous hospital, St Thomas's. With the completion of Westminster Bridge in 1750 and Blackfriars Bridge in 1769, the expansion of Southwark – and its reconstitution as part of South London – inevitably began, but it was later, as industrial developments encroached upon its ancient architecture, particularly in the guise of the London–Croydon, South Eastern, and Brighton Railways, that its marked transformations could be truly observed (and lamented by Walter Bagehot, who foresaw the borough's distinctive character subsumed into London's inexorable expansion). Broadway, a small thoroughfare which ran parallel to and north of St Thomas's Street and close to the old hospital (part of which is now a museum), has long since disappeared through demolition, and its site now lies beneath the southern section of London Bridge Station, the capital's earliest and busiest railway terminus. A commemorative blue signpost still points to the location (now a traffic tunnel) of Broadway, which now bears the name 'Stainer Street'.[10]

9 The date of Stainer's birth, 6 June 1840 has always been accepted by Stainer's family (Edward Stainer notebooks, in private possession JRS). However, Stainer's birth certificate, which was registered by his father, Registrar for the District of St Olave and St Thomas, Southwark, shows the date of his birth as being 13 June 1840. Stainer's mother, Ann, was also Informant. Edwards, who evidently went to Somerset House on 20 April 1901, while writing up his biographical article on Stainer for the *Musical Times*, discovered the discrepancy and consequently contacted J. F. R. Stainer about it. Edwards stated that the Superintendent would not admit to any error, but suggested that 'Mr Stainer (your grandfather) might perchance have made a slip in transcribing the entry for the Somerset House copy.' Correspondence between Somerset House and the Superintendent Registrar of the St Olave's District also confirmed the date of 13 June 1840. John Stainer was baptised at St Thomas's Church on 20 July 1840. (See notes of Edward Stainer, in private possession JRS.)

10 See J. Dusinberre, 'In Search of Stainer Street, Southwark', in D. Pennant, *Surge On!: Stainer Centenary Snapshot* (Woking: Pennant Publishing, 2001), 113–14. The old hospital of St Thomas's was moved to Lambeth in 1862 to make way for railway extensions.

The roots of the Stainer family (or 'Stayner' as it was formerly written down), probably of ancient Saxon origin, are found in the west country, and many of the family members can be traced to a Dorset village, Lydlinch, where some Stainers continued to reside until the twentieth century. It is virtually certain that Stainer's great grandparents were John Stainer and Mary Lovel, who were married at Henstridge, Somerset, in 1745. They had nine children, the youngest of whom, Robert, was baptised at Henstridge in 1764.[11] By the time Robert was in his twenties he had moved to Poole on the Dorset coast. With, as it appears, an eye for entrepreneurial opportunity he resettled in Wing, Buckinghamshire, in 1795 or 1796, where he married Mary Howitt under licence in the nearby village of Hanslope and enjoyed the fortunes of an innkeeper at the 'Cock Inn' in Wing between 1800 and 1805. Robert and Mary had seven children, though it seems likely that only three of them survived into adulthood.[12] The fourth child, William – John Stainer's father – was born on 22 March 1802. He was only three years old when his parents moved again, this time to Ampthill in Bedfordshire, where Robert earned his living in the wine and spirit trade, and indeed he may have continued his occupation as an innkeeper. Life as a publican was further pursued at the 'Bell Inn', Markyate Street in Hertfordshire, an advantageous location for stage-coaches on their way between London and Liverpool, but by 1818 or 1819, when Robert was well into his

[11] In the baptismal register at Henstridge, Robert is listed as being the son of John and *Elizabeth* Stainer, but this is thought by John Ranald Stainer to have been an error (see J. R. Stainer, 'Sir John Stainer's Family Line', in Pennant, *Surge On!*, 24–5). Mary Lovel, baptised at Henstridge on 25 July 1720, was the daughter of John and Elizabeth Lovel; their third child was christened Elizabeth, and it may have been this confusion with names that gave rise to the mistake. Had Mary Stainer (née Lovel) died between the births of their eighth child, James Stainer (baptised at Henstridge, 9 June (or July) 1760) and their ninth, Robert Stainer (baptised on 1 October 1764), she would surely have been buried at Lydlinch or Henstridge, but there is no record of her death at this time. However, the burial of a Mary Stainer is recorded for 6 December 1767, and this was almost certainly Robert's mother. There is also no record of a marriage of John Stainer to an Elizabeth (Edward Stainer's notebooks, in private possession JRS).

[12] Of Robert Stainer's seven children, we know that the first son, Robert, probably born in 1796, was intended for a cabinet-making apprenticeship, but for some reason did not pursue it. He avoided recruitment into the army, and assisted his father in the tallow firm. After his father's death he abandoned the business and became an Excise Officer in Liverpool. John, born on 21 September 1798, lived to a grand age and died in St Alban's in 1883. Mary, born on 27 September 1800, lived only to the age of nine and was buried at Markyate Street in 1809. A pair of twin girls, Jane and Hannah, died in infancy in 1803. The last child, Charles, was born in Wing on 8 January 1805 but survived for only two years, dying at Ampthill in January 1807. (Edward Stainer's notebooks, in private possession JRS.)

fifties, he removed his family to Southwark, where a change of commercial interest was marked by the potentially lucrative purchase of a Tallow Chandlery attached to a property (at No. 2 Broadway) owned by St Thomas's Hospital. Robert Stainer ran the tallow business himself, though he may have intended it for his eldest son (also by the name of Robert). He was a staunch churchman, a Parish Clerk, an Overseer to the Poor, a churchwarden (between 1823 and 1824), and regularly attended vestry meetings between 1820 and 1825. Both he and his wife were buried in St Thomas's churchyard, Mary Stainer in 1825, and Robert in 1832 after a stroke.

In or around 1832 Robert Stainer's original dwelling at No. 2 Broadway was taken by William Stainer, who had evidently been intended for a career in the law. Yet, though he was articled to a solicitor in King Arm's Yard, King William Street, in the City of London, this aspiration appears to have been 'spoiled' by a 'runaway' match with Ann Collier, daughter of William Delves Collier, a hostelry owner whose origins stemmed from the Huguenot weavers who settled in Spital-fields in the seventeenth century.[13] It may be that the union of William Stainer and Ann Collier did not meet with approval from Robert Stainer, for no Stainer signatures appear on the certificate of their (possibly clandestine) marriage, which was 'brought off secretly' at Christ Church, Spitalfields, on 9 November 1823.[14] William was described as a retiring, intelligent man whose nervous disposition was complemented by his wife's more extrovert demeanour.[15] To make a living he joined his brother John in the latter's cabinet-making business in Web Street, Southwark, but, after his brother decided to resettle in Markyate Street, he found employment with St Thomas's Church as a vestry clerk and registrar of births (from 1830) and parish schoolmaster (from 1834). Inheriting property from an aunt in 1854, William was able to retire from his teaching post, but he continued to discharge his church duties until his death in Southwark on 27 April 1867.

William Stainer was, by all accounts, a self-educated man. He was, according to his daughter, Ann, 'a most enthusiastic lover of music',[16] was a capable amateur flautist, a mathematician and linguist, and an ardent bibliophile, spending much of his leisure time visiting antiquarian bookshops. He and his wife had nine

---

[13] The grandfather of William Delves Collier was a William Collier, 'gentleman', who died in Chester in February 1788. He had two sons, William and Matthew. William Collier, the father of William Delves Collier, was a weaver in the areas of Spitalsfield and Shoreditch at the end of the eighteenth century, and his son certainly earned his living as a weaver before becoming the proprietor of the Rose Hostelry in Southwark. His wife, Eleanor Evitt, was also the daughter of a weaver, William Evitt. (Edward Stainer's notebooks.)

[14] Edward Stainer, in his notes, records that the source of the 'runaway match' was William Clark, William Stainer's successor as schoolmaster at St Thomas's.

[15] Edward Stainer's notebooks.

[16] Edwards, 'John Stainer', 297.

children, though three died in infancy. Of these nine, John was the eighth child. He had three surviving older sisters – Ann, Sarah and Mary – the oldest of which was Ann Stainer, born in 1825. His older brother, William, later to be a prominent clergyman to the deaf and dumb, was thirteen years his senior. John, who was so much younger, remained close to both these siblings, who did much in the early years to nurture his musical education. The Stainer house was, according to the Rev. Arthur Whitley, 'a very modest house … no green grass, no budding trees, no sound of singing birds about that neighbourhood! And yet, inside that humble dwelling-place', a sense of duty engendered by an unassailable religious conviction and close ties with the local church at St Thomas's (where all the children were baptised), fraternal affection, 'exuberance of mirth'[17] and strong familial relationships were nourished. The family all clearly learned to enjoy music through the father's self-taught interests. He played the flute in functions at the London Guildhall, and had many admirers. At home he had more than a rudimentary ability on the violin, and he would play hymn tunes on the piano (of which there were up to five in the house at one time).[18] In addition, William, who brought his cabinet-building skills to bear, constructed a small chamber organ (replete with mahogany case and gilt pipes) on which the young John used to play, and the presence of a pedal piano (with a full compass) must also have assisted the early stages of his organ technique. The instrument was almost certainly used by Ann Stainer for she held the position of organist at the chapel of Magdalen Hospital, Streatham, where, according to existing records, she never missed a single service. She was, as witnessed by her younger musical brother, a capable player: 'You will be glad to hear that Annie has really a <u>remarkably</u> good organ to play upon. I was very much pleased with her playing – she pedals so marvellously well.'[19] But, above all, John Stainer revealed musical gifts that were both precocious and prodigious and which, combined with his junior status in the family and his somewhat fragile constitution, led to 'constant care' from his eldest sister and perhaps a degree of additional protective consideration from his mother and father:[20]

> Wearied with his work among the unruly lads of that locality, he [William] would come in, snatch up his violin and solace himself with playing a hymn tune! Little Johnnie frequently came in at such a time, and would sit down at the pianoforte and accompany the good old father with this evening hymn. Of course there was plenty of merriment over it; but I could see clearly

[17] Ibid., 298.

[18] Ibid.

[19] Letter from Stainer to Elizabeth Randall, 19 September 1872, in private possession (MN).

[20] Edwards, 'John Stainer', 297.

enough that the old man was led by the influence of the little beloved disciple. Full of fun himself, a clever punster even at that early age, he nevertheless was the little child that seemed to lead them – his loving and devoted
parents. His dear mother was devotedly fond of her boy, and it would be
difficult for me to name amongst my acquaintances a more devoted, loving
family than the Stainers. To know them made you better.[21]

Since there was no organ in St Thomas's, after services were over in their own
church, William Stainer would take John to St Olave's to hear the church's huge
new instrument. As Stainer explained to Edwards: 'This was close to my old home
and I was often taken by my father, when a little boy (8–10?) to hear the concluding voluntaries at St Olave when our own service was finished at S. Thomas! You
will find an account of the then celebrated organ of S. Olave in the early editions
of Hopkins and Rimbault.'[22] The propinquity of St Olave's was indeed fortunate.
It had for almost twenty years been the home of Henry John Gauntlett, one of
England's most celebrated organists and a man whose great influence had helped
to establish the C organ compass, much preferred in Europe. Moreover, it was
through Gauntlett that a performance tradition of Mendelssohn's organ works
was instilled and promulgated through his mission to see the German System of
organs take root in Britain. Gauntlett's playing at St Olave's was renowned (as was
his advocacy of the 'Anglo-Lutheran or Protestant Organ') and the organ, the most
ambitious scheme he instituted between 1844 and 1846 (begun by H. C. Lincoln
and later completed by William Hill), boasted twenty-seven stops on the Great
Organ, ten on the Swell and three on the Pedal Organ.[23] Stainer may have heard
Gauntlett play at the tender age of six, but it is more likely that he heard Edmund
Chipp (later organist of Ely Cathedral) who, as a celebrated performer of Mendelssohn, succeeded Gauntlett in 1846. More importantly, Gauntlett's assistant had
been the polymath William Pole, a scientist and engineer by profession, and his
musical interests would later provide a profound inspiration for the young Stainer
as he embarked on the first steps of his career.

William and Ann Stainer offered their son for audition at St Paul's Cathedral in
April or May 1848,[24] shortly before his eighth birthday. 'It was because I could play
and extemporise so well that my father took me to be "tried" for a choristership',

[21] Ibid., 298.
[22] Letter from Stainer to F. G. Edwards, 5 January 1901, *GB-Lbl* Egerton 3092.
[23] See N. Thistlethwaite, *The Making of the Victorian Organ* (Cambridge: Cambridge
University Press, 1990), 189, *passim*; see also Appendix, 508–10.
[24] April or May 1848 is the date cited in Edwards, 'John Stainer', and in McNaught's
obituary in the *School Music Review* (1 May 1892, 222). The exact date of Stainer's
entry into the choir is unclear. In several recollections Stainer gave the year as 1847;
it is also the date given in George Grove's article in *Grove 1* (1883) and W. Russell,

Stainer related many years later to the musical journalist W. J. Frost.[25] Just over a year later he was admitted a full chorister in the Dean's vestry and within a short time he was regarded as the choir's most able treble voice. As Frost chronicled: '[He, Stainer] might have injured his digestion for life; half-crowns, crowns, and even half-sovereigns being tumbled into his pockets after having sung a favourite solo – coins eventually destined to provide a surfeit of sundry toothsome yet withal indigestible commodities which go to make the average boy happy.'[26]

Ingress to the choir of St Paul's Cathedral provided John Stainer with a range of important opportunities. First of all, he immediately gained access to a free liberal education, which, given his lower middle class background, was a considerable advantage, not least because it increased the prospect of later entering university or, at least, a lucrative profession; moreover, it was the one sure way of gaining a musical education which was otherwise absent in existing schools. Such education, however, had by Stainer's time of entry into the choir become an important focus of reform. This is a topic that merits some explanation and context.

In the late eighteenth century matters had come to a head when the Almoner – the cathedral officer assigned to the welfare of the choristers – dismissed the boys in protest against the inadequate financial provision made by the cathedral. A thoroughly unsatisfactory situation then transpired: many boys lived at a distance from the cathedral and were completely unsupervised other than during the two daily services or during instruction from the singing master. Appeals to the Dean went unheeded until 1812, when the choristers' welfare was undertaken by William Hawes, a lay clerk in Westminster Abbey, a violinist, and Director of Music at the English Opera House. Hawes boarded the boys, eight in number, at his house at 27 Craven Street in Charing Cross,[27] and later moved his entire household, with the addition of ten choristers from the Chapel Royal, to a new residence close by at 7 Adelphi Terrace in 1817 (also off the Strand). Hawes, who earned part of his living in the theatre, had no compunction in hiring out the boys to sing in theatres, concert halls, oratorio performances, at city dinners, and other similar functions. It was, he claimed, a means of broadening the boys' outlook,

St Paul's under Dean Church and his Associates (London: Francis Griffiths, 1922), 32. But, given his full admission to the choir on 24 June 1849 (when he was nine), Stainer more than likely began his probation in 1848 since probationary periods generally only lasted one year. See P. Charlton, *John Stainer and the Musical Life of Victorian Britain* (Newton Abbot: David & Charles, 1984), 13.

[25] W. J. Frost, 'Early Days of a Celebrated Musician: Half an Hour with Sir John Stainer', *Chums* [1889?], 647.

[26] Ibid.

[27] For some years, only the four senior boys slept at Craven Street and Adelphi Terrace, while the four juniors were day-boarders. Later all eight boarded. See G. L. Prestige, *St Paul's in its Glory* (London: SPCK, 1955), 4.

enriching their musical education, and providing them with experience.[28] His actions were by no means altruistic, since the hire of choristers attracted payments which augmented the meagre fees he received from the Cathedral. It was, nevertheless, something that was of concern to the Dean and Chapter, who by 1811 had come under attack for their lack of care and attention to the choristers. Such an issue was a matter of moral crusade for a local woman, Maria Hackett of Crosby Road, Bishopsgate, who, in that year, rebuked the Bishop of London, the Dean of St Paul's, the Canons in Residence, the Chancellor, Precentor, Junior Cardinal and Almoner in uncompromising yet deeply courteous, eloquent letters, hoping that clerical consciences would be pricked by their neglect not only of the choristers themselves but of ancient ecclesiastical statutes (studied in the British Museum) that promised proper provision.[29] Hackett, a formidable and persistent woman, pressed her case by paying (out of her own pocket) for the publication of letters she had written to the Bishop of London and the Dean of St Paul's in a pamphlet of 1812,[30] and two years later the Master of the Rolls found in her favour in a case that restored property left in trust for the choristers.[31] Hackett, who became affectionately known as the 'Chorister's Friend', was entirely unrepentant about her behaviour and made it clear that she would remain vigilant in future years about the treatment of the St Paul's choristers:

> You need not be afraid that I am at all ambitious to enter into any private correspondence on the subject. That it has not been more public has been merely from a respect to the feelings and the honour of the Chapter. I neither court their approbation nor dread their displeasure, and I wish it to be understood that it is by no means my intention to limit my solicitude to the present set of choristers.[32]

[28] J. S. Bumpus, *The Organists and Composers of St Paul's Cathedral* (London: Bowden, Hudson & Co., 1891), 137ff.

[29] Hackett's twenty-year series of petitions was initiated after she placed a fatherless boy, a Master Wintle, in the choir of St Paul's in 1811 for whom she had guardianship.

[30] See Hackett, *Letters to the Bishop of London, the Dean of St Paul's, and other dignitaries of that church on the present state of the choristers: with evidences respecting the ancient school attached to the Cathedral and observations on Saint Paul's School* (London: printed privately by Nichols, Son and Bentley, 1812). See also Hackett's *Correspondence and Evidences respecting the Ancient Collegiate School attached to St Paul's Cathedral* (London: printed privately by J. B. Nichols & Son, 1816; reprinted and revised, 1832).

[31] See T. Storey, 'Music, 1800–2002', in *St Pauls: The Cathedral Church of London, 604–2004*, ed. D. Keene, A. Burns & A. Saint (New Haven: Yale University Press, 2004), 404.

[32] J. S. Bumpus, 'Miss Hackett and the St Paul's Choristers', scrapbook [p. 165],

She also published her broader critical findings of cathedrals throughout the country in 1824; these undoubtedly made uncomfortable reading for the Church of England and its unreformed hierarchy, not least in that the challenge to an entirely male and patriarchal institution emanated not only from a member of the Church but from a branch of society which traditionally had enjoyed no influence whatsoever.[33]

By the mid-1830s, almost certainly through the moral pressure exerted by Hackett's lobbying, provision for the choirboys had improved a little. Theatre visits were now proscribed, and only properly supervised participation in oratorios or other concert work was allowed; a simple framework of education had been instituted, and a system of suitable care became more imperative for the Almoner (for which Hawes was congratulated by the Chapter):

> The boys rose at 7.30 a.m. (at 8 in winter), ran over the psalms for the day before their breakfast, which consisted of milk, bread, and butter, and so to Cathedral at 9.45. From 11 to 2 they practised music and singing; but on one morning a week the senior boys had an hour's Italian from a master supplied by Miss Hackett. Dinner was at 2, a good square meal, including meat every day, with vegetables and trimmings: half a pint of beer was served, and second glasses if desired. Evensong was at 3.15, then recreation. From 5.30 till 8 p.m. on four weekdays they had a master in to teach reading, writing, arithmetic, and the Church Catechism; but on Wednesdays their time was free, and at the week-end they were allowed to go home between Saturday Evensong and Monday Mattins, at liberty except for attendance at the Sunday services in Cathedral. Supper was at 8 (bread, butter, and beer); bed at 9. If they were engaged to sing at public dinners or in oratorios they were always accompanied, and usually back in school by 9 p.m., oratorios keeping them longer out of bed, but "seldom" after midnight.[34]

Even so, the nagging question of a proper choir-school remained on the agenda of the Dean and Chapter, not least because agitators such as Hackett, who was now assisted by an increasingly interested press and the likes of musical figures such as Elvey, continued their vocal censure. Hawes was not noted for his kindness to the

GB-Lsp. Bumpus also stated that it was Stainer who placed various of Hackett's letters at Bumpus's disposal when the latter was producing articles on the subject for the *Musical Standard*.

33 See M. Hackett, *A Brief Account of Cathedral and Collegiate Schools, with an Abstract of the Statutes and Endowments, respectfully addressed to the Dignitaries of the Established Church* (London: J. Nichols & Son, 1824).

34 Prestige, *St Paul's in its Glory*, 23.

choristers; his meeting out of corporal punishment led, on one occasion, to the removal of William Cummings:

> Mr William Hawes, of flogging notoriety, was the master of the St Paul's boys as well as of the Children of the Chapel Royal. The voice-training methods of this castigating gentleman were original and somewhat after this manner. He would get a dozen boys round him at the grand pianoforte, upon the side of which was duly deposited a whip. The smallest boys were in front, and if any boy sang a wrong note the whip was exercised upon the poor little fellow who happened to be nearest to this unfeeling tyrant. Even the buns with which dear old Miss Hackett was ever treating the St Paul's boys failed to ameliorate the stings of these constant chastisements; and matters ultimately became so outrageously cruel that Cummings's father applied to the Court of Chancery and obtained the release of his son from the whip-loving Mr Hawes.[35]

One of the most energetic of the canons, Archdeacon Hale, believed that the choirboys wasted too much of their time walking between the Cathedral and Adelphi Terrace, and that, in providing more supervised accommodation, the Almoner and the choristers needed to be domiciled in the Chapter House. Hawes remained Master of the Choristers until 1845, but at Michaelmas of that year the boys moved into the Chapter House and, after Hawes's death in 1846, Hale became the new Almoner.

The new regime, which promised to discharge its financial duties appropriately,[36] afforded a singing master, a grammar master, and a matron.[37] However, by the time Stainer was admitted to the choir as a probationer Hale's system had come to an end. In its place, the welfare of the choristers had passed to another minor canon, the Rev. J. H. Coward, who worked under the Almoner's supervision until 1853 when Hale resigned the office. Coward moved into Hale's residentiary house at 1 Amen Court where the boys were educated. They were not, however, boarded there, but were sent home at night. Though the arrangements were not ideal, particularly for the younger, more vulnerable probationers, there was a sense of stability after the disruption of the previous years. Moreover, Hale, conscious of the exigency of reform instilled by the spirit of the Cathedrals Act of 1840, and the increasing pressure of the Ecclesiastical Commissioners, oversaw the formulation of a prospectus in 1849 which consolidated the reforms achieved.[38] The prospectus not only stressed the presence of a school and a salaried grammar master (with a

---

35 'W. Cummings', *Musical Times* 39 (February 1898), 82.
36 See Chapter Minutes, 10 March 1846, *GB-Lsp*.
37 Prestige, *St Paul's in its Glory*, 48.
38 Ibid., 49.

house), but also allowances to the senior choristers of £15, to the junior choristers £12, and to probationers £5 4s. In addition each boy received daily pocket money of 1d, books and two surplices, and by 1853,[39] an apprenticing fee of £30 was made available to all boys for their careers after leaving the choir.

Stainer's routine after joining the choir was the attendance of two daily services at 9.30 a.m. and 3.15 p.m., after which he travelled home by steamboat along the Thames to Southwark. In the intervening time he and the other choristers spent three hours with the grammar master (studying Latin, arithmetic, writing and other staple skills), an hour and a half with the singing master, William Bayley, whose role was not only to train the boys for services but also to teach them musical theory, and they also received some instruction in religion. It was by no means an ideal educational framework, but Stainer, an academically intelligent youth who valued his educational opportunities, later spoke positively of the formative classical training he received at the hands of the cathedral, and acknowledged its worth as a foundation for his arts degree at Oxford.[40] Discipline and standards of behaviour and appearance seem to have been quite strictly enforced. Ineffective musical ability and development might result in dismissal, as might bad language, disobedience or indolence, and allowances might be stopped if boys arrived at the cathedral in an unkempt state.[41] Furthermore, permission had to be sought before any outside engagements were taken on, and all boys (recruited from a wide range of socio-economic backgrounds) were inculcated with a sense of privilege and honour on singing in London's metropolitan cathedral.

Stainer needed little reminding of the position he had secured in St Paul's choir. The piety of his father's background had undoubtedly instilled in him a sure measure of devotion and this sense of spiritual fervour, which genuinely motivated his life, never left him. On 24 June 1849, at the age of nine, he was fully admitted into the choir and joined the ranks of the 'junior' choristers; he was a precocious individual, hardworking and diligent; he possessed 'absolute pitch',[42] was already a capable keyboard player, and conversation, which he always enjoyed, was dominated by the discussion of church music.[43] He was, nevertheless, quite like other boys in his enjoyment of wild adventure and pranks:

> I remember on one occasion – I was a little fellow, and could not have been more than thirteen years of age at the time – I was in the boat [travelling between home and St Paul's], and nearing one of the bridges, the man at the

[39] Chapter Minutes, 9 May 1853, *GB-Lsp*.

[40] See H. Scott Holland, obituary of Sir John Stainer, *Guardian* (10 April 1901).

[41] Prestige, *St Paul's in History*, 50.

[42] See J. Stainer, 'On the Principles of Musical Notation' [5 April 1875], *Proceedings of the Musical Association* 2 (1874–5), 104.

[43] Edwards, 'John Stainer', 298.

wheel discovered that there was no one on deck to lower the funnel. There was no time to spare, and I being the only passenger within call, the skipper requested me to hold the wheel while he jumped down and succeeded in preventing the funnel smashing into the bridge. … I considered myself a man for quite a week afterwards.

I used to be a very bad boy in those days. We were strictly forbidden to climb about in St Paul's, but I often used to get up and sit on the cornice above the choir – a delinquency which, if found out by the schoolmaster, the Rev. J. H. Coward …, would have resulted in corporal punishment, in addition to the writing of certain Latin exercises.[44]

His musical abilities, especially the beauty of his treble voice and his talent as a sight-reader,[45] soon meant that he was involved at the heart of the choir's day-to-day routine as the principal soloist, a status which would help to open up opportunities of meeting others in London's musical world.

The experience and musical education of St Paul's had afforded an early and fundamental level of training to numerous indigenous musicians. Indeed, it was a view held by many in the British musical establishment that it offered the best of educations for the profession. Such a belief was espoused by George Macfarren, composer, and later Principal of the Royal Academy of Music and Professor of Music at Cambridge University:

A cathedral choir is the best cradle for a musician our country affords. I say this from the conviction, many times confirmed, that, as an average, by very far the best practical musicians – those I mean whose musical readiness gives them the air of having music as an instinct or a second nature, those who are ever prompt with their talent to produce or to perform without preparation at the requirement of the moment, those whose ears are quick, whose wits are sharp, and whose utmost ability is ever at their fingers' ends – are they who have passed their art infancy in one of our ecclesiastical arenas for constant practice.[46]

Stainer stood at the end of a long line of significant names in English music since the sixteenth century. William Byrd had reached the position of senior chorister in 1554; Thomas Morley had been in the choir, it is thought, between 1557 and 1604; Thomas Mudd was a chorister in or around 1573, and Thomas Ravenscroft in 1592. In the early eighteenth century Maurice Greene had been a member of the choir

---

44 Frost, 'Early Days of a Celebrated Musician', 647.

45 G. Grove, 'Stainer, John', in *Grove 1*.

46 J. S. Curwen, *Studies in Worship Music (Second Series)* (London: J. Curwen & Sons, 1885), 15.

(from 1706), and subsequently the organist; he was followed by William Boyce (from 1720), John Allcock (*c.* 1725) and Jonathan Battishill (from 1747). Worthy of mention in the nineteenth century are John Hopkins (cousin of John Larkin Hopkins and brother of E. J. Hopkins), who was later organist of Rochester Cathedral (from 1832), William H. Cummings, singer, scholar and future Principal of the Guildhall School of Music (from 1838), William A. Barrett, who was both a chorister (from 1846) and Vicar Choral (from 1867), Thomas Cook (from 1846), who later enjoyed a fruitful career with the Carl Rosa Opera Company between 1874 and 1894, Warwick Jordan, the organist and enthusiastic proponent of the London Gregorian Association, and Henry Gadsby, who joined the choir a year after Stainer in 1849.[47] Over forty years later Gadsby was able to recollect something of their time together in the choir:

> One of our chief diversions on our way home from school was to dance about on the timber logs seasoning in the river by Southwark Bridge, and allow ourselves to be rocked on them by the wash occasioned by the river steamers – and it was a miracle that we did not end our career in a watery grave.
>
> Stainer and I were the only choristers who accepted the offer of Mr William Bayley, the music-master of the boys, to learn harmony – a thing we never regretted. So Stainer and I plodded through Hamilton (the *superfluous* 2nd man)[48] and dear old Goss's Harmony.
>
> I well remember the happy musical evenings we used to spend together as boys at his father's house in St Thomas's Street; little Johnnie playing the Inventions and easy fugues of John Sebastian on the pianoforte. We also used to play pianoforte duets – one of the favourites being the 'Hailstone Chorus.'[49]

In addition, there was ample opportunity to get acquainted with choristers who sang with the St Paul's choristers in services which demanded an augmented choir. The Festival of the Sons of the Clergy at St Paul's was one such occasion which called for extra singers but there were numerous others around the country. Choristers were drawn from St George's Chapel, Windsor, from the chapel choirs of the Oxford and Cambridge colleges, from Westminster Abbey, the Chapel Royal and, later, St Michael's College, Tenbury, as well from other cathedrals such

---

[47] See K. I. Garrett, 'A List of Some of St Paul's Cathedral Choristers before 1873', *Guildhall Studies in London History* 1 (1974), 82–93.

[48] This comment refers to James Alexander Hamilton's widely used *A Catechism of the Rudiments of Harmony and Thorough Bass.*

[49] Edwards, 'John Stainer', 299–300.

as Winchester, Rochester and Canterbury. It was in this way, in part, that Stainer's friendship with Arthur Sullivan was ignited.

Although singing at daily services at St Paul's was undoubtedly of huge benefit to Stainer's developing musicianship and intellect, the general state and efficiency of the choir left much to be desired. During the time of Dean Copleston and the legendary Canon Sydney Smith the standard of music and choral 'deportment' had shown few signs of progress beyond the apathy of Attwood's days. Much of the blame for the indifferent mindset has been laid, all too rashly, at the door of the incumbent organist, based on contemporary notions and experiences of the role of the twentieth-century organist and choirmaster. In truth, the nineteenth-century cathedral organist at St Paul's had only modest influence on the resources at his command, on the music sung, and the level of competence shown by the choristers. Worse still, over the vicars-choral, the men of the choir, he had virtually no power. Both Thomas Attwood, who died in 1838, and John Goss, who succeeded him, were employed almost exclusively to play the organ. Control over the music rested with the Succentor, who at the time of Goss's appointment, was E. G. A. Beckwith, a minor canon. Beckwith did not see eye to eye with the Almoner, Hawes, and legal proceedings were threatened only two months after Goss had taken up his post. So bad, indeed, did things get, that Goss, finding himself in a political storm, was ordered by Chapter 'to play only such music as was enjoined by two other of the minor canons whose judgement was apparently trusted, and to observe "the strictest secrecy" about the whole matter.'[50] It was an intolerable position, and the post of Succentor appears to be been placed in abeyance for some time after this, though by 1847 Chapter wished to see a restoration of the office in order to superintend voice trials.[51] Besides the difficulties with the Succentor, Goss also had little or no jurisdiction over the arrangement for the choir except for the selection of choristers and new vicars-choral. Training and rehearsal of the boys was undertaken by the Almoner or Master of the Choristers; there were no choir practices for the full choir, and the discipline of somewhat recalcitrant vicars-choral, the singing men, remained a thorny problem which aggravated both Chapter and organist.

Moreover, a perception prevailed among the clergy that music ultimately played a secondary role in cathedrals and therefore did not require the attention demanded by its lobbyists. Such a view is clearly articulated by Sydney Smith to Hawes: 'I think the Choir of St Paul's as good as any in England – ... why not be content? you talk of competing with other Cathedrals – but Cathedrals are not to consider themselves as Rival Opera houses. ... It is enough if our music is decent

[50] Prestige, *St Paul's in its Glory*, 21.
[51] Ibid.

... it is of perfect indifference to me whether Westminster bawls louder than St Paul's; we are there to pray, and the singing is a very subordinate consideration.'[52] Hence, though conditions for the choristers may have been a matter of concern for Chapter, the reputation of St Paul's for its musical prowess was considerably less significant.

To a large extent the clergy's unresponsiveness to the standard of music in worship was encouraged by the arrangement and confined location of the services (at the East End of the cathedral), by a slovenly attitude to the liturgy and a general contempt for over-familiar ritual. John Jebb, writing in his *Enquiry into the Liturgical System of the Cathedral and Collegiate Foundations* (1843), was outraged at the level to which St Paul's had fallen, when, on expecting the celebration of Holy Communion, and the presence of numerous clergy, he had, together with other worshippers, been dismissed after the celebrants had dispersed and the altar forsaken.[53] A similar event had been witnessed by the young Frederick Temple, future Archbishop of Canterbury, who, as a young man had remained in the cathedral after Mattins for the communion service.[54] He was then accosted by a verger who, unperturbed, declared: 'I hope, sir, you are not intending to remain for the sacrament, as that will give the Minor Canon the trouble of celebrating, which otherwise he will not do.' Temple then got up and left the cathedral accordingly.[55] Stainer also recalled that, as a choirboy, the widespread attitude at morning and evening service was to get it over with:

Admittance to the Cathedral in those days (except during the hours of Divine

[52] Letter from Sydney Smith to William Hawes, 21 August 1844, *GB-Lgl* MS 10189/1.

[53] J. Jebb, *Enquiry into the Liturgical System of the Cathedral and Collegiate Foundations* (London: 1843), 521 *passim*.

[54] Before the liturgical innovations of the second half of the nineteenth century, the communion service in Anglican churches and cathedrals was much more restricted. The communion service would follow matins and the litany, and the obligatory part of the daily service would be the ante-communion which included the sermon. The second part of the service was used *only* when there was to be an actual celebration of communion, and this was a much rarer event. In musical terms this meant that the choir and organ were only used for the ante-communion service which meant singing the Sanctus as an introit, responses to the ten commandments, the responses to the Gospel, and hymns (or metrical psalms) before and after the sermon. See N. Temperley, *The Music of the English Parish Church* (Cambridge: Cambridge University Press, 1979), vol. 1, 294. At St Paul's the choir would leave the choir directly after the sermon; see W. A. Frost, *Early Recollections of St Paul's Cathedral: A Piece of Autobiography* (London: Simpkin, Marshall, Hamilton, Kent & Co., 1925), 21.

[55] See *Robert Gregory, 1819–1911: being the autobiography of Robert Gregory DD Dean of St Paul's*, ed. W. H. Hutton (London: Longmans, Green & Co., 1912), 160.

service) could only be obtained on the payment of twopence each person. It was in the interest of the vergers to speedily clear the Cathedral after Morning or Evening prayer in order to secure all the 'tuppences' they could. The Minor Canons had a share in these admission and other fees, providing they attended the service on their appointed days. If they were in their places by the time the Venite was reached their attendance was accounted good.[56]

When Stainer entered the choir he would have noticed that services in the vast edifice of the building took place in the restricted space of the east end. Services without music were held in the Morning Chapel, whereas choral ones took place in the Choir, partitioned from the rest of the cathedral by a screen on which stood the Father Smith organ. Daily services sung to a non-existent congregation, in a monastic tradition looking back to pre-Reformation times, was still quite normal. The Choir space, when full, however, could accommodate about 900 people. In terms of general activity the rest of the cathedral was virtually redundant, and the confined space in which the choir sang its largely unexciting and repetitive repertoire was a regressive influence, the dullness of which the novelist Charles Kingsley described with a grey resignation:

> The afternoon service was proceeding. The organ droned sadly in its iron cage to a few musical amateurs; some nursery-maids and foreign sailors stared about within the spiked felon's dock which shut off the body of the cathedral, and tried in vain to hear what was going on inside the choir. As a wise author – a Protestant, too – has lately said, "the scanty service rattled in the vast building like a dried kernel too small for the shell." The place breathed imbecility, and unreality, and sleepy life-in-death, while the whole nineteenth century went roaring on its way outside.[57]

Day after day the choir, dressed in the normal apparel of long surplices, buttoned up to the neck (cassocks were not worn until much later), would muddle to its place for the beginning of the service (there were no prayers, no dignified exit from the vestry, nor procession through the cathedral) replete with latecomers who would inevitably disturb what dignity existed, and there would often be heard 'a *prestissimo* rush of footsteps down the Nave, soon to be followed by the scene of a Minor Canon struggling with a corpulent verger at the entrance of the Choir in order that he (the Minor Canon) might squeeze himself in before "The Lord's Name be praised!" '[58] It was also common practice for the vicars-choral to leave

[56] Edwards, 'John Stainer', 300.
[57] D. C. Lathbury, *Correspondence on Church and Religion of William Ewart Gladstone* (London: John Murray, 1910), 193–4.
[58] Edwards, 'John Stainer', 300.

directly after the sermon, for many of the singers were engaged (either full-time or as deputies) elsewhere in other churches or the Chapel Royal. Stainer, on the point of retirement in 1888, remembered the cathedral's apathy: 'There was one canon, very much respected – I will not mention his name, because he was a kind friend to me as a boy. He said one day, "What are those boys waiting for?" It was said: "They are waiting to walk in before you in order." "I don't like processions, tell them to go in anyhow they like."'[59]

Jebb denounced the choir of St Paul's as 'degenerate' and complained at the absence of anthems and voluntaries at the morning and communions services, and the lack of an anthem when the Litany was sung.[60] There was little curb on the behaviour of the choirboys, as Henry Scott Holland remembered: 'they were weird crabbed days, when the boys could roll their pennies in a race from the Dome to the West Door, down the gaunt, solitary Nave, without fear of obstruction.'[61] Perhaps most degenerate, and antiquated to boot, was the chorister's enduring entitlement to 'spur-money', a tradition stemming from the seventeenth century, when choirboys maintained the right to claim money from any individual entering the cathedral with spurs on his boots. The practice was still in force when Stainer was a choirboy in the late 1840s![62] As Bumpus also tells us: 'When spur money was no longer to be obtained, the boys contrived to squeeze an equivalent by finding the place in the anthem-book, taking the volume to any likely-looking stranger in the stalls, and "waiting" on him until paid to go away.'[63]

One of the most systemic problems which the Dean and Chapter of St Paul's confronted, however, were the duties and status of the vicars-choral. As Prestige reminds us:

> … the vicars were the thirty deputies (as their name implies) of the mainly absentee prebendaries, and were in Holy orders: perhaps a lingering tradition of their clerical status may account for the fact that the vicars-choral were charged with reading the first lesson at the daily capitular services until Chapter transferred that duty to the minor canons in 1769. By the fourteenth century their number had dwindled to six and they were permitted to marry. But, like the minor canons, they still formed an independent body (though without having a common seal of their own); they possessed

[59] 'The Sir John Stainer Dinner', *Musical World* (4 August 1888), 611.

[60] D. Gray, 'Liturgy, 1714–2004', in *St Pauls*, ed. Keene, Burn & Saint, 355.

[61] H. Scott Holland, 'Memorial to John Stainer in St Paul's', *Musical Times* 45 (January 1904), 27.

[62] See G. P. Bevan & J. Stainer, *Handbook to the Cathedral of St Paul* (London: W. Swan Sonnenschein & Co., 1882), 72–3; see also Edwards, 'John Stainer', 300.

[63] J. S. Bumpus, *A History of English Cathedral Music, 1549–1889* (London: T. Werner Laurie, 1909), 105.

corporate estates, and each of the six enjoyed a freehold of his office. One had to be permanently represented by a deputy (paid by Chapter), since the basic stipend of the Cathedral organist was secured by making him a vicar-choral; this odd system continued until 1888.[64]

As Stainer himself declared in adulthood (though he clearly witnessed it as a chorister): '[the] independence made the vicars negligent of their ordinary duties, and careless of the reputation of their Cathedral. They attended irregularly, and were disinclined to bend to any authority whatever.'[65] Moreover, the vicars not only enjoyed a job for life, but, like the boys, had recourse to another anachronistic tradition, this time to a share of the Cupola Fund, a sum of money accrued each year by charging members of the public to see the cupola of the cathedral (it was shared out between vergers, minor canons and vicars-choral),[66] a right they only wished to see commuted if their salaries were increased accordingly.

The behaviour of the vicars was the cause of perennial scandals; the cathedral was frequently caused profound embarrassment by a combination of their inattendance, deteriorating voices and appointment of unsuitable deputies (who often failed to appear for services). Although a rule was established that at least one bass, one tenor and one alto should be present at every service (and a minor canon to keep a record of attendance), this did little to galvanise the vicars. Indeed, in 1843, when an organ recital was taking place at Christ Church, Newgate Street (a church in close vicinity to St Paul's), not one vicar-choral was seen at evensong.[67] 'It is said', Stainer recalled, 'that Handel's chorus, "For unto us a child is born," was sung on a certain Christmas Day by a handful of boys and two men!'[68] Goss, in his parlous predicament, retorted from the organ-loft: 'Do your best, and I will do the rest with the organ.'[69]

An indication of the *impasse* with the vicars-choral is revealed by the disproportionately ample space in Chapter minutes devoted to attempts to establish some method of discipline and authority. It proved largely to be a tortuous, trying and unfruitful course of action. Under a series of reforms, drafted by Sydney Smith but

64 Prestige, *St Paul's in its Glory*, 5–6.

65 Bevan & Stainer, *Handbook to the Cathedral of St Paul*, 77.

66 The Cupola Fund also charged the public incrementally for further sights, including the library, the geometrical staircase, the model-room, the whispering gallery and the two galleries outside below and above the dome; see Prestige, *St Paul's in its Glory*, 56.

67 Ibid., 22.

68 Bevan & Stainer, *Handbook to the Cathedral of St Paul*, 78. Stainer was later to remember that the piece performed at this reprehensible event was the 'Hallelujah' chorus; see Edwards, 'John Stainer', 300.

69 Prestige, *St Paul's in its Glory*, 22.

acted upon by Hale, new vicars-choral (since current ones could not be subject to the reforms) were admitted to the choir in a bid to establish unequivocally their status and obligations. Rules of employment were clearly laid down: a vicar-choral was subject to the authority of the Dean and Chapter; he must abide by the new set of regulations (as drafted by Smith) and any new ones drawn up in the future, and he must accept a retirement age of fifty-five (or earlier if Chapter considered him unfit). In addition the new recruit had to accept that some of his income tradition-ally paid by the Chapter (some £20 a year) needed to be assigned to a pension, and that he would forfeit his position if he took employment elsewhere.[70] These rules were initially accepted by the new vicars for their probationary year, but on acced-ing to their permanent positions, their colleagues, subject to the old contractual arrangements, objected on legal grounds, and Chapter was forced to set the new regulations aside. A further attempt to restrict the freedoms of the vicars took place in 1846 and 1847, when Chapter thought they could deny new vicars their right to freehold,[71] but this failed when the current vicars-choral threatened not to recognise any newcomer to vacant positions. Chapter's only recourse, therefore, was to frame a new statute, enacted in 1848, which sought to keep a stricter record of compliance with the regulations (especially of attendance) and of enforcement by summoning vicars to Chapter for explanation, but it ultimately did little to address the general *ennui* of the vicars.

With the death in 1845 of Smith and of Dean Copleston in 1849, the Chapter of St Paul's said farewell to the *ancien régime*, and felt freer to act on further reforms of the choir. In response to the more searching enquiries of the Ecclesiastical Commissioners, who had now begun to examine the predicaments of cathedral choirs in greater detail, factual answers were submitted in 1850. In these answers the lamentable state of the present choir was fully acknowledged, though at last Chapter, conscious of the cathedral's metropolitan role, were moved to curb the musical atrophy within its walls:

As to the efficiency of the choir the metropolitan cathedral from its posi-tion and dignity, the size and splendour of the edifice, the amplitude of its endowments, before they were in so large a part diverted to other purposes, ought to be the most powerful, but it is one of the feeblest in the Kingdom. This is a serious consideration, not on these grounds only, but as regards the religious state of the Metropolis. The great and increasing concourse of worshippers, especially on the Sunday afternoons, and even on week days, not of the higher and more cultivated, but of the middling ranks, the traders, especially the younger part of this class, and even of the poor; the order and

70 Ibid., 45.
71 See Chapter Minutes, 8 April 1846; see also Prestige, *St Paul's in its Glory*, 46–7.

propriety of their demeanour, the devout attention, and the interest taken in the services, cannot be fairly estimated but by those who are constantly present at those services. The Dean and Chapter will probably feel called upon to devise if possible some plan for enlarging the accommodation. But it is in vain for the Dean and Chapter to attempt to meet and to encourage this growing feeling of reverence for the cathedral services so long as their choir is in its present limited and unsatisfactory state. The Vicars Choral are only 6; and as the organist holds one place in the choir, in fact only five: on every service there ought to be three vicars on each side, at least, it is impossible physically that the present number should be in such constant daily attendance. Some augmentation either by substitutes or supplementary voices, or both, is absolutely necessary. This however the present Dean and Chapter with their restricted incomes cannot be expected to provide.

Nor need the extension of the choir eventually involve any considerable charge on the Chapter revenue. The Vicars Choral possess estates either of right or usage which, under different management would, it is thought probable, suffice to maintain a full and adequate choir. The present choir have already intimated to the Dean their readiness to surrender their estates, of course with due regard to existing vested rights. It is hoped that the Ecclesl. Comms. may have the power, and with consent to entertain the proposition, which, tho' it may require some temporary aid, until the estates shall have been raised to their improveable value, will in the end, it is believed, place the choir, by a different distribution of the funds, on an efficient footing, independent of any other source of payment. In the meantime, it is highly desirable, that a small annual sum, perhaps £150 a year, should be allowed to provide additional voices during certain services.[72]

By April 1851 Chapter had increased their request from £150 to £200. The Commissioners agreed though only after the cathedral had consented to the abolition of the two penny entrance fee and the amelioration of payments to the vicars-choral. In 1852 six additional men, or 'supernumeraries' as they were called, joined the choir on Sundays, though, regrettably, improvement in the estates of the vicars – a knotty legal problem that clearly instilled fear into members of the Chapter – remained in abeyance.[73]

The political wranglings at St Paul's in the 1840s and 1850s were symptomatic of a much larger reform-driven agenda that was sweeping Britain. Since the 1832 Reform Act under Lord Grey had swept away so many anomalies and inequities, and the Chartist movement had infused new echelons of society with an eagerness

---

[72] Chapter Minutes, 4 February 1850, *GB-Lsp*.
[73] Prestige, *St Paul's in its Glory*, 68.

for democratic inclusion, the spirit of change soon infected other institutions throughout the nation, notably the Established Church, where senior clergymen, often from an aristocratic background, could enjoy the fruits of multiple livings while others languished, as Anthony Trollope so satirically depicted in *Barchester Towers,* on a pittance.[74] Music, together with its personnel and resources, was seriously neglected, and the cathedral clergy, motivated by self-interest (including Sydney Smith who zealously opposed any transfer of funds to the choir), ultimately encouraged organists and choir to defend tenaciously what modest incomes and terms of employment they possessed. It was an acute, atrophic situation which demanded strong personalities to effect real change, but, for the moment at least, those in authority at St Paul's possessed not the will to embrace radical reforms, nor were they ready to accept the new liturgical and theological astringencies of the Anglo-Catholic revival whose attitudes to music, both choral and congregational would do so much to transform the fortunes of cathedral music in England.

As one whose musical abilities were quickly noticed, Stainer was only too well aware, even as a youth, of the casual and careless standards of the daily services. Not only would he have sung responses, services and anthems without the requisite number of parts, but he would have also observed and experienced at first hand the conservative, not to say hackneyed state of the choir's repertoire. Much of the music sung, week in, week out, was drawn from the well-established collections of Boyce's *Cathedral Music* (1760–1773) and *Fifteen Anthems* edited by Philip Hayes for the composer's widow (1780), volumes of Samuel Arnold's *Cathedral Music* (1790) and the newly edited version by Edward Rimbault of 1843, William Croft's *Musica Sacra* of 1724 (also in a later Novello edition in two volumes gifted by Bishop Copleston), Maurice Greene's *Forty Select Anthems* (1743), Nares' *Twenty Anthems* (1778) and *A morning & evening service … together with Six anthems* (1788), William Hayes' *Cathedral Music* (1795), Attwood's *Cathedral Music* by Thomas Attwood and edited by Thomas Attwood Walmisley (1852), the first volume of Thomas Pitt's *Church Music* (1788–9) and Page's three volumes of *Harmonia Sacra* (1800).[75] Other collections exist in the St Paul's Cathedral Choir Library including James Kent's *Twelve Anthems* (1773) and *A Morning & Evening Service with eight anthems,* revised and arranged by Joseph Corfe (*c.* 1777), John Camidge's *Cathedral Music* (1828), Joseph Cubitt Pring's *Eight anthems as Performed at St. Paul's Cathedral* (*c.* 1793), volumes published in the 1840s on behalf of the

---

[74] For a detailed and more wide-ranging account of cathedral reforms in the nineteenth century, see P. Barrett, *Barchester: English Cathedral Life in the Nineteenth Century* (London: SPCK, 1993).

[75] Many of the individual volumes of Boyce, Hayes, Page and Arnold, which were sung from partbooks, can still be found in the Cathedral Choir Library at St Paul's. I am grateful to Simon Hill for access to his detailed list.

Musical Antiquarian Society of William Byrd (ed. Horsley), John Dowland (ed. W. Chappell), and Orlando Gibbons (ed. Rimbault), Rimbault's editions of *Collection of Ancient Church Music Printed by the Motett Society* (1842–3) and *A Collection of Anthems … by composers of the Madrigalian Era* (1845), selected anthems of Handel (by Hugh Bond). Much sixteenth-, seventeenth- and eighteenth-century music was sung from partbooks, and this practice evidently continued until well after Stainer left the choir in the 1850s,[76] though it is also evident from the contents of the St Paul's Music Library that, after the advent of Novello's affordable publications, which were printed in score, a considerable number of Novello editions were added, notably vocal scores of Spohr (*The Fall of Babylon* and *The Last Judgment*), Mendelssohn (*St Paul* and *Elijah*), and *Purcell's Sacred Music* in the edition of 1832. Repetition of repertoire led to complacency; vicars-choral were expected to learn very little new music, so a familiarity with recurring anthems, services and chants bred an unhealthy contempt and apathy. There was also little *a cappella* music, which naturally engendered a reliance on the accompanying organ.

When Goss was appointed to the organistship of St Paul's in 1838 there is some suggestion that he hoped at least to institute some change and development of the choir's repertoire. He published *A Collection of Chants Ancient & Modern* in 1841 and edited two volumes of services and anthems with James Turle of Westminster Abbey in 1846. The former entered into current usage at St Paul's, though the volumes of anthems and services seem to have been neglected. The vicars-choral were also by no means receptive to his talents as a composer. Hostility to his fine anthem 'Blessed is the man', composed in 1842, undermined his confidence so markedly that he did not compose any further anthems until 1852, when he was commissioned to write two items for the state funeral of the Duke of Wellington.[77] Besides having to deal with an unsympathetic choir, he also experienced serious difficulties with the Dean and Chapter. Stainer, who attributed some of Goss's troubles to his own benign and unforceful temperament, recalled an awkward episode with Sydney Smith:

> On one occasion, Sidney Smith said to him, "Mr Goss, that chant this morning was what they call a minor chant?" "Yes, sir," he said. "Have no more minor chants, please, when I am in residence. I will not have any more minor music when I am in residence in future." Thereon, Goss explained that most of the compositions of the 17th Century were in the minor, and that it would cut a large hole in the music of the cathedral, but he was inexorable, "no more minor chants when I am in residence." After a time Goss

---

[76] See Frost, *Early Recollections of St Paul's Cathedral*, 18.
[77] See J. Stainer, 'Sir John Goss', *Musical Times* 21 (June 1880), 271; see also D. Gedge, 'John Goss, 1800–1880', *Musical Times* 121 (July 1980), 461.

wrote and begged that the embargo might be withdrawn, and it was, but not in a pleasant way. This was the letter withdrawing the embargo: "Since you make it a point of conscience to have music in a minor key, I give way. – Sidney Smith."[78]

Stainer was keen to exonerate Goss from negative accusations that were prevalent in the press and explained that support from Dean and Chapter had not been forthcoming when he had hoped to augment the choir:

> I should be very sorry if it were supposed that in saying the music of St. Paul's was not in a satisfactory state, I was throwing any slur whatever on the able and talented predecessor I had in Sir John Goss. I had the pleasure yesterday of an interview with his widow, who will be eighty-eight years of age in a fortnight's time, and, without my asking any question, she told me in the course of conversation what I had known before, and what I am very pleased to tell you, and that was that Sir John Goss made frequent attempts to improve the service in St. Paul's, that he continually wrote to the Dean and Chapter, and asked that he might have a larger choir, and have more discipline over them, and means of enforcing attendance. But the Dean and Chapter met him with a sort of official *non possumus*, and the family of Sir John Goss at present have in their possession letters from Bishop Copleston, who declined to take any action in the matter or accede to his wishes. I don't know that if the Dean and Chapter had wished to do it Goss was the man for it. He was too tender-hearted, and perhaps not exceedingly tenacious of his purpose. It seems in these days that a man to be a reformer, or reorganiser, ought to be constructed of affable whipcord.[79]

Similarly, the organ at St Paul's, built originally by Father Smith in 1697 and placed on the screen, was found to be under-powered for the larger annual services in the cathedral, notably those for the Charity Children and the Festival of the Sons of the Clergy. Attwood had expressed his concern in his last years as organist, during which time an octave of pedal pipes had been added,[80] but Goss was more insistent, and, though he had to contend with the unenthusiastic position of Sydney Smith,[81] he did get his way in 1849, when Bishop & Sons improved the

---

[78] 'The Sir John Stainer Dinner', 610.

[79] Ibid.

[80] See N. Plumley & A. Niland, *A History of the Organs in St Paul's Cathedral* (Oxford: Positif Press, 2001), 56–7; see also Bevan & Stainer, *Handbook to the Cathedral of St Paul*, 60.

[81] '[Goss] went to tell him [Smith] the organ was getting very antiquated, and required improvements, and additional stops, as it did in those days. But Sidney Smith said: "Well, Mr Goss, you have got a bull stop, and a tom-tit stop, and what in the world

instrument by the addition of a proper swell organ, the introduction of new key-boards for the manuals, an extension of the pedal organ to two octaves,[82] and the raising of the organ's pitch by a semitone.[83] Goss's ameliorations came about after Smith and Copleston had died and the more receptive Dean Henry Hart Milman had come to office. Milman was also keen for St Paul's to play its part during the 1851 Great Exhibition, when Goss was required to play an organ at the West End of the cathedral to accompany services (with large congregations) on Sunday afternoons.[84] Stainer's opinion of Goss as an organist was qualified by the state of the cumbersome instrument (as verified by S. S. Wesley) which he had at his disposal:

> The organs of his youth were very different instruments to those of our time, and if he were not a brilliant performer from a modern point of view, it is equally certain that many of our young organists would be utterly unable to produce the fine effects which Goss produced on an organ having two octaves of very clumsy pedals, a gamut-G swell, a 16–ft. (CCC) great organ manual, and two or three unruly composition-pedals. He always accompanied the voices (especially when *soli*) with thoroughly good taste, and his extempore voluntaries were sometimes models of grace and sweetness.[85]

Shortly before he died, Stainer, who had been asked to edit Goss's anthem 'The king shall rejoice' for Novello (in anticipation of the coronation of Edward VII), was able to give a fascinating insight into Goss's technique of registration of the organ and how achieved certain effects:

> I have ventured to make a few alterations in your transcript of Goss' Anthem.
>
> p.1 When he used <u>Gt. Diaps</u> in S. Pauls they were old <u>Smith's</u> and quite <u>soft</u>; so we must say "soft Diap. Gt."

do you want besides?" ' This quotation appeared in Stainer's after-dinner speech on leaving St Paul's (see 'The Sir John Stainer Dinner', 610), though it was only partially remembered from a speech made E. J. Hopkins to the College of Organists, subsequently printed in their *Twenty-first Annual Report* (1884–5).

[82] Bevan & Stainer, *Handbook to the Cathedral of St Paul*, 61–2.

[83] Stainer quoted the anecdote of Ouseley, who compared the St Paul organ's raised pitch with his own perfect pitch, passed onto him by the Rev. J. Hampton from Goss himself. See J. Stainer, 'The Character and Influence of the Late Sir Frederick Ouseley' [2 December 1889], *Proceedings of the Musical Association* 16 (1889–90), 26. Also reiterated in Plumley & Niland, *A History of the Organs in St Paul's Cathedral*, 58–9.

[84] Ibid., 59.

[85] Stainer, 'Sir John Goss', 271.

p.2 Goss would have played with his left hand on the <u>Choir</u>, pumping the <u>Sw</u> for his Right hand Solo! so I have marked this.

p.2 line 3. You must not use pedals with the Sw. here ("Thou hast given him") because here again old Goss would have played L.H. Ch. R.H. Gt.

p.2 bottom line. bar 4. A modern "full Sw." may mean 10 to 15 stops and a sforzando on this would startle the congregation and wake the dead! Goss intended that floppoty full chord of 6/4 to be <u>on the Choir</u>; you must remember that his swell organ only went down to [bass stave: G bottom line], and he had no coupler Sw. to Ped. of course.

By the way I am not sure that in <u>1838</u> the swell did not stop at [treble stave: G two leger lines below stave]!!! Yes, I believe <u>it did</u>.[86]

More significantly, however, Stainer greatly admired Goss as a composer of church music. As a twelve-year-old, deeply impressionable chorister, Stainer counted himself among those privileged performers at the funeral of the Duke of Wellington in 1852, when Goss's new anthem 'If we believe that Jesus died' and the dirge 'And the King said to all the people', requested by Dean Milman, were first performed publicly. Stainer vividly remembered the first time 'If we believe' was rehearsed by the substantially augmented choir in the music room at Store Street: 'When the last few bars *pianissimo* had died away, there was a profound silence for some time, so deeply had the hearts of all been touched by its truly devotional spirit. Then there gradually arose on all sides the warmest congratulation to the composer, it could hardly be termed *applause*, for it was something much more genuine and respectful.'[87] Thus, it seems, began Goss's rehabilitation as a composer of anthems, and his 'Praise the Lord, O my soul', written for the 1854 Bicentenary Festival of the Sons of the Clergy (which was probably Stainer's last occasion of this kind as a treble), was greatly admired. It is also probable that Stainer was acquainted with another of Goss's *pièces d'occasion*, the ternary processional anthem, 'O praise the Lord, laud ye the name of the Lord', a setting of verses from Psalm 135 written for the enthronement of the Bishop of London (Bishop Tate) in 1856. Stainer undoubtedly learned much from the simple diatonic style of these pieces, with their unassuming melodious felicity, uncomplicated but concise harmony, a largely eighteenth-century phraseology, and the Mozart-inspired classical equipoise of the sonata-style movements (as one finds in the two aforementioned anthems); and he received at the hands of William Bayley a sound grounding in harmony through Goss's primer, *Introduction to Harmony and Thorough Bass*

---

[86] Letter to F. G. Edwards, 15 February 1901, *GB-Lbl* Egerton 3092.
[87] Stainer, 'Sir John Goss', 270.

(probably the most widely used text in the country at that time, and the standard text used at the Royal Academy of Music, where Goss taught). The unpretentious simplicity of Goss's manner, infused with his admiration for Attwood (his teacher), Mendelssohn (whose music, in the 1840s and 1850s, stood head and shoulders above any other in England) and Spohr, would contribute significantly to the formation of Stainer's musical style.

Goss's musical acquaintances in and outside the church provided Stainer with a useful introduction to England's most prominent musicians of the era. As a young chorister he was introduced to Sir Frederick Ouseley, who, as someone devoted to the cultivation and training of boy choristers, came to inspect the choirboys. This encounter was to prove highly propitious.[88] The annual service for the Festival of the Sons of the Clergy, which involved a much augmented choir, brought him into contact with George Elvey, organist of St George's Chapel, Windsor, a popular if conservative musician whose stylistic preferences inclined towards Handel and Mendelssohn. Every year he would conduct the festival (again, the retiring Goss preferred to remain in the organ loft), an event Stainer would remember with fondness:

> My first remembrance and impression of Sir George, then Dr Elvey goes back to 1847 [*sic*] when I was admitted a chorister of S. Paul's Cathedral. At that time the Choirs of the Royal Chapel, Windsor, the Chapel Royal, St James, and Westminster Abbey used to reinforce the choir of St Paul's on the Festivals of the "Sons of the Clergy" Corporation and of the "Society for the Propagation of the Gospel". As Mr Goss presided at the organ, it was necessary to have a conductor, especially as several fine old Anthems by Gibbons and others were generally sung. The organ then stood on the Screen, and the conductor beat time from the brass Lectern in the middle of the Chancel. Dr Elvey was always conductor, and we small boys used to pay great reverence to his gorgeous Oxford hood. On one occasion he asked a senior boy to help

---

[88] Stainer notes in his paper for the Musical Association ('The Character and Influence of the Late Sir Frederick Ouseley', 33) that 'it was soon after Ouseley's appointment as Professor [of Music at Oxford University] that he came to examine the chorister boys of St Paul's, of whom I was one.' Ouseley was appointed at Oxford in 1855 at which time Stainer would have been 15 years old and hardly the 'small chorister boy' he described in his presidential speech for the *RCO Calendar* of 29 April 1889. This first meeting is more likely to have been in the early 1850s which was recorded by Maria Hackett. Indeed, Hackett maintained in a letter to Goss of December 1862 that Ouseley had examined Stainer 'and the Dean gave him a prize in consequence of a favourable report'. (See Garrett, 'A List of Some of St Paul's Cathedral Choristers before 1873', 82–93.)

him to adjust it before joining the procession: the senior boy was pale with emotion, we juniors were green with envy.

In many cases Dr Elvey conducted from memory, and only once did his memory play him false. There is a short movement in one of Dr Green's [sic] anthems "Oh, behold the works of the Lord" which is a sort of choral recitative: it is in triple measure, but Dr Elvey thought it was in quadruple measure and managed most ingeniously to get four strokes of his baton to Mr Goss' three chords on the organ. We boys of course were mightily amused at this rhythmical discrepancy, and signal was rapidly made along the line of boys, by nudging of elbows, to watch the conductor narrowly: This was done, every eye was fixed on him. I rather think we all regretted that the movement was so short! Dr Elvey took his Mus.Doc degree in 1840, the year I was born: so I was seven years old [sic] when admitted to S. Paul's, and probably was eight before I saw him. I little thought then that I should be so often in contact with him in after life, or that the richly-robed Doctor whom I held so much in awe as a child would some day prove a kind and genial friend. His tone and manner to young musicians was always that of sympathy and encouragement; and only those can fully appreciate the value of this who have like myself been a real hard worker in the rank and file of my profession.[89]

The services for the Sons of the Clergy, which always attracted a large congregation, were some of the most important musical foci at St Paul's. In the late 1840s its musical content had consisted largely of familiar repertoire (though Stainer suggests that the performance of 'fine old anthems' by Gibbons was an exciting departure from the norm), but after 1852, the festival increasingly seems to have included new works, not least by Goss himself.[90] This desire to shift away from the old, ingrained repertoire was symptomatic of Milman's new regime as Dean of St Paul's. Milman was an intellectual, an accomplished poet, historian and writer. As a broad churchman, his commitment to Anglicanism and the beauty of its liturgy and prayer book was expressed through a poetical prism and a commitment to a liberal theology (which some confused for either secularism or scepticism) much influenced by German thinking of the time.[91]

---

[89] Letter from Stainer to Miss Savory, 25 May 1894, GB-Ob MS.Eng.c.5370, fols. 127–8.

[90] Records show that, from the early 1860s, albeit after Stainer had left St Paul's, several of Goss's new anthems, including 'The Wilderness', 'Lift up thine eyes', 'Brother, thou art gone before us', and 'O give thanks', as well as evening services by Walmisley, Smart and Hopkins, were used.

[91] See D. Forbes, *The Liberal Anglican Idea of History* (Cambridge: Cambridge University Press, 1952).

His later actions, which included the use of the space under the dome of the cathedral for large congregational services from 1858, testify to his desire to make St Paul's the hub of national religious life. The service of national thanksgiving for the cessation of the cholera epidemic in November 1849 was one of the first such events to harness public attention; others followed – among them, the state funeral of J. W. Turner in 1851, populous services during the 1851 Great Exhibition, the state funeral of Wellington on 18 November 1852, the harvest service (to mark the great harvest) in October 1854 and the day of humiliation for the Crimean War, March 1855. These were services in which Stainer almost certainly participated, though others, such as the thanksgiving service for peace after the Crimean War ended (May 1856), the day of humiliation after the 'Indian Mutiny' (October 1857) and the thanksgiving service for the suppression of the 'Indian Mutiny' (May 1859), continued the trend.

The state funeral of the Duke of Wellington (which marked the end of a long and elaborate pageant from the Duke's lying-in-state at Chelsea Hospital and the procession along Horse Guards, observed by over 1,000,000 spectators) was undoubtedly one of the most remarkable services of Stainer's career as a chorister.[92] Not since Nelson's state funeral in January 1806 had there been an occasion of such national significance. Galleries were erected to accommodate a congregation exceeding 10,000, special artificial lighting (albeit imperfectly executed) was provided, and the whole cathedral, as contemporary illustrations testify, was full of dignitaries, men in uniform (including old soldiers), and a public dressed in black mourning attire. Stainer was one of eight boys prepared for the service along with those from the Chapel Royal, Westminster Abbey, and numerous other cathedrals. Rehearsals, a rare occurrence in the normal routine at St Paul's, took place at the rooms of the Royal Society, Westminster Abbey and at St Paul's on the evening of 17 November.[93] At the service the well-established funeral sentences of Croft were sung, along with chants by Lord Mornington (to Psalms 39 and 40), Goss's adaptation of the slow movement from Beethoven's Seventh Symphony for the Nunc dimittis, Goss's dirge and funeral anthem, Handel's funeral anthem 'His body is buried in peace', Mendelssohn's 'Sleepers wake! A voice is calling' from *St Paul*, though of greatest substance and pathos were the four anthems from Purcell's funeral music for Queen Mary, liturgical works deeply rooted in the tradition of English church music, yet owing to their status as *pièces d'occasion*, rarely sung. For the twelve-year-old Stainer it was a deeply memorable experience and one that would later connect with his work for the Purcell revival in the last twenty-five years of the century.

---

[92] Stainer's pass for the state occasion still survives in private possession (MN).

[93] See letters from John Goss of 3 and 7 November 1852, *GB-Lam* McCann Collection.

As Stainer grew older, and was promoted to 'senior chorister' within the choir, he found himself in much demand throughout London and elsewhere as a solo treble. In this way he almost certainly became well acquainted with standard oratorio repertoire such as Handel's *Israel in Egypt*, *Judas Maccabeus* and *Messiah*, Spohr's *The Last Judgment* and *The Fall of Babylon*, and Mendelssohn's *St Paul* and *Elijah* (indeed, it is inconceivable that he did not sing the famous treble solo in *Elijah*). Another work, new to English ears, was the *St Matthew Passion*, the first performance of which in England was pioneered by the Bach Society (founded in 1849) under William Sterndale Bennett on 6 April 1854 at the Hanover Rooms (later known as the Hanover Square Rooms). Stainer took part in this event and endeavoured to recall the rehearsals and the somewhat inadequate performance for Edwards:

> I was born in 1840 so I was only 9 years old when the Bach Society was founded. I was one among the very first of those who regularly attended rehearsals, to which I was escorted by an elder sister.
>
> The rehearsals were held in Store St. … or sometimes in Tenterden St. But I have a most vivid recollection of a series of rehearsals held in Gray and Davidson's [*sic*] Organ Factory. At these, Dr Steggall accompanied us splendidly on the organ, and once or twice in the unavoidable absence of Bennett we were conducted by Oliver May.
>
> The Misses Johnston attended regularly (there were I think two sisters), and the Passions-Musik was <u>in process</u> of translation by them, fresh sheets of lithographed music being produced at each rehearsal.
>
> I have luckily preserved my card of thanks for taking part in the first performance. It is very tasteful, the inscription being in a gothic border. I enclose a copy of the wording. Notice that they were called Hanover Rooms, not as afterwards, Hanover Square Rooms. My recollections as to the first performance are limited, I got very hot and very fatigued, and (worst of all) it was wretchedly rendered from beginning to end. Those troublesome little choruses led off by a rush of violins had been insufficiently rehearsed and were a series of catastrophes. The entrance of the strings when over-lapping the P.F. in the Recitatives was nearly every time a bungle.[94]

Bennett's performances of the *St Matthew Passion*, inspired by Mendelssohn's landmark revival in Germany in 1829, quickened the pace of the English Bach revival. Stainer's enthusiasm for Bach had already been ignited by his own domestic performances of select works from *Das wohltemperirte Clavier* – he was

---

[94] Letter from Stainer to F. G. Edwards, 6 October 1896 *GB-Lbl* Egerton 3092. Stainer's card of thanks survives in the family papers.

well able to play the Fugue in E major in Book Two from the age of seven, and extemporise with remarkable facility in Bach's style[95] – but he was also familiar with performances of Bach's increasingly popular organ works by Gauntlett and Goss's assistant at St Paul's, George Cooper, whose interpretations were said to be legendary. Moreover, in March 1852, at one of several musical parties held at the home of William Pole, the brother-in-law of Gauntlett and one-time organist at St Olave's, Southwark, Stainer sang the alto part (as part of a small chorus of twenty-five singers) in the first complete performance of Bach's *Magnificat* in England, as well as in several cantatas (which again must have been their first hearing).[96] Stainer much admired the pioneering spirit of Pole and many years later was keen to stress to Edwards his long-forgotten work:

> None of the papers have [*sic*] alluded to the late Dr Pole's efforts to introduce music practically unknown, 50 years ago. e.g. he used to make MS parts with his own hands and have parties in his house to try Bach's Cantatas (then not easy to get), also, works by Mozart, and also of the early Italian composers and others. As I used to go there and sing them as a child, I recall the pleasure he gave to many. He was a pioneer in the difficulty [*sic*] task of teaching people what they <u>ought</u> to like, and this should not be forgotten.[97]

These experiences of Bach, at a time when new editions and performances of his music were steadily gaining ground, were a major formative influence on Stainer, and his later championship of Bach's organ works, the *St Matthew Passion*, the *Christmas Oratorio* and other works undoubtedly stemmed from the 1850s.

Concurrent with his Bach encounters, Stainer was also introduced to other notable musical personalities. After the 1851 Great Exhibition the Willis organ had been transferred to and installed at Winchester Cathedral at the instigation of its famous (if notorious) organist, S. S. Wesley. On the occasion of the organ's opening, Stainer, along with other boys from St Paul's, Westminster and the Chapel Royal joined the Winchester choristers for a major service at which Wesley's anthem 'Ascribe unto the Lord' was sung. Stainer remembered with some vividness the event and Wesley's quirky yet apposite interpretation:

> … it was at the opening of the new Willis organ at Winchester in 1852 or 3 that "Ascribe unto the Lord" was performed, I presume for the first time. I was then 12 or 13 years old as the case may be. At the rehearsal in the Cathedral, Wesley could not get the combined choirs (S. Paul's, Westminster,

95 Edwards, 'John Stainer', 298, *passim*.
96 See W. Pole, *Some Short Reminiscences of Events in my Life and Works* (London: private publication, 1898), 10.
97 Letter from Stainer to F. G. Edwards, 3 January 1901, *GB-Bl* Egerton 3092, fol. 126.

Royal Chapel) to take the movement "As for the gods of the heathen" rapidly enough. So he came down into the body of the church, leaving one of his assistants to play (?Garrett or Arnold), and beat time with a stick on the side of a choirbook, a device which left no doubt as to the position of the down-beats! We all thought it a great scramble at the pace he took it, but of course he was right, and I have always kept it up to his pace. But I am sorry to say this movement is often quite spoilt, – being slowly dragged along by those who are ignorant of the composer's intention.[98]

Though Stainer was to find Wesley's argumentative personality irritating and lacking in pragmatism, he greatly admired Wesley's church music, which is evinced not only by the performances he oversaw as a choirmaster, but also the influence exerted on his own music by Wesley's treatment of dissonance.

The service at Winchester was only one of numerous external events that Stainer attended. Madrigal-singing in London and other urban centres of Britain (not least Manchester, Dublin and Bristol) had remained an extremely popular social focus among the middle and upper classes. New works had continued to be published, and the membership of societies, encouraged by the combination of informality and entertainment (which usually included the imbibing of alcoholic beverages and annual dinners) flourished during the nineteenth century; moreover, the societies invariably attracted men of substantial musical standing to conduct their rehearsals and concerts. The Madrigal Society of London, a long-standing institution and reckoned to be the oldest musical association in Europe, had been in existence since 1741, when it had been founded by John Immyns, a member of the Academy of Ancient Music. A society of relatively small membership (about thirty) met regularly, enjoyed the conviviality of monthly dinners and boasted among its members Sir John Hawkins the musical historian, Jonathan Battishill, E. T. Warren, Thomas Arne, Benjamin Cooke and William Horsley. By 1811 it began to offer prizes for original madrigalian compositions (which attracted such composers as Samuel Wesley, W. Linley and W. Beale) and by the 1830s it was recognised as one of the most select musical societies in London, numbering among its members George Cooper, James Turle (of Westminster Abbey), Vincent Novello and James Calkin. Stainer gained an introduction to the Society probably through the introduction of Goss, who took an active interest in the composition of madrigals (his *Collection of Glees and a Madrigal for 4 and 5 voices* enjoyed a modicum of popularity, and the first of the collection, Ossian's hymn 'O those whose beams' was highly regarded) and for years he participated in the Society's companionable proceedings. In January 1884, during a paper given by Sir George

[98] Letter from Stainer to F. G. Edwards, 12 April 1900, Novello collection.

Macfarren at the Musical Association, Stainer recalled singing under Cipriani Potter:

> I well remember, as a boy, when I was called in at the great festivals to take part in those concerts, the extraordinary effect which his [Potter's] appearance had on me. I was very pleased to hear that Professor Macfarren had not even forgotten those shirt-collars which always interested me very much. We used to watch him at these evenings, conducting, and we boys used to be very much interested as to which side of the collar would come down first. He was a very good conductor of Madrigals as of everything else when he once began, but was sometimes rather bothered, I suppose, by being asked by the members, "Mr Potter, what is about the time of this Madrigal?" He used to say, "This is about the time – one – two," and then when he commenced it the beat would be something quite different, so that the actual time differed very much from that which he gave beforehand. One other thing, although it has very little to do with Mr Potter, may be of some interest. As a conductor he used to play a wooden pitch pipe, which I have the honour to play now as his successor, though I do not use it very often for the same reason that made it comical in those days – the note varied enormously according to the pressure of wind you gave it. He used to begin with a loud pressure, and as it died away the note was considerably flattened; on one occasion he blew it in the usual way and said, "Gentlemen, that note is G," when a voice said, "Mr Potter, which end of it?"[99]

Such experience as he gained both from the affable and social intercourse that the performance of madrigals encouraged, the production of new works (by Goss, Pearsall, Lahee, Leslie and others), and the study of new editions of madrigals, especially those by Wilbye, Weelkes and Morley, firmly established his love of, and lifelong attachment to, the madrigal genre, both as a vehicle of recreation and as a vibrant creative idiom.

In 1851, owing to the need for a capable treble voice, Charles Steggall, a busy London organist, prevailed on Stainer to sing the soprano solos in the Cambridge performance of his doctoral exercise.[100] Walmisley, organist at King's, Trinity and St John's Colleges, was unable to recommend a suitable voice from the chapel

---

99 G. A. Macfarren, 'Cipriani Potter: His Life and Work' [7 January 1884], *Proceedings of the Musical Association* 10 (1883–4), 54–5.

100 Stainer maintained in a postcard to Edwards of 7 October 1896 (*GB-Lbl* Egerton 3092) that he had first met Steggall 'at one of those early rehearsals' of the Bach Society. This may have been before Steggall's doctoral exercise of 1851, in which case Stainer may have begun to attend rehearsals of the Bach Society from its inception in 1849.

choirs, so Stainer was asked to go to Cambridge in 1851. Both his musical and academic prowess were instantly recognised:

> Not only his beautiful voice, but his general personality and manner, made a great impression in the University town, and I remember Professor Walmisley being much taken with him. Looking at him admiringly during lunch after the rehearsals, he turned to me with: 'What a sweet child it is, and what a pretty little pipe it's got!'
>
> I remember, too, that at the dinner my father gave to the London contingent of singers (several from the R.A.M.), Sterndale Bennett, W. G. Cusins, W. F. Low, and others, who had come to hear my work, how he was noticed by everyone and how readily he answered a question in Latin, jokingly made by an undergraduate, who, by-the-bye, showed his appreciation by handing half-a-crown across the table. From that time I took the greatest interest in the boy who, till he went to Tenbury, frequently visited me.[101]

Stainer retained a high opinion of Steggall's abilities as an organist, and for a short time also took counterpoint lessons from him.[102]

At about the same time, he became acquainted with the young Arthur Sullivan, who was two years his junior and a chorister at the Chapel Royal. Sullivan maintained that it was in 1854: 'As boys we spent a good deal of time together; we spent our half-holidays – the only time we had to spend. Both of us being of "a musical turn," as they say, we discussed music and musical matters [and] the compositions of the great masters.'[103] It is, however, possible that the two were acquainted earlier as fellow organ pupils of George Cooper.[104]

When Stainer began to learn the organ formally is unclear, but it was probably in the early 1850s, when he was physically able to negotiate the pedal-board. Lessons, which were too financially onerous for Stainer's father, were paid for by Maria Hackett. (Stainer had become one of her favourite musical *protégés*.) Instruction usually took place at Cooper's other place of employment, St Sepulchre's Church, Holborn Viaduct (known as the musicians' church), where Stainer is also known to have assisted. Teaching must have been systematic and rigorous. Cooper was

---

[101] Edwards, 'John Stainer', 300.

[102] Ibid., 301.

[103] 'The Sir John Stainer Dinner', 613.

[104] Another pupil of George Cooper was Walter Parratt, who was Stainer's junior by only one year. Parratt took lessons from Cooper at St Sepulchre's, and on one occasion, while Stainer was still a chorister, played the anthem for the service at St Paul's where he met Goss. (See D. Tovey & G. Parratt, *Walter Parratt: Master of the Music* (London: Oxford University Press, 1941), 27.) The two later met at Tenbury (Tovey & Parratt, 46).

well known as a capable instructor, and his *Organist's Manual* had been published in 1851. Sometime later, in 1863, he also published his *Introduction to the Organ*, which still enjoyed currency in the 1890s when it was revised by John Frederick Bridge.

Like Steggall, Cooper noticed Stainer's talent early and was equally impressed with Sullivan's promise. 'How I should like you two boys to race one another in life', he was once heard prophetically to remark when they were in his company.[105] The two young men were often to be found together, and on one occasion, after Stainer had left the St Paul's choir, he and Sullivan found themselves sharing the organ-loft in the cathedral with Goss:

> In 1855 or 1856, when the organ at S. Paul's still stood in its original position on the screen, and the organist played with his back against the choir-organ, there was a space on each side of the organ loft which had a seat where three or four visitors could sit during service. These spaces were hidden by dark red curtains, but on Sunday afternoons when Mr Goss permitted a few friends to join him, the curtains were thrown open so that his visitors could have a view of the choir and congregation, and a very pretty sight it was. During the short interval which elapsed between my choristership and my call to S. Michael's College, Tenbury, I was on several occasions one of the favoured few who were invited by Mr Goss to sit in the organ loft. One Sunday afternoon he asked me to cross the further side, because he expected some one else. I of course obeyed, by sitting on the organ-stool and wriggling along it, for this was the only means of moving from one side to the other except to shut off the "pedal-pipes" and walk across the pedals. This last method of transit was that always adopted by Mr Goss. The other visitors duly arrived before the commencement of service; they were little Arthur Sullivan and two ladies who had kindly brought him in their carriage. During the sermon Goss having said a few words to Sullivan crossed over to speak to me; but alas, the dear man had forgotten to shut off the pedal-pipes, and he had taken two steps on the pedal-clavier before he realised that he was the cause of the alarming thunderings which were frightening the congregation and putting a temporary pause in the sermon. He completely lost his presence of mind, and was unable to decide whether to go backwards or forwards. Brought to his senses by the sustained roar, continued his walk, or rather trot, towards me; when he sat down in a nervous perspiration and mopped his face while the dome was still echoing with the deep rolling sounds of his unpremeditated pedal fantasia. This story will be quite devoid of interest except to organists, and the occurrence has probably been

---

[105] Edwards, 'John Stainer', 301.

entirely forgotten by all those who were present; but I reminded Sullivan of it many years afterwards and we both recalled our boyish comment on it – "what a joke, wasn't it"![106]

Stainer was often asked to deputise at St Paul's when Goss and Cooper were indisposed. This was, however, only piecemeal work, and he sought other employment as an organist in local churches. He did not have long to wait. The schoolmaster, the Rev. J. H. Coward, was rector at the little Wren church of St Benet's, Paul's Wharf, in Upper Thames Street (a St Paul's living and close to the cathedral), and the organistship there was closely overseen by both Goss and Cooper (who had once been organist there between 1833 and 1838). The job had become vacant in April 1855, when the present organist had not been re-elected to the position,[107] and by October it had been resolved to employ the fifteen-year-old Stainer until Easter 1856 at the rate of £30 per annum.[108] This six-monthly contract was quickly renewed, and by April 1857 he was still in post, having been re-elected together with the churchwardens and other officers. At the same time, Stainer's salary of £30 was confirmed at the same rate as previous years, though, because he was a minor, it had to be paid through the Rev. Coward to Stainer's father.[109]

Though employment at St Benet's was useful experience for Stainer, it seems clear that Goss and Cooper, and Coward for that matter, knew that it was only a temporary apprenticeship, and that a more auspicious position would soon be offered to him. That opportunity soon occurred in the late summer (probably late August) of 1857, when Stainer was deputising at the afternoon service at St Paul's. During the service Ouseley had appeared in the organ loft and watched Stainer accompany the music 'from the old "scores" '.[110] Stainer maintained that in the summer of 1857 Ouseley had come to St Paul's to consult Goss and Cooper in his search for a replacement organist at St Michael's College, Tenbury, and, hoping to find either man at the organ console, had been surprised to encounter Stainer instead. That same evening he received a letter offering him the position of organist

[106] Among the letters to F. G. Edwards (fol. 149) in GB-Lbl Egerton 3092.

[107] 10 April 1855, Vestry Minutes, St Benet's and Paul's Wharf, GB-Lgl Ms 877/4.

[108] 17 April 1855, Vestry Minutes, St Benet's and Paul's Wharf, GB-Lgl Ms 877/4: 'Resolved, That the Rector, be requested to obtain the Services, of Mr Stainer [colour of ink indicates later insertion of name] as Organist, till Easter next.'

[109] 16 April 1857, Vestry Minutes, St Benet's and Paul's Wharf, GB-Lgl Ms 877/4: 'Resolved that the Organist's Salary be continued at £30 per annum, and that the Church Wardes be authorized (during the Minority of Mr John Stayner [sic]) to pay the same to the Revd J. H. Coward [Rector and Minor Canon] upon his producing quarterly the receipt of the Father of the said Mr John Stayner.'

[110] Stainer, 'The Character and Influence of the Late Sir Frederick Ouseley', 34. See also The College of Organists 25th Annual Report 1888–9, 33,

at Ouseley's new pioneering institution.[111] But whether Ouseley's visit had indeed been impromptu is hard to say, for it is evident that, in 1855, during another of his choirboy inspections, he had met Stainer at an opportune moment, just as he was leaving the choir:

> I shall never forget the nervousness with which I approached this musical and clerical dignitary when summoned to meet him in the drawing-room of our master, the Rev. J. H. Coward. But I played a Prelude and Fugue by Bach, from the "forty-eight," by memory, and, at its conclusion, Sir Frederick gave me a few words of good advice and much kindly encouragement.[112]

From this evidence it is quite plausible that, in the knowledge of Stainer's existence and talent, Ouseley had in fact come to St Paul's to 'head-hunt' the brilliant young organist who was now available for employment. Whatever the real truth of the episode, Stainer took little time to make up his mind. On 3 September 1857 he tendered his resignation at St Benet's,[113] and shortly afterwards was on his way to the Worcestershire countryside to become Ouseley's assistant and Tenbury's second organist. At only seventeen years of age his career as one of Britain's most significant church musicians had begun in earnest.[114]

---

[111] Stainer, 'The Character and Influence of the Late Sir Frederick Ouseley'. Edwards ('John Stainer', 301) recounts that Ouseley had appeared in the organ-loft at the morning service of the eventful day, and that Stainer had, according to his sister (Annie Stainer), arrived home for dinner in the knowledge that Ouseley wanted an organist for Tenbury. Ouseley had then attended afternoon service and offered the position to Stainer on the spot.

[112] Stainer, 'The Character and Influence of the Late Sir Frederick Ouseley'.

[113] 3 September 1857, Vestry Minutes, St Benet's and Paul's Wharf, *GB-Lgl* Ms 877/4.

[114] See Rev. F. T. Havergal, *Memorials of Frederick Arthur Gore Ouseley* (London: Ellis & Elvey, 1889), 65. Havergal confirms that Stainer arrived at Tenbury for the Michaelmas Term. It is erroneously stated in Russell, *St Paul's under Dean Church*, that Stainer began work at Tenbury in 1858.

II ❧ 1857–1859

'I Saw the Lord':
Ouseley and Tenbury

> In 1857 I found myself, after a railway journey to Worcester and then twenty
> miles on the top of a coach, settled in the charming building which he [Ouse-
> ley] had raised at his own cost for the advancement of church music. From
> it a short cloister led into a church of beautiful design, rich in carved wood-
> work and stained glass, containing a fine organ, and served by an admirable
> choir. Here, day by day, choral services of a high standard of excellence were
> maintained.[1]

STAINER appositely described his decision to undertake the assistantship at
Tenbury as 'a turning-point in [his] life'.[2] There were of course great musical
opportunities afforded by his employment there; apart from services, he had much
time for organ practice, private study and the extraordinary luxury of individual
tuition from Ouseley. But the wider experience offered by the almost monasti-
cal isolation of Tenbury, a unique establishment of a college attached to a parish
church,[3] was a new kind of ecclesiastical discipline shaped by its founder's vision
of church music as a quintessential and ordered component of Christian worship, rather than the tolerated appendage that it had become in so many services
throughout the country. For Stainer, whose only experiences had been of political
turmoil and liturgical malaise at St Paul's, Tenbury offered a quite new and deeply
influential perspective that would ultimately crystallise his view of church music
for the rest of his life.

St Michael's, Tenbury, had materialised after years of spiritual, emotional and
physical gestation on Ouseley's part. The son of a baronet, he had been educated
privately under the tutelage of a clergyman, the Rev. James Joyce, before embarking on his studies at Christ Church, Oxford, in 1843. A year later, at the age of
nineteen, his father died; as the only son, he came into a substantial inheritance,
a fortune which in time allowed him to realise a steadily coalescing fusion of
his education and career. He took his B.A. at Oxford in 1846 (and M.A. in 1849),

---

[1] J. Stainer, 'The Character and Influence of the Late Sir Frederick Ouseley', *Proceedings of the Musical Association* 16 (1889–90), 34.

[2] Ibid.

[3] See D. Bland, *Ouseley and his Angels: The Life of St Michael's College, Tenbury and
its Founder* (Windsor: private publication, 2000), 62.

and, having established his musical credentials within the university, he sought to accomplish two important strands of his life. One was to study for a Mus.Bac. degree at Oxford, the other was to seek ordination. In 1850 he took his music degree. This caused some consternation among some in the university. Why, with a M.A. from Oxford, would he wish to take a lower degree (the Mus.Bac.) and a musical degree at that?[4] But this controversy paled into significance in comparison with the chequered history of his early days as a clergyman. Between 1846 and 1849 Ouseley, who lived in Lowndes Street, sang in the choir of the nearby St Paul's Church in Knightsbridge which had been opened in 1843 in an affluent and highly fashionable part of London with a congregation largely drawn from the population of Belgravia. Its vicar, the Rev. W. J. E. Bennett, was an enthusiastic student of Tractarian developments in Oxford during the 1830s (a movement which drew its name from the *Tracts for the Times*, sermons delivered in St Mary the Virgin, Oxford's university church, by John Henry Newman, John Keble and Edward Pusey). Indeed, Bennett was not only an adherent to the original theological tenets of Tractarianism but he was an enthusiastic devotee both of the ceremonial innovations which had begun to be introduced by John Bloxam at Littlemore near Oxford in 1837 and the scholarly research into worship and architecture of the Cambridge Camden Society, founded in 1839. St Paul's Knightsbridge was symptomatic of all that Tractarians and ecclesiologists held dear. Gothic in design, with Perpendicular windows, it conformed with those new church-building ideals that were sweeping England's religious revival. Within its walls, a surpliced choir sang at the east end, just outside the chancel. Ceremony took pride of place, prayers and responses were intoned, lighted candles were proudly visible, the eastward stance at the altar was observed at communion, and music was accepted as a vital dimension of worship.

In 1849 Ouseley was ordained deacon at St Paul's on Trinity Sunday by Bishop Blomfield, Bishop of London, and was licensed there as a curate. St Paul's was a demanding parish; on Sundays congregations were large (with no fewer than 1,700 parishioners attending in the morning – 120 of whom remained for communion after Mattins and the Litany – and 1,200 in the evening) and the southern extremity of the parish at Pimlico, where many poor resided, was the focus of much work for both Bennett and his young curate. Indeed, Bennett petitioned the wealthy members of his parish in Knightsbridge to finance the building of church and a school at Pimlico which would not only minister to the poor but would also expand the same style of worship as practised at St Paul's and provide accommodation in the form of a college for priests and choristers. In 1847 the

---

4 See F. W. Joyce, *The Life of the Rev. Sir F. A. G. Ouseley* (London: Methuen & Co., 1896), 85.

school in Pimlico was opened, and Bennett and his family soon moved into the clergy-house attached to the half-built church together with his curates, Ouseley, Laurence Tutiett, Henry Fyffe and G. F. de Gex. Fyffe and Gex would become life-long friends of Ouseley and play an important role in the formation of Tenbury.

St Barnabas, Pimlico, was consecrated by the Bishop of London on 11 June 1850. The sixteen choral services held there during its first week drew numerous High Church activists including Keble, Pusey, J. M. Neale and Bishop Wilberforce of Oxford. Music for the Dedication Festival was superintended by the Rev. Thomas Helmore, who acted as Precentor and brought in additional choristers from West-minster Abbey and the Chapel Royal. Holy Communion was celebrated every day with a full choir; Gregorian chant was sung; and those attending services included many clergy curious to observe the High Church manner for use in their own parishes.[5] Yet, although St Paul's and St Barnabas's were veritable models of the new Tractarian 'method' – whose precepts were to restore order, dignity, reverence and mystery to the Anglican liturgy – they became the focus of serious political antipathy for those who believed that Rome was gaining a foot in the door, a sus-picion fuelled by Lord John Russell's 'Papal Aggression' in September 1850, when Pope Pius IX established a new province of the Roman Catholic Church with an Archbishop at Westminster and twelve bishops under his authority.

Ouseley, who retained something of the old eighteenth-century 'High and Dry' conservatism (which, in cleaving to traditional Anglicanism and the Prayer Book, disliked Romish innovations), was uncomfortable with the Anglo-Catholic prac-tices at St Paul's and St Barnabas's, and he felt saved in his deacon's orders from 'doing many things sorely *against* [*his*] *conscience*'.[6] Nor did he share the ecclesio-logical affinity for Gregorian chant, a repertoire he disliked. Yet, though he con-templated leaving the parish, he was loath to if it meant bringing criticism upon Bennett, who was by then the butt of much invective from enemies in the press and among the Church of England itself. 'No Popery' riots broke out in November 1850, and St Barnabas's was attacked by a mob. Threats were made to the clergy, and services were cancelled when menacing mobs threatened to disrupt them:

> We had every reason to be certain of a more violent attack on the Sunday the 17th [November], so we took every precaution to be prepared for it, nor were they superfluous. The 8 am and 9 am Services went off quietly; but at 10.30 am, the mob began to collect, but luckily our own congregation were seated in time. Nothing in the church happened before the Sermon, but during it a prodigious yell was heard without, which frightened some of our people much. The church was crammed to suffocation, and a body of

[5] See *The Parish Choir* 3 (1850), 116–19.
[6] Joyce, *Life of Ouseley*, 64.

staunch friends were stationed up the body of the nave to prevent any attack on the chancel. When the sermon was concluded, and the Non-Communicants prepared to retire, a violent rush was made by the populace outside; and doubtless, had they succeeded in their attempt, our beautiful edifice would have been dismantled, and our lives endangered. We know that was their object; but it pleased God to defeat their sacrilegious intention. The well-affected within were too strong for them, 100 policemen succeeded in quelling the mob without, sufficiently to let the congregation retire. The organist, by my direction, played "Full Organ" the whole time, to drown the row, which had no small effect in preventing the disaffected from communicating with one another. In about forty minutes, the church was at length cleared. It was truly gratifying to see the very large number of Communicants who remained to thank God in this way for His Almighty protection.[7]

The commotion at Pimlico led swiftly to Bennett's resignation; this was followed soon afterwards by those of Ouseley, Fyffe and Gex.

Ouseley felt some responsibility for the choristers at St Barnabas's; he agreed that they should continue to be educated, fed and boarded at his own expense at Lovehill House, Langley Marish, near Slough, under the care of his friend Fyffe, while their musical education was superintended by John Hampton, one of the oldest choristers. Ouseley, who felt somewhat traumatised by the St Barnabas débâcle, elected to travel abroad in order to recuperate. On the Continent he took time to consider his position in the church and to dwell on the role of music within his ministry.[8]

Ouseley's Continental travels took him to Portugal, Spain and Italy, where he was distinctly unimpressed with the church music, an opinion which cumulatively helped to confirm in his mind an antipathy to Romanism:

Oh! How wretchedly disappointed I have been with the musick in Rome! On Palm Sunday there was a beautiful Mass of Palestrina's; and during Holy Week I heard beautiful Misereres and Lamentations by Palestrina, Bai, Allegri, and Baini; also on Easter Day a very fine Mass by Siciliani – all first-rate composers. But these Romans can't sing their own musick! They have fine voices (Basses and Tenors, that is), but the … Trebles are *execrable*.[9]

Northern Europe, however, was much more inspiring, and in Munich, Leipzig and

[7] Ibid., 65–6.

[8] Ouseley explained to Joyce that it had been 'the invariable and tyrannical rule of [his] Bishop, [to] take Priest's Orders at Christmas [1850]' but leaving St Barnabas's so precipitately had meant that he remained unordained as a priest. (See Joyce, *Life of Ouseley*, 64.)

[9] Joyce, *Life of Ouseley*, 71.

Dresden his impression of the well-trained choristers served to encourage his own aspirations to form a model choir with properly educated and trained choristers from a higher class of society:

> In my humble opinion it is very desirable indeed to raise the position of our English Choir boys. *Now* they are too often mere rabble, and what refinement of style can we expect from such materials? ... Now, my choral scheme will tend, maybe, by God's blessing, to improve this state of things. I hope also that by instituting a model choir I may supply another great deficiency, i.e. Choir *men*, brought up as Choristers, who shall know how to be reverent and devout in Church; singing not for their own sake, but for God's glory; ... Now there is a great lack of good *chaunting clergy* in Church of England. No man can be so fit to perform the Priest's part well, in a Choral Service, as he who has been brought up as a Chorister boy.[10]

On Ouseley's return to England, towards the end of 1851, the small choral community of six choristers and three probationers that he had helped to fund under Fyffe and Hampton at Langley Marish continued to pursue its musical ideal, and a number of Ouseley's organist friends, notably Goss, Cooper, E. G. Monk, Corfe and the young Walter Parratt,[11] visited to sing and play.[12] After much deliberation he resolved to found a collegiate institution on the outskirts of Tenbury Wells, Worcestershire, close to the borders of Herefordshire and Shropshire. With financial assistance from local people, and the subtle repulsion of opposition to the scheme from some (which included the vicar of Tenbury), the church, designed and built by Henry Woodyer, was consecrated in 1856, a year after Ouseley had been appointed Professor of Music at Oxford (having successfully taken his D.Mus. at the university in 1854) and Precentor of Hereford Cathedral (having been ordained priest two days beforehand).

When Stainer arrived at St Michael's College, Tenbury, in October 1857 the college buildings had been in use for only about six months, the church interior (rich in carved woodwork and stain glass) was unfinished, the church grounds were still recovering from their recent repositories of alabaster blocks and other materials; there was no garden or planted trees; and there were serious difficulties with the Flight & Robson organ in the church.[13] Nevertheless, the regime of daily choral services was under way; the staff and boys ate regular meals in the dining-hall (staff at high table and boys in the main body of the hall); and the choristers were

[10] Ibid., 77–8.

[11] D. Tovey & W. Parratt, *Walter Parratt: Master of the Music* (London: Oxford University Press, 1941), 46.

[12] J. Hampden, *Reminiscences*, Hereford Cathedral Library D483.

[13] Bland, *Ouseley and his Angels*, 62.

educated between morning and evening services, a period which included two hours of piano lessons every afternoon given by Stainer himself. The boys each had their own cubicle; they wore gowns to classes; there was a library; outdoor sports were encouraged (in which Stainer keenly participated); and, within reasonable bounds, boys were able to take part in rural activities such as fishing and beating for the local shoots. The Tenbury staff and choristers were initially taken aback by the youthfulness of their new organist, among them John Hampton (one of the original choristers from Langley Marish and now one of the men) who was the same age as Stainer:

> I can well remember our astonishment when he first appeared among us. … He looked too young for the post, which we considered to be so very important. However, Sir Frederick assured us that 'he would do,' and we soon found that was true. All the while he was here I believe he was most sincerely loved by us all, and he was forward to help everyone with whom he came in contact. The curate, a first-rate mathematician, read with him and formed a very high opinion of his capabilities. We thought him bumptious, but we soon found that we were mistaken, for he was humble enough and seemed glad to be plainly spoken to by any whom he conceived had a right to speak.[14]

Although Ouseley took full responsibility for the management, discipline and financial welfare of the college (which included preparation of the boys for confirmation), all musical matters, including the rehearsal of the choir, were left to the organist. For Stainer the entire arrangement of Tenbury, its atmosphere, a regular salary, and the time it afforded for study were highly amenable, while the idealistic vision to which the institution remained resolutely faithful chimed with his own aspirations:

> In these utilitarian days it would seem to many a great waste of resources that splendid musical services should regularly take place on week-days in a church, with no congregation to participate in them or enjoy them. But Ouseley never viewed it in this light. The services, he said, were for the glory of God, and the offering would be none the less acceptable to Him because it came from an out-of-the-way spot in a remote country district.[15]

The isolation of Tenbury might, in other circumstances, have proved to be stultifying for a young organist of Stainer's talent, but the peculiar opportunities it offered at this juncture of his career were considerably advantageous. Besides

[14] F. G. Edwards, 'John Stainer', *Musical Times* 39 (May 1901), 301–2.
[15] Stainer, 'The Character and Influence of the Late Sir Frederick Ouseley', 34.

the routine of daily services, practices, the performance of voluntaries and the 'cathedral' ambience of the college, Stainer found himself in an ideal position to develop his interests as a performer and as a composer of church music with an able choir at hand to perform it. The organ at Tenbury, though unfinished when the church was opened, was potentially an impressive instrument designed by Ouseley himself, and part of that tradition of large 'insular' instruments built in England during the 1850s. Constructed by Flight & Robson (who had built the organ at St Barnabas's, Pimlico), the manuals showed an unusual feature of the time to extend down to CC and up as far as g³ across the Great, Swell and Choir,[16] and a pedal specification of a 32-foot Pyramydon, 16-foot Open Diapason, a 12-foot Quint and a Principal 8-foot.[17] As Thistlethwaite has posited, 'it was probably the last long-compass organ to be built in England.'[18] This organ, with its fifty-six stops, of course gave Stainer a much greater range than he had known at St Paul's, but he must have also recognised that he was playing on an instrument of an older era. He found himself at an important juncture where organ-building and performing techniques were changing. The long compass of the Tenbury instrument tended to reflect a prevalent view among organists of the 1830s and 1840s that the pedal was an adjunct to the manual, and although there were well-known 'pedalists' – S. S. Wesley, R. Prescott Stewart, and George Cooper, Stainer's organ teacher – there were many who felt that the CC compass of the manual made the pedal organ redundant.[19] Stainer, however, was of a younger generation, keen to develop his pedal technique and to exploit the colourful, dramatic possibilities of the organ as a more romantic, indeed orchestral instrument (a fact confirmed by his earliest forays into anthem composition). In addition he was fully aware of the emerging tradition of the German organ method, favoured by Frederick Davison, William Hill and Gauntlett, the performance of Bach's organ works, of which his teacher, George Cooper, was an avid exponent and editor, and the need to use pedals for the execution of Mendelssohn's 'modern' organ sonatas.

The regular presence of Ouseley at Tenbury meant that Stainer was exposed at first hand to the rationale of the Tenbury 'experiment' and to the ideals of Ouseley's vision of church music. Stainer was to learn much from his mentor's example, and, as surviving correspondence reveals, he was to be a sounding-board for Ouseley's battles with the press and with resistant clergymen who both failed to appreciate the importance of music in worship and refused to see the benefit of musical guidance from those more expert:

[16] See N. Thistlethwaite, *The Making of the Victorian Organ* (Cambridge: Cambridge University Press, 1990), 95.

[17] Ibid., 101.

[18] Ibid., 105.

[19] Ibid., 97.

What riles me most is the assertion that clergymen are bound not to be musicians, or to take a part in the ordering of musical services. This seems to me to strike a fatal blow at all hope of choral improvement – Unless the clergy themselves take it up, it can never be accomplished. But unless they are musicians themselves they can only injure the choral cause, even if they attempt to promote it. But they cannot be expected to become musicians unless professional musicians aid them, teach them, encourage them, and co-operate with them. The writers in the Mus[ical] Stand[ard] do the contrary of all this – ergo – they are impeding this improvement of church music in England. Is not that logically correct?[20]

Stainer also had immediate recourse, free of charge, to technical and historical instruction from a senior Oxford (albeit non-resident) academic, a phenomenally valuable source of guidance towards his desire to study for a music degree. Such assistance as Stainer gained systematically in harmony and counterpoint from Ouseley may in part be gauged by the primers, *A Treatise on Harmony* (1868), *A Treatise on Counterpoint, Canon and Fugue, based on Cherubini* (1869) and *A Treatise on Musical Form* (1875), which Ouseley later published in Oxford, and the authoritative articles he produced for the first edition of *Grove's Dictionary of Music and Musicians*. On music of a more contemporary nature, Ouseley was more reticent. Writing to Stainer a few years later, after his pupil had left Tenbury, he admitted his inability to comprehend late Beethoven: 'I will look at the Sonata of Beethoven's you name. I am not sure which it is, till I look. I confess I am often unable to understand his latest works. But that may be my stupidity.'[21] In addition to his predilection for technical stringency, Ouseley was also an enthusiastic antiquarian and an ardent student of musical history, a fact not only manifested in his termly lectures at Oxford, but even more remarkably in his extraordinary library of primary and secondary sources, particularly of Italian sixteenth- and seventeenth-century vocal music. Stainer's evenings at Tenbury, when not devoted to organ practice, composition or private study, were passed in the company of Ouseley in which he was able to develop a profound acquaintance with this rare material:

In the splendid musical library he had collected there was a rich store of pure vocal masses of the Italian school in MS. in the old clefs, including not only the soprano and alto, but often also the now obsolete mezzo-soprano and baritone clefs. At that time he had not found opportunities of going carefully through these, and, most fortunately for me, I was asked constantly

---

[20] Letter from Ouseley to Stainer, n.d., *GB-Lbl* Add. MS 62121, fol. 3.
[21] Letter from Ouseley to Stainer, 4 February 1865, *GB-Lbl* Add. MS 62121, fol. 6.

to play them through to him, he turning over, and from time to time making critical remarks. I gained much from this almost unique chance of studying the vocal writers from, say, 1550 to 1700.[22]

Ouseley's library was indeed a rare phenomenon, and today it remains one of the most important and extensive collections ever made by a private individual. His particular interest in early English church music led him to collect an extensive range of Tudor and Stuart composers, including Fairfax, Sheppard, Tallis, Byrd, Weelkes, Morley, Gibbons, Tomkins and Henry Lawes, the Batten Organ Book, and also a unique eighteenth-century copy of a Caroline arrangement of Tallis's forty–part motet 'Spem in alium'. Sacred and secular English music of the later seventeenth, eighteenth and nineteenth centuries was well represented, with works by Blow (notably his Coronation anthems), Purcell (a copy of *Dido and Aeneas*), Arne (his oratorio *Judith*), Arnold, Travers, Greene, Boyce, Handel (his *Acis and Galatea* and the score of *Messiah* used by the composer at its first performance in Dublin) and Crotch (whose oratorios *The Captivity of Judah* and *Palestine* Ouseley much admired). Among the Continental music of the seventeenth and eighteenth centuries were oratorios and church works by Pergolesi, Jommelli, Clari, Perez, Caffaro, Durante, Leo, Marcello, Colonna, Fago, Hasse, cantatas and operatic music by Cimarosa, J. C. Bach, and Mayr, more than a dozen operas by Paisiello, and numerous copies of the famous settings of the 'Miserere' by Gregorio Allegri (including the famous *abbellimenti*) and Tomasso Bai.[23] Such a rich source

---

[22] Stainer, 'The Character and Influence of the Late Sir Frederick Ouseley', 34.

[23] In the event of the closure of St Michael's College, Ouseley had indicated that he wished his library to be housed in the Bodleian Library, Oxford. The manuscript collection of the library came to the Bodleian in 1978 and became the property of the library after the college's closure in 1985. With regard to the printed material in the collection, some of this was sold off since some of the items were already possessed by the Bodleian. However, the Bodleian was determined to retain the library and raised £180,000 to prevent it from being broken up. The first catalogue of Tenbury manuscripts was published in 1934 by Editions de L'Oiseau Lyre, Paris and compiled by E. H. Fellowes (with additions, amendments and annotations by Watkins Shaw), who also provided a first supplement to the catalogue. A second edition, with additions, amendments and annotations was first published on microfilm in 1981 by Harvester Press Microform Publications Ltd, Brighton. A second supplement was made by Watkins Shaw. After Ouseley's death in 1889 the collection of manuscripts was bequeathed by him to St Michael's College, Tenbury. A catalogue was made, careless in the eyes of Fellowes, by Bumpus (where books and manuscripts were catalogued together). The Rev. E. H. Swann (Warden at Tenbury) asked the Rev. Surtees Talbot to make a catalogue and put the library in order, but the task got no further, since only three weeks after beginning the task, in the spring of 1918, Talbot died. Later that year Fellowes was asked to take on the task and he began it afresh.

of material helped to formed Ouseley's picture of musical history, one which informed his termly lectures at Oxford and his future papers for the Musical Association.[24] For Stainer, who had free access to this material on a daily basis, it was a heaven-sent opportunity to be able to study musical history without recourse to the British Museum.

In addition to his antiquarian interest in church music, Ouseley, self-taught on the guitar, loved to perform on the instrument and to accompany himself in popular Italian and Spanish songs. Stainer eventually received as a gift a guitar and an arrangement of the first prelude of Bach's '48' together with a dedication and recommendation that, with regular practice (which Stainer duly effected), 'he might excel on the guitar no less than on the organ'.[25] Ouseley also encouraged the singing of madrigals in leisure hours. He had done this with the choristers at Langley Marish, but at Tenbury, with its ready supply of old music, there were more plentiful opportunities to sing Italian and English repertoire from the sixteenth and early seventeenth centuries in four, five and six parts, and pieces from Ouseley's library were readily copied into partbooks.[26] Already familiar with madrigalian works and other secular material from his participation in the London Madrigal Society, Stainer felt a natural affinity with this type of music-making and, according to John Hampton, may well have composed at least three madrigals for domestic use at Tenbury which were later published in Oxford in 1864.[27]

Two of them were clearly influenced by his familiarity with Morley's balletts. Both 'The Queen of May' and 'Why so pale' (which sets Suckling's much-used lyric) are simple designs with 'fa la' refrains. The Queen of May', in six parts (SSATTB), shows impressive handling of texture, manipulation of textual stress and effective use of female–male 'antiphony' between upper and lower 'choirs' in the refrain. Stainer also provides subtle contrast in each distinctive verse, especially in the last, where a shift to the tonic minor and an injection of dissonance cleverly underpin a fleeting moment of sorrow. The quizzical, strophic 'Why so pale and wan fond lover' is rather more ambitious and distinctive. Irregular phraseology and a degree of tonal fluidity enhance a series of 'questioning' musical gestures – an imperfect cadence approached through an augmented sixth ('Prithee why so pale?'), an ambiguous diminished seventh and a further half-close accompanied

---

[24] See Ouseley's Oxford lectures 1858–88, *GB-Ob* Tenbury Collection MS 1453.

[25] Edwards, 'John Stainer', 302.

[26] See partbooks in the Tenbury collection, *GB-Ob* MSS 945–54.

[27] See Edwards, 'John Stainer', 301. The partbooks contain three madrigals – 'The Queen of May' [MSS 945–6 and 951–4] , 'Why so pale' [MSS 945–54] and 'Love's servile lot' [MSS 945–54; only MS 945 and 948 for first and second treble are copied out; the rest only bear the title] – published in Oxford, though when they were copied is uncertain.

by a significant ritenuto – which are resolved by a refrain in the major mode. With each refrain, in an expanded six-part texture (from the original SATB), Stainer shows considerable polyphonic flair as he inverts his various contrapuntal strands, the last being most elaborate of all (Example 1).

Homophony rather than polyphony and the rapid descending chordal movement governs the character of 'Love's servile lot', a setting of a lyric by Robert Southwell. (It was a style that Warlock and Moeran were to ape many years later in the *Capriol* Suite and the *Songs of Springtime*.) Like 'Prithee, why so pale', the mood is one of dark, passionate humour, amplified in the final verse where, like 'Why so pale', Stainer increases the texture from four voices to six for a much variegated conclusion enhanced by chromaticism, an infusion of polyphony, the dissonant colour of the 'English cadence' and the thoroughly 'romantic' final close (replete with dominant eleventh).

As a fast-developing and impressionable youth in his late teens, Stainer was almost certainly impressed by Ouseley's promotion of madrigal-singing and composition, his love of musical history, and his taste for antiquarian research. Yet he also clearly realised at Tenbury that he did not share his mentor's aesthetic outlook on the future of church music. Ouseley was a disciple of his Oxford predecessor, William Crotch, and an advocate of the aesthetic principles laid out in Crotch's Oxford lectures, the *Substance of several courses of lectures in music, read in the University of Oxford, and in the Metropolis*, published in 1831, though based on his lectures given between 1800 and 1804, and in 1820. Deriving much of his aesthetic scheme from analogies with Sir Joshua Reynold's *Discourses*, written between 1769–90, and thereby pertaining largely to eighteenth-century notions of art, Crotch's views of music, which were defined by reference to the styles of the 'Sublime' (spiritual grandeur and aspiration, intellectual rigour, equipoise of structure and tonality), the 'Beautiful' (classical grace, lyricism, charm and the 'affecting' of the emotions), and 'Ornamental' (a lighter style, more heavily dependent on caprice, and the emerging instrumental idiom) bore relation to the levels of intellectual application required to create them.[28] Crotch's outlook was ultimately pessimistic; he perceived music as being in decline, and that the very reverse of his established hierarchy was in the ascendant. In one sense he was right. At the time that he was forming his aesthetic ideas – at the very beginning of the nineteenth century – the maelstrom of musical debate was rapidly outstripping older eighteenth-century shibboleths such as the superiority of vocal music over instrumental. Perhaps more alarming to many was the emergence of secularism (a product of

---

[28] For a more extensive account and analysis of Crotch's writings, see H. L. Irving, *Ancients and Moderns: William Crotch and the Development of Classical Music* (Aldershot: Ashgate, 1999).

Example 1. Madrigal 'Prithee, why so pale' ('Encouragement to a lover') – conclusion

the Enlightenment and the turbulence of the revolutions in America and France),
to which was closely allied the rising supremacy of instrumental music.

Crotch's viewpoint, and Ouseley's after him, was largely consistent with the
reaction articulated by the Caecilian-Bündnisse (Cecilian Leagues) in Bavaria
and Austria at the end of the eighteenth century. Besides a desire to restore the
authority of the church, the liturgy, and traditional religious sentiment, the Cecilians longed for a return to a 'pure' church music with little or no instrumental
participation. A definition of a 'true church music' had begun to emerge in the
works of J. F. Reichardt, A. W. von Schlegel, K. A. von Mastiaux, Herder and J. A. P.
Schulz, a new reverence for Fux's *stile antico*, and a burgeoning rediscovery of the
music of Palestrina, whose style attempted to define a new sense of devotion and
'unworldliness'. All of these combined to give momentum to the reactionary, anti-
Romantic principles of the Cecilians, who deplored the evolution of the opera and
the concert hall as the new cathedrals of the bourgeoisie, and their ideals spread
to Protestant northern Germany, France and Switzerland. With Regensburg as the
hub of the Cecilian movement, the fervour for 'pure' church music spawned editions of early music (edited by scholars such as F. X. Haberl), influential treatises
such as A. F. J. Thibaut's *Über Reinheit der Tonkunst* (1825) and Carl Proske's *Die
Verbesserung der Domkirchenmusik* (1829–30), and a large repertoire of ecclesiastical works that failed to rise above a banal pastiche of sixteenth- and seventeenth-
century models. Crotch's *dictum* expressed much the same aesthetic consequence
for church music in England:

> 'And must we, then, have no new church music?' Yes; but no new style: noth-
> ing which recommends itself for its novelty, or reminds us of what we hear at
> the parade, the concert, and the theatre. Much new music may be produced
> in the sacred style; though to equal what has already been produced will not
> be found so easy as may perhaps be imagined.[29]

By 1831, when a compendium of Crotch's lectures was in print, the same principles were effectively enunciated by the Gresham Prize, funded by no other than
Maria Hackett, who was also an adherent of Crotch's 'sublime' precept. As Gatens
has pointed out, the Gresham Prize gave a fillip to Crotch's cause. He, with two
confederates, William Horsley and R. S. Stevens, formed the judging panel, so that
it was inevitable that applicants would feel compelled to conform to his principles
if they were to be successful. Those that took a different line, such as S. S. Wesley,
were doomed to failure.[30] Ouseley, and other conservatives such as Elvey, while

---

[29] W. Crotch, *Substance of Several Courses of Lectures in Music, Read in the University
of Oxford, and in the Metropolis* (London, 1831), 83.

[30] See W. J. Gatens, *Victorian Cathedral Music in Theory and Practice* (Cambridge:
Cambridge University Press, 1986), 66.

they may not have adhered as rigidly to Crotch's views, nevertheless held up his principles as their fundamental credo. Indeed, Ouseley publicly declared his undying allegiance to Crotch in his papers for the Church Congresses at Manchester and Leeds,[31] and his lectures given at Oxford as late as the 1880s.[32] Ouseley viewed secular influences on church music with deep unease, and contemporary developments were denounced. In church music he believed steadfastly in the values of sixteenth- and seventeenth-century cathedral music (values which, incidentally, had been reinforced by his Continental travels to southern and northern Germany in the 1850s); Handelian oratorio was the touchstone of large-scale choral music, and for instrumental music Mozart was the limit of his stylistic outlook.

Among Crotch's and Ouseley's fiercest critics were Gauntlett and S. S. Wesley; they were conjoined by Stainer, who, even with his youth, fundamentally rejected his teacher's *dicta* and attributed Ouseley's lack of success as a composer to the excessive constraints he placed upon himself. For that, Stainer later asserted, 'Dr Crotch must be blamed', and he condemned the false analogy of Reynold's *Discourses* with musical art:

> Ouseley thoroughly imbibed the spirit of Crotch's "Lectures." In these Crotch traces the history of music as if analogous to the arts of painting and architecture. Other arts, he argues, have reached a culminating point of excellence, and then have gone into decadence; therefore the art of music is in a similar condition. As a sequel, students are advised to *imitate* the compositions of the so-called "best period" of style. Crotch was an ardent admirer of Sir Joshua Reynolds' "Discourses," and his Oxford lectures are simply larded with quotations from Sir Joshua. …
>
> I know no more sad example of the fallacy of the argument by analogy than this creed of Crotch – that music had seen its best days. If you remember that Crotch began to lecture publicly in 1801, or thereabouts, you will at once see what a very false prophet he has proved to be.[33]

Instead, Stainer offered a much broader, liberal and catholic philosophy of music which surely must have crystallised early in his career, and was quite probably forming during his time at Tenbury:

> We musicians are not yet called upon to retrace our steps, for our many-sided and wonderful art seems again and again to burst afresh and find new room for vigorous growth. Of course, imitation of the past in music is a

31 See *Proceedings of the Church Congress, Manchester*, 161–72, and *Leeds*, 326–34.
32 See Ouseley's Oxford lectures, *GB-Ob* Tenbury MS 1453, 'The Art of Musical Criticism' (1881) and 'A Lecture on Church Music' (11 March 1885).
33 Stainer, 'The Character and Influence of the Late Sir Frederick Ouseley', 37.

necessary process of pupillage; but, to look upon it as an end in itself, is surely destructive to all progress and expansion. The imitator is, after all, no better than a mere mechanic; the ultimate function of the true artist is not to imitate the old, but to create the new. In order to do so, he must, indeed, tread old paths, but not for the purpose of loitering in them, only in order to trace them up to the very front of the present. There is one insidious temptation which often draws gifted men into the ranks of mere imitators; it is this: the general rock of mankind will always prefer an imitation to an attempt at novelty, for the very obvious reason that the public finds it easy to criticise an imitation, whereas only a select and cultured few are capable of gauging the true merits of what is unfamiliar.[34]

It is evident, however, that Stainer felt duty-bound to conform to Ouseley's aesthetic limitations for the purposes of entering for his B.Mus. degree at Oxford. For this purpose Stainer had only to submit an exercise (Ouseley's institution of formal written examinations was not introduced until 1862) conforming to established rubric which, if approved, had then to be performed in the University. Stainer's exercise, *Praise the Lord, O my soul*, a setting of selected texts from Psalm 103, was completed on 19 October 1858. In virtually all aspects the work, including the 'Cherubinian' contrapuntal stringencies that Ouseley was to impose on the formal written papers, was a 'Crotchian' imitation with little to commend it. The overture, a neo-Baroque 'introduction and fugue' modelled on the 'French Overture' of *Messiah* and other Handelian introductory essays to oratorios, is uninspired, though no doubt Ouseley and his Choragus, Charles Steggall, saw some technical merit in the augmentation of the fugal subject towards the close. The choruses, set in the obligatory yet somewhat archaic five parts, are dull and stylistically sterile, though the central choral fugue 'The Lord hath prepared his seat in heaven' has a degree of rhythmic vigour in its subject and countersubject, but the modest merits of this material are only thrown into relief by the banality of the closing 'Amen' fugue, which again must have found its source in *Messiah*. Having matriculated at Christ Church College, Stainer oversaw the performance of his cantata on 9 June 1859 in the Sheldonian Theatre, Oxford, with Ouseley present; the degree was conferred the following day. He was just nineteen years of age. In 1856, under the unreformed statute, Leighton Hayne, organist of Queen's College, had taken his degree at the age of twenty; this had been the subject of some note in *Jackson's Oxford Journal*.[35] Stainer had not only emulated Hayne, but he was also the youngest ever successful candidate of a B.Mus. – though this 'record' was soon to be

[34] Ibid., 37–8.

[35] See S. Wollenberg, *Music at Oxford in the Eighteenth and Nineteenth Centuries* (Oxford: Oxford University Press, 2001), 114.

trounced in 1866, when under Ouseley's reformed system of examinations Parry was to gain his B.Mus. at the age of eighteen.

Conservatism may have been an expedient means of achieving his musical degree, but Stainer was of no mind to mimic Ouseley's seventeenth- and eighteenth-century imitations in his first works for the church. Though he was happy to assimilate elements of the 'sublime', the grandiose effects of Handelian oratorio, and the melodic grace of the classical style, his object was, as he was to enunciate on numerous occasions, to integrate these ideas within the boundaries of new stylistic developments, an artistic philosophy which he would live out in the very first phase of his creative output. In 1858, the same year that his exercise was completed, he composed three anthems with the choir of Tenbury in mind: 'The morning stars sang together', 'I saw the Lord', and 'The righteous live for evermore', all of them substantial creative and imaginative essays in a multi-sectional 'verse' idiom deriving much of their harmonic vocabulary from the music of Mendelssohn and Spohr. Stainer would also evince a phraseological manner essentially classical in its regularity (which he seems to have inherited from Goss), modulatory processes and tonal behaviour from a knowledge of Beethoven and Schubert, an imaginative assimilation of Bachian counterpoint and a sense of dissonance at times comparable with the experimental progressions of S. S. Wesley. These things considered, Stainer still held his style within the 'equilibrium' of the 'ecclesiastical style' which, driven by an innate sense of faith and propriety, attempted to maintain a balance of solemnity, an avoidance of extremes, and a moderated sense of theatricality, where, as Gauntlett once pronounced, one should 'not transgress the bounds of religious fervour, and reverential joy'.[36]

'The morning stars sang together' was included in the first volume of Ouseley's *Special Anthems for Certain Seasons and Festivals of the United Church of England and Ireland*, published in 1861. Ouseley's volume was intended to provide a repertoire of modern anthems for the festivals of the church year, a practice hitherto ignored by many churches and cathedrals but one applauded by the Tractarians. The anthems were also designed to cover a wide range of abilities from the village church to the cathedral, and from the liturgical constraints of the introit to the large-scale anthem. 'The morning stars' was a large-scale affair, typical perhaps of Stainer's youthful ambition. Written for Christmas Day, and dedicated to George Cooper, the anthem took its title and first line from the book of Job (Ch. 38 v. 7), though the focus of the text is from Luke's gospel (Ch. 2 v. 11), 'For unto you is born this day in the city of David a Saviour, which is Christ the Lord', taken from the scene of the shepherds. The anthem was conceived as a broad ternary form in

---

[36] H. J. Gauntlett, 'English Ecclesiastical Composers of the Present Age', *Musical World* 21 (5 Aug 1836), ii: 113.

which two slow-moving choruses (in four parts), the second an almost *verbatim* repeat of the first, flank a central verse for five solo voices. Stainer's conception of the chorus, which is throughout uniformly antiphonal and homophonic in delivery (between Cantoris and Decani), was clearly an evocation of angels answering back and forth. The impression too, is one of timeless sublimity and majesty, portrayed by the slow-moving harmonic rhythm, prevalence of pedal points, and the spatial dimension of the (almost Renaissance-like) antiphony. The first choral paragraph, which seeks to emphasise the angelic multitude by the 'endless' repetition of the text, embarks from A major, but concludes in the subdominant, D. This allows Stainer to indulge in a Schubertian shift (through the unison D) to B flat (Example 2) which, with the accumulation of the full choir at *ff*, gives greatest impact to the presentation of the gospel text. Stainer's recovery to A major is deftly effected through F major and its relative D minor (which invokes the return of the text from Job and its concomitant antiphony), and the final section, in which the full choir present the gospel text once again, is the tonal reverse of the opening section in that it embarks from the subdominant and concludes by buoyantly rising the fifth to A. For the verse in the dominant, E major, Stainer selected his text from Isaiah (Ch. 66 v. 10 and part of v. 12) and opted for a simple binary structure (repeated) in a contrasting and more perceptibly classical style, which, in looking back to Goss and Attwood, amply demonstrates the indebtedness of so much English church music to Mozart.[37]

'The righteous live for evermore', an anthem for general use, setting vv. 15 and 16 from the book Wisdom, is a tripartite 'ABC' scheme. 'A' effectively constitutes an introduction using the homophonic and phraseological idiom of the hymn, though even here Stainer surprises us with an unexpected detour to D major, a goodly distance from the tonic E. The verse, like 'The morning stars', is overtly classical in demeanour, binary in structure (AAB plus coda) and couched in the dominant (B major). Introduction and verse, however, are preparation for the 'sublime' statement of the final, five-part fugue ('For with His right hand') back in the tonic. Stainer's exposition, replete with regular fugal entries and countersubject, is somewhat prosaic, though some interest is generated by the tonal progress of the fugue towards the flat submediant (C major), an event which triggers an episode of much slower note values (a Bachian technique filtered through Mendelssohn). This moment of repose functions as a transition back to E major which is announced by augmentation of the subject (in the bass) and a stretto in the upper voices. This structural confluence marks the climax of the fugue proper, though the most dramatic point is the quasi-Handelian apotheosis, marked by a

---

[37] See N. Temperley, 'Mozart's Influence on English Music', *Music & Letters* 42 (1961), 307–18.

Example 2. Anthem: 'The morning stars sang together' (transition from D to B flat)

return to the slower note values, a passing memory of C major, and a thoroughly Romantic restoration of E major by way of its 6/4.

More remarkable and bolder than either of these anthems, however, was Stainer's anthem for Trinity Sunday, 'I saw the Lord', composed in 1858, but not published until 1865, when it was accepted by Novello, and in 1866 in the second volume of Ouseley's *Special Anthems for Certain Seasons*. Though it followed the same tripartite scheme as 'The righteous live', its entire conception was more original in its manipulation of well-established musical paradigms; this is evident in its transformation of the 'verse' style-form, the unconventional use of fugue as a rhetorical device, the unusual tonal scheme, and the striking dialectic of drama and serenity which is articulated by the anthem's larger architectural plan. The first and second sections of 'I saw the Lord' were conceived as a vivid exposition of Isaiah's visionary text (Ch. 6 vv. 1–4) for eight-part choir,[38] to which a tranquil fugue and chorale (in fact a form more closely approaching a Bachian chorale prelude) acts as a major foil in its setting of the last verse of the Latin hymn 'Ave, colenda Trinitas' in John David Chambers' recent translation ('O Trinity! O Unity! Be present as we worship Thee') from his *Psalter* published in 1852.[39] The tonal design is also deftly executed. G, coloured by extensive use of both its major and minor modes (a Schubertian device utilised with great power as a means of striking modulation) underpins both the first and second sections of the anthem, concluding on the dominant. However, at the close of the second, and most dramatic section (with its famous climactic statement 'And the house was fillèd with smoke'), Stainer gives more weight to the dominant through its 'modulatory' plagal cadence (all the more unexpected after the extended tonic pedal of G over no less than ten bars) and which provides the necessary conduit for the final section in its serene D major.

Perhaps the most arresting feature of 'I saw the Lord' is its masterly use of harmony, chromaticism and modulation, all of which betray Stainer's affinity with Romanticism. The opening 'proclamation', which moves from a major statement of the arpeggiated material to a minor one, establishes a generative process germane to the first section. Through the fluctuation to the minor mode and a cycle of fifths, F major is reached by bar 7, though a further step of a fifth (on B flat) allows an augmented sixth to bring us to the dominant of D and what seems like an imminent return to G (Example 3a). This is sidestepped, however, by an unanticipated shift to C which signals further development of the initial material using the same major–minor process, one which also concludes on its dominant (bar 22), giving way to an imitative passage and 'codetta' (Example 3b). These two strands of material pave the way for a further chromatic statement (strongly suggestive of Spohr) in which the outer voices rise stepwise through an octave from G minor to the dominant of D (Example 3c). A cadence into D at this juncture

---

[38] The only autograph of 'I saw the Lord' survives in *GB-Ob* Tenbury 1352. A significant feature of this manuscript is that Stainer's origination was initially for SSAATTBB (each part taken by Decani and Cantoris respectively) which was used in Ouseley's volume of 1866. The origination for Novello's published edition was SATB SATB double choir, which may have come about through the extensive use of antiphonal exchange within the eight-part choral texture. Furthermore, there are considerably more dynamics, accents, tied notes and registrational instructions in the published version and there is one choral passage in the manuscript, originally conceived as being *a cappella*, where the organ has been added (bars 54–8).

[39] Chambers' translation, slightly revised, later appeared in his *Lauda Syon* of 1857. It may have been this publication that Stainer knew, given its propinquity to the composition of 'I saw the Lord.'

Example 3. Anthem: 'I saw the Lord': (a) arrival at the dominant of D (bar 9);
(b) codetta: 'above it stood the seraphims'; (c) 'each one had six wings'; (d) 'Holy, holy, holy';
(e) 'the whole earth is full of His glory'; (f) 'And the posts of the door mov'd'; (g) 'And the
house was filled with smoke'

Example 3 continued

(c)

each one   had six   wings;   with   twain   he cov-er'd his   face,

each one   had six   wings;

(d)

Ho - ly,   Ho - ly,   Ho - - ly

Ho - ly,

Example 3 continued

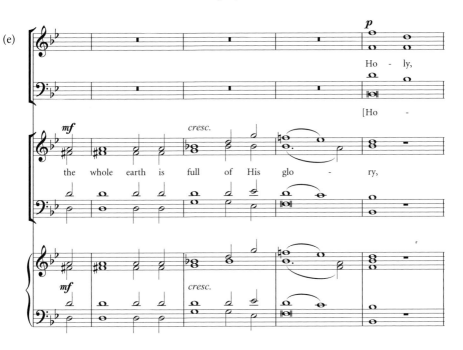

Example 3 continued

seems inevitable but for an entirely unexpected move to F sharp minor, a change of tonal direction which powerfully underscores the new text ('Holy, holy, holy'). The distance of F sharp minor from the original tonic, G, serves to heighten the musical genuflection (Example 3d) but at the same time its slower, descending arpeggios have the effect of calming the chromatic turbulence of the preceding section. Stainer's subsequent recovery of G minor is also quite masterly. The first of two sequential antiphonal statements takes us to D major; the second (with Schubertian panache) to B flat (Example 3e), at which point a reprise presents two statements of the 'genuflective' material, initially in the major mode (B flat) and, most fittingly to end, in the more familiar G minor. In no more than twenty-six bars the tonal distance travelled has been remarkable and compares readily with any of the experiments of Spohr and S. S. Wesley. Moreover, such was the striking force of this episode, it is not surprising that Stainer should have chosen to revisit the material later on in the anthem.

For the portentous second section, Stainer continued to build on the dramatic proclivity of the first part with its attitudinising chromaticism; indeed, the opening unison statements for chorus ('And the posts of the door mov'd') are derived from the 'codetta' material (Example 3f, compare 3b) in diminution. The imitative material that follows, in eight parts over an extended tonic pedal, is also inhabited by chromatic voice-leading; but what is most striking here is Stainer's handling of diatonic dissonance which, in accordance with the violence of the text ('And the house was fillèd with smoke'), rises to a high degree of intensity (Example 3g). Stainer would almost certainly have been familiar with seventeenth-century essays in dissonance in the Italian sacred music of Carissimi, Lotti and Caldara, in the Restoration music of Blow and Purcell, Michael Haydn's archaic church works, and Mozart's well known 'Ave verum', though much of the 'heightened' dissonance employed here was probably gleaned from examples in S. S. Wesley (as in anthems such as 'Ascribe unto the Lord' or 'Let us lift up are heart').

The style of Stainer's lyrical fugue (which rhetorically does not sound like a fugue at all), presented in the manner of a 'verse' and sung throughout by solo voices, was also probably garnered from the examples of S. S. Wesley's euphonious fugal finales (such as one finds in 'Let us lift up our heart'). In fact the four phrases of the fugue subject, across the irregular expanse of nine bars, have the deportment of a hymn tune save for their wider vocal range and the intriguing tonal property of embarking from D major and concluding in B minor. The alto's answer, which should mark the introduction of the dominant, is instead in F sharp minor (bars 10–11), and though A major is stated *en passant* (bars 11–12), F sharp predominates. This ambiguity between tonic and relative continues with the tenor entry whose way is prepared by a return to B minor (bar 18). Deftly, however, Stainer steers us obliquely back to D (bars 19–20), though this is only temporary, for B minor again asserts itself at the subject's close (bar 27). Irregularly, Stainer does not introduce the fourth entry of his exposition (for bass) at this stage. Unconventionally this is introduced after a radical shift to the Neapolitan (bar 29) initiates a cycle of fifths flatwise which brings us to B flat (bar 32). In accordance with the tonal properties of the subject, the bass's entry cadences in G, though Stainer, showing his full command of contemporary harmonic apparatus, deflects the cadence to D. At this point he administers his *coup de maître* by recalling the 'genuflection' from the first section of the anthem ('Holy, holy, holy, The whole earth is full of His glory') sung twice by the chorus. This is presented as a counterpoint (indeed more in the manner of a chorale *cantus firmus*) to the fugue (the recapitulation of whose subject, now for all four soloists, is marked by a return to D major) and the wonderfully expansive 'free' material of the coda.

'I saw the Lord' was an exceptional, bold and original essay exhibiting a rare confidence from one so young and relatively inexperienced. Besides its impressive technical assurance in which well-tried style-forms (such as fugue) are employed with fresh vigour and imagination, the larger architecture of the anthem is closer to the concept of a miniature cantata (a perception, incidentally, Stainer was to apply to S. S. Wesley's larger anthems such as 'Let us lift up our heart'). Moreover, the artifice of the anthem, with its inventive tonal behaviour, cyclic dimension, and thematic integration, reveals a conception unusual in nineteenth-century English church music where, through Stainer's handling of vocal technique, is, beyond question, nineteenth-century instrumental procedures are distinctly prevalent. Such thinking was to emerge in many of Stainer's later ecclesiastical works.

'Drop down, Ye Heavens, from Above':
Oxford (1)

T HE facility, artifice and brilliant technique of 'I saw the Lord', a prodigious, indeed precocious exhibition by such a young man, undoubtedly impressed Ouseley even if he may have been out of sympathy with the anthem's contemporary style. Ouseley, however, must have sensed that, for all its conducive attributes, Tenbury was too isolated a spot for Stainer to pursue his musical career and that, before long, his pupil would be looking for fresh and more advantageous opportunities elsewhere.

Such an opportunity presented itself at the end of 1859 when the post of organist and *informator choristarum* became vacant at Magdalen College, Oxford, after the resignation of Benjamin Blyth on 1 December,[1] and after his assistant, E. Vine Hall, turned down the offer to replace him.[2] The post was available through open competition. Among those who put themselves forward for consideration with appropriate testimonials were Samuel Reay (a one-time chorister of Durham Cathedral and organist of Radley College), George Mursell Garrett (formerly a chorister at New College, Oxford under Stephen Elvey, and now organist at St John's College, Cambridge) and George Benjamin Arnold (a pupil of S. S. Wesley

---

[1] Watkins Shaw refers to Blyth's 'early retirement' (see W. Shaw, *The Succession of Organists* (Oxford: Clarendon Press, 1991), 384), but Frederic Bulley's diary (*GB-Omc*) not only tells us that Blyth actually resigned (see copy of letter of resignation, 1 December 1859) but that, after a prior warning (16 May 1859) there was a need to suspend him (11 June 1859) which, after a period when others took on his duties, he resumed his post (16 October 1859) for about six weeks until his resignation. Bloxam recalled in October 1883 that Blyth's departure had been 'under such painful circumstances that [he, Bloxam] had not the heart to make any memorandum.' (*GB-Omc* MS 444). Blyth retired to Whitchurch in 1860 but he continued to participate in Magdalen music including the Magdalen Vagabonds, a fact which indicates that he had not been ostracised by the college. For the rest of the term in December 1859, Blyth's place was taken by Vine Hall.

[2] See E. Vine Hall, *The Magdalen Vagabonds: A History of their Doings*, unpub. *GB-Omc* which contains the following remarks: 'Frederic Bulley even stated: "… he [Vine Hall] might have been appointed Organist of Magdalen College, at the last vacancy, if he had felt inclined to accept that office …" ' Vine Hall was also offered the organistships at Exeter College (in 1859) and New College (1860).

and organist of St Mary's, Torquay).[3] Stainer's appointment to the post was by no means a foregone conclusion. Reay (b. 1822), Arnold (b. 1832) and Garrett (b. 1834) were older, more experienced professionals and came with testimonials from eminent church musicians; next to them, Stainer, with only just over two years at Tenbury, and not even twenty years of age, must have seemed almost absurdly young to the President of Magdalen, Frederic Bulley. However, Stainer, who could already boast of an Oxford music degree, came with excellent testimonials, one of them from Ouseley who commanded respect within the University as the Professor of Music.

In the event, Bulley, who was an intelligent, astute, if conservative personality, with a reputation as having been a first-rate tutor at Oxford and a stalwart supporter of the choir, elected to audition three of his four applicants, among whom was Stainer. He was summoned at short notice to Magdalen on 22 December (it being the only free day before the Christmas vacation) that he 'might perform the organ duty in the Chapel ... at 10, or at 4, or both'.[4] Stainer attended his audition and Bulley was pleased to write to Ouseley on Boxing Day that he considered the young organist the most suitable man for the job, but, given his youth and relative inexperience, felt reluctant to give him an open-ended contract. Instead, a three-month agreement was offered in order to see whether he had the ability to train the choristers, manage the Lay Clerks, all of whom were of more senior years, and cope with the daily pressures of chapel services. After this period a full contract would be offered if his abilities proved satisfactory. Ouseley was kept informed of these contractual terms, presumably on the basis that, should Stainer not prove acceptable, his pupil could return to Tenbury:

Dear Sir Frederic [*sic*],

Of three candidates to whom I have given leave to compete for the Organist's place at Magdalen, Mr Stainer is the only one who appears to me to be fitted for the office.

He is, in my opinion, a person of good taste and judgement, and capable of considerable development. But of this I need further proof. It remains to be proved also whether he is efficient as a teacher and superintendent of the

---

[3] Bulley's diary also alludes to a 'Mr Redhead of Aylesbury' who, having assisted with the services during the period immediately after Blyth's resignation in December 1859, may have been auditioned (see diary of Frederic Bulley, 15 December 1859 and 20 December 1859). A 'Dr Read' of Salisbury also expressed an interest in the post in March 1860.

[4] Diary of Frederic Bulley, 20 December 1859. See also letter from Bulley to Stainer, 20 December 1859, in private possession (JRS).

Quire. And this I propose to ascertain by a trial of three months, at the end of which time, if he gives satisfaction, he will be formally admitted.

The Stipend for the first year will be £120 with an increase, if the President thinks fit, of £10 per annum afterwards, until the income reaches £150.[5]

In fact the terms of Bulley's contract were a little more stringent, since Stainer was required to promise 'to resign at any time before Xmas 1860 if requested to do so by the President'. He was also required 'to attend in Chapel on Fridays as well as other days taking his seat with the Clerks and superintending the Quire' and 'to provide himself with lodgings at his own expense'.[6]

Stainer accepted Bulley's terms and agreed to make himself available to begin work on Saturday 28 January 1860.[7] As the day arrived, Bulley wrote to confirm arrangements for his first service, his accommodation and board:

> I write to inform you that the Choristers return to College on Saturday next, and that the Choral Service in Chapel will re-commence on Sunday next, the early service being at eight o clock. At early prayers on Sundays and Saints Days the Communion Service only is chanted.
>
> I have provided lodgings for you in Merton St at the house of my servant Skinner, where I hope you will be comfortable.
>
> If you prefer dining in Hall to dining at your lodgings, you might be allowed to battell [the account of a member of a college at Oxford for provisions and board] at your own expense at the Clerks' table.
>
> If you will call upon me immediately on your arrival, I will give you any further instructions which you may require.
>
> I shall feel obliged to you to let me know on what day it will be convenient to you to come to Oxford, that my servant may have everything in readiness for you.[8]

Stainer began his duties accordingly, and, after the three months' trial period had elapsed, Bulley was not in a position immediately to make up his mind. So, on 27 April 1860 he wrote to Ouseley 'to enquire whether he would object to Mr Stainer's remaining at Magdalen until the middle of July, supposing that I would engage to give him a final answer at that time. Said that I believed this arrangement would be very likely to be attended with a favourable result.'[9] In fact Stainer's performance must have been well nigh exemplary, for he immediately formed a

5 Letter from Bulley to Ouseley, 26 December 1859, in private possession (JRS).

6 Conditions, in Bulley's handwriting, n.d., in private possession (JRS).

7 Diary of Frederic Bulley, 1 January 1860.

8 Letter from Bulley to Stainer, 23 January 1860, in private possession (JRS).

9 Diary of Frederic Bulley, 27 April 1860.

rapport with the choristers as one, many years later, attested: 'One of the *very* first to see and know "Mr." Stainer, at Magdalen, was myself. Directly we choristers saw him and heard him we adored him and did so ever after. Over and above his unapproachable playing, he was one of the very few touched with the radiance of the inner life of sacred music.'[10]

By the middle of May, Bulley was ready to admit Stainer on a full contract,[11] and by July the *Oxford Chronicle* was ready to announce 'the newly appointed and highly accomplished organist, Mr Steiner [*sic*]'.[12] £120 would continue to be his salary (with increases as the President saw fit); Stainer would be expected to reside outside the College; and he was expected to be present in the Quire on Fridays 'to lead the boys' (when organ accompaniment was traditionally not used).[13] More-over, if he wished to pursue a degree while at Oxford, lectures were not to interfere with his duties.

Stainer's desire to sit for a B.A. degree at Oxford, even though he already pos-sessed a B.Mus., almost certainly stemmed from his desire for greater social status. Although the B.Mus. carried some weight within his profession, in the Univer-sity itself music had for many years languished as a second-class degree. Not only was the Professor of Music a non-resident office, but so were those studying for the degree. No tutoring of music took place in Oxford and it was the job of the Professor, with his Choragus and an external academic or specialist, to examine the exercises. Stainer, for one, had been examined in just this way. However, with Ouseley's appointment at Oxford in 1855, music began to enjoy some augmenta-tion in reputation. To an appreciable extent this must be attributed to Ouseley's social position, for, among the senior academic circles of the University, music was not a subject for someone of his rank and wealth. As W. Tuckwell recollected:

> I shall recall later on the consternation felt among the older men of Oxford, when Ouseley, baronet, gentleman commoner, Master of Arts, condescended to become Doctor of Music; and we all remember Mr. Osborne's contempt for the "Honourables" to whom his daughter introduced him – "Lords, indeed? Why, at one of her swarreys I saw one of 'em speak to a damn fiddler, a fellar I despise."[14]

---

[10] F. G. Edwards, 'John Stainer', *Musical Times* 39 (May 1901), 303.

[11] Stainer was officially admitted as organist at Magdalen on 13 May 1860; see W. D. Macray, *A Register of the Members of St Mary Magdalen College, Oxford from the Foundation of the College* vii (London: Henry Frowde, 1894–1915), 99.

[12] *Oxford Chronicle*, 14 July 1860.

[13] *Oxford Chronicle*, 18 May 1860. These conditions bear Stainer's signature of agree-ment (JRS).

[14] W. Tuckwell, *Reminiscences of Oxford* (London: Smith, Elder & Co., 1907), 73.

Ouseley's status gave similar *gravitas* to the Professorship of Music, which had virtually no profile under his predecessor, Sir Henry Bishop, and the standing of the music degrees also began to rise after he reformed them in 1862 by introducing written papers (involving a critical and historical knowledge of the subject in addition to the exercise). This change in the fortunes of music, albeit relatively modest, also reflected other major reforms that had been the focus of controversy in the University since the early 1850s.

On Stainer's arrival in Oxford in 1860 the University and colleges were in the process of reacting to two government commissions – the first initiated in 1850 and concluded in 1852 (in the report known as 'the Blue Book'), the second (as the result of the general lack of co-operation of the first) in 1854 and which lasted four years until 1858. The Commissions had materialized in much the same way as had the Ecclesiastical Commission of the 1830s. Statutes at Oxford had barely changed since the seventeenth century of Archbishop Laud:

> [It was] a privileged oracle of the *ancien regime* looking to the state for the maintenance of its exclusive rights, and requiting its obligations by its public pronouncements, its influence upon the clergy, and the election of members of parliament similar in social character to those of the early Hanoverian period, but wholly different in their disposition towards the political order.[15]

Colleges had turned their backs on their original eleemosynary principles; no longer were the poor of society given proper educational consideration as dictated by former statutes. 'Even in the seventeenth century there had been between 400 and 500 poor students, many of them at Magdalen, All Souls and New College which now received small numbers and men of a very different kind.'[16] Governance of the University had atrophied: it was dominated by Heads of Colleges and Houses rather than by professorial chairs (which were largely irrelevant) and the pursuit of research; Convocation, where important reforms could be effected, was distorted by reactionary 'country' clergymen who were brought up to Oxford to vote down any reform that threatened to diminish religious influence (actions which were often contrary to the wishes of those actually working in the University); fellowships were so restrictive as to be open only to men of particular schools or a locality, and it was often obligatory for a fellow to be in holy orders; celibate Anglican clergymen dominated the colleges both as fellows and heads, and while a few of them took on the responsibility of teaching undergraduates, most saw their fellowships as little more than a welcome financial springboard to begin their careers in the church.

---

[15] W. R. Ward, *Victorian Oxford* (London: Frank Cass & Co., 1965), xiii.
[16] Ibid., 161.

What is more, the entire system suited the clergymen. Although other subjects such as Medicine, Law, Classics or even Languages were possible channels in which a fellow might forge a career, Colleges had no 'in house' application of these disciplines, whereas most colleges owned large numbers of advowsons which entitled them to appoint clergymen to college livings, positions which were offered to fellows in holy orders, some of whom (but by no means all) might be scholars of Theology. To complete the Church of England's monopoly, all undergraduates had to subscribe to the Thirty-Nine Articles and be communicant members of the Anglican Church (the so-called 'religious tests') which excluded both Dissenters and Roman Catholics.[17]

But liberal reformers, among them W. E. Gladstone, Member of Parliament for the University, supported radical changes which would shake the ecclesiastical ascendancy to its foundations. Fundamental questions such as Oxford's academic standing in the field of knowledge were posed by radical 'liberal' journals such as the *Edinburgh Review*, not least because Oxford was lagging so far behind Continental universities, especially those in Germany. In this regard, a powerful discourse raged about the importance of science (a discourse defined by the onrush of secularism and the Darwin revolution) and the appointment of new professorships. The Commission's desire to create new professorships derived essentially from the want of specialist expertise. Both Oxford and Cambridge, with their emphases on college tutoring (and coaching), relied on tutors to teach a range of subjects in which they held only a slender knowledge. In founding new professorial chairs, the universities would encourage a hierarchy in which professors would lead their subjects of study and research. College fellows (whose places would be accessible for the first time to open competition and academic merit) and readers would also form part of this hierarchy as would the tutors, and with the new system would come a career structure in which those entering at the bottom could aspire to reach a more senior goal with commensurate financial rewards; added to which, new professorial positions would also widen the curriculum and provide a cutting edge to the university's flagging academic influence.

Reaction to the changes recommended by the Commission was initially hostile from both colleges and Hebdomadal Board (the governing council at Oxford University), but after the recommendations of the 1854 Commission (which ultimately had legislative power, through the Oxford Act, to force change if necessary), the order of the day was compromise. Fellowships were partially opened up as each college made its case for reluctant change, and funds more generously spent on academically unproductive fellowships were redirected towards the creation

[17] See A. J. Engel, *From Clergyman to Don: The Rise of the Academic Profession in Nineteenth-Century Oxford* (Oxford: Clarendon Press, 1983), 2–6.

of more scholarships, demyships (a form of scholarship specifically at Magdalen) and facilities for gentlemen commoners (those students without a scholarship). Colleges looked for concessions (such as New College and Jesus), but a few, such as St John's, tried to push this spirit of compromise to its limits. Refusing to give way to the Commission's demand for reform, St John's was ultimately punished for its obstinacy by direct action from the Privy Council, who forced change upon the college.[18]

Routh, the long-standing President of Magdalen, made it clear that the Commission's reforms were a betrayal of the statutes established by the College's Founder, but he was prepared 'to accept such proposals as might, in accordance with the statutes, be agreed upon by the President and Fellows jointly'.[19] Little alteration took place until Routh's death in 1854, at the age of ninety-nine (he had been President for sixty-three years), but with the election of Bulley in January 1855, and the help of government legislation, change was effected to support four new professorships, in Moral and Metaphysical Philosophy (its first appointee, incidentally, being H. L. Mansel, later Dean of St Paul's Cathedral), Chemistry, Mineralogy and Physical Geography, the more generous funding of Demyships and Exhibitions, and, perhaps most radically, the opening up of places to non-foundation commoners of which Magdalen was able to admit as many as it could realistically accommodate.[20] By 1858 the number of Commoners had grown, but with the increase of Demyships and Exhibitioners, this growth was only gradual.

Stainer almost certainly hoped that matriculation at Magdalen might be a possibility. He was, like many middle-class young men of his time, eagerly aspiring to the status of a 'gentleman' and to the ideal of ruling-class egalitarianism quintessential to the Victorian concept of professional work.[21] But there were numerous reasons why Bulley could not oblige, as he made clear in a letter to Ouseley after Stainer's appointment: 'If Mr Stainer wishes to matriculate, he must do so at some other College or Hall. 1st Because I could not place him in the Commoners' List at Magdalen for some time to come; and if I could do so, the expenses of a Commoner here are probably more than he could afford, the Commoners being for the most part people of independent means, tho' the system pursued is economical considering the class for whom it is intended.'[22] Clearly, then, there were not enough Commoners' places in Magdalen, nor, as Bulley evidently appraised, could Stainer, with his lower middle-class background, meet the cost of accommodation

---

[18] Ibid., 58–9.

[19] H. A. Wilson, *Magdalen College* (Chippenham: Antony Rowe, 1899; repr. London: Routledge/Thoemmes Press, 1998), 248.

[20] Ibid., 255–7.

[21] Engel, *From Clergyman to Don*, 11.

[22] Letter from Bulley to Ouseley, 26 December 1859, in private possession (JRS).

there. But, perhaps more importantly, Bulley liked to maintain a separation between undergraduates and choristers (a policy decision well founded in light of the Symonds affair in 1862, detailed below). 'I wish to keep the choristers as clear as possible from contact with the undergraduates of the College, which', he explained, 'would be next to impossible if the Organist were one of them.'[23] (And, of course, Stainer, who was not yet twenty, had all the appearance of an undergraduate.) Bulley did, however, promise that Stainer would be granted a room in Magdalen for musical practice and the possibility that he might 'migrate' to Magdalen after graduation. In the mean time he recommended St Edmund Hall as a place where he might matriculate and which would be eminently more affordable for a man of his slender means.[24] Stainer took Bulley's advice and matriculated at St Edmund Hall in 1861.

The Magdalen College that Stainer confronted, when he arrived in late January 1860, may have begun to embrace reform, but it was nevertheless still a conservative institution whose celibate fellows were predominantly in holy orders.[25] One of the most prominent of these was the great antiquarian John Rouse Bloxam, whom W. Tuckwell described as the 'incarnation of all that was ideal in the College, its medievalism, sentiment, piety, [and] was the first man to appear in Oxford wearing the long collarless coat, white stock, high waistcoat, which forms nowadays the inartistic clerical uniform.'[26] It was an apt depiction of a cleric who believed implicitly in the value of Magdalen as an ecclesiastical seat of learning, enhanced by its sense of isolation and comfortable existence:

> [Magdalen was] one of those great semi-monastic establishments which are peculiar to this country; and however slight their intrinsic value, considered as contributions to the stock of knowledge, may be, they will serve at least to shew, by their number and variety, what might be accomplished by persons gifted with greater energy and more profound attainments, through the aid of foundations, in which exemption from domestic cares, and a liberal provision for all the reasonable wants of a celibate life, afford such facilities for the indulgence of either literary or scientific tastes.[27]

[23] Ibid.

[24] Ibid.

[25] Statistics reveal that in 1860 Magdalen's fellows numbered twenty-eight among the clerical and only eight among the lay. By 1867 the numbers – sixteen clerical and fifteen lay – were almost equal, though by 1872, when Stainer left Magdalen, the clerical fellows still outnumbered the lay by eighteen to eleven. By contrast, University College had seven lay fellows in 1860 to only four clerical, a ratio more typical of the university.

[26] Tuckwell, *Reminiscences of Oxford*, 165.

[27] J. R. Bloxam, *A Register of the Presidents, Fellows, Demies, Instructors in Grammar*

As well as being a diligent antiquary and ardent chronicler of Magdalen College's history, Bloxam was an enthusiastic Tractarian and ritualist. As a Demy at Magdalen between 1830 and 1835, Bloxam would have been accustomed to the conservative stance of its high churchmen (which, at that time, included its President, Routh), where the Church of England's traditions and liturgy formed the basis of their worship and veneration, and their theological convictions derived much from the Caroline period.[28] Henry Best, a Fellow between 1792 and 1797, observed that George Horne, Magdalen's President between 1768 and 1791, 'even bowed to the altar on leaving the chapel without any dread lest the picture of Christ bearing the Cross, by Ludovico Caracci, should convict him of idolatry. Here we all turned towards the altar during the recital of the Creed.'[29] Horne was also known to observe fasting, he occasionally exercised private confession, and lighted candles were placed on the altar at the celebration of the Eucharist.[30] Routh, who succeeded Horne, continued many of these traditions and made known his admiration for Archbishop William Laud. With the Tractarian controversies of the 1830s, however, many of the clergymen fellows at Magdalen became interested in the wave of new theological thinking which it engendered, even if they chose, as Routh did, not to call themseleves 'Tractarian'.

Bloxam, on the other hand, who was made a fellow at Magdalen in 1835, became an avid Tractarian, and, more significantly, he was also eager to see the richness of ceremonial restored to the Anglican liturgy. At Littlemore in 1837, where he was curate under Newman, he exercised his ritualist energies with considerable zeal, reviving the use of the stole over both shoulders. He also added candlesticks to the altar; there was an elaborately bound bible and a wooden offertory basin, instruments of ritual which, according to his own recollections, he used at Magdalen (where he also wore a cope and stole in chapel).[31] Bloxam resisted the temptation to convert to Rome, but he retained his Anglo-Catholic ritualist enthusiasms to the end, and his influence was appreciable. His deep interest in neo-Gothic architecture (he was a prominent member of the Oxford Society for Promoting the Study of Gothic Architecture) led to the construction of Pugin's new gateway to the college, and his rooms were richly decorated (which 'bore a striking resemblance

and in Music, Chaplains, Clerks, Choristers and other members of Saint Mary Magdalen College in the University of Oxford from the foundation of the College to the year 1857 (Oxford: James Parker & Co., 1881), 197–8.

[28] See R. D. Middleton, *Dr Routh* (London: Oxford University Press, 1938), 140–2.

[29] H. Best, *Four Years in France* (London, 1826), 8–9.

[30] See P. B. Nockles, *The Oxford Movement in Context: Anglican High Churchmanship, 1760–1857* (Cambridge: Cambridge University Press, 1994), 184–5, 211, 249.

[31] See 'Collections' compiled on J. H. Newman by Bloxam, *GB-Omc* MS 304, 185; also see Middleton, *Dr Routh*, 34.

to a small oratory').[32] He devoted much time to the conduct and detail of music and worship in the Chapel, which involved the ordering of choristers' day-to-day lives through ritual, prayer and procession. Bloxam left Magdalen in 1862, but the legacy of 'high church' devotion lived on in the Deans of Divinity, notably the Rev. John Rigaud (who had been curate at St Mary Magdalene, Oxford, then (and now) very high church) and James Edwin Millard, the headmaster of Magdalen School.

The Anglo-Catholic stance at Magdalen meant that music was considered an important component of college and chapel life. In 1855 the college invested in a new organ (at the instigation of Blyth) built by one of Britain's most progressive firms, Gray & Davison. The instrument, very much based on the emerging concept of the 'concert organ', was constructed on the principles with which the firm had first experimented at Glasgow City Hall. As Thistlethwaite has indicated, the Glasgow organ represented 'the first application in this country of Cavaillé-Coll's "increasing pressure" system',[33] and was designed to enhance the quality and volume of the reed stops (especially in the upper registers); there was also a much greater variety of registers on the Swell and two harmonic flutes on the Great. The new organ at Magdalen included the 'increasing pressure' system on the Great fluework,[34] and a high-pressure tromba. The four-manual design of the organ, though relatively small, embraced other innovations tried out at Glasgow such as a tremulant, a pneumatic lever and octave couplers, and the orchestral notion of the instrument, which was now intended to perform equally well for the music of Bach on the one hand and arrangements of orchestral music on the other, was emphasised by imaginative registers on the Choir and Solo organs.[35]

For Stainer, the organ, tuned to a system of equal temperament (at that time an innovation to English organs), offered not only a major opportunity to develop his potential as a virtuoso performer, but also, and perhaps more significantly, to extend his approach to orchestral registration, both for the purposes of performing orchestral music on the organ and for accompaniment of choral works where the organ could substitute more than satisfactorily for the orchestra. In these skills and as improviser, Stainer established his reputation as one of England's foremost performers, though, on his own admission, he considered that W. T. Best, organist of Liverpool Town Hall, 'stood alone'.[36] Nevertheless, Stainer was to draw approbation for his improvisations before the service and for his voluntaries of Bach and

[32] *The Collected Letters of A. W. N. Pugin*, vol. 1: *1830–1842*, ed. M. Belcher (Oxford: Oxford University Press, 2001), 379.

[33] N. Thistlethwaite, *The Making of the Victorian Organ* (Cambridge: Cambridge University Press, 1990), 278.

[34] Ibid., 279.

[35] Ibid., 281–2.

[36] J. M. Levien, *Impressions of W. T. Best* (London: Novello & Co., 1942), 29.

Mendelssohn, and before his first year was out he was undoubtedly recognised as the finest organist Oxford had seen in many generations.

Edward Chapman, tutor, one of Magdalen's steadily growing number of lay Fellows, and later a Member of Parliament and keen music-lover, was often invited into the organ loft of the chapel to witness the service. His memories of Stainer's abilities as an accompanist remained vivid:

> I shall never forget my many sittings with him in the organ loft of the College Chapel during evening service. His accompaniment of the Psalms and his impromptu before the anthem were the like of which I have never heard before or since, and I do not hesitate to say that many of these impromptus exceed in beauty any of his written compositions. With bowed head and closed eyes he would on the soft stops seem gently to unfold the theme of the coming anthem, working out and expanding its ramifications with exquisite delicacy, then coming to the end, his face would light up as though emerging from a far off dreamland, and, with head erect he would conclude, and glide into the anthem. It is most difficult to describe his accompaniment of the Psalms. The chant first simply played through, say, on the choir organ, would then become a wonderfully harmonized interpretation of the words, no brilliant dashing execution; but if I may call it an inverted and dispersed harmony on the solo or choir organ, no two verses alike, but sustaining and truly <u>accompanying</u> the choir, ending with a cathedral custom on which he always prided himself – viz., the introduction of the lower pedal notes in the verse before the <u>Gloria Patri</u>.[37]

Such facility endeared Stainer not only to the Oxford clergy but also to the Vice-Chancellor, Dr Jeune. The University Church of St Mary the Virgin had been without an organist since the death of Stephen Elvey in October 1860; Jeune appointed Stainer to the post of University Organist (in preference to others such as Corfe at Christ Church and Arnold at New College), a position considered a major honour. Stainer took up his duties there in 1861, duties which involved a regular Sunday morning service (after that at Magdalen) during term time on the church's historic seventeenth-century 'Father' Smith organ.[38]

In addition to the major expenditure exacted by the installation of its new organ, Magdalen College, through the offices of both Routh and Bloxam, took a healthy interest in the continuance and welfare of the choir. Though an immovable conservative in most matters, Routh had given sanction to Bloxam, as Dean

---

37 Edwards, 'John Stainer', 308.

38 The 'Father' Smith organ at St Mary the Virgin was tragically destroyed by fire in 1947. A new organ was built by J. W. Walker, though this was replaced in 1987 by another instrument, built by Metzler Orgelbau of Zurich.

of Divinity, to implement serious reforms to Magdalen School in the wake of those made by Arnold at Rugby since the 1820s. Originally boys at the school had received their education at the old Lodgings of the Principal of Magdalen Hall, but by November 1843 Bloxam had resolved that a new school would be erected on the site of a popular inn (the Greyhound) at the corner of Longwall, adjacent to the college, as well as a house (at No. 58, High Street) for the Headmaster, sixteen choristers and other boarders. Legal objections were made which held up progress until 1849, when work commenced, but in May 1851 the new school, a fine example of Victorian Gothic designed by J. C. Buckler, was opened and new and more competent teachers were employed.

Among this first wave of new teachers was James Elwin Millard, who, having won the friendship of Bloxam, was appointed Headmaster in 1846 after the resignation of William Henderson. A keen 'advanced High Churchman',[39] Millard carried the school into a new era and saw it expand both in number and buildings before he retired in 1864. The School then passed into the hands of R. H. Hill, who did much to improve the standard of education by employing university teachers as part-time masters, by expanding the number of available scholarships, and by broadening the curriculum to include science (for which a laboratory was built by Millard).

For many choristers, school life at Magdalen, save for the endemic bullying, was a happy experience, as was later intimated by the historian J. R. Green:

> The College was a poem in itself; its dim cloisters, its noble chapel, its smooth lawns, its park with the deer browsing beneath venerable elms, its "walks" with Addison's Walk in the midst of them, but where we boys thought less of Addison than of wasps' nests and craw-fishing. Of all Oxford colleges it was the loveliest and the most secluded from the outer world, and though I can laugh now at the indolence and uselessness of the collegiate life of my boy-days, my boyish imagination was overpowered by the solemn services, the white-robed choir, the long train of divines and fellows, and the president – moving like some mysterious dream of the past among the punier creatures of the present.[40]

Lewis Tuckwell, inaugurated as a chorister in 1847 (and regarded as one of the most beautiful trebles the choir had ever known), later a tenor Lay Clerk, and Precentor of Magdalen chapel until 1877 (before taking a college living at the Oxfordshire village of Standlake), also recalled that the choristers 'were kindly treated, well fed, and never over-worked. Sundays and all Saints Days were holidays.

---

[39] R. S. Stanier, *Magdalen School: A History of Magdalen College School, Oxford* (Oxford: Basil Blackwell, 1958), 157.

[40] Ibid., 170.

On these no work was required of us but only such as belonged to the performance of the Chapel Services.'[41]

Bloxam's interest in the enhanced role of the choir meant that both the day-to-day workings of the choir and special days, as those cited by Tuckwell, were executed with particular care. Services took place every day: Mattins at 10.00 a.m. and Evensong at 4.30 p.m. (this changed to 5.00 p.m. in 1863). Choral Communion was less regular, but it nevertheless took place on an appreciable number of important Sundays and feast days throughout the church year.[42]

Besides singing at these services, choristers were expected to undertake various ceremonial duties. The Chapel-bill for the week was always written out by one of the choristers appointed for the purpose, and copies delivered to the President, Vice-President and Dean of Divinity; also for the Senior Common Room, the Ante-chapel, the Vestry and the Organ-loft. Choristers who sat nearest the President and Vice-President's stalls in Chapel were required to point out the Anthem for those officers during the First Lesson. Senior Choristers were ordered to give notice of the celebration of the Holy Communion by going round to all members of the College, who were present, on the preceding Sunday during the Second Lesson and were also obliged to bring a bill of the attendance of Clerks and Choristers during the preceding week to the Dean of Divinity every Monday morning, which after revision by him, was delivered to the President.[43]

But what the choristers looked forward to with greatest relish were the *special* days in the college's tradition which Bloxam maintained with a notable assiduity. The first was May Morning, a ceremony which particularly appealed to Bloxam's antiquarian sensibilities and which he refashioned into the form still used today.

[41] L. Tuckwell, *Old Magdalen Days 1847–1877 by a Former Chorister* (Oxford: B. H. Blackwell, 1913), 11. All choristers at Magdalen received free education and accommodation in accordance with the first statutes of the college in 1480. Choristerships often proved to be a significant way of assisting intelligent children from poorer backgrounds. The 'Greene Exhibition', for example, was designed go to a chorister 'of the best deserts for music, learning and manners, – and of the greatest poverty of parents'; see *GB-Omc* CP/2/63 Committee meetings & reports 1867, fols. 87–89r. It was also often the case that choristerships were offered to sons of poorer clergymen, especially from college livings.

[42] In 1863 Choral Communion is noted to have taken place in Magdalen chapel on the second Sunday after the meeting of the chapel in the October Term, Advent Sunday, Christmas Day, First Sunday in Lent, Fifth Saturday in Lent, Easter Day, Second Sunday in Easter Term, Ascension Day, Whitsunday, St Mary Magdalene's Day (choral service up to the Offertory); see *Directorium Magdalenense in usum decani in sacra theologia* MDCCCLXIII *Curavit* JACOBUS ELWIN MILLARD. *Coll: Magd: Socius et Decanus in Sacr: Theol: 1863*, GB-Omc MS 765.

[43] Ibid.

The choristers were expected to rise at 4.30 a.m. and make their way with the Lay Clerks and organist, all surpliced, to the top of Magdalen tower. On the stroke of 5.00 a.m. the choir sang the Latin Hymn 'Te Deum Patrem' (the 'Hymnus Eucharisticus' by Benjamin Rogers). After the music was over, the boys went down to the Organist's room and had breakfast worthy of the occasion. The choristers received special pocket money; they swam, had fun, were permitted to ring the bells, and then returned at 2.00 p.m. for the May Day dinner. The dinner, at which the toast 'Floreat Magdalena' was sung,[44] was sumptuous and hosted by Bloxam.

The Great Gaudy Day, on 22 July, marking the feast of St Mary Magdalene, signalled the end of term for the choristers. The 10.00 a.m. service was fully choral at which Goss's 'Praise the Lord O my soul' was usually sung. The choristers, in their gowns, sang Grace at the end of the fulsome evening dinner, took supper in the Junior Common Room, received Gaudy Money and (as was permitted in those days) the four senior choristers received a bottle of port.[45]

But perhaps most memorable to the choristers, and for which Bloxam must be fully credited, were the Christmas celebrations which were arranged specially for the choristers who had to remain behind for Christmas Day after the other boys at Magdalen School had gone home for the holidays. Tuckwell clearly recollected Christmases at Magdalen with special fondness:

> The Dons did indeed lay themselves out to make us happy during those few days, most of which were spent in some party or other in the College rooms. But that which far eclipsed them all was the Christmas Eve party in the College Hall. It was instituted by Dr. Bloxam somewhere late in the "thirties" or early in the "forties". All that I can testify is that in 1847 it was in existence, and was held in Dr. B.'s private rooms, to which I have referred above. It soon became so popular that he was petitioned to transfer it to the College Hall, but the exact date of the change I do not know. After the 10 a.m. Service on that day we had to attend a rehearsal for the music of the evening party, but in the afternoon some of our number met Dr. B. at a shop called the Civet Cat to choose sixteen presents for the evening, for this was from the first intended to be a Choristers' Party. It was for *them* the High Table was spread. *They* alone partook of the frumenty [hulled wheat boiled in milk and seasoned with cinnamon and sugar], mince-pies and mulled wine, which we called *negus*, the other guests having to be content with humbler fare. For *them*, too, the Christmas-tree was provided and the presents purchased, whilst the sixteen silk bags, suspended from the tree,

---

44 A version of 'Magdalena floreat' for tenors and basses was later composed by Stainer and is still sung at the college on special feast days.

45 See Tuckwell, *Old Magdalen Days*, 15.

and known each to contain half-a-crown, were for *their* benefit, as was well understood by all present.[46]

Between 9 and 10 the choirboys sang the first part of *Messiah* accompanied by the organist on the piano. Supper followed, the Christmas-tree lighted, and presents given out. Everyone having eaten, the choristers then sang a number of carols from the SPCK collection, including 'Christmas comes, the time of gladness' and 'From the hallowed belfry tower', after which, on the stroke of midnight, the 'Gloria in excelsis Deo', attributed to Pergolesi was sung; this was concluded by a Christmas peal of bells 'when the Loving Cup was passed round and the guests dispersed, after many a handshaking and hearty wishes for the festival now ushered in.'[47]

By 1860, when Stainer had arrived in post, the tradition of Christmas at Magdalen had become well established, as is evident from Bulley's diaries. Indeed, by 1861 the entertainment had, as Darwall-Smith tells us, become a major fixture of the College year, being attended by Chaplains and Fellows, sometimes by the Vice-Chancellor and his guests, and, by 1871, by forty members of the College, eighty guests, and, in the gallery, forty-two ladies.[48] Stainer, who, during his period at Magdalen, steadily began to develop a fascination for melody and song from the Middle Ages to the present, adored the traditional festivities. His interest in Christmas carols would soon manifest itself in publications that would bring him national renown as well as an appreciable income in royalties.

The standard of chapel music which Stainer found at Magdalen in 1860 was generally good. In addition to the sixteen choristers, who were well trained, the eight Lay Clerks, many of them former choristers, latterly clergymen or men preparing for holy orders, were of fair ability and were employed under conditions more conducive to discipline than Stainer had known in his former days at St Paul's.[49] The Lay Clerks received an annual stipend of £110 a year for singing two daily services, the Gaudy on 22 July, the May Morning ceremony and any Graces

---

[46] Ibid., 15–17. See also R. Darwall-Smith, 'Magdalen and the Rediscovery of Christmas', *Magdalen College Record* (2001), 92–102.

[47] Ibid., 17–18.

[48] Darwall-Smith, 'Magdalen and the Rediscovery of Christmas', 95. The entertainment on Christmas Eve remained a fixture at Magdalen until 1965, when it was moved to 19 December.

[49] *GB-Omc* MS 827 (Portraits of Choristers, Clerks and Chaplains of Magdalen College) gives ample evidence of this trend for choristers and Lay Clerks who later became Chaplains, Fellows of Magdalen or clergymen (who were appointed to college livings). Among these were Lewis Tuckwell, William Macray, E. M. Acock, Edward Vine Hall, and Compton Reade. James Millard, Headmaster of Magdalen School from 1846, had been a chorister, a Demy between 1842 and 1853, and a Fellow from 1853. It was also common for choristers to become Lay Clerks. Blyth was himself a chorister at Magdalen between 1835 and 1841, and sang as a Lay

in Hall for which they were required. Vacations were generous: a fortnight at Christmas, a few days at Easter, and about twelve weeks from 23 July until term began in October. After thirty years' service, all retiring Clerks received half-pay as their pension.

Stainer's own position as organist and *informator choristarum* was freehold (a job he held for life), and he was permitted by order of the President to hold practices at his discretion, a regulation enforced since May 1858. Stainer undoubtedly took full advantage of this statute. Like at St Paul's, the Lay Clerks were familiar with the repetitive repertoire they sang from day to day, and practices were probably rare occurrences. Blyth evidently demanded change towards the end of his tenure, but Stainer, with the inclusion of new anthems and service music in his sights, considered the obligation of regular practices for Lay Clerks as *de rigueur*, a fact reinforced, one suspects, by the reiteration of the order in writing by Bulley to Stainer.[50] His new regime would insist on a schedule of rehearsals for both choristers and men, a *modus operandi* which, by force of his persuasive personality, and by the results he achieved, drew approbation from the Lay Clerks and from the President and Fellows.[51] In addition he appears to have head-hunted his old St Paul's chorister friend, William Alexander Barrett (who had been principal alto at St Andrew's, Wells Street) to fill the same role in Magdalen chapel. Barrett was admitted to the choir in 1861.

After only a few years at Magdalen, Stainer had brought the choir up to new level of attainment. Henry Scott Holland, later a colleague of Stainer's at St Paul's Cathedral, recalled the 'fragrance and magic … of that wonderful music' at Magdalen;[52] the *Guardian* claimed that Stainer had 'raised the choir to a higher standard than had hitherto been known in the Anglican Church';[53] and Stainer himself was clearly pleased with the phenomenon he had created in Oxford. More to the point, the niches of the reredos, left empty after the chapel's restoration in the 1830s (on the grounds that filling them might be considered too idolatrous),

Clerk between 1842 and 1845. Several of Stainer's choristers went on to become Lay Clerks during his tenure as organist.

[50] The order – 'That the singing men be required to attend the practisings of the Quire, when required by the Organist' – signed by Bulley, survives among Stainer's papers (JRS).

[51] Such was Stainer's insistence on practice for the choristers that, by 1866, Bulley was moved to request that the organist should endeavour to 'limit as far as practicable (but at his discretion) the musical practice of the Choristers to three hours in the week, each practice not to exceed one hour in duration.' See Diary of Frederic Bulley, 30 May 1866 (Amendment of Regulation No. 2, May 21), *GB-Omc*.

[52] 'Unveiling of the Stainer Memorial at St Paul's Cathedral', *Musical Times* 45 (January 1904), 27.

[53] *Guardian*, 2 April 1901.

were now being populated with statues of Old Testament characters: 'Our Chapel is so much improved by the filling up of the "niches", that it is creating quite a "sensation." '[54] The same sense of initiative was also reflected in the College agreeing to invest in a rehearsal organ for the Vestry Room.[55]

The legacy of Blyth's musical regime at Magdalen was one entirely familiar to Stainer from both St Paul's and Tenbury. The same diet of sixteenth-, seventeenth- and eighteenth-century material, determined by the collections of Boyce, Hayes and Arnold, was mixed with a conservative sprinkling of Ouseley and Crotch, the occasional anthem of Goss and S. S. Wesley, and extracts from the choral works of Spohr and Mendelssohn; the service music was even more conservative, with the sole exception of S. S. Wesley in E. This is evident from the music lists which have survived for the 1850s, but none, alas, survives for the period of Stainer's appointment. From an existing directory, compiled by Millard, Dean of Divinity, we can nevertheless adduce that Stainer intended not so much to expand the repertoire at Magdalen (though he did include some of his own music and that of Sullivan), but to develop a more systematic schedule of service music for ordinary days to be sung from month to month by a choir ready and technically able to sing service music every day.[56]

1st week	2nd week	3rd week	4th week
Rogers in D or in A minor (Eve)	Aldrich in G	Rogers in F	King in F
Boyce in A Heathcote in G	Boyce in C Goss in E	Travers in F	Croft in A King in D
Gates in F Kelway in B or Stainer in E flat	Sullivan in D (Te Deum only)	Stainer in C (Te Deum only) Wesley in F	Nares in F or Turle in D
Hopkins in F Rogers in E minor	Kempton in B flat	Gibbons in F	Creyghton in B flat
Farrant in G	Tallis in D	Rogers in D	Aldrich in G or Ouseley in E flat
King in C	Ouseley in E flat	Stainer in A Cook in G minor	Ouseley in A or Creyghton in E

---

[54] Letter from Stainer to Palmer, 10 May 1865; in private possession (RN).

[55] Diary of Frederic Bulley, 16 May 1867, *GB-Omc*.

[56] Millard's *Directorium Magdalenense* (*GB-Omc* MS 765) reveals that Stainer had originally sketched a system of service music for ordinary days over a three-week period (the sketch survives in Stainer's hand in pencil pp. 76–7). This system was evidently modified to a four-week system, presumably by Millard (see pp. 80–2) which also included a list of canticles for festival Sundays (which included Wesley in E, Macfarren in E flat and Elvey in A). The directory is dated 1863 when the volume was begun, but there are numerous later additions and emendations which undoubtedly relate to the later 1860s and early 1870s.

The date of this scheme is uncertain, but the presence of Stainer's Evening Service in E flat suggests that it may be as late as 1870, when Lewis Tuckwell had taken over as Precentor.[57]

An elaborate plan was drawn up for the psalms, in which two schemes of chants functioned on alternate months as well as one for 'Proper Psalms' for Christmas Day, Easter Day, Ascension Day, Whit-Sunday, and Commemoration Days. In addition a list of separate chants (together with an appendix of additional chants, presumably added later), both single and double, were assembled, many of which, by Goss, E. J. Hopkins, S. S. Wesley, Elvey, Ouseley, and W. H. Gladstone, reflected Stainer's desire to update the chant repertoire. (The list also included Stainer's chants paraphrasing Beethoven and Spohr, a technique he had drawn from Goss's single-chant paraphrase of the slow movement of Beethoven's Seventh Symphony and Turle's paraphrase of 'Lord God of heaven and earth' from Spohr's *Last Judgment*.)[58] This expression for liturgical order, quintessential to the Tractarian concern for externals, was also reflected in the clear instructions provided for the canticles (such as the use of the Benedicite during Lent, instead of the Te Deum, and the proscription of the Benedictus on St John the Baptist's Day, when it formed the text of the Gospel, and on 18 February, 17 June and 15 October, when it formed the text of the Second Lesson at Mattins).

The most articulate manifestation of Tractarianism in the Magdalen directory was the list of anthems clearly categorised for apposite Sundays and feast days in the church year. As a Tractarian-led institution, Magdalen may well have insisted on this practice before the 1860s, but with Stainer's arrival the discipline of the anthem and its liturgical function seems, by degrees, to have grown and diversified. At first the college authorities (namely the President, Vice-President and Dean of Divinity) seem to have responded negatively to change. A college order, entered into the directory, of 10 December 1863 stipulates 'that no anthems not in the general Collection (or appendix) be appointed. That the words of all new Anthems be first allowed of by the President, Vice-President and Dean of Divinity'. But, in time, the college gradually relaxed its views until 1870, when, under the aegis of Lewis Tuckwell's Precentorship, a new order of 10 July allowed for a 'new arrangement of Anthems (forming Appendix 2) as proposed by Mr Tuckwell be carried out under his guidance'. Among Stainer's range of anthems were a

---

[57] The later date of this scheme would appear to be confirmed by the fact that it had been an earlier practice of the choir (elucidated in Millard's directory) to sing the Morning Canticles to chants on Wednesdays and Fridays.

[58] See *St Paul's Cathedral Chant Book* (1878), no. 99 (Goss) and Turle (104). Stainer's paraphrases of the slow movement from Beethoven's 'Pathétique' Sonata and the treble solo 'All glory to the Lamb that died' from Spohr's *Last Judgment* may be found in the same book (see nos. 63 and 62 respectively).

substantial array of modern English compositions by S. S. Wesley (with 'Blessed be the God and Father', 'Cast me not away', 'Ascribe unto the Lord', 'O Lord my God', 'O give thanks', 'The wilderness', 'Thou wilt keep him in perfect peace', 'Thou judge of quick and dead' (from 'Let us lift up our heart') and 'He shall swallow up death in victory' (from 'O Lord, thou art my God'),[59] Goss's anthems from the late 1850s and 1860s ('These are they which follow the Lamb', 'Christ our Passover', 'O praise the Lord of heaven' and 'Stand up and bless the Lord'), Barnby, Barrett, Dykes and Sterndale Bennett, favourites such as Mozart's 'Ave verum', Attwood's 'Come Holy Ghost and 'Turn thee again', extracts from Spohr's *Last Judgment* as well as the more conservative fare of Ouseley, Steggall and Elvey.

How soon Stainer's own anthems found their way into the music lists at Magdalen is not known, but in 1861 the first volume of Ouseley's *Special Anthems for Certain Seasons* was published by Robert Cocks & Co. in London, bringing into the public domain 'The morning stars sang together' and another anthem, 'The Lord is in His holy temple'. A 'sublime' five-part fugue, 'The Lord is in His holy temple', endeavours to be a bold, muscular representation of Habakkuk (Ch. 2 v. 20), in stark contrast to the hushed manner of Stanford's interpretation many years later at the conclusion of 'For lo, I raise up'. The expositional portion of this anthem, like the fugue of 'The righteous live', is routine, though some interest is generated by the detour to the flat mediant (F major) and the augmentation of the subject divided between soprano and tenor. Yet, for all its technical polish, contrapuntal industry and Handelian *élan* (characterised by the *fortissimo* bass entry in its highest register), the fugue retains the air of a worthy degree exercise.

Two smaller anthems, 'For a small moment have I forsaken Thee' and 'Deliver me, O Lord', written in 1862 and 1863 respectively, reveal sides of Stainer that were to appear with greater aplomb in his more mature works. 'Deliver me, O Lord' was commissioned by Thomas Lloyd Fowle, a self-taught local musician in Winchester, for his *Parochial Anthems by the Cathedral Musicians of 1863*, a publication which included works by seventeen other composers, including Gauntlett, Spark, Barnby, Elvey, Macfarren, Ouseley, Leslie and Fowle himself. In keeping within the spirit of Fowle's 'parochial' remit, Stainer produced an unassuming miniature, uniformly homophonic in texture and technically undemanding (much of the soprano line is conjunct in its melodic motion). Nevertheless, the piece is by no means banal. Though the through-composed structure is periodic in its number of phrases,

[59] It is likely that Magdalen owned copies of S. S. Wesley's *Anthems* of 1853; a number of the contents appear in the music lists of the later 1850s. However, it is notable that revisions of these anthems, published by Hall, Virtue & Co. and Novello, were issued during the 1860s or early 1870s (see P. Horton, *Samuel Sebastian Wesley: A Life* (Oxford: Oxford University Press, 2004), 334–6), which the college may well have purchased at Stainer's insistence.

individual phrase-lengths are, paradoxically, irregular (4+6+4+6+8+4+4+7). Moreover, this feature is further enhanced by the unusual tonal behaviour. Tonicisation (into E flat major) is reserved until the final strain, while C minor, which emerges from the ambiguous opening (note the half close and perfect cadence in the first two phrases) also has a part to play in the final phrase, where its passing reference fittingly points up the text ('bring my soul out of trouble').

'For a small moment' was dedicated to his friend and colleague Dr Charles William Corfe, organist of Christ Church Cathedral and choragus to Ouseley. For all its Goss-like classical simplicity (in a binary form that contrasts the tonic minor and major of E), most striking about this plaintive short anthem is Stainer's handling of a more Romantic, emotionally charged chromatic language. This is not only evident in the detailed progressions and poignant suspensions (e.g. bars 4–5), but also in the climaxes of both sections, the first which arrives on the dominant of G sharp (forestalled by the interrupted cadence) and the second, more dramatic still, which achieves C major – each climax also acquiring effect through its particular context.

Stainer's most ambitious liturgical works of this first period at Magdalen were the two multi-sectioned verse anthems, 'They were lovely and pleasant in their lives' (written for the feast of St Simon and St Jude) and 'Drop down, ye heavens from above' (for the feast of the Annunciation). These two anthems were intended, with 'I saw the Lord', to be included in the second volume of Ouseley's *Special Anthems*, which Ouseley hoped to bring out in 1865. 'As to the anthems', he urged to Stainer, 'I should be really obliged if you would send them to me at once: for the book ought to be out before Easter.'[60] In the end the *Anthems* were published the following year.

In both these essays Stainer, more technically assured, evinced a wider diversity of styles. The opening section of 'They were lovely', a verse SATB, was one such instance. An abridged sonata structure (a rare example in Stainer's output) once again took its lead from the models of Goss, but its execution showed considerable subtlety. Both first and second subjects unusually conclude in different keys from their point of departure – the first subject from G major to B minor, the second from the dominant of D to the dominant of E – and maintain a sense of seamless continuity through the avoidance of unequivocal cadence. The recapitulation, which also avoids the platitude of a perfect cadence back to the tonic, is also beautifully effected by the conversion of the dominant of E to V⁷b of C (bars 32–3). Stainer's alteration of his thematic material to facilitate the return of the second subject in the tonic is masterly, as is the simultaneity of first- and second-subject material as the crucial agents of final tonicisation (bars 50–2). Prominent within

[60] Letter from Ouseley to Stainer, 4 February 1865, *GB-Lbl* Add. MS 62121, fol. 6.

the first subject of the opening movement, B minor forms the key of the more turbulent verse for two basses ('As gold in the furnace'). This is a powerful movement, reminiscent of S. S. Wesley by dint of its dramatic organ accompaniment and bold chromatic progressions. But perhaps most striking is the introduction of the Neapolitan for the closing phase of the movement, where Stainer undoubtedly intended to intensify the vivid imagery of the text ('like sparks among the stubble'). Such a device must surely have been imbibed from S. S. Wesley's compelling verse for solo bass in his anthem 'Let us lift up our heart', itself a highly original sonata movement set in the same key and whose use of the Neapolitan raises the anthem to new heights of harmonic modernity. For the conclusion to 'They were lovely', Stainer once again opted for a 'sublime' fugue, inspired by the acclamatory text of Ecclesiasticus (Ch. 24 v. 24). Here the treatment of the fugue subject is more fertile, particularly in the use of close imitation and *stretti* which gives a greater propulsion to the counterpoint.

By comparison, 'Drop down, ye heavens from above' explores a more archaic, austere church style. This is copiously demonstrated by Stainer's studied counterpoint in six parts, yet executed with a surprising freedom. The two preludial bars for organ introduce two seminal components – an angular subject (with fitting verisimilitude) sounded on a Swell reed (a feature surely emanating from the Magdalen organ's high pressure reed stops) and a pedal countersubject descending through the interval of a fourth (Example 4a). These two elements are liberally worked out over the next twenty-four bars, the angular subject in choral imitation, the solo reed stop providing a free fifth contrapuntal voice, and the pedal a sixth, reiterating the countersubject (see bars 3–5, 5–7, 13–15). More significantly, within his contrapuntal matrix Stainer exhibits an impressive handling of diatonic dissonance (comparable with the intensity of S. S. Wesley), particularly at the apex of the registral ascent of all six voices, which signals the reprise of the opening bars with the subject in augmentation (in the bass) as well as in its original form at

Example 4. Anthem: 'Drop down, ye heavens, from above: (a) opening organ statement; (b) climax of first section with bass augmentation; (c) 'full of grace are thy lips' (diatonic progressions);   (d) 'because God hath blessed thee for ever' (chromatic progressions)

(a)

Example 4 continued

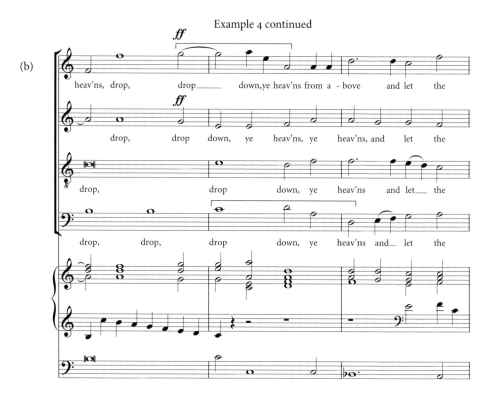

(b)

the twelfth (Example 4b). A recitative for solo and chorus (employing Luke's well-known text) provides the conduit to an earnest fugue which retains interest not only in Stainer's treatment of fugal entries (not least the entry in the major at bars 31–4) but also in the episodic material that supersedes the initial countersubject to become a dominant feature in the second half of the structure (especially above the concluding dominant pedal). The major form of the subject and its secondary countersubject ultimately become the focus of the final phase of the anthem and once again ignites Stainer's predilection for diatonic dissonance (Example 4c), though we are also reminded of the composer's colourful command of chromaticism in a progression he most likely derived from his madrigal 'Dry your sweet cheeks', composed at much the same time (Example 4d).

The direction of music in Magdalen chapel and services at St Mary the Virgin were the staple of Stainer's earnings. They were duties he evidently carried out with conspicuous professionalism, for Bulley (whose son sang as a chorister in the chapel choir) saw fit to increase his stipend annually by £10 from 1861, an award supplemented in February 1862 by the college's allowance of his rent.[61] Life had some routine. In addition to the two daily services and regular rehearsals, there

[61] See the diary of Frederic Bulley, 11 February 1862, *GB-Omc.*

Example 4 continued

were lectures and tutorials to attend, time for private study and visits home to Southwark to see his family during the vacations. In Oxford he attended Ouseley's termly lectures – on musical pitch, fugue, the history and characteristics of madrigals, and the old Italian school of sacred music – much of which was relevant to his studies for the Mus.Doc. and to the formation of his practical theories of

Example 4 continued

(d) be - cause God hath bless - ed thee for ev - er, God hath

bless - ed thee for ev - er, God hath bless - ed thee for ev - er.

harmony and equal temperament. Stainer, though very much detained by his work in Oxford, remained close to his former mentor. He visited Tenbury for the annual Commemoration service (often with Tuckwell) and renewed his friendship with Sullivan, who also attended. On 2 December 1863 the annual choral festival for the Choir Benevolent Fund took place in Christ Church Cathedral. Corfe conducted while both Stainer and Ouseley presided at the organ. Two years later Stainer offered to help Ouseley at Tenbury during August. Ouseley was delighted and was keen to hurry his old pupil to complete his contribution for the second volume of his *Special Anthems*: 'Nothing could please me more than to have you here during August next, as otherwise I believe I should be absolutely alone. As to pecuniary arrangements (if you will have it so), at the rate of £40 a year, one month would be £3.6s.8d. Shall that be our arrangement?'[62]

In 1862 Stainer must have been aware of a rather nasty blackmail case which involved a Probationer Fellow, John Addington Symonds, who was accused of

---

[62] Letter from Ouseley to Stainer, 4 February 1865, *GB-Lbl* Add. MS 62121, fol. 6.

aiding and abetting an undergraduate bent on 'pursuing' one of the Magdalen choristers. Supporting references from Balliol (Symonds' former college) and from the master, Jowett, were not enough to mollify Magdalen's more conservative college council (who anyway mistrusted the more liberal leanings of Balliol and Jowett) from treating the case with contempt. Instead, having decided that there was a *prime facie* case to answer, Magdalen required Symonds to defend himself against allegations made in a series of letters sent by the undergraduate to six of the Fellows, and though Symonds' name was ultimately cleared, and the undergraduate dismissed from Oxford in disgrace, Symonds felt compelled to resign his Fellowship after his health failed.[63] Stainer, it seems, was kept at arm's length from the unsavoury episode. The boy in question, a certain Walter Goolden, would later become a tenor Lay Clerk in the Magdalen choir and a dedicatee of one of Stainer's songs, 'Insufficiency'.

In the same year as the Symonds case, Stainer became more actively involved in secular music-making in the college. Glee- and madrigal-singing were important extra-mural activities in the city and university. Prominent in its nineteenth-century history, and particularly active in the 1830s, 40s and 50s, had been the Oxford Motett and Madrigal Society, run by Corfe, who also succeeded to the position of conductor of the University Amateur Musical Society after Stephen Elvey's death. By the 1860s, however, concerts in individual colleges as well as in public city venues were becoming a common feature of Oxford life.[64] Stainer inherited the conductorship of the Magdalen Madrigal Society from Blyth, who had been its conductor for many years.

The Society largely confined its musical activities to the College Hall but did occasionally sing elsewhere. Concerts were often given for charitable purposes. One such occasion was on 3 December 1862 for the Lancashire Relief Fund, at which money was raised to help the unemployed of the northern cotton mills (a crisis caused by the blockade of the Confederate states during the American Civil War). Others were given in aid of the Summertown Infants School Fund on 25 February 1865 and The Radcliffe Infirmary.[65] One or two of the concerts were linked with college events – May Day and Commemoration Day[66] – but, in the

---

[63] For a fuller account of this episode, see *The Memoirs of John Addington Symonds*, ed. P. G. Kurth (London: Hutchinson, 1984), 130–4.

[64] For an overview of concert life in Oxford colleges during the 1860s, see S. Wollenberg, *Music at Oxford in the Eighteenth and Nineteenth Centuries* (Oxford: Oxford University Press, 2001), 189–95.

[65] See *GB-Omc* MSS 984 (Summertown School Fund) and 985 (Radcliffe Infirmary).

[66] See *GB-Omc* MSS 982 (May Day concert, 1863) and 984 (Commemoration Day, 17 June 1868). Chapman remembered that madrigal-singing in College Hall was a major annual event under Stainer's leadership. (See Edwards, 'John Stainer', 307.)

main, concerts were given purely for the amusement of the singers.[67] At least two concerts were given outside the college: one in November 1866 in the University music room (to raise money for the new organ in St Giles's Church), and another not long after, on New Year's Eve, in the Pump Room at Leamington.

Programmes for these concerts reflected Stainer's tastes for both the 'ancient' and 'modern'. Among the 'ancient' were the Elizabethan madrigalists, Benet, Ward, Gibbons, Ford, Morley, Dowland, Weelkes and Wilbye, and Continental madrigals by Donato, Marenzio, Palestrina and Waelrunt; there were glees by Boyce, Bishop, Webbe, Hatton, Walmisley and Henry Smart, partsongs by Mendelssohn, but, most notably, there was a prolixity of more modern madrigals, ranging from Linley's 'Let me careless' of the eighteenth century, to those of John Barnett ('Merrily wake Music's measure'), Goss ('Ossian's Hymn to the Sun'), Pearsall (who was extensively represented by 'Allen a Dale', 'Light of my soul', 'It was upon a springtide day', 'Nymphs are sporting', 'Lay a garland', 'T'other morning', 'Sir Patrick Spens', 'Who shall win my lady fair', the ballad dialogue 'The King sits in Dunfermline town' and, of course, the arrangement of 'In dulci jubilo', a perennial favourite), and several of Stainer's own compositions. This repertoire was the staple diet, but from time to time they also sang larger works, including Handel's *Alexander's Feast* and Mendelssohn's Psalm 42.

Many of the singers of the Magdalen Madrigal Society, with invited guests and choristers, came together during the vacations to sing in a vocal group styling themselves the 'Magdalen Vagabonds'. They 'obtained their name for their intent to "wander" from place to place earning a few coins from the pockets of natives of the various places which they visit'.[68] 'Earning a few coins', however, was for charitable purposes, namely for raising funds for the restoration or renovation of church buildings around the country with a preference for churches which were specifically Magdalen livings. The idea of the 'Vagabonds' was proposed by the Rev. Compton Reade, one of the chaplains of Magdalen and a capable bass, on the basis that the group would meet and sing concerts for a week directly after Christmas and in July and August after the Great Gaudy. The first concert, organised

---

[67] For copies of surviving programmes of the Magdalen College Madrigal Society, see *GB-Omc* MSS 982, 984–6.

[68] Vine Hall, *The Magdalen Vagabonds*. Vine Hall had been chorister at Magdalen between 1845 and 1855, an academic Lay Clerk (1855–9) and Assistant Organist (1858–9). He later became Precentor of Worcester Cathedral (1877–90). His history of the 'Magdalen Vagabonds' was completed in 1909, shortly before his death. In accordance with his wishes, it was subsequently sent to Lady Stainer by Vine Hall's widow (see letter of 22 July 1909, *GB-Omc*) with the dedication 'To Lady Stainer these pages are inscribed in memory of Sir John Stainer, Organist of Magdalen, and S. Paul's Cathedral, the kindest of friends and the most illustrious member of the far-famed Magdalen Vagabonds.'

by Reade, took place at St Peter's, Titchfield, in July 1862 and was a small affair involving Stainer, Tuckwell and three Magdalen choristers. The event proved to be a particularly happy one for Stainer, as Tuckwell recounted:

> Whilst John Stainer was conducting a certain glee, the door at the further end of the room was opened, the noise of which caused him to look round, and we saw him to our great surprise bound from the platform up to him who was the cause of the interruption, and in his great joy almost embrace him. He was a short, grey-haired, kind-looking old gentleman, whom we assumed to be some near relation, perhaps his grandfather; it was no other than Sir John Goss, his former master, and at that time Organist of St. Paul's Cathedral, who was so well-known even then to all lovers of Church music. The glee that we were then singing was one of his best known compositions, "There is beauty on the mountains," which he insisted on hearing us sing over again. He was staying with some friends at Fareham, and was pledged to return to them for dinner, and therefore was unable to be at the concert.[69]

In 1863 the 'Vagabonds' made a return visit to Hampshire with their numbers augmented. Among them were Barrett, Blyth (who became a long-standing member), T. Marsh Everett (a Lay Clerk), E. M. Acock (chaplain at Magdalen and Christ Church) and the Rev. J. A. Lambert (a fine basso profundo). As time went on they were joined by Corfe and W. Davies (a Lay Clerk from St Paul's Cathedral). Concerts in 1863 were given on 31 July in the Old Town Hall at Romsey; the whole party later adjourned to the Abbey Church, where they listened to Stainer playing the organ. As a memorial to their trip, the whole party was photographed in the New Forest at the Rufus Stone. In December 1863 the 'Vagabonds' made their first post-Christmas foray, this time visiting churches in Maidenhead, Wokingham and Henley. In July 1864 Titchfield and Romsey enjoyed a further visit, while in December members of the group travelled north to Rugby and east to Frampton church near Boston in Lincolnshire, where, on both occasions, they sang carols. In the summer of he following year (1865) concerts were given at Reading Town Hall (for Pangbourne Church), where Stainer also played two solos on the organ, Basingstoke, Yeovil (for the Infirmary), Taunton (at the London Hotel) to raise money for the hospital, and Leamington. With the exception of Taunton, when he had to return to Oxford, Stainer conducted all these concerts, which took place in a convivial atmosphere.

Of a more intimate nature than the 'Vagabonds' was yet another, smaller vocal assemblage which called itself the 'Maltese Glee Club'. The surviving minute books state, with 'tongue in cheek' that 'A meeting was held at Magd. Coll on Feb 6th 1865

---

[69] Tuckwell, *Old Magdalen Days*, 85.

for the purpose of forming a Glee Club, there being nothing of the kind at that time in Oxford, the various College Madrigal Societies, and the moribund University Amateur ditto counting for nothing.'[70] Its founding members were Stainer (who was dubbed its conductor), Reade (who was President), Acock (Vice-President), Barrett (Secretary) and Edward Handley (Treasurer), a Commoner at Magdalen. Meetings were held on Fridays in members' rooms and refreshments were limited to beer or other malt liquor at the expense of the host of the evening. It was from this aspect of the gatherings – to consume beer after singing for an hour and a half – that the group derived its name (and not the Mediterranean island, though all members wore a Maltese Cross as an emblem of membership).

The first meeting was held in the President's rooms on Friday, 10 February 1865 (at which Stainer could not be present), and the Club met for the rest of the term, supplementing its weekly gatherings by assisting one of its members, Handley, with a concert at the Music Room, Holywell Street on 23 February (which Stainer directed) and a special dinner at the Clarendon Hotel on 16 March. Honorary members were steadily elected, including Tuckwell, Blyth, Frank Walker (a Vicar-Choral at St Paul's Cathedral), Vine Hall and Ouseley (who was proposed by Stainer). Yet by May Stainer already found the commitment of regular meetings too onerous and explained to Barrett: 'Will you be good enough to state to the Maltese meeting tonight that I have asked Dr Corfe (and he has most kindly consented) to take sole musical charge of the club – if not "for good" at all events while my hands are so full of work. I feel greatly indebted to him for relieving me of duty, and I am sure "the club" will also duly appreciate his venerable help.'[71] Stainer attended a further meeting on 2 June, but thereafter he was largely absent, and during the following term he was absent save for an 'extra night' on 6 December. The Maltese Glee Club, which gradually saw a depletion in its membership, struggled on throughout February and March 1866, but on 7 May, when the Minute Book ends, the Club presumably folded.

There were a number of likely reasons for Stainer's absence from the Maltese Glee Club. We know from correspondence with Ouseley that he was due to submit final versions of three anthems for publication in the second volume of *Special Anthems*. In addition, he, no doubt stimulated by his participation in the Magdalen College Madrigal Society, the 'Vagabonds' and the Maltese Glee Club, had continued to compose madrigals since leaving Tenbury; indeed, some of them were performed by the Magdalen College Madrigal Society.[72] Having completed a set

---

[70] Minutes of the Maltese Glee Club, *GB-Omc*, 1.

[71] Minutes of Maltese Glee Club, letter from Stainer to Barrett, 19 May [1865], *GB-Omc*.

[72] The exact date of composition of the eight madrigals is not known, though, as was

of eight, Stainer decided to publish them in Oxford by private subscription in 1865. The list of subscribers reveals both the extent of his reputation and the degree to which he had developed a network of friends, musicians and academic colleagues. There were numerous names from among Magdalen's clerical and lay dons, as well as Frederic Bulley. The Rev. C. Adams subscribed on behalf of the choir of New College; Philip Armes (organist at Durham Cathedral) subscribed, as did E. H. Thorne (organist at Chichester). Among other musicians were Blyth, his former teacher George Cooper, Steggall, Elvey, Corfe, Langdon Colborne (Stainer's successor at Tenbury) and, of course, Ouseley himself, who had anticipated the publication with eagerness. 'I anxiously await the receipt of your madrigals', he related to Stainer in February 1865, 'for I have always particularly admired those of them which I have heard.'[73] Copies were bought from among the academic fraternity of Oxford by the classical scholar Henry Nettleship and the Professor of Astronomy, W. F. Donkin, both ardent amateur musicians and friends; one copy was purchased by his brother, William Stainer, who by now was Superintendent of the Manchester Society for the adult Deaf and Dumb, and two copies were purchased by Thomas Randall, a local Liberal politician and prominent public figure in Oxford who was soon to become Stainer's father-in-law.

Stainer's collection of madrigals, published by Houghton & Tuke, is practically unknown – since there is only one surviving printed copy[74] – yet it is a compelling testimony to the author's growing creative ambitions and contains some of his boldest and most inventive unaccompanied vocal works. The three madrigals already discussed, and possibly written at Tenbury, have a lighter, vivacious demeanour, but the remaining five reveal a more intense, earnest manner both in their emotional deportment and in their scale and style.

The five-part (SSATB) 'Love not me for comely grace' was clearly modelled on the more deliberately archaic style of Pearsall, with its opening close imitation

mentioned in Chapter 2, it has been conjectured that 'Why so pale', 'The Queen of May' and 'Love's servile lot' may have been composed at Tenbury. 'The Queen of May' was performed for the first time publicly at Oxford by the Magdalen College Madrigal Society most appropriately on May Day 1863. 'Disappointment' was evidently completed by mid-June 1864, since it appeared in a MCMS concert on 8 June 1864. 'Why so pale and wan' was sung in a programme of 21 June 1865 along with the first hearing of 'The frozen heart', which was repeated at another MCMS concert on 30 November 1865. There is no surviving evidence that the largest madrigals, 'Dry your sweet cheek' and 'The Castle by the Sea' were ever publicly performed.

73 Letter from Ouseley to Stainer, 4 February 1865 *GB-Lbl* Add. MS 62121 fol. 6. As an indication of his support for Stainer, Ouseley purchased no fewer than six copies.

74 The single surviving copy is in the Tenbury collection (*GB-Ob* MS 1352).

Example 5. Madrigal: 'Love not me for comely grace' (opening)

and distinctly 'nineteenth-century' dissonance (Example 5). For the most part gentle and sonorous, the madrigal is couched in a richly lyrical E major, which is so telling at the outset and in the closing imitative episode ('Keep therefore a true woman's eye'), though at the more tormented heart of the piece, predominantly homophonic in texture, Stainer takes us to the dominant minor (B minor), and indulges in a brief moment of self-quotation from 'I saw the Lord' (in the same key – see bars 16–23).

Of a much more turbulent nature is 'The frozen heart', also for the same disposition of five voices. Here Stainer lends a vivid imagery to the opening text ('I freeze') with searing repetitions of the dominant minor ninth, and continues the harmonic intensity with a series of striking gestures including the dominant minor thirteenth ('For pitties sake'), a diversion to the Neapolitan, and an anguished imitative point ('I'll drink down flames') which chromatically rises to the first climax of the madrigal. Half-closing on the dominant of E, Stainer provides a transitional moment of calm ('but if so be') before launching into the final polyphonic paragraph ('I'd rather keepe this frost and snow') which evokes a sense of chilling severity through its deployment of an almost Fuxian style of invertible counterpoint (the last page is an extraordinary *coup de maitre*) and double suspensions. The dissonance of the ensuing descending sequences is mirrored by a registral ascent at the close which is almost neo-Purcellian in its use of the augmented mediant chord, though the subsequent harmonic progressions and suspensions are genuinely romantic (Example 6).

For his second six-part madrigal (SSATBB), 'Disappointment', Stainer took the opening and closing eight lines from the once highly popular 'Pastoral Ballad IV' of

Example 6. Madrigal: 'The frozen heart' (conclusion)

the eighteenth-century poet, William Shenstone, to form a structure of two verses with refrain. For the verses Stainer used essentially the same dolorous, Wilbye-like music to evoke a sense of desolation instigated by a faithless lover, while the two-line refrain, in the tonic major, is subject to substantial tonal reworking (compare bars 42–67 and 122–46).

For his setting for eight voices (SSAATTBB) of 'Comfort to a lady upon the death of her husband' ('Dry your sweet cheek') from Herrick's *Hesperides*, Stainer chose to illustrate the text's fluctuation between sorrow and the peace and resolve of a new beginning through a constant tonal fluctuation of F major (the tonic) and its relative D minor. This is encapsulated within the progressions of the first four bars, but the 'contest' is maintained throughout the madrigal in such moments as the first climax in bar 7 (on the dominant of D, replete with minor thirteenth); the radiant return to the dominant of F in bar 14 ('suns guild the aire again'); the powerful 6/4 of F after the tumultuous chromatic progressions of the 'chaffing sea' in bar 23; the stormy dominant pedal of D ('winds have their time to rage') in bars 27–33; the restoration of F in bars 35–45 and the affirmation of F in bars 46–55 (though note the interrupted cadence in bar 47); the startling juxtaposition and accentuation of the dominant of D in bars 56–9 immediately after a half-close in F (bar 55), and the equally arresting recovery of F in bar 59 which finally gives rise to a cadence in bar 60 and tonic stability for the remaining six bars.

Stainer's manipulation of key is one outstanding feature of this impressive madrigal but another is undoubtedly the richer sonority of eight voices, the textural impact of which powerfully accentuates contrasting moments of serenity, passion and climax. This can be felt in bar 7, where the sound of the full ensemble is first experienced, but it is also telling in bar 14 where Stainer's handling of diatonic dissonance is highly inventive (Example 7). Moreover, in the most hot-blooded passage that immediately follows (bars 17–24) the composer once again reveals his propensity for chromatic harmony which is enhanced here by the contrary motion of the outer voices and the truly 'modern' retrieval of the tonic as a secondary climax in bars 23–4. Other passages worthy of note are the impassioned statement ('Upon your cheek sat ysicles awhile') in bars 52–3 which makes use of enhanced dominant harmony (note especially the dominant eleventh in bar 53), the 'fortissimo' juxtaposition of the dominant of D in bar 56, and the radiant accumulation of all eight voices in the coda (bars 60–6).

Although 'Dry your sweet cheek' is perhaps the most tonally involuted madrigal of the collection, the most elaborate is 'The Castle by the Sea', a ten-part setting of Longfellow's poem from his prose romance, *Hyperion*, based on Johann Ludwig Uhland's lyric 'Das Schloß am Meere'. The deeply melancholy ballad has a biting irony worthy of Heine. Cast in the form of a dialogue, it tells of a glorious, romantic, Gothic castle towering above the sea, enshrouded in mist, 'in the

Example 7. Madrigal: 'Dry your sweet cheek'

evening's crimson glow'. However, we learn by degrees in the subsequent narrative, that, contrary to the expectant sound of joyous minstrels and the regal vision of the 'king and his royal bride', the sound of weeping is heard as the 'ancient parents' mourn, 'moving slow, in weeds of woe, No maiden was by their side!' Stainer responds to the narrative by dividing the 'question and answer' of the dialogue between two five-part choirs, bringing them together to express the anguished paradox of the final verse.

Stainer builds in a sense of tension through his skilful manipulation of key and mode:

Text	vv. 1–2	v. 3	v. 4	v. 5	vv. 6–7	v. 8
Choir	Choir 1	Choir 2	Choir 1	Choir 2	Choir 1	Choirs 1 & 2
Key	G	G → b	G	e, F → V of G	G	g
Section	A	B	A	C	D	E

Choir 1, who lead with the question, are linked with tonal stability and an opulent diatonicism. The 'answers' of Choir 2, on the other hand, are associated with increasing tonal dissolution, dissonance and expressive chromaticism. For example, in verse 3, Stainer quits the dominant of E minor for C major, which is then interpreted as the Neapolitan of B, a key whose arrival is enunciated by two emotionally charged suspensions (Example 8a). In verse 5, Choir 2 also quits E minor, but this time the sorrowful 'wail' is marked by an unexpected sortie to F major and a further series of expressive dissonances, not least the initial dominant eleventh marked *sf* (bars 62–3), which provides a deeply moving comment (Example 8b). For the final verse, marked 'Adagio', the Gothic atmosphere intensifies as the mode changes to G minor, and the sense of mourning is magnified by the joining of the two choirs into a full ten parts, creating a projection of a massive granite-like, architectural edifice. Such an impression is also enhanced by Stainer's marked harmonic deceleration and his combination of an ecclesiastical, Renaissance-like style with a Romantic harmonic vocabulary. It is a powerful vision and one worthy of comparison with the *a cappella* work of Schumann and Cornelius. Indeed, such pieces as these seem to transcend the older madrigal form and even the partsong, having more in common with the secular motets of Cornelius (such as those of Op. 11 published in 1871 and *Die Vätergruft* of 1874, which also include settings of Uhland).

Example 8. Madrigal: 'The Castle by the Sea':
(a) dissonance of modulation to B minor); (b) emotional *peripeteia*

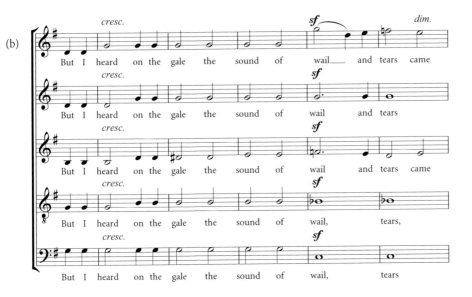

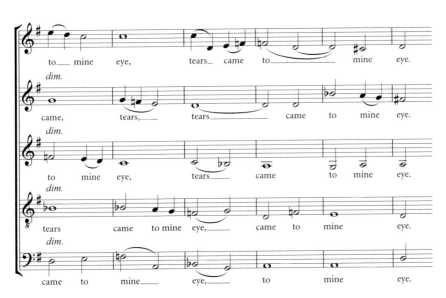

Besides the madrigals that he opted to publish by subscription, Stainer also entered a further work for the much-publicised Bristol Madrigal Society prize in 1864. Thanks largely to the work of Robert Lucas Pearsall, who helped inaugurate the Society in 1837 during one of his brief sojourns to England (he having settled abroad in Germany and later Switzerland), the Bristol Madrigal Society had developed a national cachet for its performances of a wide repertoire of English and Italian madrigals (as well as a broad corpus of Pearsall's work) and its

Example 9. Madrigal: 'Like as a ship':
(a) climactic progressions based on IV[7]; (b) conclusion

reputation rivalled that of the of the much older London Madrigal Society. The prize therefore carried a degree of prestige and consequently attracted no fewer than ninety-five entries. Stainer's entry, bearing his Greek logo from Aristophanes' *The Frogs*, was not among the winners; the prizes went to men of greater maturity and a more conservative style. First prize of £25 went to Henry Leslie's six-part setting of Thomas Watson's 'Thine eyes so bright'; second prize of £15 was offered to W. J. Westbrook for his five-part setting of 'All is not gold that shineth bright in show' (from *England's Helicon*); and third prize of £10 went to Henry Lahee for his six-part setting of Pope's 'Hark, how the birds on ev'ry bloomy spray'. All were duly published by Novello; Stainer's madrigal was never published and there is no surviving evidence of a performance.

'Like as a ship that through the ocean wide', a setting of the twenty-fourth sonnet from Spenser's *Amoretti*, is a further remarkable example of Stainer's work in the idiom. A substantial through-composed work in eight parts, the madrigal

Example 9 (a) continued

was conceived in three sections, the first two being linked as part of the 'octave' of the sonnet form, the third, in accordance with the six-line 'turn', functioning as an extended conclusion. The emotional turmoil of Spenser's first eight lines is aptly portrayed in the first forty-seven bars of music, the first section (of twenty-three bars) being dominated by a stormy passage that carries us from D minor to the dominant, A, and a second, faster section, dictated essentially by a rising chromatic bass, which (replete with a series of inverted augmented sixths) brings us back to V of A. It is in the slower 'turn', however, where arguably Stainer's finest music is located. Embarking in a more positive mood, from A major, the paragraph increasingly darkens as we modulate to B minor (via its affecting Neapolitan), and though there is a fleeting glimpse of optimism, suggested by the brief statement of D major ('Till then I wander') with its uncanny clusters of sound, D minor reasserts itself in a doleful series of progressions based around IV^7 and its first inversion (Example 9a). But most heart-rending of all is Stainer's final anguished

Example 9 continued:

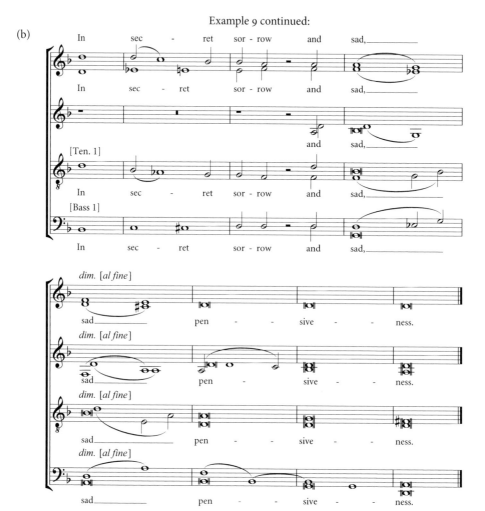

statement where the chromatic progressions have a modernity comparable with the late nineteenth century (Example 9b).

At much the same time that Stainer was pouring his creative energy into the madrigal, he was also showing some interest in song. A somewhat banal setting of 'When all the world was young lad' from Charles Kingsley's *The Water-Babies* probably dates from 1863, the year of Kingsley's publication.[75] Two love songs, of more musical merit, may possibly date from this time – a setting of Coleridge's 'Maid of my love, sweet Genevieve' and 'Rest', the latter a setting of a common-place poem but interpreted with some delicacy, not least in the touching modal

75 The manuscript watermark of 1863 also suggests this date of composition. Another undated setting of Kingsley, 'O! that we two were maying', from *The Saint's Tragedy*, may have been written much earlier, judging by the immaturity of the handwriting.

alteration from E minor to major that accompanies the 'religious' change of mood, and the legerdemain of the shift to the submediant before the end. A further love song, 'To sigh, yet feel no pain', which is more reminiscent of Mendelssohn, is also undated, but, from its dedication to 'E C R', Elizabeth Cecil Randall, it must date from 1865 or before. The unpublished song also bears a letter, written from Magdalen College, which accompanied the manuscript:

My dear Mrs Randall,

I send with this a song which I have this morning indited for your young lady. The words are very old, and <u>very beautiful</u> – the author's name is – I am sorry to say – unknown.

If she doesn't "fancy" it, tell her to commit it to "the devouring element." It is to be sung at a "goodish" pace. I hope your cold is better.

Ever yours sincerely
John Stainer[76]

P.S. Ask the young lady to withold [sic] her verdict till she knows it quite well.

The circumstances of Stainer's romance are unknown, but he was clearly head-over-heels in love. 'I hope Mrs Randall has returned safely from Torquay – tomorrow I shall perhaps have the pleasure of seeing her again, and *you* also my dear love, I find as difficult now to part from you for a few hours – as I once did for a few days – weeks or even – months!!!'[77] 'To sigh yet feel no pain' was undoubtedly a love-offering to his future wife, who by 1865 was his fiancée and very much a distraction from his normal duties, including his regular Sunday morning service at the University Church: 'Unless I can find some one to play the concluding voluntary at the University Sermon tomorrow – I shall not be with you till half-past twelve – if I <u>can</u> find such a foolish person I shall be with you at half past eleven.'[78]

Marrying into the Randall family, who not only had means, a fine property at Grandpont House in Oxford, and pre-eminence within the body politic of Oxford, gave the twenty-five-year-old Stainer further social elevation. That he was evidently conscious of the Randalls' higher social and pecuniary station, and of the humbler

[76] Letter from Stainer to Mrs Elizabeth Randall, undated [February 1865?], in private possession (JRS). Stainer had in fact taken his text from Thomas Moore's unsuccessful operetta *M.P. or The Bluestocking*.

[77] Letter from Stainer to Elizabeth Randall, 2 November [1865], in private possession (MN).

[78] Letter from Stainer to Elizabeth Randall, 31 October [1865], in private possession (MN).

disposition of his own origins, is evident from a letter written to 'Lizzie' who had visited Stainer's parents in Southwark not long before their marriage in December 1865:

> Having made up my mind to write to you tonight and to trudge off to Post with it I was not a little pleased to find your dear letter lying on my table, especially as it tells me of the entire recovery of your finger and of your kindness in paying the old folks a visit. I hope the sublime magnificence of their palatial residence didn't make you very uncomfortable!!! I think I ought to feel very thankful that God has so blessed and prospered me in life as to give them the pleasure of seeing me hold a better position than themselves. I am happy to say I never feel tempted to feel pride or conceit on this score. I can only say – may <u>our</u> children reach a position ten times as good as the capital one <u>we</u> start with. Can anything give greater pleasure to parents in their old age?[79]

Elevation of status was also on Stainer's mind in an academic sense. After being examined in law and history at the Schola jurisprudentiae (now part of the Bodleian Library) in 1864,[80] he received his B.A. (as an ordinary degree without honours) which enabled him to take his M.A. in May 1866,[81] a degree which allowed additional college rights, such as dining in Hall.'[82] The gaining of his degree undoubtedly gave Stainer a new 'egalitarian' social standing with other 'gentlemen', but he was also aware that the higher degree of Mus.Doc. would confirm his status within the university, not least because Ouseley was keen to recruit his protégé as an examiner. In fact Ouseley was not only eager to enlist Stainer's assistance but, as he made clear to him in February 1865, he already cherished hopes that Stainer might soon succeed him: 'I have set my heart resigning my Professorship in your favour as soon as you are M.A. and Mus.Doc. I think I could probably secure it for you, if I managed discreetly. This is <u>confidential</u>.'[83]

Ouseley's scheme did not come about for another twenty-four years, but, undoubtedly encouraged by his mentor's belief in him, Stainer thought he might stand a chance of filling the Reid Professorship of Music at the University of Edinburgh, vacated on the death of John Donaldson. The appointment attracted no fewer than twenty-one candidates, among them Ebenezer Prout, Macfarren,

[79] Letter from Stainer to Elizabeth Randall, 7 December [1865], in private possession (MN).
[80] See letter from Stainer to F. G. Edwards, 11 January 1901, *GB-Lbl* Egerton 3092, fol. 130.
[81] Diary of Frederic Bulley, 19 May 1866, *GB-Omc.*
[82] Diary of Frederic Bulley, 19 February 1866 *GB-Omc.*
[83] Letter from Ouseley to Stainer, 4 February 1865, *GB-Lbl* MS 62121, fol. 6.

John Hatton, Henry Wylde, Gauntlett, John Hullah, Herbert Oakeley and several from the Continent.[84] Robert Prescott Stewart, already Professor of Music at the University of Dublin, 'intended to stand, but was at the last moment dissuaded'.[85] Stainer received some support from the press, not least because of his prowess as a performer, but the real competition seems to have been between Hullah, who not only had credentials as an educator but also as a theoretician and historian, and Oakeley, who had decided to put his name forward after seeking the counsel of S. S. Wesley.[86] Oakeley's application arrived with the university about ten days before the meeting of the board on 2 November and with it followed an 'active canvas of the electoral body … by the friends of the newcomer'.[87] At the meeting, chaired by Gladstone, Rector of Edinburgh University, the vote was reduced to one between Hullah and Oakeley, in which Oakeley prevailed by five votes to three. The decision provoked not only disappointment but consternation among the supporters of Hullah and of several of the other candidates, largely on the basis that Oakeley had little experience or reputation. Yet, in spite of the disquiet expressed in the press, the appointment of Oakeley was accepted. 'For the sake of the popularity of the Professorship, we might have wished that some of the candidates, whose merits have already been tested by time, had been selected', reported the *Musical Times*; 'but we must not commit the injustice of ignoring the fact that not only has Mr. Oakeley furnished very excellent testimonials from distinguished musicians (amongst the rest from Dr. S. S. Wesley), but he has published a large number of vocal works, chiefly sacred, many of which, as Dr. Buck affirms, are often performed at Norwich.'[88]

Wesley's involvement in Oakeley's appointment could hardly have pleased Stainer. In May 1865 he was introduced to Wesley at St Mary Redcliffe, Bristol, during a choral festival; it was not an auspicious meeting and Stainer recalled Wesley's contumelious character:

> Dr Wesley was present at the rehearsal and I had the pleasure of being introduced to him – did I say pleasure? he by no means gave me a good impression. He seemed a very eccentric and rather disagreeable man who would evidently have given his ears to have said something sarcastic to me during our interview of twenty seconds – only he hadn't a chance.[89]

84 *The Times*, 16 October 1865.

85 E. M. Oakeley, *The Life of Sir Herbert Stanley Oakeley* (London: George Allen, 1904), 110.

86 Ibid.

87 *The Times*, 6 November 1865.

88 P. Scholes, *The Mirror of Music, 1844–1944: A Century of Musical Life in Britain as Reflected in the Pages of the Musical Times* (London: Novello & Co., 1947), 663.

89 Letter from Stainer to Palmer, 10 May 1865, in private possession (RN).

It was an impression that Stainer retained throughout his life. He continued to admire Wesley as a composer and musician, but as an 'officer of the church' he always considered that Wesley was too consumed with grievances. It was a criticism he also levelled at Gauntlett: 'Like many other of these high-flyers, he [Gauntlett] thought grumbling was as good as work. Wesley was another; he was at three Cathedrals and left each in a worse musical state than he found it.'[90]

While awaiting the decision of the Edinburgh board, Stainer was immersed in arrangements for his Mus.Doc. It had been necessary to wait for the regulation period of five years before entering for the higher degree, but in that time he had gained a new confidence in his technical and creative powers as well as a broader knowledge of past and present musical repertoire. He was granted the proper permission from the President of Magdalen to take his degree,[91] and his exercise, an oratorio, *Gideon*, for soloists, chorus and orchestra, approved by Ouseley and Corfe, was duly performed (as was required) on 8 November 1865.

His preparation for the performance of his oratorio involved not only marshalling members of the Magdalen and other chapel choirs, and a soprano soloist, Emma Jenkin, from London, but also an orchestra for which he obtained help from Alexander R. Reinagle, organist of St Peter in the East in Oxford, and a well-known local violinist and cellist.[92] A good rehearsal on 2 November augured well, as he reported to Elizabeth Randall: 'You will be glad to hear that the rehearsal this morning was most satisfactory. I must confess to have been quite delighted with my own music!! The Overture sounds just what I hoped it would when I first scored it – you will [I] know be pleased with it. Didn't the first violin "slash" into it!! The prima donna "Madame Jenkini" has run through her parts entirely to my satisfaction.'[93] The performance of *Gideon* was scheduled to take place in the Hall of Magdalen College, but such was Stainer's popularity and renown within the university, and the expectation that a more sophisticated work was to be heard, that huge numbers of spectators arrived in the college who simply could not be accommodated. So reported the *Oxford Journal*:

> The exercise, however, being of a much more elaborate character than usual, it excited great interest; the Hall, consequently, was crowded before the appointed hour, the staircase was packed, and the cloisters were rapidly filling when the Vice-Chancellor, who had had considerable difficulty

90 Letter from Stainer to F. G. Edwards, 6 November 1899, *GB-Lbl* MS Egerton 3092, fol. 95.

91 Letter from Bulley to Stainer, 7 November 1865, in private possession (JRS).

92 See Wollenberg, *Music at Oxford*, 168, *passim*. Reinagle is best known today for his hymn tune 'St Peter', used several times in *Hymns Ancient & Modern*.

93 Letter from Stainer to Elizabeth Randall, 2 November 1865, in private possession (MN).

in effecting ingress, adjourned the performance to the [Sheldonian] Theatre, it being next to impossible for all the performers to make their way through the crowd. The galleries of the Theatre were soon well filled and Mr Stainer, the Vice-Chancellor and Sir Frederick Ouseley were warmly cheered on entering.[94]

In fact it had been Stainer who had appealed to the Vice-Chancellor to change the venue, a quite unprecedented happening in Oxford's musical history though 'it was somewhat amusing to see, as the company passed up High Street, some of the undergraduates in their zeal shouldering the music stands in the "flit"'.[95]

Though the performance of *Gideon* was well attended, its reception was generally modest and, notwithstanding the publication of the vocal score by Novello (in what was probably a limited edition), its importance was no more than provincial. The *Oxford Times* claimed that 'throughout the piece the master mind of the composer was developed, which was illustrated by the rounds of applause drawn from the audience, comprising the musical talent of the university and city';[96] some found merit in Emma Jenkins' solo arias,[97] while the ultra-conservative critic of the *Orchestra* used his opportunity to rail against what he perceived as the insidious, indeed secular modernisms of Stainer's style by comparing it directly with Crotch's *Palestine*. There 'the style is always dignified and elevated. There is no Zampa-like overture in the oratorio of "Palestine." In the oratorio under review there is no harmony, no dignity, no elegance; nothing to show solid acquirement, extensive reading or erudite research. ... "Palestine" yet lives. "Gideon" is dead.'[98] But, in spite of its local support and approbation, *Gideon* did not break through into the oratorio market so markedly circumscribed by Handel, Haydn, Mendelssohn and Spohr, and has remained unperformed since its one and only hearing.

Gideon may have been written to satisfy the rubric of an examination (which demanded a secular or sacred vocal work with orchestral accompaniment lasting between 40 and 60 minutes), but, unlike his more conservatively 'compliant' cantata for the Mus.Bac., Stainer's doctoral exercise showed a more confident, expansive composer. The story of Gideon offered all the traditional components and imperatives quintessential to the Handelian and Mendelssohnian Old Testament oratorio. With its central theme of complete dependence on God for delivery from the raiding Midianties, the plot allowed for emotions of despair, supplication,

---

94 *Oxford Journal*, 11 November 1865.
95 *Oxford Chronicle*, 11 November 1865.
96 *Oxford Times*, 11 November 1865.
97 *University Herald*, 11 November 1865.
98 *The Orchestra*, 30 June 1866.

reflection and prayer, fear, resolve and triumph, not to mention the miracles of the flesh and unleavened cakes, the fleece, and the final Israelite defeat of the Midianite thousands by an army of only three hundred, in a battle scene reserved until the end of the oratorio. Such an array of sentiment gave ample opportunity for a variety of solo work, and, most importantly for the 'English' oratorio genre, for the chorus. Following the model of *Elijah* and other Birmingham oratorios, *Gideon* is divided into two distinct and substantial halves, the first half closing with the miracle of the fleece and the dew (at a time when delivery from the Midianites seems hopeless), the second with the battle and victory.

The variety of techniques within Stainer's choruses is worthy of note. Arguably the simplest structure is the choral lament (No. 3) in E minor of Part I ('Remember, O Lord, what is come upon us'), which, though an uncomplicated ternary design, nevertheless surprises us with the central paragraph in C (and then for much of the time in the minor mode), and the memory of this E–C relationship (I–VIb–I) is nicely encapsulated in the last six bars. A similar ternary scheme is deployed in the Duet and Chorus (No. 19 – 'O Lord we have sinned'), where the chorus (as the voices of the Israelites) sing a form of unison *cantus firmus* against the main thematic material of the orchestra. The soprano duet forms the basis of the central paragraph before all forces conjoin in the reprise – the sopranos uniting with the orchestra while the choir once again provide the *cantus firmus*. The *cantus firmus* technique also plays a part in No. 6, where, as the voice of God, it functions as a counterpoint to a lyrical duet for soprano and tenor, the entire structure being flanked by choral recitative. Two of the choruses make use of chorales, revealing Stainer's indebtedness to Bach, filtered through Mendelssohn. In both instances the chorale is used as a means of spiritual reflection and is closely linked with the evolution of Gideon's trust in God. In No. 20 (which recounts the miracle of the fleece) Gideon's two entreaties are 'answered' each time by the full choir, but, to give added intensity to the revelation of God's intervention, the repeat is transposed up a tone from F to G. A comparable scheme can be found in No. 27 ('Thou who broughtest Thy people from the land of Egypt'), though with a more radical tonal plan. Gideon's accompanied recitative embarks from a resplendent B major, but for the chorale, sung by the soldier tenors and basses, the key shifts to E flat major. Even more unexpectedly, a repeat of the material, commencing in E flat, does not mirror the initial tonal process but is instead raised a semitone to E major. The effect is impressive. The main choral pillars of *Gideon* are, however, the dramatic, more freely constructed double choruses, such as one finds in No. 15, which narrates the miracle of the flesh and unleavened cakes; here Stainer surely modelled the theatrical opening and tranquil conclusion on 'Behold, God the Lord passed by!' from *Elijah*, and Mendelssohn's 'Baal! Hear and answer' must have proved a useful paradigm for No. 10 ('Baal Lord of earth and sky') not least in the lead Stainer took from Mendelssohn's orchestral accompaniment. A similar effect must also have been in Stainer's mind for No. 21, which dramatically opens Part II, though here, as part of the most extended choral structure of the work, it forms part of a preludial ternary form (replete with central solo quintet) to a 'sublime' and well-composed double fugue, one which has more fluency and drive than the rather more prosaic fugue that ends the oratorio and whose limited effect is weakened by the somewhat emasculate battle scene, a musical *locus* in which Stainer is clearly uneasy.

Although the choral parts of *Gideon* are architecturally more imposing, some of Stainer's most successful and distinctive music is situated in the solo sections, where the chromatic influence of Spohr is at its most conspicuous. The chastising tenor aria (No. 5), in ternary form, has a strikingly expressive, tangential opening on its dominant ninth, which is deftly manipulated at the reprise as part of a tonal recovery from the central section's F major. Besides making extensive use of the Neapolitan, the soprano aria in B minor (No. 8 – 'When the enemy shall come in like a flood') probes as far as F major before returning via D minor. But perhaps most noteworthy is the euphoniously penitential Trio (No. 25 – 'Behold we come unto Thee') in F major where, in the first episode of the rondo design, Stainer indulges in a set of modulations which move upward sequentially through a series of minor thirds from C minor, through E flat minor, to V of F sharp, before easing onto a 6/4 of F and the restoration of the tonic. Such harmonic boldness is comparable with S. S. Wesley.

Stainer proceeded to his degree on 9 November 1865.[99] Fellows and other members of Magdalen College were evidently delighted that their organist had successfully taken the degree, and then at only twenty-five years of age. Not since Philip Hayes, who had been organist at Magdalen between 1776 and 1797 (and Professor of Music in the University) had a Magdalen organist boasted of such qualifications. As a mark of their admiration, a set of doctoral robes (a very expensive commodity, no doubt well beyond Stainer's pocket) were purchased for their colleague:

> We beg to offer you our warmest congratulations on your recent degree, and to request your acceptance of the appropriate robes, as a mark of sincere personal regard for yourself and high appreciation of your most successful efforts to sustain the musical reputation of this College and of the University of Oxford.[100]

Stainer was delighted at the gesture, as he reported to Elizabeth: 'I have just received

---

[99] Diary of Frederic Bulley, 9 November 1865, *GB-Omc*.
[100] Edwards, 'John Stainer', 303.

the formal document – asking me to accept a set of robes – and must own to being exceedingly pleased to find it signed by 46 names – all Magd: men.'[101]

Glowing with the kudos of his new degree, and a salary of £180,[102] Stainer married Elizabeth Randall at St Aldate's Church in Oxford on 27 December 1865; Ouseley presided at the ceremony and the marriage certificate was signed by Thomas Randall and Stainer's youngest sister, Henrietta. It was a close and loving union; the couple shared a strong Christian faith, a love of books, the arts and of travel, especially on the European continent. They moved into accommodation at 64 High Street in Oxford, close to Magdalen College, and after only ten months they saw the birth of their first child on 2 October 1866, named John Frederick Randall after his father, after Ouseley (who attended the christening on 4 December) and his mother's maiden name. Over the next five years the Stainer family was rapidly augmented by another four children. Elizabeth Cecil (known as 'Cecie') was born on 19 November 1867, Ellie on 13 October 1868, Edward on 16 December 1869, and Charles Lewis on 8 June 1871. It was a contented and happy household; Stainer adored his children and, having come from a large family (unlike his wife who had but one brother, Thomas, who died at twenty-one), he was accustomed to the love and inner strength that family bonds engendered. While his wife was expecting 'Cecie', his father died in April 1867 at Wimborne in a property he had inherited from a cousin in 1854; he was buried in the graveyard of the Minster.

Life seemed set fair, yet one thing troubled Stainer: he suffered from poor sight. 'My eyes are beginning to show symptoms of collapse', he wrote to Elizabeth not long before their marriage.[103] Eye strain appears to have dogged him throughout his professional life and the relatively poor illumination afforded by candlelight in organ lofts can only have contributed to his problem. Some uncertainty surrounds Stainer's eyesight. It has been often recorded that he lost the use of one eye in a childhood accident,[104] though this is questioned by some descendants of the Stainer family who maintain that he possessed a 'lazy eye', a congenital complaint

---

[101] Letter from Stainer to Elizabeth Randall, 7 December 1865, in private possession (MN).

[102] Stainer had received his rise in salary from £150 to £180 in March 1865; see diary of Frederic Bulley, 28 March 1865, *GB-Omc*.

[103] Letter from Stainer to Elizabeth Randall, 7 December 1865, in private possession (MN).

[104] Russell, in his *St Paul's under Dean Church and his Associates* (London: Francis Griffiths, 1922) attests to Stainer's 'use of one eye', though gives no further circumstantial detail. W. A. Frost (*Early Recollections of St Paul's Cathedral* (London: Simpkin, Marshall, Hamilton, Kent & Co., 1925), 62) also states that one eye had been 'injured by an accident in his childhood', and only one eye 'was of any use to him', though again he gives no further description of how impaired Stainer's vision was or the nature of the affliction.

confused with the serious accident suffered by his brother, William Stainer, who lost an eye in 1880:

> Since I wrote, William has had a bad accident to his left eye. As he was shutting some shutters in one of his new Homes a heavy rod of iron fell right into his eye and completely crushed it. This was on Friday. Of course I was with him the same evening. Yesterday (Saturday) I took Power and an experienced assistant to see him, and Power decided directly he saw the wound, that it would be necessary to entirely remove the crushed eye in order to save his good <u>right eye</u>. He was then and there placed under chloroform and the operation was most skilfully and successfully performed. When I left him he was perfectly happy and calm. Today (Sunday) Power says he is in excellent progress and that barring one glass eye he will in a week or two be as well as ever. I too have seen him today and all is evidently going on well. He has had very little pain, and there is no anxiety at all about his speedy recovery. He has had a narrow escape of even more serious injury. He has been very calm and plucky.[105]

The fact that Stainer refers to the plural – 'eyes' – in his letter to his wife-to-be suggests that he was in possession of both, but that his vision was clearly suffering from strain, whether he enjoyed sight in both eyes or only one. In any event we know that Stainer's sight was seriously impaired, that it was a matter of serious concern throughout his career, and a crucial element in his decision to retire from St Paul's Cathedral in 1888.

As soon as Stainer had gained his Mus.Doc., Ouseley recruited him as an examiner alongside himself and Corfe for the Oxford music degrees. Such a move proved auspicious for the young Hubert Parry, still a schoolboy at Eton, who came up to Oxford to look around the university in May 1866. Parry, who had made Stainer's acquaintance briefly at the Gloucester Three Choirs Festival in 1865, attended evensong at Magdalen on several occasions. 'Stainer played the last 3 movements of the Sonata in B flat (Mendelssohn) afterwards most gloriously', he recorded in his diary, 'and brought out the "Tuba mirabilis" tremendously in the last strain.'[106] Two days later Parry, whom Stainer quickly recognised as 'bright, intelligent, and talented',[107] visited Magdalen again, tried the organ, and sought advice from Stainer about how he should approach his forthcoming Mus.Bac. examinations.[108]

---

[105] Letter from Stainer to Elizabeth Stainer, 15 February 1880, in private possession (JRS).

[106] Diary of Hubert Parry, 20 May 1866, *ShP*.

[107] Letter from Stainer to F. G. Edwards, 6 June 1898, *GB-Lbl* MS Egerton 3092, fol. 40.

[108] Diary of Hubert Parry, 22 May 1866, *ShP*.

The two young men met again in the following December, first at a musical party at the home of Professor W. F. Donkin (an able amateur cellist) and later at the Scola Musicae, where he was to sit his written papers. These were duly passed and the exercise was given on 21 February 1866. By then Parry had arrived at Oxford as an undergraduate at Exeter College and the relationship between the two men passed from a more formal one to one of intimate friendship and mutual respect. Among other candidates whom Stainer examined were William Pole, who took his Mus. Bac. degree in 1867, and J. Frederick Bridge in 1868.

Stainer's role as university examiner added to an increasing diversification of musical employment which, besides consolidating his close association with the city and university, extended his reputation beyond Oxford to London and the wider nation. As a teacher, he took on the tuition of Oxford students, especially on the subjects of harmony and the organ, for which he claimed a special, practical interest. In this regard he was an important influence on the young Charles Harford Lloyd, who came up to Oxford in 1868. 'I can hardly express my gratitude to Stainer', Lloyd recollected. 'He gave me a term's lessons in harmony, but beyond that I gained an experience of untold value to me in watching him as he played the organ and accompanied in his own inimitable manner.'[109] He had organ pupils, among them, George Clement Martin (with whom he would have a long professional relationship), and he served as mentor to J. Frederick Bridge, whom he met by chance at Holy Trinity Church, Windsor, in or around 1865 on visiting the Revs. Henry and Stephen Hawtrey (who were close friends of Stainer's Oxford colleague W. F. Donkin) where Bridge was a young organist.[110] Bridge had hoped to enter Oxford as an undergraduate, and applied for an organistship at Queen's College, but after being turned down, he resolved to take his Mus.Bac. and apply for organist posts elsewhere. Eventually a post at Manchester Cathedral came up, and Stainer was happy to act as a principal referee: 'I have much pleasure in bearing testimony to the general musical ability of Mr Bridge; he is an excellent organist, and from the manner in which his own choir performed his exercise for a musical degree in the Sheldonian Theatre, all who heard it must have formed the highest opinion of his skill in training Choirs. In every way I believe him to be fully qualified for the post he now seeks.'[111] Bridge's application was successful. On hearing the news, Stainer was delighted: 'I hope the lateness of my congratulations on your 'promotion' will not

[109] F. G. Edwards, 'Charles Harford Lloyd', *Musical Times* 40 (June 1899), 370.
[110] J. F. Bridge, *A Westminster Pilgrim* (London: Novello & Co., Hutchinson & Co., 1918), 4.
[111] Letter from Stainer to the Appointment Committee of Manchester Cathedral, received 25 February 1869, in private possession (JRS).

make you think them less sincere. I shall be very glad to hear all about your choir, organ etc.'[112]

In the second half of the 1860s Stainer's reputation as an organist and church musician was nationally established. There are numerous instances of his being asked to advise on new organs for parish churches and private houses. In May 1865 he was asked to play at a choral festival at St Mary Redcliffe in Bristol. The experience of an unwieldy organ and clerical conductors provoked a colourful letter to a friend:

> Yesterday I provided the College with a deputy and went to play at a Choral Festival at S. Mary Redcliffe? – 600 voices!!!
>
> Two clergymen conducted (not of course both at once) – and beat time with up beats for down! – diagonal "slashes", both arms and a foot "going it" at the same time – with a stick the size of an ordinary umbrella!! Then I ventured to look into the looking glass to see if I was in time with the conductor – or rather if he were in time with me (for I took the law pretty much into my hands) – I could see a surplice and hood performing a certain number of circumgyrations and the stick representing a figure of this shape
>
> [scribbled figure]
>
> If I could only have guessed which was the upbeat and which the down – I should have been happy – but apart from chaff – the whole thing went very well. The effect of some of the unison music being very fine. Do you know the church? The Organ is at the West end and the choirs were in the chancel and transepts – that is to say about 150 feet from the Organ! – Now commiserate with me. The Organ had no pedal pipes – and the pedals were coupled irrevocably and perpetually to the great organ! So when you wanted to play on the Choir Organ – all the stops on the Great had to be put in until the bass of the Grt was = the Choir! and as if to add insult to one's sufferings there were no composition pedals so all alterations of stops had to be done "vi et armis" (which being interpreted signifies "with a bang and with both arms").
>
> The organist of the church was very civil and did the duties of a composition pedal for me. An account of the Swell organ will interest you. This noble institution rejoiced in the marvellous compass of 2½ octaves! – Fiddle G to D – hardly enough to tempt musical fingers to run riot. …
>
> I forgot to state one peculiarity of the organ at S. Mary Redcliffe – there was no coupler Sw: to Grt: but there was a swell to Choir and also Choir to Grt – so by drawing both the object could be attained – only unfortunately

---

[112] Letter from Stainer to Bridge, 11 November [1869], in private possession (JRS).

the Ch^{r.} didn't pull the swell notes quite down and the Grt: didn't push the Ch^{r.} notes quite – so about one note in 6 on the swell spoke properly. Bells are going for Chapel – so adieu.[113]

In December 1865, shortly before his marriage, he played, to some acclaim, at the Reading Town Hall, during a visit made by the Vagabonds in aid of Pangbourne Church. In 1867 he was asked by Lord Waterpark, of Doveridge Hall, Derbyshire, to assist with the design of the organ (by Steele & Kay of Stoke-on-Trent) in the local church of St Cuthbert's, Doveridge. In April of the same year his services as organist were requested for the fourth annual festival of the associated choirs of the Archdeaconry of Worcester, at St Lawrence Church, Evesham, though the death of his father intervened. (S. S. Wesley, who was close by in Gloucester, took his place.) On 27 September he was asked to preside at the full choral services to mark the opening of the new Nicholson organ at Holy Trinity Church, Worcester (and afterwards to share in a recital of organ music with Ouseley, Parratt and A. J. Caldicott). 'I shall be delighted to run over and do my best to "show off" your Organ at the time you name', he wrote to the Holy Trinity authorities. 'I should of course like to have a "canter" with your choirs. Most heartily do I congratulate you on your speedy prospect of "doubling the pleasures and halving the cares" of this life.'[114] The occasion also included a commission, the anthem 'Sing a song of praise' from the Rev. W. Rayson (Sacrist of Worcester Cathedral and honorary secretary for the Worcester Choral Association), which was sung at the special evensong, and repeated at the morning service on 29 September (at which Stainer also participated). Stainer was also asked to preside at the opening of the new organ of Quebec Chapel, Bryanston Street, London on 5 July 1868.[115]

Perhaps the most telling indication of Stainer's national repute was his employment by Grove to perform solo organ works – a new departure – in the Saturday Concerts at the Crystal Palace. On 7 November 1868 he appeared for the first time in a programme of overtures by Rossini and Mendelssohn, Beethoven's Fourth Symphony and vocal numbers by Spohr, Benedict, Mendelssohn, Meyerbeer and Rossini and played Mendelssohn's Fourth Organ Sonata and Bach's 'Pedal Fugue' in G minor. The occasion not only introduced him to August Manns, conductor of the Crystal Palace Orchestra, but also to J. W. Davison, critic of the *Musical World*. 'The experiment of an organ performance was entirely successful, thanks to the admirable playing of Dr. Stainer. The organist of Magdalen College is a master of his instrument. Neither the Sonata of Mendelssohn nor the Fugue of

---

[113] Letter from Stainer to Palmer, 10 May 1865, in private possession (RN).

[114] Letter from Stainer to [Rev. W. Rayson], n.d., Worcester Cathedral Chapter Library.

[115] *Musical Times* (January 1901), 24.

Bach presented any mechanical difficulties that were not conquered with perfect ease.'[116] Stainer was hired again by Grove, three years later, on 11 November 1871, to play similar repertoire – Mendelssohn's Sixth Organ Sonata and Bach's Prelude and Fugue in C major – an appearance which was, this time, preludial to further appearances as a soloist with the Crystal Palace Orchestra in 1872 and 1874 and as a 'choral' organist in oratorio (a role where the organist supported the chorus by playing their parts) for both Manns and Joseph Barnby.

In addition to his career as an organist and church musician, there is much evidence that Stainer took the ample opportunity to study music more closely, particularly through the works of Mozart, Beethoven, Schubert, Schumann, Spohr, Brahms and Wagner. The young Parry for one was elated by the works that formed Stainer's more adventurous voluntaries; he noted in his diary that 'Stainer played the most sublime thing by Mozart afterwards' (which was probably the late Fantasia and Fugue in F minor).[117] And a few weeks later Schumann's late Bach-inspired music was on offer: 'Stainer played for me, my eye, such a fugue. The last of Schumann's set of 6. It is one of the finest things I ever heard in my life; and I must speedily attempt its better acquaintance.'[118] Stainer's broad appetite for late eighteenth- and nineteenth-century music is evident both from an impressive range of musical materials he drew on for his *Theory of Harmony*, published in 1871, and the transcriptions of instrumental music (published by Novello in five sets) he made for the organ between 1869 and 1872 which included the Adagio from Beethoven's String Quintet Op. 4, the overture to Handel's *Semele*, the first movement from Haydn's Symphony No. 104, the Andante from Schubert's Piano Sonata Op. 120, the Sinfonia from Spohr's *Last Judgment*, and the Adagio espressivo of Schumann's Second Symphony. In 1869 he also arranged a march by the virtuoso pianist Agnes Zimmerman. 'I look forward with such pleasure to hearing your arrangement of my March', she wrote from London; 'Could you possibly play it to me next Friday at about 12.30? or a little before one o'clock?'[119] These pieces alone evince a man who was in no way circumscribed by his working ecclesiastical environment, but was hungry to imbibe the new musical developments of Europe and to celebrate new and promising indigenous works on offer at the nation's choral festivals.

He was a regular visitor to the Three Choirs Festivals, where he met Ouseley, Dykes, Parry and Sullivan. Of Sullivan's talent he held a high opinion, but he harboured doubts about the direction in which his friend's potential was developing. Depth and invention were being sacrificed, so he thought, to popularism and the

---

[116] *Musical World*, 14 November 1868.
[117] Diary of Hubert Parry, 11 March 1867, *GB-ShP*.
[118] Diary of Hubert Parry, 2 April 1867, *GB-ShP*.
[119] Letter from Agnes Zimmerman to Stainer, 13 February 1869, *GB-Lcm*.

economic temptations of commercial publishers. It was a view confirmed after hearing *The Prodigal Son* at Worcester in 1869:

> I heard the Prodigal Son at Worcester – the instrumentation throughout is charming – but as a whole the work lacks 'bottom' – you understand me. The melodies are graceful but not always original. It will keep afloat until the publishers have made a good thing of it, then ____! It is as good as the Woman of Samaria [by Sterndale Bennett's] – and very much in the same sugar candy style.
>
> I do wish dear Sullivan would put his thumb to his nose – to the public and critics, – and write for 'the future'.
>
> The later works of Mendelssohn and Beethoven, and all the works of poor neglected Schubert and tardily-acknowledged Schumann – all point to the future of music. Sullivan ought (I feel that he is a great man and could do so) to begin where they left off – regardless of encores and banknotes.[120]

Participation in the charitable work of the 'Vagabonds' continued. During the summer of 1866 Stainer and his new wife accompanied the group back to Romsey, which headed a tour to Ryde, Taunton, Yeovil and Leamington, the latter including a service in Whitnash Church the day after the concert. In 1867 they returned to Whitnash, Rugby and Reading, but also made visits to Wellingborough, Marlow and Eton, where they raised money for the reredos and chancel of the chapel. After Christmas of 1868 they sang at several venues in Rugby, including a choral service of music for men's voices arranged by Stainer in Holy Trinity Church. They also travelled to Husband's Bosworth, Birmingham, Lutterworth, as well as familiar haunts at Taunton, Leamington and Whitnash Church, where on 23 July they sang Stainer's Communion Service in A and Goss's 'Praise the Lord O my soul'. Rugby was again the setting for another summer concert in July 1869, before they travelled, on a much more wide-ranging tour than ever, to Northampton, Romsey (where they took a picnic in the New Forest), Wokingham, Folkestone, Bridgewater, Butleigh and Glastonbury, as well as a visit to Tenbury on 29 September for the Dedication Festival. Their tour of 1870 took them back to Taunton, Leamington, Romsey as well as Hereford. In Romsey Abbey, which incorporated a pleasant afternoon at Broadlands, home of the lately deceased Lord Palmerston, they sang two services which included Sullivan's recently published Service in D and S. S. Wesley's 'The Wilderness'. After Romsey they made their way to Reading and included a return visit to Glastonbury as well as Cheddar. Stainer's last tour with the Vagabonds took place during the Christmas vacation of 1871 and early 1872.

---

[120] Letter from Stainer to J. F. Bridge, 11 September [1869], in private possession (JRS).

Favoured locations of Rugby and Leamington were settings for concerts, but they also incorporated a visit to the Warwickshire town of Coleshill, as well as new venues in Hampshire – Alton, Southampton (where they sang a choral service in St Peter's Church on 10 January 1872) and Ringwood; and to round off the tour the singers gave a charity concert at St Thomas's Hospital in London, Stainer's old stamping ground.

In Oxford Stainer's musical life flourished and the level of activity increased markedly; indeed, Hugh Allen, among others, credited Stainer with propelling sacred music in the city into a new era.[121] He assisted, usually as organist, with Oxford Diocesan Festivals, which occurred annually at Christ Church Cathedral. For the laying of the foundation stone at Keble College, on 25 April 1868, he was asked to superintend the music for the service. For the installation of the Marquess of Salisbury as the new Chancellor of Oxford, on 18 June 1870 he and Corfe under-took the direction of an orchestral concert comprising Mendelssohn's Overture *A Midsummer Night's Dream*, Weber's *Jubilee Overture* and two works by Beethoven, the Violin Concerto and the 'Pastoral' Symphony. Ouseley and Corfe 'were loudly cheered and a tremendous burst of applause greeted the mention of Dr Stainer whilst at the same time a wag lightly requested that the Choragus ... give the com-pany a Corfe mixture!'[122] He assisted Corfe with the University Amateur Musical Society, the university's most long-standing musical institution, but was the main force in founding or reviving several choirs in the city. He was made honorary conductor of the Oxford Orpheus Society in 1863, a group of singers who evidently maintained a deep affection for him (as is shown by the choir's generous testi-monial when he relinquished the post in 1872), and founded the Oxford Philhar-monic Society in 1866. The Oxford Philharmonic, a choir of 200 singers, gave their first concert on 21 March 1867 with the first public hearing in Oxford of *Elijah*. Certain difficulties with the Philharmonic committee appear to have compelled Stainer to give up the conductorship to James Taylor, organist of New College,[123] though he did participate in the first concert as the harmonium player. Stainer also helped to revive the fortunes of the Oxford Choral Society (founded by Crotch in 1819) which had declined in recent years, and this organisation was very much a rival to the Philharmonic. Stainer also relinquished the conductorship of this body to W. H. Allchin, a local musician, who also took over the Orpheus Society after Stainer's departure from Oxford.

[121] H. P. Allen [under the name of C. Rootham, who read the paper in Allen's absence], 'Music in the Universities' [25 April 1922], *Proceedings of the Royal Musical Associa-tion* 48 (1921–2), 102.

[122] P. Charlton, *John Stainer and the Musical Life of Victorian Britain* (Newton Abbot: David & Charles, 1984), 30.

[123] Ibid., 28 and n. 23.

At Magdalen the Madrigal Society went on giving concerts in the College Hall (where Stainer's new song 'Jilted' was given on 22 June 1870), and the Chapel Choir gave charity concerts in aid of the restoration of Headington Church on 18 June 1867 and, again, for St Thomas's Hospital on 20 June 1872. The latter, held in the hospital's Court Room, was billed as a 'Concert of English Vocal Music … by past and present members of the Choir of St Mary Magdalen College, Oxford.'

In addition to his participation in the secular musical life of Magdalen, Stainer also found himself involved in the musical life of Exeter College. In 1862 Exeter College had celebrated the fact that its Music Society (ECMS) had emerged from virtual insolvency, four-fifths of the college members participated, and a performance of Haydn's *Creation* (the first time ever performed by a college society) had confirmed the college as 'the most musical in the university'.[124] By 1863, however, after a series of clerical conductors, the society's committee felt it necessary to recruit a more qualified and experienced conductor. Stainer first appears as the conductor in October 1864 and was instrumental in giving a highly successful Commemoration Concert in June 1865, a programme which included choruses from Mendelssohn's *Antigone*. Nevertheless, with the appointment of a new chapel organist, F. Scotson Clark (by all accounts a somewhat feeble musician and performer), the ECMS felt obliged to employ him as conductor on a termly basis. The December concert of 1865 was fair, but during the following term a debate arose about reappointing Clark which ultimately provoked the motion to reappoint Stainer (who was re-elected by thirty-two votes to seven). Misgivings about Stainer's non-membership of the college, and the possible slighting of the regular college organist persisted into 1868, but by then Stainer had engendered so much satisfaction in the society's activities that he was annually reappointed. During the course of his conductorship of the ECMS Stainer directed performances of the 'Spring' section from Haydn's *Seasons*, Mendelssohn's cantata *Sons of Art*, the *Festgesang* and selections from *Oedipus at Colonnus*. Moreover, as he related to Edwards many years later, he was particularly proud at having given the first hearing of Schumann's *Das Glück von Edenhall* in his own English adaptation (later published by Novello) with Parry's assistance:

> While he [Parry] was an undergraduate of Exeter Coll. I was conductor of the Exeter College Musical Society, and Parry played occasionally pianoforte solos, and accompanied songs and other things admirably. It may interest you to know that I adapted Schumann's Cantata "The Luck of Edenhall" to English words for performance by the Exeter Coll. "Musical Soc^y. and that

124 Minutes of the Exeter College Musical Society, Report of 1 November 1862, GB-Oexc.

Parry played (of course excellently) and I conducted – the first performance of this cantata in this country.[125]

The Exeter College concerts also featured new works by Parry, and two new songs by Stainer, 'Insufficiency' (8 December 1869) and 'Loyal Death' (21 June 1870), sung by J. M. Davenport and Frank Pownall respectively. Pownall would later be the dedicatee of a further song, 'Unbeloved', composed in 1871. All were published by Novello. Critical reception of the songs was mixed. 'Insufficiency' was described as 'a most eccentric song; full of phrases of the purest melody, but so strangely vague in what is usually called 'tonality' as to cause a feeling of restlessness which, although somewhat in character with the impassioned poetry, leaves an unsatisfactory impression upon the ear.' And it was quite evident that Stainer's feeling for unconventional progressions left the critic somewhat baffled:

> The passage marked "Lento" has a melancholy wail, in excellent keeping with the poetry; but we can not say that we like the manner in which the return to the original key is effected, an opinion which we think will be shared by our musical readers when we say that the [flat] 4/2 on A flat is succeeded by the 6/4 on A natural in D major (the melody dropping from B flat to A natural) and that theme is then continued in this key.[126]

'Loyal Death', dedicated to another Magdalen Lay Clerk, J. Swire, drew a more favourable review, even though Stainer's shift from A flat to B major was reproached as being 'a bit sudden'.[127] 'Unbeloved', taken from *Songs and Ballads* by the free-thinking, radical Victorian poet Gerald Massey and published in London in 1854, was much more sophisticated, deploying an imaginative, sonata-like structure. Stainer's first two verses (like a repeated exposition) establish a contrast of material between two tempos of 'Adagio' (3/4) and 'Andante' (9/8) and two keys (F and D) as if to define the delineation between the lover and his unattainable beloved. A more impassioned 'Allegro agitato' becomes more tonally dissolute before opening material in F major is reasserted for the final verse. Here also the D major 'second subject' is restated boldly in the tonic, though Stainer provides a telling memory of the former contrasting tonality of D as if to remind of the lover's once youthful ardour.

Stainer's relationship with the publishing house of Novello, already healthy after the publication of his first cluster of anthems, became ever closer in the mid-1860s, indeed to the point where he rarely ever had to look to another publisher for the dissemination of his work. Henry Littleton, for his part, also sensed that,

[125] Letter from Stainer to Edwards, 6 June 1898, *GB-Bl* Egerton 3092, fol. 41.

[126] *Musical Times* 11 (1870), 276.

[127] *Musical Times* 11 (1870), 404.

given the commercial potential of his cheap editions combined with the growing demand from parish churches (which had led the way in the new Tractarian revival), Stainer's music had huge marketable prospects. The first major indication of this occurred in 1867 with the publication of the first series of *Christmas Carols Old and New*, which Stainer compiled with the help of the Rev. Henry Ramsden Bramley, High Church conservative, Fellow and Tutor at Magdalen, who provided not only many translations from Latin but also a number of original (though not particularly distinguished) verses.

The carols were almost certainly an expression of Stainer's antiquarian love of old song and melody, an interest that he would sustain and research throughout his life, and one that would be manifested in the magnificent library of song that he developed. Such a fascination was no doubt inherited both from his father and from the example of Ouseley. Stainer was also fully aware of Christmas as an increasingly popular religious festival. As Andrew Parrott and Hugh Keyte have suggested: ' "The Victorian reinvention" of Christmas was in reality more the compression of the traditional celebrations of the old Twelve Days into two or three, and the conversion of what had always been a period of communal festivity into a more inward-looking celebration of the family.'[128] This, mingled with the antiquarian zeal for recapturing, indeed idealising, Christmases 'of old', fuelled the publication of traditional carols during the first part of the nineteenth century for parish use, and the 'rediscovery' of old carols that had appeared in chap-books and broadsides from the eighteenth and early nineteenth centuries. Highly influential were two Cornish antiquarians, Davies Gilbert (who published *Some Ancient Christmas Carols* in 1822) and William Sandys (whose *Christmas Carols, Ancient and Modern* appeared in 1833) whose work was adapted by a number of successors, among them, J. M. Neale and Thomas Helmore (their *Carols for Christmas-tide* of 1853–4, from *Piae Cantiones* of 1582), Edmund Sedding (his nine *Antient Christmas Carols* of 1860), Joshua Sylvester (*A Garland of Christmas Carols Ancient and Modern* of 1861), Edward Francis Rimbault (*A Collection of Old Christmas Carols* and *A Little Book of Christmas Carols* of 1861 and 1863 respectively) and William Husk (*Songs of the Nativity: being Christmas Carols, Ancient & Modern* of 1864).[129] During the second half of the nineteenth century this burgeoning of curiosity for the traditional carol – the pastoral vision of Victorian domestic bliss, the cosy Christmas fireside and, of course, Bloxam's tradition of Christmas celebrations at Magdalen – chimed with Stainer's sensibilities. Whether any of his carols were

---

[128] *The New Oxford Book of Carols*, ed. H. Keyte & A. Parrott (Oxford: Oxford University Press, 1992), xxi.

[129] That Stainer knew these publications well is evident from the *Catalogue of English Song Books Forming a Portion of the Library of Sir John Stainer* (London: printed for private circulation by Novello, 1891).

sung at the Magdalen Christmas entertainments is not known, but what is certain is that the 'Vagabonds' were in the habit of singing carols during their tours directly after Christmas, and there is evidence that they sang at least one of Stainer's original pieces – 'Jesu, hail!' – at Leamington on 26 December 1865.[130]

Of the twenty carols published in the first series, eight were traditional and adapted from earlier sources. These included 'God rest you merry Gentlemen', 'A Virgin unspotted', 'The seven joys of Mary', 'A child this day is born' and 'The first Nowell'; the old English tune of 'Greensleeves' appeared to William Chatterton Dix's words 'What child is this', and the collection *Carols for Christmastide* by Neale and Helmore furnished 'Good Christian men rejoice' and 'Good King Wenceslas'. All appeared in Stainer's harmonisations, several of which, notably 'The first Nowell', remain common currency to this day. Contemporary carols by Elvey, Steggall, Maria Tiddeman, S. C. Hamerton, Arthur H. Brown, Dykes, Barnby and Ouseley constituted the remaining twelve, though only two of these – Dykes's charming setting of E. Caswall's 'Sleep, holy Babe' and Barnby's Gounodesque lullaby 'When I view the Mother holding' – had real distinctive character. Stainer had hoped that Sullivan might contribute, and sent him two texts including 'Sleep, holy Babe' (which Dykes eventually set), but his hands were full, as a letter to Stainer, who was holidaying in Scotland in September 1867, indicates:

> You are a happy man to have the means and leisure to move about in the most lovely part of Scotland. You will return like a giant refreshed. I on the contrary am compelled to return here after a short and broken holiday to get through a heap of work which is on my hands.
>
> I am afraid I cannot help you with regard to the Carols for I have so many commissions still uncompleted that all my time is taken up, and in plain terms I don't think it would be worth your while to indemnify me for the time and thought I should have to bestow on the work nor indeed should I wish it from such an old friend. If I were less busy, and did not depend upon any compositions for half my income nearly I would do it with the greatest pleasure.
>
> "Sleep! Holy Babe" is the best of the two I think (without the last two verses). The other is rather affected. I have been at Birmingham and Hereford, and look upon music just at present as a loathsome Art![131]

Stainer may not have succeeded in persuading Sullivan to contribute to the first series of carols, but the publication enjoyed overwhelming success, and thousands of copies were sold, so Sullivan was able to contribute to a second series, published

---

[130] See Vine Hall, *The Magdalen Vagabonds*.
[131] Letter from Sullivan to Stainer, 3 September 1867, *US-NYpm*.

by Routledge and Novello in 1871 (with illustrations engraved by the Brothers Dalziel), which added another twenty-two carols to the original twenty. This time Stainer included ten traditional carols in his own harmonisations, among them 'The Lord at first did Adam make' ('A Carol for Christmas Eve'), which was taken from Davies Gilbert's collection (where it was similarly entitled 'For Christmas Eve'), 'The Holly and the Ivy' set to an old French tune, 'God's dear Son', 'The Waits' Song' and 'The Babe of Bethlehem' (all taken from Rimbault's collection), 'The Cherry Tree Carol' (though a different tune from the familiar one that appeared in Husk), 'The Wassail Song' (the text appeared in Husk, the tune was from Yorkshire), and 'Dives and Lazarus' (though a different tune from those published in the later *Oxford Book of Carols*). Among the modern carols, Goss's 'Hymn for Christmas Day', better known as the setting of Caswall's 'See amid the winter's snow', was the only one to find a permanent place in later carol books, though at least three others – Barnby's 'Cradle-Song of the Blessed Virgin', Dykes's 'Christmas Song' ('Once again O blessed time') and Stainer's 'The Child Jesus in the Garden' (somewhat evocative of Gounod or Adam) – deserve to be better known.

Though Littleton was clearly delighted with the commercial success of Stainer's and Bramley's collaboration, at least one of Stainer's competitors, Rimbault, and his publisher, Chappell's, was furious and accused Stainer of plagiarism. 'Mess[rs] Chappell & Co. complain that you have copied some of your carols from a publication edited by Dr Rimbault', wrote a somewhat unsettled Littleton in January 1872; 'will you kindly write to me on the subject and oblige.'[132] Rimbault's complaints were as follows:

No. 21   The Lord at first had Adam made

This version of the tune was made by me from Carols 1 and 2 in Davies Gilbert's Ancient Christmas Carols c. 1823. It is copied verbatim from my book, No. 3.

No. 23   The Holly and the Ivy

I found this tune in an old Lute Book and translated it from the tablature. The idea of adapting it to these words was my own. It is copied verbatim from my book, No. 9.

No. 24   The moon shines bright

I noted this tune from the singing of a farmer in Lancashire, altered it and adapted it to these words. The idea of fitting it to carol words is mine. It is copied verbatim from my book, No. 20.

---

[132] Letter from Henry Littleton to Stainer, 9 January 1872, *GB-Lbl* Add. MS 62121, fol. 14.

No. 29   God's dear son

Copied <u>verbatim</u> from my collection, No. 18.

No. 31   The Babe of Bethlehem

I noted this tune <u>for the first time</u>, and <u>adapted it to the words, with which it had no previous connection</u>. The last eight bars <u>are my composition</u>, to suit it to the carol words. It is copied <u>verbatim</u> from my book, No. 6.[133]

Stainer's rejoinder to Littleton rejected each of Rimbault's complaints in turn, not least indicating that traditional tunes were public property and that his own arrangements differed markedly in their harmonisations:

I have received your note enclosing Dr Rimbault's complaints as to our making use of carols from his book. I will answer his complaints seriatim on my own behalf and that of Mr Bramley.

He says No. 21 'The Lord at first' is copied from his book (No. 3) <u>verbatim</u>. This is not the case. If he had compared the words he would have at once seen the variations. The harmonies are new. Davies Gilbert's collection claimed our attention from the first, and was carefully examined.

He says No. 23 'The Holly and the Ivy' is copied <u>verbatim</u> from No. 9 of his book. This is not the case. A comparison will show our words to have been obtained from a separate source. The proper words of the chorus being omitted in his collection. The harmonies are new. The air is called by Dr Rimbault an 'Old French Carol Tune'. We have repeated his statement.

He says 24 'The moon shines bright' is copied from his No. 20 – <u>verbatim</u> – whereas a comparison will show … we have printed <u>10 verses</u> from an independent source – whilst he has printed only <u>five</u>. The harmonies are new.

He says No. 29 'God's dear son' is copied <u>verbatim</u> from his No. 18 – whereas the second stanza in our book does not occur in his. The harmonies are new.

With regard to No. 31 'The Babe of Bethlehem' which he says is copied <u>verbatim</u> from his No. 6 – All that need be said is that he has called it <u>Traditional</u> (Kent). A reliable authority – we repeated this statement. Had we had the least idea that "Traditional" signified "partly composed by Rimbault" we should have either asked his permission to print it or have omitted it altogether. We thought all traditional melodies were public property.[134]

---

[133] Letter from Rimbault to Henry Littleton, 2 January 1872, *GB-Lbl* Add. MS 62121, fol. 15.

[134] Letter from Stainer to Littleton, n.d. [January 1872], *GB-Lbl* Add. MS 62121, fol. 12.

Stainer's rebuttal saw an end to the matter, and allowed Novello to pursue an aggressive policy of advertisement for the carols, one which soon led to the publication being a fixture of each Christmas. Stainer's musical arrangements were entirely pragmatic. Their simple harmonisations, highly adaptable and expertly crafted for accompaniment on the organ or piano, were intended for the archetypal parish church choir or even for the drawing-room, while the subject matter of the carols themselves was uncontroversial, popular and eminently performable. Magdalen College, so Keyte and Parrott have argued, 'occupied a place in the public mind analogous to that of King's College, Cambridge, today',[135] and opened the way for cathedrals, which had largely ignored or set their face against the carol repertoire, to include them in their services. In this regard, Stainer would once again be instrumental in helping to set new trends.

The popular 'parish' dimension of the carols was also reflected in other practical ecclesiastical works of the mid- to late 1860s. The *Magdalen Psalter*, which provided pointings for the Psalms, Canticles and the Athanasian Creed, was published in Oxford in 1868 by Stainer in collaboration with Lewis Tuckwell. It was immediately adopted by Magdalen Chapel,[136] by Christ Church Cathedral, by several other chapels and metropolitan churches in Oxford, by many of the larger public schools, and by diocesan festivals, the demand of which led to the issue of several further editions. Moreover, in January 1867, the system of pointing in the psalter (where a bold typeface was used to mark specially stressed syllables on reciting notes) became the subject of a more discursive article for the *Musical Times* in which Stainer attempted to demonstrate the true though complex relationship between the seemingly anomalous seven-bar structure of single and double chants and the regular eight-bar periodicity of classical melody.[137]

In 1865 Stainer produced his first hymn tune, 'Hail the day that sees him rise', which appeared the same year in *Hymns for the Church of England with Proper Tunes* (musically edited by Steggall).[138] Two years later he wrote 'Sudeley' for the Rev. Brown-Borthwick's *Supplemental Hymn and Tune Book* (1868), a tune which demonstrates some considerable melodic artifice in its phraseology. Also composed for *Hymns for the Church of England* in 1869, and also included in the enlarged edition of 1875, was 'Dies Judicii', a muscular setting of Thomas of Celano's Advent

[135] *New Oxford Book of Carols*, xxi.

[136] See diary of Frederic Bulley, 22 May 1868, *GB-Omc*.

[137] See J. Stainer, 'On the Rhythmical Form of the Anglican Chant', *Musical Times* 13 (January 1872), 335–8. By way of demonstrating his theory, Stainer ultimately hoped that chant would become the repository of a greatly enlarged reservoir of melody (see p. 338).

[138] This hymn for Ascensiontide also appears in Millard's list of anthems, and was evidently sung at Magdalen.

irregular three-line verses ('Day of wrath! O day of mourning!'), intensified by Stainer's striking chromaticisms. Though too young to contribute to the first edition of *Hymns Ancient & Modern* in 1861, Stainer was enthusiastically signed up by Monk and Ouseley for the supplementary edition of 1868, to which he contributed five tunes – 'Emmanuel', 'Nativitas', 'Magdalena', 'Iona' and, probably best known of all, 'Charity' (a setting of 'Gracious spirit, Holy Ghost' by Charles Wordsworth, classical scholar and Bishop of St Andrews) – to the additional 112 hymns. In 1868 he also contributed a single tune, 'Damiani', thoroughly reminiscent of Dykes's 'Melita' ('Eternal Father strong to save') in the sequential chromaticisms of its last line, to the *Sarum Hymnal* (successor to the *Salisbury Hymn Book*) edited by Lord Nelson, J. R. Woodford and J. A. Dayman (the musical editor), but a year later his services were called on more substantially by Joseph Barnby who had been co-opted as the musical editor by William Cooke and Benjamin Webb for *The Hymnary*, a hymnal published in 1870. For this Stainer produced five tunes – 'Dawn', 'Matins', 'Celano', 'The Haven' and, arguably the best, 'Wondrous Love'; 'Crux Beata', an unusual tune set to J. M. Neale's 'Are thy toils and woes increasing' was composed for the revised edition in 1872. Only one tune, 'Colomba Sancta', written in 1871, was unpublished.[139]

The production of carols and hymns was supplemented by other 'parish' liturgical music. A congregational Te Deum in C (on which Parry no doubt modelled his early Service in D dedicated to Stainer), set largely for unison choir, was regularly sung at Magdalen as part of Millard's four-week schedule of morning canticles, as was the largely unpublished 'Magdalen' Service in A composed in or around 1866.[140] Though by no means a characterful work in terms of its thematic material – much of the unison material does at times seem to meander – the Service in A does reveal that Stainer was attempting to lend some form of thematic and tonal cohesion to both individual and cumulative structures. For the 'genuflection' in the Te Deum ('Holy, holy, holy'), the foray to C major is one that occurs repeatedly in other movements, and its significance as a tonality is thrown into relief particularly in the section before the conclusion, when it is touched on again in juxtaposition to C sharp minor (see 'Day by day we magnify Thee'). C major is the first important detour in the Benedictus, and in the Sanctus becomes a vehicle to move further flat to F. Both C and F form the emotional epicentre of the Creed, and F constitutes an important 'memory' before the conclusion. In the Magnificat one is aware of the thematic reworking of both the opening material of the Te Deum and the Creed, and the first detour to C ('the lowliness of his handmaiden'), given the context of past recurrences, now seems a logical and integral shift. Similarly in the

---

[139] See J. Stainer, *Hymn Tunes*, no. 71 (London: Novello & Co., 1900), 123.
[140] Most of the 'Magdalen' Service remains unpublished, though the Kyrie and Creed were later published by Novello.

Nunc dimittis, F major is allowed to make its mark early on, at the end of the first line of text ('According to Thy word'), and the key dominates the rest of the text until the return of A for the Gloria (which, incidentally, relates to thematic material of the Benedictus), and even then, for the fugato that ensues, Stainer takes us increasingly flatwise as far as F before finally restoring A.

Of a similar 'parish' orientation was the verse anthem 'Sing a song of praise', written for the Worcester Choral Association. The first section, an abridged sonata, shows the influence of Goss, as does the classical semi-chorus in the relative minor, while in the final section, Stainer evidently tried to ape, in a very concentrated duration, a Handelian 'Hallelujah' style of chorus to equal the anthem's role as a *pièce d'occasion*. A similar tripartite anthem, 'What are these that are arrayed in white robes?', was composed in or around 1871 for the choir of All Saints, Lathbury, Buckinghamshire, a church in the Oxford diocese. More distinctive than 'Sing a song of praise', this anthem makes much of the contrast between the acclamatory mood of the opening and a more penitential lyricism ('These are they which came out of great tribulation'). Stainer chooses to state this contradistinction a second time, and in so doing, gives greater weight and melodious euphony to the tranquil close ('and God shall wipe away all tears'), pathetically articulated by the sequential falling sevenths of the solo sopranos and the harmonised reiteration for full choir. In addition to this anthem literature, Stainer also published in 1867 *The Gregorian Tones with their endings harmonized in various ways*, a compilation of tones and accompaniments used in Merton College Chapel in Oxford designed to be used in a parish context. Moreover, being further-ranging than other Gregorian publications of the period, it sought to provide a major assortment of terminations to the chanting tones. In fact Stainer admitted in his short preface that it was both impossible and impracticable to provide more than a few examples of the 'infinite variety of harmonies which may be added to the Gregorian Tones.'[141] And yet, as he demonstrated in his extensive 'Table of Tones with their Endings', there were considerable possibilities for more daring chromatic harmony, including the use of diminished sevenths and augmented sixths, chords verging on the theatrical for the more puritan advocates of *echt* church music.[142]

Of the music more obviously intended for the English cathedral and collegiate environment, Stainer produced two substantial anthems. The first, 'Lead, kindly light', was composed in 1868. Though the anthem was conceived as a gentle, indeed pastoral, evocation of Newman's well-known text, in which Stainer's classical melodic gift was given full and affecting utterance, the mystical dimension

---

[141] J. Stainer, *The Gregorian Tones with their Endings Harmonized in Various Ways* (London: Novello & Co., 1867), 1.

[142] See also B. Zon, *The English Plainchant Revival* (Oxford: Oxford University Press, 1999), 300–1.

of Newman's poetry is also a central thread, epitomised by the modulations of the opening statement, where an immediate shift away from the tonic, E flat, takes us first to F minor, then A flat, and finally to a half close in the tonic. The lyrical theme and its accompanying harmonic formula are repeated twice over in an ever-enriching contrapuntal texture before Stainer takes us, in a manner thoroughly reminiscent of Schubert, to the flat mediant, G flat major (a 'purple patch' that vividly illustrates 'the night is dark'), before settling in the dominant. The reprise is also handled with true legerdemain, both in the way Stainer incorporates the initial modulations and in the handling of fresh contrapuntal strands. The verse, for solo treble or tenor, is couched in B major, a reflection of Stainer's increasing predilection for third relationships in his larger liturgical structures. This is, like those verses of S. S. Wesley's extended anthems, more of an aria in terms of its emotional breadth and rhetoric, and the tonal scope of the piece which explores the flat submediant (G major) in conjunction with the dominant ('I lov'd the garish day') again reveals the composer's thoroughly Romantic penchant for harmony, as do the touching references to the Neapolitan (C major) and the flat mediant (D major) in the coda, and the variation of the refrain ('Lead Thou me on'), heard first deploying the major subdominant, and on the second hearing, the minor. But perhaps most intricately subtle is Stainer's final section, where melodic and harmonic motives from the two previous sections are fused and reworked within the 'variation' context of the first section. As a balancing gesture Stainer presents new secondary material ('And in the morn those angel faces smile'), though even this continues to gravitate to the more melancholy hues of F minor, and it is this key that marks the final climax ('Which I have lov'd long since') before the coda, yearningly wistful in its understatement.

Stainer's other major verse anthem of this period, the larger 'Awake, awake, put on thy strength', sets verses from Isaiah (Ch. 3 vv. 1–2, 7–10). Dedicated to the Rev. J. R. G. Taylor, Succentor of Hereford Cathedral, a colleague of Ouseley's, an able alto and an honorary member of the 'Vagabonds', it is conjectured to date from 1871. Though less thematically cogent than 'Lead, kindly light', 'Awake, awake' contains some fine music. The first section, for full choir, is a carefully proportioned rondo structure whose main thematic strand reiterates the text of the anthem's title. A similarly conceived rondo design inhabits the third section ('Break forth into joy'), and the rondo theme is subsequently transformed and reworked in the more lively triple-time coda, a version which reminds us that the theme itself is ultimately derived from the first section of the anthem. The gem of the piece, however, is the verse for semichorus, 'How beautiful upon the mountains' in the third-related key of D major. In a similar manner to the last section of 'I saw the Lord', Stainer draws on the unusual rhetoric of the slow lyrical fugue, giving us a full exposition and an additional fifth entry (in the soprano) of the euphonious fugal subject. In conjunction with the fugal 'melody' – for that is what it is in terms of its rhetorical delivery – is a regular countersubject ('that publisheth peace') whose material forms the basis of the central paragraph. Stainer's reprise of the fugal subject, which is now presented as a series of imitative entries, is given additional piquancy by the supporting tonic pedal in the organ, and by the dissonance of the subdominant-inflected harmony. The countersubject, absent during the series of imitative entries, is finally presented at the very close, sung in unison.

In addition to anthems, Stainer also produced two settings of the evening canticles which were published in 1870. The one in E flat, which was regularly sung at Magdalen, was later to become part of his first comprehensive Morning, Communion and Evening Service, and showed some advance on the A major service of the mid-1860s in terms of the quality and contrast of its material, and in the equilibrium of the 'full' and 'verse' design. Just as in the earlier service, Stainer also linked the glorias of the Magnificat and Nunc dimittis in terms of thematic material, and also used a paraphrased version to begin the Nunc dimittis. More sophisticated, however, was the Evening Service in E, which, though clearly modelled on the E flat Service in terms of its episodic structure and contrast of choral forces, reveals a more integrated approach to tonality. This is clearly evident in the 'genuflection' ('Holy, holy, holy') which, while anticipated by a similar rhetorical device of a half close, moves more radically to the flat mediant (G major) rather than the more traditional supertonic so conspicuous in the E flat setting. G major also significantly returns for the last two lines of text ('He remembering His mercy') before the gloria, whose restatement of E major is announced tangentially from G and by an organ reprise of the choir's opening material. In addition to the flat mediant, Stainer also makes colourful use of the flat submediant (C major) as adjuncts to the dominant in both the Magnificat and Nunc dimittis, and the glorias make prominent, indeed dramatic, use of the Neapolitan before the final cadence.

Stainer's most extended secular work, undated but presumably composed during the 1860s, was a string quartet dedicated to the Savilian Professor of Astronomy at Oxford, W. F. Donkin. A true 'Renaissance man', Donkin was an important scientific and cultural magnet at Oxford. As a professional scientist and mathematician, he contributed papers to *Philosophical Transactions* and was close to George Boole, who acknowledged Donkin's work in his *Treatise on Differential Equations* of 1859. His contribution as an astronomer is often measured by the important paper he read to the Royal Astronomical Society entitled 'The secular acceleration of the moon's mean motion' (printed in the society's *Monthly Notices* in 1861), but he also retained a deep interest in both theoretical and practical music, and it was his intention to produce a large treatise on acoustics in three parts which covered both the science of sound as well as its application within present-day theory and practice. Only the first part, *Acoustics* (pub. 1870), was completed by his death in November 1869. Donkin's family was actively musical: W. P. Donkin was a fine pianist; W. E. Donkin, a celebrated amateur violinist, was a Fellow of Exeter College, President of the ECMS from 1870, and an important performer with his brother at the University Musical Club. W. F. Donkin himself took part in a great deal of music in Oxford, and was even known to compose. On his death Stainer rearranged a setting of the Latin hymn 'Justorum animae' for performance in Magdalen Chapel. Writing to his friend, Henry Acland, he explained ruefully: 'I am afraid his family were <u>not</u> pleased with me for this, and I have always regretted having done so. Although I feel bound to tell you that on hearing the whole sung as an Anthem in Magd: Chapel, only a few weeks ago, I thought it <u>most</u> effective.'[143] Donkin cultivated a close friendship with Ouseley, with Joachim (who often visited Oxford to perform), and with the musical circles at Cambridge.

In his capacity as a keen performer of chamber music, Donkin held parties at his home which became well known among Oxford's musical fraternities. In December 1866 Parry recorded attending one such party, where he met both Stainer, Taylor and Ouseley, who had one of his quartets performed the same evening specially written for the occasion.[144] Given the dedication of Stainer's Quartet in E minor, it seems more than likely that it was written for one of these musical parties. The scale of the work suggests that Stainer, like Ouseley before him, took his lead from the works of Mozart, and, perhaps in light of the structural freedom of some of the movements, from Beethoven's Op. 18 set. (Parry's two early quartets of 1867 and 1868 have the same classical orientation.) The first movement, made up of a slow introduction and sonata movement, is largely conventional in treatment, as is the short dance movement (a Minuet). The slow movement, however, is far from the traditional classical conceptions in its 'fantasy' exploration of one central theme across a broad range of contrasting keys and instrumental registers (perhaps owing something to Haydn's *Seven Last Words*), and the finale attempts to combine elements of sonata rondo with fugue in a most energetic and eccentric design.

Donkin's 'domestic' concerts were almost certainly points of contact both for the musical *cognoscenti* of Oxford but also for the university's Liberal wing of reforming intellectuals with whom Stainer enjoyed increasing acquaintance. Donkin's work on acoustics was complemented by the work of the physicist R. H. Bosanquet at St John's, a colleague whom Stainer regarded highly and who would be associated closely with several of his future musicological ventures. Among his other distinguished academic acquaintances were Henry Acland, Henry Halford

[143] Letter from Stainer to Henry Acland, 26 Oct [no year], *GB-Ob* MS Acland d.80, fols. 108–9.
[144] Diary of Hubert Parry, 4 Dec 1866 *GB-ShP.*

Vaughan (the Regius Professor of Modern History), and the Balliol reformers Arthur Stanley (the specialist on German theology and later Dean of Westminster) and Benjamin Jowett (who was deeply influenced by the philosophies of Hegel and Bauer). In addition there were the Latin scholars John Conington and Henry Nettleship, the theologian Mark Pattison, and the Sanskrit scholar Max Müller.

Perhaps of all these, Müller was one of his closest friends. Born in Dessau, and named Max after the male protagonist in Weber's *Der Freischütz*, Müller was the only son of the popular German lyric poet Wilhelm Müller, set by many of his composer compatriots including Schubert (notably the song-cycles *Die schöne Müllerin* and *Die Winterreise*), Mendelssohn and Schumann. Müller had settled in Oxford in 1848, but his future had been secured in the university when he was appointed deputy Taylorian Professor of Modern European Languages. He succeeded to the full chair in 1854, became a naturalised British citizen the following year, but in 1860 was involved in controversy when one of his mentors, Horace Hayman Wilson, Boden Professor of Sanskrit died. Müller was expected to fill the vacant chair, but at a time when Oxford elections could still be determined by the clerical mass of university MAs, his liberal Lutheranism and lack of concern for the church's struggle to maintain its influence within the university were less palatable than the conventional religious views of the opposing, and far less able, candidate, Monier Williams. Indeed, the election, which drew many of the country clergy to Oxford in December 1860, amply foreshadowed the ensuing battle between contemporary sacred and secular forces in the university, the anachronism of Oxford's systems of academic election and the burning need for reform. It proved to be one of the 'high-water' marks in the Established Church's vain attempt to retain its declining control: Williams was elected with 833 votes to Müller's 610, much to the latter's bitter disappointment. But in time Oxford made amends by creating a brand new chair of comparative philology for him in 1868. Given that all previous chairs in the university had been established by private or royal benefaction, Müller's new appointment, founded solely by the university, was a major *coup* for him. Müller was one of Oxford's most intellectually lively personalities, known both for his scholarship and for his abilities as a fine pianist. Stainer greatly admired him, as a letter, written many years later, to F. G. Edwards attests:

> You ought in the next M.T. to have a nice article on Max Müller. He was a really good musician and when I first knew him (40 years ago) a capital pianist. Did you ever see his Musical Reminiscences (a short pamphlet)? My copy has <u>his autograph</u>, I can't lend it. If you want to read it you must come here – <u>please</u>. Much of it <u>could</u> and <u>should</u> be quoted. It was printed for private circulation only.

You ought also to give a list of the great composers who set his father's beautiful lyrics. Schumann, Mendelssohn, and many others.[145]

Such admiration was also reflected in the dedication of Stainer's first major theoretical work, published by Rivington's in Oxford in 1871, *A Theory of Harmony Founded on the Tempered Scale*, which bears the inscription: 'Dedicated to Max Müller, who, though unable to devote himself to the art of music, owing to the claims made on his time by other fields of labour, forgets not to encourage by his sympathy and kindness those who are pressing forward in its path.' It seems evident from this statement of homage that Müller took a keen interest in Stainer's theoretical research, and, more than likely, encouraged the author to publish his findings. Furthermore it is significant that Stainer chose to place an epigraph from Donkin's *Acoustics* on the title-page (for the second edition), which succinctly encapsulated the *raison d'être* of his work.[146] As to the actual origins of the treatise, Stainer admitted that much of the text had been drawn from practical experience by way of 'notes used by the author in giving lectures to classes of University men'.[147]

The motivation to produce *A Theory of Harmony* appears to have been fuelled by a number of important circumstances. As mentioned above, research into the science of sound had gathered considerable momentum since the seminal works of scholars such as E. F. F. Chladni in the early nineteenth century. There were many scientists working in the area in mid-nineteenth-century Britain, such as Donkin, Bosanquet and William Spottiswoode, but there were important figures on the Continent, above all Helmholtz, who published his highly influential *Die Lehre von dem Tonempfindungen* in 1863 (later to act as the basis of William Pole's *The Philosophy of Music*). As part of this research, the science of the musical scale became the object of physical investigation, and speculation arose as to the foundations of the scale in nature and the natural harmonic series.

Just as the scientific debate was entering a more sophisticated stage of technological enquiry, music was entering a more intensely chromatic phase with the music of Schumann, Spohr, Liszt, Chopin and Wagner, having already drawn inspiration from the practices of Beethoven, Schubert and Weber. Such developments had, in themselves, challenged the manufacturers, particularly of pianos and organs, to adopt the system of equal temperament rather than older and less

---

145 Postcard from Stainer to F. G. Edwards, 4 November 1900 *GB-Lbl* Egerton 3092 fol. 115.

146 'The whole structure of modern music is founded on the possibility of educating the ear not merely to tolerate or ignore, but even in some degree to take pleasure in slight deviations from the perfection of the diatonic scale.'

147 J. Stainer, *A Theory of Harmony Founded on the Tempered Scale* (London, Oxford and Cambridge: Rivingtons, 1871), x.

flexible systems of just temperament. Alfred Hipkins, for example, won over the firm of Broadwoods to equal temperament in the 1840s, and though equal temperament was resisted by English organ builders until after the Great Exhibition of 1851, it was steadily adopted by most firms thereafter – indeed, the organ at Magdalen was one of the first wave of instruments to be tuned to the system in the mid-1850s.

The emergence of more intensely chromatic harmony excited considerable debate. Among the scientific theoreticians, some, such as Thomas Perronet Thompson, in his *Principles of Just Intonation*, emphatically rejected the tendencies of chromatic harmony as being contrary to the 'acoustical laws' of the enharmonic scale.[148] Allied with the notion of these 'acoustical laws' were the production of treatises on harmony which endeavoured to reconcile harmonic theory with the harmonic series. This was evident in Alfred Day's *Treatise on Harmony*, completed in 1842, which remained a text of major influence in Britain throughout the nineteenth century, as is confirmed by Parry's article on Day for the first edition of *Grove's Dictionary of Music and Musicians*. Macfarren resigned temporarily from the Royal Academy after espousing Day's theories for the teaching of harmony, and Day's work (which Macfarren edited for a later edition of 1885) was clearly influential in Macfarren's own *Rudiments of Harmony* (1860) and *Six Lectures on Harmony* (1867). In the wake of Macfarren's work came Ouseley's *Treatise on Harmony* of 1868, which was widely used as a teaching tool. Here Ouseley wanted to try to steer what he perceived as a central course, by presenting a series of practical rules which were nevertheless 'founded in nature' and scientific theory (a fact underlined by the provision of a topographical chart supplied at the end of the book by William Pole comparing 'Natural Harmonics' and the 'True Scale' with 'Equal Temperament'):

> So many treatises on Harmony have appeared since the beginning of this century, that some apology is perhaps due for adding yet one more to the number. The author must plead as his apology, the conviction that although the existing treatises on the subject contain much very valuable matter, yet all seem to him to be either founded on erroneous principles, or faulty in arrangement. Some mix up together the elements of Harmony, Counterpoint, and Pianoforte-practice; others start from principles not based on nature, but too often contradicted by the now better ascertained phenomena

---

[148] The 'enharmonic scale' is one containing intervals of less than a semitone in order to accommodate the ratios of Just Intonation. Simple enharmonic keyboards, not uncommon in the sixteenth and seventeenth centuries, had more than twelve divisions in the octave in order to facilitate modulations to tonalities up to three flats or four sharps (where pitches such as A flat and G sharp were distinct).

of acoustics; others repudiate physical sciences altogether, and treat Music as though it were only an emotional art. The present volume tries to avoid these and other similar errors.[149]

Stainer, who was clearly interested in the development of chromatic harmony and, through application, its stylistic potential, strongly believed that past attempts to reconcile nature and harmonic theory were based on false premises. In the preface to the first edition he quite pugnaciously outlines his objections and argues that those still advocating, in both theory and practice, an enharmonic scale are not in effect being true to reality:

> Modern music owes much of its beauty to the use of "doubtful chords [the term is taken from Thompson];" that is, chords which belong equally to more than one key. Now, if an enharmonic scale were feasible, such chords could not exist, because mathematical correctness of ratio would make every chord strictly in tune in one key, instead of allowing it to be somewhat out of tune in several keys. The whole of our musical literature, from the works of Bach to those of Wagner, would therefore be unavailable for instruments with an enharmonic scale.
>
> It is said voices and instruments of the violin class, not only can, but do make use of an enharmonic scale. This is tantamount to saying that singers and violinists, when reading from a separate part, know whether a note they are sounding is used by the composer according to its apparent notation, or as part of a chord of a different nature, or as both interchangeably; and not only this, but are also aware in each case what the fundamental sound is, from which the ratios of vibrations are calculated, and what is the exact ratio of the note they are sounding, and in defiance of notation are altering the pitch of the sound, or in other words are making two or more notes out of the one before them, so as to adapt it to its various combinations. Such a statement may be taken for what it is worth, although it should be said that many practised musicians who believe themselves endowed with an instinct leading to such marvellous results, will be found on examination to have formed for themselves this so-called instinct from the harmonic laws of the tempered scale.
>
> Musicians, therefore, have evidently this dilemma before them, either they must adopt an enharmonic scale and sacrifice the existing musical literature, or, if they wish to retain the literature, they must give up the theory of an enharmonic scale.[150]

---

[149] F. A. G. Ouseley, *Treatise on Harmony* (Oxford: Clarendon Press, 1868), vii.

[150] Stainer, *A Theory of Harmony Founded on the Tempered Scale*, vii–viii.

Stainer believed wholeheartedly that forming a theory of harmony on both equal temperament and the laws of nature (as Ouseley had attempted) were irreconcilable and 'mutually destructive', and that the only satisfactory system was to establish a theory of harmony based on the tempered scale. 'The tempered scale', he admitted, 'is certainly out of tune, and will not bear to have its proportions exhibited to an audience with better eyes than ears on a white screen',[151] but the reality of composers' ability to enjoy the tempered scale's compromise seemed out of all proportion to the 'imaginary pain' of certain theorists. Only, Stainer argued, when musical mathematicians have concurred on the exact number of divisions necessary in the octave, and instruments have been invented on which the new scale can be played, and, moreover, a system of notation has been invented for performers and composers, 'then it will be time enough to found a Theory of Harmony on a mathematical basis'.[152]

Of paramount importance in Stainer's theory was the interval of the third – 'practically [no intervals] are of so great value in harmony as the third' he postulated on his theory of intervals,[153] and, in so doing, established his own nomenclature, abolishing the terminology of 'perfect' and 'imperfect' intervals where the octave, fifth and fourth were termed 'major' and 'minor' in the same manner as all other intervals. This nomenclature, as he himself later recognised, never caught on, and, in his later primer on *Harmony*, was forced to restore the old classification of intervals. Similarly he preferred the use of the term 'superdominant' for the sixth degree of the scale (advocating the abolition of the term 'submediant') and the 'subtonic' for the leading-note. As for chords themselves, he advocated within his tempered system that the interval of a third was the quintessence of modern harmony:

> Until the interval of a third is allowed to be the basis of all harmony, no theory of music can possibly be formed which will be true to facts. The old veneration for the perfections of the fourth and fifth, hardly yet extinct, helped to degrade thirds by calling them imperfect intervals; yet the greater number of those lovely chords which ravish us so much, and furnish us with an endless source of modulation (such as the chord of the diminished seventh and its inversions), contain neither the interval of a fourth or fifth between any of the component notes. All are thirds, or their inversions, sixths. If any interval ever deserved to be called perfect, it is the third.[154]

And from this assertion, Stainer based his system on the two fundamental chords

[151] Ibid., ix.
[152] Ibid.
[153] Ibid., 12.
[154] Ibid., 15.

of the tonic and dominant and the superimposition of thirds placed above them as far as the thirteenth (in both their major and minor forms), beginning with the chord 'of the fifth' (the full triad) and moving upwards by each third.

Function and resolution of these harmonies is subsequently given fulsome demonstration through the use of musical examples from eighteenth- and nineteenth-century repertoire. Perhaps of greatest interest here is the extent of Stainer's examples drawn not only from the well-known repertoire of Mozart symphonies, Beethoven's piano sonatas, overtures and symphonies, Handel and Mendelssohn oratorios, Spohr's oratorios, Rossini's choral works, Schumann's songs, Chopin's piano music and Gounod's operas (notably *Faust*), but also from works little known in England, namely Bach's Mass in B minor (whose first English performance took place in London in 1876), Schumann's symphonies and *Paradise and the Peri* (which Stanford later premiered at Cambridge) and Brahms' *Alto Rhapsody*.[155]

Following this exposition of fundamentals, Stainer endeavoured to explain the process of related harmonies (derived largely from the tonic and dominant chords already discussed), suspensions, chromatic chords such as the augmented sixth (though out of this arose somewhat verbose and tortuous definitions), Neapolitan harmony, pedal notes (or 'sustained notes' as Stainer termed them), the significance of auxiliary notes within harmonic progressions, and processes of modulation. Stainer's conclusion, which summarises his findings and provides the student with tailor-made exercises for the application of his theory, also usefully contains further postulations that 'the art is perpetually striving to reach beyond the "conventional;" and in consequence of this, that new combinations, at first considered illegitimate, are being from time to time recognised. That there are no fixed laws, and, consequently, no "license" [*sic*] to break them.'[156] Moreover, Stainer leaves us with his own moral imperative that, though melody be more limited in its expansion than harmony, it is to the melody (which 'imparts a much higher pleasure than is obtained from the contemplation of that bare outline called the "tune"') that educated musicians should aspire. Indeed, he further avowed that harmony was to be used as a means of 'beautifying melody, not of superseding it', and, by inference, that a refinement of melody and harmony, as an interdependent art, formed the beginnings of a larger matrix of musical mastery, the study of form.[157]

Stainer's treatise undoubtedly generated substantial interest. Within a year Rivington's were required to print a second edition, and by 1875 Stainer produced

[155] Examples from Wagner's *Tannhäuser*, Brahms's *Schicksalslied* and Verdi's Requiem appeared in the updated third edition.
[156] Ibid., 166.
[157] Ibid., 169.

a third edition, this time published by Novello.[158] However, the attention paid to the book could be measured not only by its positive reception (evident from the 'propaganda' press citations of the advertisements) but also by the controversy it generated. Those wedded to acoustical theories of harmony (such as Thompson), to Day's long-standing treatise (notably Macfarren), or to theories which incorporated elements of just and equal temperament, were critical of the discourse Stainer had ignited, accusing him of dismissing the value of contemporary acoustical research and of earlier treatises on harmony. Some, however, found much in Stainer's treatise worthy of praise. Writing to his friend Robert Bridges, Gerald Manley Hopkins described it as 'a great step forward and has quite a daylight, a *grand jour*, of sense'.[159] Bernard Shaw, by no means an apologist for the university world from which Stainer emanated, was nevertheless extremely supportive of the rational thinking exhibited in Stainer's work and congratulated the author for succumbing 'to an acute sense of commonsense, [by investing] Day's system with that quality in the only modern treatise on harmony I have ever recommended anyone to open.'[160] In particular Shaw admired the broad span of musical evidence, especially those examples taken from Wagner. In 1910 he recalled how, as a young man, it was Stainer's treatise alone that had proclaimed the advances of Wagner's harmonic practices:

> … in my time nobody except Stainer did anything but explain that Wagner's practice was "wrong" and that everything depended on your having correct views as to the true root of the chord of the supertonic, all this nonsense about roots being the result of a wildly absurd attempt to dress up the good old rule-of-thumb thoroughbass with Helmholtz's discovery of overtones, partial ones, combination tones, and the like.[161]

And it was Shaw's perception of Wagner's instinctive understanding of harmonic 'progress' that led him to berate Macfarren's own harmonic theories and his fervent advocacy of Day's treatise:

> Meanwhile Wagner, working by ear, heedless of Day, was immensely

---

[158] When the fifth edition was published in 1876, the title was altered to *A Treatise on Harmony and the Classification of Chords*, and this form of the book was published in a number of further editions.

[159] See M. Allis, 'Bridges, Parry and the *Invocation*', in *Nineteenth-Century British Music Studies*, vol. 2, ed. J. Dibble & B. Zon (Aldershot: Ashgate, 2002), 307.

[160] B. Shaw, 'Specialists in Singing', *The World*, 16 November 1892, in *Shaw's Music*, vol. 2, ed. D. H. Laurance (London: The Bodley Head, 1981), 739.

[161] B. Shaw, 'The Reminiscences of a Quinquagenarian' [6 December 1910], *Proceedings of the Musical Association* 37 (1910–11), 19; also in *Shaw's Music*, vol. 3, ed. D. H. Laurance (London: The Bodley Head, 1981), 626.

enlarging the harmonic stock-in-trade of the profession. Macfarren kept on proving that the Wagnerian procedure was improper, until at last one could not help admiring the resolute conviction with which the veteran professor, old, blind, and hopelessly in the wrong, would still rise to utter his protest whenever there was an opening for it.[162]

Stainer's response to the criticisms launched at his theory was to include in his second edition not only the original preface to the first edition but also a second preface in which he attempted to reinforce his first principles. Though in no way conceding his argument that acoustical laws and practical harmony were ultimately separate issues, he took the trouble to recognise the value of scientific research into sound as a necessary part of any musician's education. Nevertheless, he remained adamant that the narrow views of 'scientific musicians' of contemporary harmony were impractical, inconclusive and essentially irrelevant:

> I maintain that the all-important duty of scientific musicians is to give to the world the natural Scale, and that having been done, and the Scale having become the material (as it were) of a musical literature, then begins the duty of the *writer on Harmony* [Stainer's italics], then must he set about discovering by what processes the notes of the Scale have been manipulated into works of Art. But what answer does the practical musician get who asks scientific men "what is the true Scale?" As a matter of fact there are as many answers as writers on the subject.[163]

Stainer stood by his practical vision of harmony as a phenomenon that could not suffer the enharmonic felicities that some scientists wished to impose upon music, especially the music of his contemporaries.

> In Beethoven, Spohr, Rossini, Schumann, Gounod, Wagner, and numerous other authors, passages occur which, when given to two parts simultaneously, are in one case in a nomenclature of sharps, in the other of flats; of course, it was intended that they should sound as if in *one* key. But scientifically both cannot be right, then which part is to give way? And who, I ask, will undertake to re-edit the modern musical classics with these necessary corrections?[164]

To these questions, Stainer submitted, no satisfactory answer was forthcoming. As for his theory of superimposed thirds, a theory rejected by the critic of the *Musical*

[162] Shaw, 'Specialists in Singing', 739.
[163] J. Stainer, *A Theory of Harmony Founded on the Tempered Scale*, 2nd edn (London, Oxford and Cambridge: Rivingtons, 1872), xi.
[164] Ibid., xii.

Times as a breach of 'scientific truths',[165] he understood the controversial nature of his discoveries, but retorted that if this was not a correct description of the 'sound-ladder' now in current use, he challenged his critics to prove their own theories with recourse to the music of modern masters.

In fact, Stainer's belief in the practical veracity of the Tempered Scale and his own theories was essentially based on a more fundamental theory that the scale itself was entirely empirical. To support this view he quoted William Pole's view that 'the scale so formed is entirely empirical, the notes having no harmonical relation to each other, and consequently all intervals formed thereby being more or less out of "of tune." '[166] Indeed, Stainer went further and declared that the scale itself was entirely arbitrary, a view which in itself caused offence, but, as he was quick to point out, his standpoint was based on an examination of scales from many different cultures, ancient and modern, and the assertion 'nature gives an affinity of sounds between any note and its octave, and poor mortals cannot make use of more than a very limited number of them.'[167] In conclusion to his preface to the second edition of his treatise, Stainer ultimately made it clear that a principal stimulus to write his work had emerged through the false premises of studying acoustics for his degree, and from teaching prospective candidates at Oxford:

> Having passed as a student through the prescribed course of so-called scientific instruction, and finding it to fall utterly short of its promises, and to be incapable of accounting for modern musical progressions, I determined to begin at the other end, and try to draw a system for musical classics. Such being the case I protest against the statement that I have no guiding principles, but that all is assumption. This charge can only be laid against me by those who are ignorant of the immense value which inductive arguments possess.[168]

By the time *A Theory of Harmony* reached its third edition in 1875, Stainer decided to remove the titular reference to the Tempered Scale, explaining in a new preface that he believed his theory was 'perfectly applicable to the system of just intonation, and because 'the attitude of scientific men to modern chromatic music has ceased to be that of hostility, inasmuch as they see that their system will never be adopted as long as it threatens the existence of a single masterpiece in musical literature, while, on the other hand, it will be universally accepted when it renders such works capable of more perfect performance.'[169] Clearly he believed that, at

---

[165] *Musical Times* 13 (January 1872), 341.
[166] Stainer, *A Theory of Harmony Founded on the Tempered Scale*, 2nd edn, xiii.
[167] Ibid.
[168] Ibid., xv.
[169] J. Stainer, *A Theory of Harmony*, 3rd edn (London: Novello & Co., 1875), vii.

last, he had triumphed over the pedants, though his treatise did not enjoy the longevity or recognition for which he had hoped, and, in spite of its 'commonsense' approach, musical institutions preferred to adhere to the well entrenched theories of Day and the primers of Macfarren and Prout.

It is an interesting and significant paradox that, while Stainer thrived on the liberal atmosphere of Oxford's intellectuals, especially Donkin, Acland and Müller, and the reformist zeal which produced *A Theory of Harmony*, his propinquity to church music also meant that he retained major conservative sympathies with the Tractarians who had, after all, been the main force of opposition to reform in Oxford, particularly to the abolition of religious tests and the transformation of convocation away from the domination of clergymen.

Much of the opposition had been led by Henry Parry Liddon, a protégé of Pusey and Keble, whom, as Vice-Principal at St Edmund's Hall and as a prominent preacher at the University Church, Stainer knew well, both in the capacity of don and tutor. Liddon's presence at Oxford was considerable. A former vice-principal of the Anglican theological college at Cuddesdon, he was renowned for his New Testament lectures in Christ Church hall, his Bampton Lectures (a series founded for the exposition and defence of the Christian faith) in 1866 on 'The Divinity of Our Lord and Saviour Jesus Christ' (a highly popular publication which ran to fifteen editions), his extensive Lenten lectures at St James's, Piccadilly, in 1870, which thrilled London's middle classes (later published as *Some Elements of Religion* in 1872), his abilities as a theologian and scholar, and for his magnetic style as a preacher in the University Church and Christ Church Cathedral in the late 1860s. Liddon's reputation at Oxford was undoubtedly influential in his appointment in April 1870 by Gladstone (who was then Prime Minister) to a canonry at St Paul's Cathedral, a position to which was added the Ireland Professorship of Scripture at Oxford. Liddon's time thereafter would be spent partly in London and partly in Oxford until he resigned the professorship in 1882. At Oxford he had unquestionably exerted his influence as a Tractarian on the religious devotion of Stainer, but on arriving at St Paul's he would prove to have an even more critical impact both on Stainer's career and, indirectly, on the future prosperity of the English cathedral tradition and its support of music as both a liturgical and spiritual agency.

IV ❧ 1872–1882

Reform and National Renown:
St Paul's Cathedral (2)

Tнеrе is no surviving evidence to suggest that Stainer aspired to leave Oxford. By 1871 Bulley had seen to it that he was on a salary of £200. This sum, however, was not considerable, and with a wife and five children to provide for (and another expected – Elizabeth Stainer was pregnant with a sixth child in January 1872), it seems likely that Stainer was looking for a higher-paying job. Nevertheless, Oxford was an amicable, comfortable and intellectually stimulating environment which he did not consider giving up unless a new and more rewarding opportunity presented itself.

In 1871 Stainer was invited to join the Rev. John Bacchus Dykes, W. H. Monk, Sir Henry Baker and the Rev. G. W. Huntingford on the committee of the revised *Hymns Ancient & Modern*. During August of that year Stainer went up to Monkland near Leominster to spend time with his colleagues, painstakingly going through the tunes of the hymnal to see what should be jettisoned and what should be retained.[1] 'No greater privilege have I ever had', Stainer later recalled, of participating on that committee, and with the encouragement and enthusiasm of Dykes and Monk for the hymn genre he declared: 'I plunged deeply into the fascinating study of hymnody, and have lost no opportunity of employing myself as a humble labourer in a sphere congenial and dear to me from the time of my childhood.'[2] The matter of hymn tunes and hymn texts instigated some correspondence between Stainer and Liddon in September 1871 as is evidenced by the following letter from Stainer:

> I have had a talk with Dr. Bright about the Hymns. Our difficulty, I find, will be to get good translations of the words, the music of which we wish to use. The list I took to him was pared down to three! – but this need not be the limit of the number used by us, if only you will be so kind as to see him (on your return to Oxford) and see what sets of <u>words</u> are available – I will then use the Tunes set to them from your book.[3]

---

[1] See *Life and Letters of John Bacchus Dykes*, ed. J. T. Fowler (London: John Murray, 1897), 150.

[2] J. Stainer, *Hymn Tunes* (London: Novello & Co., 1900), iii.

[3] Letter from Stainer to Henry Parry Liddon, 15 September [1871], *GB-Okc*.

The same letter also divulged the fact that a letter from Liddon had also raised the matter of music at St Paul's and that major reform was anticipated. Stainer, a recent visitor to St Paul's to see how the fabric of the building was advancing, had managed to obtain an interview with the Succentor, the Rev. W. C. Fynes Webber, a Minor Canon since 1850 and Succentor since 1856, who remembered Stainer from his days as a chorister at the cathedral. 'I was in London the other day', Stainer related to Liddon (his manner still suggesting that of pupil to teacher), 'and at a time of day when I did not expect to meet anyone, I went to see how St Pauls was progressing; however, I came across Mr Webber and had a chat with him in the Vestry, on the subject to which you alluded in your letter.'[4] The conversation with Webber clearly concerned the possibility that the post of organist at St Paul's could quite soon be vacant – Goss had evidently indicated that he might resign – and that the vacancy would be connected with major reforms driven by the regime of the newly appointed team to the St Paul's Chapter, Robert Gregory, Richard William Church (the new Dean) and, of course, Liddon. More significantly, Stainer's letter to Liddon intimates that, though nothing official had yet taken its course (since Goss had not yet tendered his resignation), the prospect of his employment at St Paul's had been privately discussed. Moreover, Stainer made it clear that he was ready and willing to consider the post:

> Of course year by year my ties to Oxford become stronger, owing to the kindness I receive on every side – indeed if I were to consult my personal comfort, I should not for one moment contemplate leaving the place – but I am ready to go wherever a sense of duty tells me I ought to go. So when the time comes, if it ever should come, when I am asked to cut asunder all that links me to this place – you will find me ready to go and prepared to do my best. The future organist of your cathedral will have very up-hill work before him – and very little chance of success unless he is backed up well by a one-minded and compact Chapter. I feel I could be of use. I should hope in time to entirely alter your wretched <u>style</u> of music. Some little time since my wife came with me to afternoon service at St Pauls, and after our zealous and hearty services in Oxford – she was <u>horrified</u> at the coldness and carelessness shewn in the metropolitan cathedral. Of course this letter is strictly

---

4 Ibid. It is also perhaps significant that Stainer's reconnection with St Paul's had taken place in late 1870 when he was requested to join the Musical Subcommittee of the Executive Committee of the 'St Paul's Completion Fund' (which included Fynes Webber, Sparrow Simpson, Goss, Cooper, Turle, Ouseley, Elvey, Sterndale Bennett, Hopkins and Willis), a body 'formed to report on the best mode of arranging the Musical Services of the Cathedral, in connection with its decorations.' (See *GB-Lsp* Dugdale 907.) Stainer attended at least one meeting of this body on 16 December 1870.

private. Your kindness to me for many years has been so uniform that I write to you as to a friend.[5]

Stainer had quite clearly discussed the matter with Bridge at Manchester, for the latter had evidently expressed an interest in applying for the Magdalen post if and when it was subsequently vacated. Stainer's advice was negative:

Although Magd: ought to consider you a real 'catch' – if you give up your present position for my old shoes – I should consider you nothing short of a donkey. Nothing like plain speech! You would have half the income! a worse choir! and twice the responsibility – coupled with a most expensive place to live in. This is private. … If you can make cock-sure of your MA – the case is slightly different – but only slightly.[6]

By the end of November 1871 Goss's resignation, anticipated by the Dean and Chapter at St Paul's, was finally tendered:

After upwards of 33 years service at the cathedral it has come to my knowledge that the Dean and Chapter consider it expedient for the interests of the church that the duties of Organist should be undertaken and discharged by one individual in future; and that, in view of proposed changes involving a large increase of services, the whole time of the Organist should be placed at their disposal.

At my advanced age (I shall shortly enter upon my 72nd year), and with my many other engagements, which I could not, if I would, terminate abruptly, I feel that I cannot offer to do much more than I am enabled to do at present, but that I ought not to suffer any selfish feeling to interfere with the duty I owe to the church which I have so long served to the best of my power, and to which I hope, with the help of God, to devote my remaining energies.

Under these circumstances I should wish to take any course that may commend itself to the wishes of the Dean and Chapter, provided they will allow me to retain during the remainder of my days the title of Organist, and the small Income (some £250 per annum) which I have hitherto received from the Cathedral. It would be most mortifying both to myself and to my family and friends for me to have to relinquish the former; it would be unprecedented under the circumstances, and would be sure to call forth remarks which would tend to lower me in the estimation of the public, on whose good opinion I shall still be dependent in a great degree.

---

[5] Ibid.

[6] Letter from Stainer to J. F. Bridge, 3 October 1871, in private possession (JRS).

With regard to the question of pension, I will only state that I have been a working man all my life, that I have brought up a large and expensive family, and that I have been unable to make anything like an adequate provision for my old age.

With these few remarks I feel that I may leave myself in the hands of the Dean and Chapter in the full conviction that they will neither allow one who has so long done faithful service in their Cathedral to suffer pecuniary loss, nor recommend him or require him to take any step which will be derogatory to the high position he has always held, or detract from his fair fame.[7]

Goss's resignation was accepted along with the conditions that he was able to retain the title of 'Organist of St Paul's' (so long as he agreed not to interfere with the organ or choir of the cathedral), his income of £250, and, until his death, his privileges as a Vicar Choral without the responsibility of providing for any of its duties. Having agreed terms with the outgoing organist, Chapter, with its mind firmly fixed on its favoured new appointment, raised the salary of the organist to £400 on the condition that he 'undertake the whole musical instruction and superintendence of the cathedral choir; that he is available whenever his services are needed at the cathedral, and that he accepts no other appointment.'[8]

With the public announcement of Goss's resignation in December, George Cooper, Goss's assistant for twenty-eight years, wrote to Chapter:

In a letter received yesterday from Mr Goss he tells me it is his intention to resign his position as Organist of your Cathedral. At his suggestion I write at once to offer myself as his successor.

I beg most respectfully to inform you that I was appointed Deputy Organist in the year 1838 when Mr Goss became Organist of the Cathedral. I had however been in the habit of taking the service previous to this date during the lifetime of Mr Attwood when I was about 12 years of age. I therefore may fairly claim to have devoted the greater portion of my life to the service of the Cathedral without at the same time being at all adequately remunerated for the same.

I am quite aware that should I obtain the honour I am seeking at your hands I should have to resign two most important appointments that I hold namely that of Organist and Choir master of Her Majesty's Chapel Royal, St James's, as well as that of Organist of St Sepulchre's Church, where the appointment has been in my family for more than a century.

---

[7] Letter from Goss to Dean Church, 30 November 1871, St Paul's Chapter Minutes, *GB-Lsp.*

[8] Chapter Minutes, 30 November 1871, *GB-Lsp.*

> I beg respectfully to be informed of the duties that would devolve on the new Organist and also what stipend he would receive.[9]

Whether Chapter discussed the matter of duties with Cooper is unknown; he was still only fifty-one, a thoroughly able and experienced organist (notably more competent than Goss), and no doubt promised future valuable years of service. He also had the support of some of the Vicars Choral and Goss himself, and there was no doubt some degree of expectation that the sub-organist would succeed the organist, just as Goss had succeeded Attwood in 1838. But the determination of the Dean, Gregory and Liddon (who appears to have been the principal conduit between the St Paul's Chapter and Stainer) was unwavering.[10] They wanted a new, young man of like mind who would help to implement their new vision. Immediately following Cooper's letter, the Chapter Minutes, devoid of any further deliberation such as the question of advertising the post, shortlisting or even interviewing candidates, categorically announced the decision: 'Resolved that Dr John Stainer be elected Organist of St Paul's Cathedral at a salary of £400 a year commencing at Lady Day next.'[11] The offer was speedily communicated to Stainer, who, on 23 December, wrote to Liddon that he would attend a meeting of Chapter to discuss details before making up his mind:

> I shall hope to present myself at the Chapter meeting on Thursday. I should like to hear certain details as to the future management of the Choir and other matters. When all has been fully talked over I shall be able to give a reply to the offer of the Dean and Chapter which is so kindly worded.[12]

Stainer and the St Paul's Chapter convened on 28 December 1871, after which he accepted the post along with the authorisation, if Stainer agreed, to appoint George Cooper as his assistant. Moreover, as is evident from his future activities and employment, he was able to forge an agreement with Chapter to undertake work outside the cathedral so long as it did not conflict with the new more extensive duties they outlined. More importantly, Stainer's commitment to his new post was galvanised by the assurances of staunch moral and financial support by Chapter in order to carry through major reforms and expansion. This was quite clearly a crucial factor, as he divulged to his friend, J. S. Egerton:

---

[9] Letter from George Cooper to the Dean and Chapter of St Paul's, 22 December 1871, Chapter Minutes, *GB-Lsp*.

[10] Liddon's role as the prime-mover in brining Stainer to St Paul's from Oxford was confirmed years later by Henry Scott Holland; see H. S. Holland, *A Bundle of Memories* (London: Wells Gardner, Darton & Co., 1915), 83.

[11] Chapter Minutes, 22 December 1871 *GB-Lsp*.

[12] Letter from Stainer to Liddon, 23 December 1871, *GB-Okc*.

Many thanks for your very kind letter – I ought to have answered it before – but I have had so very much to do. I trust to be able by steady and quiet work to make the services at St Paul's something like what they should be. The Dean and Chapter (best in England) are prepared to back me up to any extent. The responsibility of the post will not be shirked by me, I assure you. In a few years if I am spared I hope with God's help to let you hear a really fine performance there.

Funds are being squeezed out of the Eccles: Commissioners for a very large Choir – probably 3 times as numerous as now. Only <u>time</u> is required for such vast changes.

The organ will be <u>very</u> fine – and although not encumbered with spare room in the organ-loft I shall hope to see you up with me someday.[13]

The news of his appointment reached the press early in the new year, at which time Stainer promptly tendered his resignation to Magdalen College; it was received with some solemnity, as Bulley recorded in his diary: 'That the College wish to express to Dr Stainer their regret at losing him, and their sense of the great zeal and ability which he has shown both as Organist and Master of the Choir during his twelve years tenure of office.'[14] As a tribute to Stainer's work at the college, the British artist, Briton Riviere, made a gift of Stainer's portrait, which was presented to Magdalen in July.[15] As a further indication of their high regard for him, the Magdalen dons and undergraduates presented him with a magnificent suite of Sèvres ornaments (which later adorned his drawing-room mantelpiece in Amen Court at St Paul's). The Exeter College Musical Society presented him with a conductor's ivory baton (which also still survives) for which Stainer expressed his sincere gratitude:

Be so kind as to give my best thanks to the members of the E.C.M.S. for the very handsome present they have sent me. I cannot tell you how pleased I am with it. I certainly do not deserve to have any such present bestowed on me – as it was (I assure you) always a <u>pleasure</u> to me to direct such a cheerful and hardworking set of men as your College sent up. I shall value the baton greatly – and it will constantly remind me of those whom I have left in Oxford – for whom I have feelings of genuine regard and gratitude.[16]

[13] Letter from Stainer to J. S. Egerton, 12 March [1872], in private possession (JRS).

[14] Diary of Frederic Bulley, 12 March 1872, GB-Omc.

[15] Riviere's portrait is mentioned in W. D. Macray, *Register of the Members of St Mary Magdalen College, Oxford*, vol. 7: *Fellows, 1882–1910* (London, 1911), but this is not in the present list of pictures and portraits at Magdalen.

[16] Letter from Stainer to the President of the ECMS, 28 April [1872], Minutes of the ECMS, GB-Oec.

Others, such as Dykes, with whom Stainer was actively working as a colleague (until Dykes's unexpected death in 1873), knew that Oxford would miss Stainer's dynamism in all areas of musical and religious life: 'as a Churchman and a musician he is the very man for the post … [and] he will be very much missed in Oxford.'[17] A good deal of the ecclesiastical press were delighted to see Stainer accede to Goss's job, and glad to see that he took a moderate line on the matter of Gregorian chant:

> A profound musician, a facile composer, and a very fine executant, he is, in a word, one of the most accomplished representative men of the present generation of organists. In addition to his professional qualifications he is an M.A. of Oxford, a member of Congregation, and a man of some literary culture. … As regards chanting, and the selection of music generally for the Church service, Dr. Stainer is, we believe, of the mind of Dr. Dykes, preferring the *via media*.[18]

Parry, who had left Oxford in 1870, and was now living the life – albeit temporarily – of an underwriter at Lloyds, was quick both to congratulate and reassure his friend that, in quitting Oxford, the capital would bring new and more challenging opportunities as well as more immediate interaction with the musical profession:

> My dear old Professor,
>
> I really can't express to you how delighted I was at seeing by accident in the papers your translation to the see of St Pauls. Of course one must feel sorry for poor Oxford, but from every other point of view one must congratulate oneself and the country as well as you.
>
> Oneself because one will be sure to see you oftener at the Crystal Palace and such like places of musicians resort, and for the world because London is much more the right sphere of action for people like you, and you will have much larger opportunities of doing good. For yourself I am sure it is quite the best thing possible; I don't know whether it will be quite as agreeable a life as Oxford – but that is not of much account when a man has special work in the world to do.
>
> I feel almost inclined to fancy you and Barrett cooperating in the work of regeneration in which direction his pen and influence are always straight.
>
> I hope we shall see you before long, and hear you too. If you ever have time do write me a line, though ever short to say how you like the prospect, how you are etc etc for I haven't heard of you for such a very long time.

[17] *Life and Letters of John Bacchus Dykes*, 157.
[18] *Church Bells*, 13 January 1872, 4.

Remember me to the Mrs please. I think you will be rather sad leaving the associations of Magdalen organ and Oxford life. Never mind; we must always look forwards, not backwards.[19]

Severance with Oxford was inevitably sad, but in his wake Stainer not only left his mark as the principal regenerator of musical life in the university, a fact confirmed by Hugh Allen, one of his professorial successors, but also in persuading Walter Parratt, only eight months his junior, to quit his post at Wigan Parish Church (which was probably better paid) for the soon-to-be-vacant position at Magdalen on the grounds that the post would bring him greater status. In spite of Stainer's support, however, Parratt fretted that he was not qualified:

[Parratt] arrived [at Magdalen for his interview and trial] very unwell, nervous and depressed. He announced that he was going back by the next train, saying that for him, a poor provincial organist, without degrees and reputation, to aim at such a post at the University was an act of folly and presumption. Luckily his scruples were overcome enough for him to stay the night, and with the help of a chemist, who prescribed for stage fright and internal disturbance, he got to bed, and in the morning was well enough to face the President, Dr. Bulley. The first interview and trial were decisive – nobody else would do – and he was appointed.[20]

Yet there was by no means a public consensus supporting Stainer's appointment at St Paul's. The fact that Cooper, whose abilities as an organist had always been viewed more positively than those of Goss, had been passed over in favour of a much younger man rankled with some, while others thought it a continuing scandal that Stainer had been appointed without competition. Opposition went on for several years; a gentleman signing himself 'Old School' contributed a series of letters hostile to Stainer in the *Musical Standard* in which he accused him of being an organist but not a true church musician, as well as dredging up the old allegations of Tractarian bias in his appointment by the Dean and Chapter.[21]

Stainer did duty as organist for the last time in Magdalen Chapel on Palm Sunday, 24 March 1872,[22] and, having procured temporary accommodation in

[19] Letter from Parry to Stainer, 5 January 1872, in private possession (MN).

[20] D. Tovey & G. Parratt, *Walter Parratt: Master of the Music* (London: Oxford University Press, 1941), 46. Stainer was succeeded at the University Church by James Taylor, organist of New College who held the position until his death in August 1900.

[21] See *Musical Standard*, 30 September (220), 28 October (284), 18 and 25 November (333 and 347), and 23 December (411–12).

[22] Diary of Frederic Bulley, 24 March 1872, *GB-Omc*. Stainer was succeeded at Tenbury by Langdon Colborne, another pupil of George Cooper.

London, the very next day assumed his new position at St Paul's. He was to embark on a task of musical reform not witnessed at St Paul's since the Restoration, yet he was also to find himself part of a much larger wave of change sweeping the cathedral, one that had been gathering pace since the early 1860s.

Milman, who had been Dean while Stainer was a chorister at St Paul's, had been the instrument of some major changes in the cathedral, changes that would prove to be of significant benefit to Stainer on his arrival. He had been moderately successful, unlike Hale before him, in securing funds from the Ecclesiastical Commissioners for the doubling of choirmen on Sundays. More significantly, however, it was Milman who oversaw the introduction of evening services under the dome (a space already enhanced by the restoration of Thornhill's paintings) which commenced on 28 November (Advent Sunday) 1858. So attracted was the public to the event that, in spite of 2,500 chairs packed in for the occasion, there was insufficient room; 'Ludgate Hill was blocked; and a sensational number of persons, variously reckoned at anything from 10,000 to 100,000, failed to win an entrance.'[23] In consequence the services were continued until Easter, and, henceforth every year a fresh series of Sunday evening services was instituted from January until Easter. For these services a large voluntary choir, ready to sing chants, hymns and anthems, was recruited to lead the singing and sat in the transept on a semicircular platform, directed by a Vicar Choral.

With the huge appeal of the Sunday evening services, Chapter was inevitably forced to incur the expense of purchasing additional chairs for the burgeoning congregation, and since the augmentation of congregational singing now dwarfed the power of an organ accustomed to accompanying a small body of singers, it was decided that the instrument should be enlarged, and, with Goss's blessing, the work was entrusted to William Hill, who took down the organ in September 1859. Although £1,000 was originally envisaged, Hill later submitted a much more ambitious plan for a four-manual instrument with sixty-four stops at a cost of £2,200.[24] This plan was not adopted, but in the mean time more radical ideas had been looming, where the entire organ and screen would be removed and the organ resited in the choir. The decision was undoubtedly a controversial one, and Chapter reserved its final decision until 18 January 1860, after recommendations from the 'General Committee for the direction of the Church' were made. In March 1860 F. C. Penrose, the cathedral's Surveyor of the Fabric, submitted his report, in which he reiterated the points of the Committee's resolutions to remove both organ and screen.

---

[23] G. L. Prestige, *St Paul's in its Glory* (London: SPCK, 1955), 80–1.

[24] N. Plumley & A. Niland, *A History of the Organs in St Paul's Cathedral* (Oxford: Positif Press, 2001), 65.

In his report Penrose noted that, with the organ's absence, there had been so much appreciation of the new vistas opened up in the building that there was a disinclination to put the organ back in its original position. He also claimed (from early plans preserved at Oriel College, Oxford) that there was indisputable evidence of Wren's intention to place the organ under one of the arches on the north side, though proper evidence for this is strenuously denied by Plumley and Niland, who suggest that Penrose may 'have been guilty of assembling information to suit his own and his employers' agenda';[25] more to the point, however, appears to have been the leaning of the Dean and Chapter to join a trend already prevalent in other cathedrals and substantial parish churches for liberating long vistas which had begun at Hereford in 1842, and followed by Durham, Ely, Wimborne and, contemporary with St Paul's in 1860, Chichester, Bristol, St Patrick's, Dublin, and Ludlow. Lichfield, Worcester, Bath, Tewksbury, Salisbury and Peterborough followed suit between 1861 and 1883.[26] The resiting of the organ under the second archway of the choir on the north side largely circumscribed its use for the area of the choir rather than for effective use in the dome, a fact confirmed by W. A. Frost, who sang as a chorister in the 1860 Festival of the Sons of the Clergy: 'It [the organ] was too far away to accompany a Choir under the dome, and so the music was entirely unaccompanied.'[27]

Realising rather late in the day the musical consequences of their actions, the Dean and Chapter purchased a four-manual organ built by William Hill of sizeable proportions from the Panopticon of Science and Art in Leicester Square which was placed on a gallery (ironically the old screen used to support the old Smith-Wren organ) in the south transept. An official opening of this organ was marked by a performance of *Messiah* in the cathedral at the patronal festival on 25 January 1861.

When Stainer arrived at St Paul's the Panopticon organ in the south transept was still in place, though interest in its improvement had been overtaken by a new scheme, apparently initiated in 1870 by a minor canon, William Sparrow Simpson (and not Henry Willis as has been supposed),[28] to move the original organ to the

---

[25] Ibid., 70. It also seems that, from surviving evidence, by no means all the Chapter – notably among them the Succentor Fynes Webber and the Rev. Dr William Sparrow Simpson, a minor canon at the time – were in favour of this change. (See Plumley & Niland, *A History of the Organs in St Paul's Cathedral*, 82, 98.)

[26] Ibid., 71.

[27] W. A. Frost, *Early Recollections of St Paul's Cathedral* (London: Simpkin, Marshall, Hamilton, Kent & Co., 1925), 10.

[28] Plumley & Niland, *A History of the Organs in St Paul's Cathedral*, 98. However, Sparrow Simpson, like many others, generally preferred the organ to be restored to the screen.

west end of the choir and to divide it into two. Willis, who had been entrusted with work on the St Paul's organ in 1863 after some dissatisfaction with Hill's work,[29] was viewed with considerable favour at St Paul's, and took up this new scheme with alacrity. The result of his endeavour, which was ultimately a major entrepreneurial risk, proved hugely successful, and no one admired his work more than Stainer. The organ, however, was by no means complete when Stainer set foot in the cathedral on 25 March 1872. Indeed, from 5 February to 23 March the building had been closed to the public, though it had been opened the once for the huge Thanksgiving Service for the Recovery of the Prince of Wales on 27 February 1872. For this the manuals of the Willis organ – the pedals were not ready – were probably used though the Panopticon instrument was played by Cooper. Which organ Goss played is uncertain, but what is clear is that this auspicious occasion (for which he wrote his grand Te Deum) effectively marked his departure from the cathedral.

Milman died in 1868 and in his place Henry Longueville Mansel, a theologian philosopher from Oxford, was appointed Dean. Mansel remained in his office for only three years; he died in 1871, but during that time he oversaw the institution of Saturday chapter meetings and the observance of the Patronal festival on 25 January. Mansel's death formed part of a major turnover of clerical personnel at St Paul's. In November 1868 Robert Gregory, vicar of St Mary-the-less, Lambeth, replaced Weldon Champneys, who had been appointed Dean of Litchfield; Liddon, who arrived in April 1870, replaced Thomas Dale, who was the new Dean of Rochester; the scholarly Joseph Barber Lightfoot filled the place vacated by the death of Henry Melville in March 1871; and Richard William Church, formerly of Oriel College and vicar of Whatley near Frome in Somerset, was installed as Dean on 17 October 1871 after Mansel's death in August.

Lightfoot's interests as a scholar meant that his attentions to reform at St Paul's were minor, but the triumvirate of Gregory, Liddon and Church – all of them dyed-in-the-wool Tractarians – were to provide a matrix of complementary talents. Gregory, a High Church Tory (and appointed by Disraeli), whose arrival at St Paul's by no means drew the approbation of his colleagues, was no great thinker or scholar, but his organisational abilities, his talent for finance, and his desire for discipline, brought a new razor-sharp edge to the conduct and deportment of the cathedral, especially in its worldly business. Liddon's prowess was as a preacher, and after his first sermon in the cathedral, which attracted large crowds, it was necessary in future for him to preach from a pulpit under the dome. From here he habitually gave his homilies for the next twenty years, which, though long and largely orthodox in theology, were deeply engaging for the quality of his voice and

---

[29] Ibid., 77.

delivery. Public approbation of his sermons can be measured also by the popularity of the collections *Easter at St Paul's*, *Advent at St Paul's* and *Christmastide at St Paul's*, published in 1885, 1888 and 1889 respectively.

Church's appointment, like that of Liddon, was by Gladstone, who, as an admirer of Church's abilities as a scholar, had tried on more than one occasion to confer preferment upon him. It was Church's germane desire to make St Paul's both a metropolitan and national focus that Gladstone wholeheartedly applauded. He knew, however, that change was to be hard won, as he admitted to his friend Thomas Mozley in August 1871:

> It is clear that what I am to come in for is very tough practical business, and that I am not to be as other Deans have been. It is to set St Paul's in order, as the great English Cathedral, before the eyes of the country. I mean that this is what Gladstone has in view, and what Liddon, Gregory, and partially Lightfoot expect of their Dean. I have three things before me: (1) To make a bargain with the Ecclesiastical Commission about the whole future revenues of St Paul's, and get from them what will be necessary for the works and wants, material and others, of the <u>reformed</u> Cathedral. (2) To carry on the architectural restoration, for which a quarter of a million is the sum demanded. (3) To fight and reduce to order a refractory and difficult staff of singing men etc., strong in their charters and inherited abuses. I don't mean that all this is to be done single-handed, but the responsibility will fall on the Dean'[30]

Although Church played his part, it was Gregory who decided to take on the Vicars Choral. His resolve was fired initially by a more than casual installation 'on a specially dark evening of the shortest day of the year, after the four o'clock service' in the oppressive blackness of the empty cathedral.[31] With only his wife and children permitted to remain, he was led by a verger and Archdeacon Hale to the high altar: 'we walked to the high altar at the extreme east end of the Cathedral, and then the usual service was read by the Archdeacon, and I was placed in a chair instead of a stall, and we returned to the vestry. A more miserable and disgracefully slovenly service I never saw.'[32] Gregory was warned by his fellow canons that his predecessors had entertained similar feelings of indignation and reform, but that St Paul's was 'an Augean Stable that nobody on earth can sweep, therefore let

[30] M. C. Church (ed.), *Life and Letters of Dean Church* (London: Macmillan & Co., 1895), 200.

[31] R. Gregory, *Robert Gregory, 1819–1911: being the autobiography of Robert Gregory DD Dean of St Paul's*, ed. W. H. Hutton (London: Longmans, Green & Co., 1912), 157.

[32] Ibid.

things take their course, and do not trouble about them.'[33] But Gregory was not be put off. On All Saints Day in 1869 he was infuriated by the poor attendance of choirmen and publicly chastised them in the south aisle where they tradition-ally vested. It was a scene that reached the national newspapers. Scandalised by the publicity, Chapter accepted Hale's proposal to revive the 'discipline Chapter' which used to sit every Saturday; it was a first brave step in attempting to bring the ncorrigible Vicars into line.

In the intervening years between Stainer's departure as a chorister at St Paul's and his arrival in March 1872, the conduct of the choir and its standard of singing had improved little. The six supernumeraries, appointed in 1852, had dwindled to four. In 1870 a fifth was added and salaries were increased, though there was the additional duty of singing on weekdays as well as Sundays. The regulations to which the supernumeraries were compelled to adhere were detailed,[34] but the Vicars Choral, zealously aware of their independence, were far from willing to sub-ject themselves to new duties or constraints. It had also been a well-established tra-dition, for reasons of tenure and salary, that the Organist occupied one of the six positions of Vicars Choral, his place being taken by a 'permanent' deputy paid for by Chapter. As mentioned above, Goss agitated for the continuance of his status as a Vicar Choral after his retirement, and Stainer, fully cognisant of the benefits it would bring, took full advantage of the custom.[35] In terms of their behaviour and attendance, the Vicars Choral were still unpredictable, insubordinate and, frankly, contemptuous of Chapter. Several voices had outlived their usefulness and the boys were weak, as was noted in an article for the *Musical Standard* of 14 January 1871:

> The choir consisted of ten men's voices and thirteen boys' and babies' voices. Of the five men sitting on the north side, No. 1 was a bass voice, rather thin, but good; 2 bass, very good; 3, tenor, may have been good, but worth noth-ing now, except in a chorus; 4, tenor, very good; 5, alto, weak, but fair tone. Boys and babies, north side; with the exception of No. 1 and the soloist in the anthem, not worth a nap. South side, five men; No. 1, bass, passable; 2, tenor,

---

[33] Ibid., 158.

[34] See Chapter Minutes, 4 May 1871, *GB-Lsp*.

[35] Prestige, *St Paul's in its Glory*, 151–3. This was agreed after Stainer's meeting with Chapter on 28 December 1871. After the death of a Vicar Choral created a vacancy in January 1873, Stainer acceded to the freehold, though he was much criticised for it by the *Musical Standard* (22 February 1873, 115), and Walker, who trained the boys claimed that it had been promised to him during the time of Archdeacon Hale (see Frost, *Early Recollections of St Paul's Cathedral*, 39–40). Unlike Goss, who retained his position after retirement, Stainer agreed to resign his when he left St Paul's in 1888.

good; 3, supposed to be a tenor, but might be anything you liked except a chorister, but if he is one more shame to those in authority; 4, young alto voice of good quality; 5, alto, has been very good, but fading now. Boys and babies, south side; except No. 2 and one of the babies – as before; in fact the trebles, with the exceptions mentioned would hardly be considered good enough for the meanest church in London, or indeed anywhere else; and truly the man who is supposed to form a choir out of such material is to be pitied.[36]

Besides the poor singing, which attracted the invective of 'wretched', 'tedious' and even 'disgraceful',[37] a further scathing criticism was the repetition of anthems. Blame was levelled at Fred Walker, a Vicar Choral, who trained the choristers: 'I fear one main cause of the small stock of services and anthems is the laziness of the master of the boys. It is far easier for him to take them frequently over a small list, which they must know almost by heart, than to go to the trouble of teaching them new things.'[38] Moreover, *The Choir* did not underestimate the size of Stainer's task: 'The choir, as they showed last Sunday afternoon, cannot even sing the Amens with ordinary care and decency, and thus the task lying before the Doctor is no ordinary one.'[39] But responsibility also lay with Fynes Webber, the Succentor who chose the music. His limited, indeed unenterprising taste, was soon the subject of disparagement in a further article for the *Musical Standard* by 'One who Knows', who attempted not only to restore Walker's reputation but also to suggest that the repertoire required urgent scrutiny.[40]

The resurrection of the Saturday Chapter meetings paints a vivid picture of the *laissez-faire* attitude of the old regime and the choir's (often alarming) indiscipline. In January 1871 the Succentor was asked to publicise in the cathedral every week a list of anthems, and 'was further requested to set anthems which might be as far as possible in harmony with the teaching of the seasons of the church, as ordered in the Prayer Book'.[41] The Succentor's efforts left much to be desired in terms of presentation, but even with this new *modus operandi* subversion often took place when poor attendance meant that anthems had to be changed during the service itself:

---

[36] *Musical Standard*, 14 January 1871, 16–17.

[37] Ibid.

[38] *Musical Standard*, 11 February 1871, 75.

[39] *The Choir*, 6 January 1872, 3.

[40] See *Musical Standard*, 25 February 1871, 87–8.

[41] Weekly Chapter Minutes, 7 January 1871 GB-Lsp. The Succentor also sent the lists of the music sung on Sundays to the *Musical Times* and *The Choir*, though it was not until 1873, after it was proposed by Stainer, that a full weekly list was printed.

Mr Goss attended to explain a stoppage in the service yesterday. It was resolved that 'every deputy singing in the choir shall be requested to notify to the verger in attendance for what member of the choir he is acting as deputy. It was also resolved that in case it be found absolutely necessary, from the sudden indisposition of any single, or other urgent cause, to change the service or anthem appointed for the day, sufficient notice must be given of the proposed change, not only to the Minor Canon in waiting, but also to the Dean or to the Canon in Residence, before the commencement of the service and the cause of the change explained. ... But it cannot be allowed that any change should be made during the service, or during the passage from the vestries to the Choir.[42]

Similarly the Succentor himself bewailed the woeful and inexplicable inattendance of crucial voices, or of confusion between the organist and choir:

The Succentor complained that there was no counter-tenor on Tuesday or Wednesday morning, and that the anthem had to be changed in the service on Thursday evening through the Organist being without a copy, while on Tuesday he played the wrong anthem. The Succentor also complained of the playing of the organ on Wednesday evening.[43]

This lamentable state of affairs remained unchanged throughout 1871 and showed no signs of abating upon Stainer's arrival. Indeed, the position of the Vicars Choral epitomised an apathy engendered by decades of neglect and general indifference. Thomas Francis seemed to cultivate an obstinate recalcitrance which frequently brought him before the admonishing Weekly Chapter, and he seemed to relish the prospect of combat whenever change to his circumstances beckoned; William Winn (who conducted the Special Evening Choir and the annual service for the Sons of the Clergy) was an able bass, but others were failing, including Charles Lockey, who was represented by a permanent deputy.

The advent of Stainer's presence at St Paul's in March 1872 has, as Storey has made amply clear, brought with it numerous confusions and inaccuracies reinforced by Fellowes' article published in *English Church Music* in January 1951.[44] It is often supposed that he was responsible for the rebuilding of the organ,[45] but, as we have seen, work was well under way by the time he arrived, and though Willis took a further year or more to install the 32-foot and 8-foot pipes and composition

---

[42] Ibid., 14 January 1871.

[43] Ibid., 28 January 1871.

[44] See T. Storey, 'The Music of St Paul's Cathedral: The Origins and Development of the Modern Cathedral Choir', vol. 1 (MMus diss., Durham University, 1998), 1–15.

[45] See P. Barrett, *Barchester: English Cathedral Life in the Nineteenth Century* (London: SPCK, 1993), 179.

mechanism,[46] much of it was available for use and not in the disrepair Fellowes describes.[47]

Hostility to Stainer's appointment has already been alluded to: some felt that Cooper had been ungraciously passed over, and that Stainer had acceded to his position without audition; but there were also those, so Fellowes claims, who considered that partisanship (rather than merit) had been at work, on the grounds of Stainer's High Church bias. According to Fellowes, after Stainer took office, a figure was supposed to have appeared in the organ-loft one day to exclaim 'Of course we all know why you are appointed; it is not because you can play the organ; any one can see that you can't. ... It is obviously because you are a High Churchman.'[48] Such an outburst may articulate the general antagonism that the press maintained towards St Paul's, particularly to the more ritualist tendencies of the Dean and Chapter, and indeed a nostalgia for the 'good old days' of Goss.

In 1871 this antagonism rose to new heights when the Purchas Judgment (made by the Privy Council) outlawed the eastward position of the celebrant at holy communion.[49] Gregory and Liddon refused to recognize the judgement and their resolve prevailed when the Bishop of London refused to enforce the decision in spite of pressure from the Church Association (the representative body of the Anglican Church's Evangelical wing). Yet there is certainly no evidence of any hostility to Stainer within the cathedral or of any bitterness from Cooper.

There is also the claim by Fellowes that the Special Choir decided to resign in a body 'and on the following Sunday sat in a row in the front of the Dome, expecting a breakdown'.[50] No evidence exists of this event either in any of the chronicles, nor, as one might expect, in the press coverage. Shortly after Stainer's arrival in March, the Special Choir disbanded, as it always did at Easter, having sung for its customary period since the previous January. This practice had existed since 1861, along with an annual dinner paid for by Chapter. The Chapter Minutes of 1872 record thanks to the Special Choir and payment of the cheque for dinner, noting that the organist wished 'to reconstruct the choir in such a way as he may think will best conduce to its efficiency. Should therefore any members of the existing volunteer choir wish to continue their services, the Chapter would be glad if they would communicate with Dr Stainer.'[51] Thereafter Stainer oversaw significant changes. The Special Choir, entirely voluntary and numbering 200 mixed voices or more,

[46] *Musical Standard*, 8 March 1873, 147.

[47] See E. Fellowes, 'Sir John Stainer', *English Church Music* 21/1 (January 1951), 7.

[48] Ibid.

[49] See W. J. Sparrow Simpson, *The History of the Anglo-Catholic Revival from 1845* (London: George Allen & Unwin, 1932), 135–8.

[50] Fellowes, 'Sir John Stainer', 7.

[51] Chapter Minutes, 18 April 1872 *GB-Lsp*.

had been accustomed to sit in the south transept, below the Panopticon organ on a platform before a congregation facing southwards. But once the chancel had been reconstructed, its choirstalls were brought into service and, through pressure of space, a smaller choir of surpliced cathedral boys and men (a significant corpus being readmitted from the former choir) sang for the service.[52] These took place on every Sunday throughout the year. Stress was placed on a congregational ethos more akin to a parish church rather than a cathedral, and the musical repertoire was essentially chants and hymns. While not marking any protest from the choir, the *Musical Standard* noted that:

> The first definite step in the reform of the choral arrangements at St Paul's Cathedral was taken on Sunday evening last, when the choristers, nearly seventy strong, took their place in the stalls at the entrance to the choir instead of on the orchestra formerly used under the monster organ. Another important alteration consisted in the substitution of a hymn from Hymns Ancient and Modern in the place of the anthem.[53]

Stainer retained a particular affection for the Special Choir, which he rehearsed every Friday evening. Wherever possible he attended the annual dinner, included the singers as a body in the large-scale performances in the cathedral, and, as Storey points out, he maintained musical interest by varying the sacred repertoire with secular works.[54] The Special Choir also provided him with a more tangible link with the cathedral's congregation, and, like the Tractarians, he cherished the proper ordered participation of congregations in hymn-singing. On this question, and the matter of the positioning of the organ and choir for congregational singing he held particular and concise opinions:

> Speaking generally, I should say that an organ placed behind a congregation gives more support to their voices than when in front: but I also think that there are other reasons besides musical reasons for this. There can be no doubt that when a congregation can *see* a choir (whether surpliced or not) there is a natural tendency to *listen* rather than to *take part*. When however a choir and organ are behind a congregation, this temptation ceases to exist, and the congregation feels compelled, (I might almost say *driven*) to exert itself in the music.

[52] From January 1873 women no longer sang in the choir; on this point Charlton (p. 58) appears to have been confused.

[53] *The Choir*, 11 January 1873, 18. A decision to replace the anthem with a hymn had been made as early as 16 May 1871 (see Chapter Minutes) when the Chapter resolved to adopt the strongly Tractarian *Hymns Ancient & Modern* as the sole hymnal for the cathedral.

[54] Storey, 'The Music of St Paul's Cathedral', 11.

You ask about St Paul's: it is in many ways an exceptional place. In hymn-singing I find that the sound of the choir and organ (as now placed) passes up the Dome and down again to the ears of the people sitting between the centre of the back of the Dome-floor: hence they "drag" dreadfully; and I can see no remedy for this. But nevertheless we sometimes have some magnificent congregational singing in St Paul's especially at our simple quasi-parochial Sunday-evening services.[55]

As for the main cathedral choir, musical and behavioural standards rose slowly and with a resistance that must have steadily sapped Stainer's energy. Liddon, like Gregory, was moved to chastise the men in the summer of 1873, though he did so without the public humiliation that Gregory had exacted in 1869:

I have had a large part of the choir into the vestry this morning, and have talked to them at length about behaviour in church. Specially on these points: (1) standing about and talking in their surplices, before Service; (2) talking to each other when going to the Choir; (3) sitting during the Prayers; (4) talking and sending notes to each other during Service, on matters <u>not</u> connected with Service; (5) irreverence at Holy Communion just before and after receiving. On this point I went at length into the intentions of the Chapter in insisting on having communicants; we wanted <u>religious</u> men first; then, if we could get them, accomplished musicians.[56]

Progress was sluggish, but, as Stainer recollected to Fellowes many years later, he had assured Dean Church it would take him three years before improvements were really perceptible. 'He and the Chapter waited patiently', so Stainer recalled, 'and fortunately, we began to turn the corner at the close of the second year!'[57] In achieving this amelioration, Stainer read a report to the Saturday Chapter on 6 July 1872. This, together with a similar report from the Succentor, was laid more officially before Chapter in printed form on 14 October 1872 and, since its sole concern was the Vicars Choral, a copy was sent to each of them.[58]

The first part of the report was written by Webber, who had witnessed the inertia of the choir since Stainer's time as a chorister. In it he detailed the financial circumstances of the Vicars Choral and vain attempts of Chapter to control their attendance over thirty years, including a meticulous analysis of it over nine months commencing at Michaelmas 1871. The results were discouraging, so much

55 Letter from Stainer to Edwards, 12 October 1886, *GB-Lbl* Egerton 3092, fol. 1.
56 J. O. Johnston, *Life and Letters of Henry Parry Liddon* (London: Longmans, Green & Co., 1904), 141.
57 Letter from Stainer to Fellowes, 14 April 1900, *GB-Ooc*.
58 Chapter Minutes, 14 October 1872, *GB-Lsp*.

so that for the six weeks between 5 February and 23 March 1872, while the cathedral had been closed in preparation for the Royal Thanksgiving, not one Vicar Choral would agree to sing in person at Christ Church, Newgate Street (the alternative venue designated by Chapter), and only three by deputy.[59] 'These gentlemen', Webber noted, 'still practically claim the right to stay away when and as long as they like, to send or not to send their deputies, and, above all, to treat Sunday as they do the week-days, so that hardly ever is the choir without absentees ...'[60] Perennial excuses made by the Vicars Choral – vocal ailments and residence at a distance from the cathedral – were rejected by Webber, especially the latter. 'Two hours a day only are required at St Paul's, instead of eight or nine in any other service ... and they enjoy a holiday of more than one-third of their whole time, and by employing a deputy can make it more that one-half.'[61] Indeed, Webber attributed the poor attitude of the Vicars Choral to the very circumstances that gave them security, a fact observable in deputies, who, after obtaining a position of Vicar Choral, had fallen into the habits of their predecessors. Webber finally concluded, not surprisingly, that the system could not be suffered any longer; the Vicars Choral received an appreciable income from public resources for the service of the public, yet had disproportionate power to defy both the cathedral authorities and, perhaps more importantly, public opinion. 'The system of corporate and freehold tenure', he insisted, 'has been abundantly tried and found wanting, and it would seem that nothing short of its extinction will meet the increasing demand for a really efficient Choir at St Paul's Cathedral.'[62]

Stainer's report was even more hard-hitting. He began by listing the wretched standards and bad habits which he had encountered:

I think I may be excused if I first point out the unsatisfactory state in which, on my arrival, I found everything connected with the Choir. The ordinary Responses, and even the "Amens" were sung in a hurried and careless manner, no copy of the music to them was in existence, and the traditions which individual members of the Choir attempted to follow were often conflicting. The Psalms for the day were recited at a pace which entirely destroyed their meaning and beauty, and, no pointed Psalter being in use, each singer divided the words and adapted them to the chant, in any way he thought best. The copies of the Chants were insufficient, and if the chant were changed to suit the character of the words, the Choir took some little

[59] W. C. F. Webber & J. Stainer, *Reports on the Choir of St Paul's Cathedral* (London: Rivingtons, 1872), 9.

[60] Ibid., 8.

[61] Ibid., 9–10.

[62] Ibid., 11.

time to discover what the new chant was. A more serious fault was, that both Services and Anthems were sung at such a rapid pace, as to render anything like musical expression impossible.[63]

Stainer then proceeded to catalogue his responses to these engrained problems:

> You were kind enough to call together immediately a Committee which had sometime previously been nominated by you (but which had not met), to consider the best means of improving the singing of the Responses and Psalms, and in accordance with their Report, adopted by an almost unanimous vote. I wrote out a copy of the music to the Responses, which has been printed, and for about a fortnight has been in the hands of the Choir. A Pointed Psalter was also provided for each singer, and although the pointing selected is not on the best system, yet it is found better than no system at all. A collection of chants arranged for daily use has been printed as is now in use. The full result of these changes has scarcely yet been felt. It is hoped that the pace at which the Services and Anthems are <u>now</u> sung (especially the former) is more suitable to the dignity of the music and the size of the building.[64]

But the main target of his criticism were the Vicars Choral and the powerless position of the Dean and Chapter. Early in April 1872 Stainer had invited all members of the choir to attend a general choir practice.[65] This was evidently a novelty:

> The five Supernumeraries readily gave their consent, and were present at the first practice, but no Vicar Choral attended. At the general practices afterwards held, one Vicar Choral attended, and on one occasion another Vicar Choral sent to say that he would have attended but for an important engagement. The Supernumeraries have always been present, and have shown much attention and zeal. These general practices have taken place at intervals of about three weeks, but though they have done some good, their effect has been much lessened by the absence from them of elder members of the Choir. I do not hesitate to say that unless <u>all</u> the singers can be made to attend, a high standard of musical performance can <u>never</u> be reached.

---

63 Ibid., 14.

64 Ibid., 14–15.

65 These practices took place in a new room built on the first floor of the belfry tower (at a cost of £250) at the instigation of Gregory in 1870. See W. M. Atkins, 'The Age of Reform: 1831–1934', in *A History of St Paul's Cathedral and the Men Associated with it*, ed. W. R. Matthews & W. M. Atkins (London: Phoenix House, 1957), 267.

I purpose, as soon as a full attendance can be secured, to hold these practices weekly.[66]

This was Stainer's first major reform, but he offered one other Draconian suggestion, namely that if Chapter could not enforce this change and assert its proper authority, then extinction of the positions of Vicars Choral should be allowed to run its course or an Act of Parliament invoked for abolition of the corporation. Stainer clearly preferred the latter, believing that if the statistics were laid before Members of Parliament, the House of Commons would readily consent to the destruction of an anachronistic constitution. Moreover, he rightly held the view that the revenue of the Vicars Choral, some £1,400 annually, would be more effectively used to employ up to twelve voices, thus enlarging the choir for the cathedral's cavernous space. Yet he admitted ruefully that:

> Even if the Choir could be greatly enlarged from other resources, a really good state of musical discipline would be unattainable so long as the influential nucleus of the Choir consisted of a body of gentlemen having the power of singing when they like, how they like, and of attending in person even when unable to sing at all.

Ultimately, however, Stainer looked to Chapter to assert their rightful authority, for, if that were carried out, he would then properly admit full responsibility for the musical efficiency of the choir and, quite selflessly, sacrifice his promised right to a Vicar Choralship.[67] In the event, Chapter demurred from either of Stainer's proposals, perhaps from a desire to implement reforms with some immediacy rather than endure another rancorous dispute.[68] But the message to the present Vicars Choral was clear – their conduct was to be more stringently monitored, and though there were sporadic periods of inattendance (especially by Francis, who, with a chequered career of chastisement and suspension, remained defiant to the end), their deportment, as the Weekly Chapter minutes attest, began by modest degrees to improve, helped by a scheme of fines (which Gregory implemented with characteristic determination),[69] a stricter regime of appointing deputies (whom

[66] Ibid., 16–17.

[67] Ibid., 20.

[68] Abolition of the Vicars Choral was finally implemented by Act of Parliament in 1931. In the mean time, Chapter treated promotion to the positions of Vicars Choral as a reward for longevity of service.

[69] Such was Gregory's strict implementation of discipline that 'he quashed a choir-man's excuse for lateness, punishable under the statutes by a fine, with the promise that were the delinquent to fall down dead on the steps of the Cathedral on his way to service, his widow should be fined for his non-attendance' (Prestige, St Paul's in its Glory, 99).

Chapter had to approve), a reinvigorated sense of discipline, including Stainer's desired weekly choir practice,[70] and, perhaps most crucially, the winning influence of Stainer's personality. It was, however, a gradual process in which Stainer was prepared, with commendable patience, to bide his time.

Thanks to the success of Gregory's negotiations with the Ecclesiastical Commissioners, funds for the choir became available for a variety of purposes. In December 1872 eight new men, identified as Assistant Vicars Choral, were auditioned and placed in a contributory pension scheme, with a retirement age of sixty.[71] The same conditions were negotiated for the five Supernumeraries, while the Vicars Choral, though retaining their freehold, were given a pay rise (and funds from the commuted Cupola Find, finally settled in 1874), no doubt as an incentive to mend their ways. In late March the Rev. Coward agreed to the transfer of the Almonry estate to the Ecclesiastical Commissioners and the relinquishing of his office of Almoner; this paved the way for the appointment on 26 June 1872 of the Rev. Alfred Barff as a proper Master of the Choir Boys (or Master Grammatices as was his formal office).[72] (It comes as no surprise that Barff was a friend of Liddon's and had been chaplain at Cuddesdon during Liddon's time as Vice-Principal.)

The notion of a proper dedicated building for the choir boys had been discussed for years by Chapter, but by 1871 the matter had at last been delegated to the cathedral surveyor to find a suitable site. In January 1873 eleven additional choirboys were auditioned and housed for the moment in 1 Amen Court, while the existing twelve continued as day-boys; in the best Tractarian tradition they were admitted formally by special service on 8 March. This brought the total of choristers to twenty-three; this number remained until the new choir school in Carter Lane (on the site of the ancient Choral Grammar School), finished towards the end of 1874, was opened in early 1875; at that time a further fifteen boys were adjoined. All thirty-eight (thirty choristers and eight probationers) were then housed and educated at the school free of charge. How Maria Hackett must have smiled as Stainer and the Dean showed her around the school as it neared completion;[73] she died, nine days short of her ninety-first birthday, on 5 November 1874; the choir, at their

---

[70] Frost (*Early Recollections of St Paul's Cathedral*, 47) notes that the weekly choir practice was not implemented immediately, and that, for the Sunday anthem, Stainer initially would request a practice before the service.

[71] Another Assistant Vicar Choral was appointed after a Vicar Choral died and Stainer took the vacant freehold; it was a position Stainer took very seriously, for when the organ was not required for services, notably on Good Friday, he would take his place in the choir with the rest of the men and boys.

[72] Chapter Minutes, 22 March 1873, *GB-Lsp*.

[73] *Musical Times* 41 (May 1900), 303.

own request and expense, attended at her burial at Highgate Cemetery five days later.[74]

Hackett would have thoroughly endorsed the new conditions for the choristers, not only because the proper resources were being devoted to their welfare, but also because Stainer, her former protégé, saw to it that one half of the boys should enjoy a free afternoon alternately on Saturdays,[75] and all the boys could be excused on Wednesday afternoons after October 1873 (this later moved to Thursdays in February 1875) while the men sang the service. In addition, during the summer months of August and September, one half of the choristers enjoyed a month's holiday while the other half sang in the cathedral, a practice which was also later extended to Christmas and Easter. Crucially, however, Stainer, with the tenacious assistance of Gregory, had realised his goal of a large choir to lead day-to-day worship in St Paul's. The sound of this body of singers, its strength and potential, remained close to his heart, and he firmly believed that the financial support given to St Paul's needed to be applied to other English cathedrals: 'The real want', he told Fellowes, 'is larger and better choirs; more <u>money</u> in fact.'[76]

During this time the singing of the boys became a focus for major improvement. Some of the music chosen for them was evidently too difficult, and there was at least one occasion where their lack of mastery led to the anthem of the day being replaced by something easier. Much of the singing was careless, rushed and undisciplined, which drew criticism from the Dean on more than one occasion, and with the addition of the new boys in 1873 the task of training undoubtedly became more onerous for Fred Walker, who, as a Professor of Singing at the Royal Academy of Music (RAM), had trained the original twelve boys since 1867. This was soon recognised by Chapter, who concluded that, for the moment, they would remunerate Walker's labour with an additional £50 until such time as the appointment of a proper Singing Master was effected.[77] In June 1874 Chapter agreed to appoint Stainer's former organ and harmony pupil at Magdalen, George Clement Martin, to this position; two years later, on the death of George Cooper, Martin became Assistant Organist.

Discipline of the boys also proved a more arduous undertaking, at least to begin with. One boy was suspended for a fortnight in April 1873, another suspended indefinitely (though he was given a further chance a month later), and one boy, already expelled from the Temple Church, was given his marching orders in

[74] A cenotaph to her memory was erected in St Paul's in March 1877 from subscription, raised by the choristers and the work of Stainer and Barrett.

[75] Weekly Chapter Minutes, 15 March 1873, *GB-Lsp*.

[76] Postcard from Stainer to Fellowes, 6 November 1899, *GB-Ooc*.

[77] Chapter Minutes, 1 March 1873, *GB-Lsp*.

February 1874. This eventually led to the narrowing of the pool from which boys were selected, as Liddon noted in May 1878:

> We have found it necessary to make another change. The boys *were*, almost all of them, the sons of tradesmen – we have been driven to admit only the sons of gentlemen, chiefly of poor clergymen. Not merely the cockney pronunciation in church, but weightier reasons made this restriction necessary; although in *the abstract* I regretted the change, as partly cutting off the Cathedral from the sympathies of the people. But the event has justified our decision. Having once made up our minds as to what had to be done, we got rid of our old boys as quickly as we could, without doing an injustice. ... This plan sometimes forfeits a good voice, but in the end it is of the greatest advantage to the choir – as *now* admission is considered a very great privilege, and no parent would think of interference with our rules.[78]

These improvements to the state of music powerfully reflected the general mood of reform that was sweeping the cathedral. Sunday evening services with the voluntary choir, now all male, were continuous throughout the year; the new Lectionary was adopted, a choral celebration of Communion was implemented every Sunday morning, and, later, in addition to Good Friday, services on Fridays were sung without organ (except during the Paschal season and Saints' Days);[79] the Willis organ was completed, which, in Stainer's opinion rendered the Panopticon organ redundant (it was put up for sale in July 1872); the bearing of the choir was formalised by more orderly processions (accompanied by an organ voluntary), prayers before and after the service, and the wearing of cassocks became obligatory for the boys in 1873 and the men in 1874, while clean surplices were provided at the expense of the Cathedral. Perhaps most significantly, Stainer's desire of having the music lists printed weekly and distributed to the choir and throughout the cathedral was fully realised by the beginning of 1873.[80]

Although Stainer must be credited with much of the change in music at St Paul's in the early years of his regime, it would be well to remember that it was Webber, the Succentor, who was ultimately responsible for what was sung. He was a keen singer and was President of the London Church Choir Association; yet, one suspects that he was accustomed to a repetitive repertoire, and broached musical reform with some trepidation. To this end he resisted, with the exception of 'Jesu, our Lord', Stainer's early attempts to introduce the works of Gounod. But the

---

[78] Johnston, *Life and Letters of Henry Parry Liddon*, 142–3.

[79] Weekly Chapter Minutes, 20 April 1878, *GB-Lsp*.

[80] Weekly Chapter Minutes, 21 December 1872, *GB-Lsp*. The initial desire was to emulate Barnby's scheme at St Andrew's, Wells Street, by having the lists printed monthly.

augmentation of the choir inevitably imposed important changes. During 1872, when the choir remained in its old form, the repertoire of works was drawn from the seventeenth and eighteenth centuries. However, from January 1873, when the provision of music became a new imperative (no longer could the cathedral rely on the old bound volumes of music for the men, and copied partbooks for the boys), a substantial amount of 'old' repertoire was dropped, never to be revived. As Storey has informed us, eighteen Morning, six Communion, fourteen Evening Services and sixty-seven anthems were purged, and a good deal of the Georgian repertoire discarded. This, to a considerable extent, reflected Stainer's general dislike of the latter, but the exigencies of the new circumstances – a larger choir in a much bigger space – militated against the suitability of lengthy solo verses and a numerous choir with little singing to do.[81]

Stainer first articulated his musical and practical objections in a paper read before the Church Congress at Leeds in 1872, but he reserved his greatest opprobrium for the *Handbook to the Cathedral of St Paul* in 1882, in which he considered the effect of the post-Restoration models to be injurious:

> The effect on English Church music was disastrous. There can be no mistake about the characteristics of Anglo-French music; anthems in this style have generally little independent symphonies on the organ called *ritornelli*; the chief part of the performance is nearly always allotted to a trio for an alto, tenor, and bass voice, interspersed with solos; all the movements are broken up into short sentences, and there is frequent change from duple to triple measure; above all things, they possess strongly-marked rhythm, frequently quite commonplace and vulgar, but which no doubt gave great pleasure to the restored royal toes as they beat time on the floor of the chapel of St James's Palace.

In not wishing to be misunderstood, not least with the gradual reawakening of national interest in the music of Purcell, Stainer readily admitted to an admiration of the best in the work of Humfrey, Blow and Purcell, but he had an aversion to their imitators and to the monopoly they enjoyed in cathedrals for more than century: 'Indeed, so strongly has it left its mark that many persons still uphold it as the true Cathedral style, and are weak enough to call it distinctively English simply because no other nation was so foolish as to borrow it from the French.' Yet Stainer conceded that conditions at St Paul's had formerly rendered this style of music practical and attractive:

> It must, however, be said in extenuation of the popularity of this style of music, that pieces for *soli* voices were thoroughly adapted for our small collegiate

---

[81] Storey, 'The Music of St Paul's Cathedral', 16, *passim*.

chapels [here no doubt Stainer recalled his experiences at Magdalen], and for that small portion of many of our cathedrals cut off and formed into a separate church by an organ-screen. In the days when the organ of St Paul's separated the chancel from the rest of the Church only seven hundred persons could attend the service, and that not without inconvenience. For this limited space six Vicars Choral and twelve boys could supply the requisite music with fairly good effect, and this was the only choir the Cathedral possessed until within the last quarter of a century.[82]

Still, under Webber, the reduced repertoire, much of it by Greene, Boyce, Blow and Croft, meant that repetition of pieces intensified, though Stainer was able to introduce a few novelties, such as his own 'Lead, kindly light', Thorne's 'God so loved the world' and Mozart's 'Jesu, Word of God incarnate'. In the case of service music, much of the reform followed in the wake of liturgical reforms made by Chapter's desire to see the spirit and dignity of the Book of Common Prayer restored. After many years of neglect the Benedicite was introduced for the penitential seasons of Advent and Lent, and the Benedictus for the majority of Morning services. To this end, Stainer leapt at the opportunity to introduce Gounod's setting of the Benedictus (which remained a hugely popular setting at St Paul's until the First World War), added his own settings in A and E flat, as well as to those of the 3rd Gregorian and 6th Tones), and other composers, among them Goss, Calkin, Garrett and Turle, soon came up with their own settings to append to their originally existing settings of the Morning Service.

With Chapter's decision to establish a regular Sunday choral celebration of Communion, service music, which had largely meant only settings of the Responses to the Commandments and the Creed (the choir formerly departed after the sermon), and the Sanctus, if used, sung as an introit, now required a more rounded conception which included not only the Sanctus but the Gloria, Gospel responses, Sursum Corda and final Amen.[83] Chapter's decision rendered much of the cathedral's communion repertoire obsolete and what repertoire was available – by Ouseley (in A), Barnby (in E), Garrett (in D), Monk (in C) and Stainer (in E flat – added to his already existing Evening Service) provided the staple diet until 1876. As for the music for the Evening Service, some expurgations were made, but the reduced repertoire witnessed only the additions of Gadsby in C and Dykes in F, and, by sheer necessity, ATTB settings by Stainer (in D) and Gadsby (in A) were

[82] G. P. Bevan & J. Stainer, *Handbook to the Cathedral of St Paul* (London: W. Swan Sonnenschein & Co., 1882), 75–6.

[83] Because the Sanctus was now properly included in its proper place within the communion celebration, Stainer included an 'Introit' in his E flat service as a means of separating matins and the litany beforehand.

introduced for the 'men only' services implemented in 1873, an innovation which met with some approbation by the press.[84]

Between 1870 and 1877 Stainer's conception of service music began to change. His Evening Service in E flat, written at Magdalen in or around 1870, exuded moments of harmonic richness and passages of delightful lyricism such as the verse 'And His mercy is on them that fear Him' (Example 10). Both the Magnificat and Nunc dimittis were through-composed entities, having simple tonal structures (barely straying from the areas of the relative minor and subdominant) and an unadventurous organ part consistently doubling the vocal lines. Yet, like its contemporary setting in E major, it exudes a new confidence in its word-setting and its well-chosen use of harmonies to enhance meaning and emotion (e.g. the climactic 'shall call be blessed' and the gentle, yearning 'Abraham and His seed forever'). Indeed, one wonders whether the service had some influence on Stanford's later setting in B flat of 1879, for not only is there a strong connection between Stainer's E flat frame in triple time and the lyrical subdominent episode in quadruple metre, but there is also a striking similarity in the duple time of Stainer's sedate gloria which Stanford likewise introduced at the close of his settings of the Benedictus, Jubilate Deo and Nunc dimittis. This, of course, remains a matter of conjecture, but we do know that Stanford knew Stainer's service well for it was often sung at Trinity College, Cambridge where he became organist after 1873.

With the Evening Service in A major, composed for the Sons of the Clergy in 1873, Stainer became bolder in his treatment. Conceived for orchestra, the role of the organ accompaniment took on a new life as is evidenced by the striking opening and the prominent position of the orchestra in the musical structure (indeed, at times it is the organ that provides musical momentum rather than the choir or soloist). The procedure of setting 'And His mercy' as a lyrical verse with chorus is once again followed in the Magnificat, though this time it is placed in the flat submediant, F major. This contrasting relationship had been used in the Nunc dimittis of the 'Magdalen' Service, where its role had been one principally of tonal contrast within a simple ternary scheme. Here, however, its function is as a 'second subject' which is allowed to recapitulate in a subtly transformed guise on the dominant of A ('He rememb'ring His mercy), preparing the way for the reprise in the tonic (as Stanford does in in his B flat Magnificat) of the opening material in the Gloria. The Nunc dimittis, like its E flat counterpart, is entirely through-composed. More significant here, however, is the tonal divergence to F ('in peace according to Thy word'), which clearly makes reference back to the same tonal contrast in the Magnificat.

---

[84] See *The Choir*, 18 October 1873, 238. Stainer's service was a regular item, being sung six times in 1873, thirteen times in 1874 and eleven times in 1875; see Storey, 'The Music of St Paul's Cathedral', ii, 167.

Example 10. Service in E flat: Magnificat (central verse)

Example 11. Service in E flat: Nicene Creed: 'He suffered and was buried'

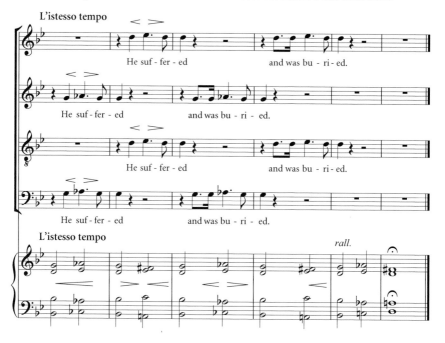

This heightened sense of tonal relationships was one that Stainer would explore with greater intensity in later settings of the Canticles. There are indications of this in the Morning and Communion Service in E flat probably composed in 1874. Here the Te Deum presents a striking matrix of contrasts in the structure between E flat ('We praise Thee, O God'), D major ('Holy, holy' holy') and B flat ('Thou art the King of glory'). This same interrelationship is repeated in the Credo, and the Offertory sentences explore the same keys. In addition the 'closing' effect of the reprise of opening material (employed in the Magnificat) is regularly deployed, which, in the case of the Te Deum, occurs with arresting modifications (notably the climactic shift to the Neapolitan just before the final cadence).

In the composition of the Morning and Communion portions of the A major Service (composed *c.* 1877), the manipulation of tonal relationships and thematic material was even more sophisticated. The Te Deum, set in A major, is a broad ternary scheme in the which the opening part sets up a thematic design (A–B–C–B–D). This is subsequently contrasted by a central paragraph in D, a key highly significant to the larger scheme of the service in general. The final section, set entirely in the tonic, is a truncated form of the first part. Stainer also set the Benedictus in A major, but for the Communion Service the two major parts, the Credo and Gloria (linked by their common reprises), are couched in D major, as if anticipated by the tonal dialectic of the Te Deum; and the Sanctus, set in A, appropriately exploits the setting of 'Holy, holy, holy' from the Te Deum. This enhanced net-work of thematic and tonal relationships combined with a more cohesive concept of form begins to lend the Service as a whole a more 'instrumental' sensibility and begins to move in the direction of Stanford's *Gesamtkunstwerk* notion of the musical service. Similarly the chromatic intensity of the A major Service builds on those passages of a distinctly secular style in the E flat Service. The incarna-tion clause of the Nicene Creed ('and was incarnate of the Virgin Mary') of the E flat Service, with its 'song-like' accompaniment and lush progressions, brings to mind Gounod's and Massenet's *mélodies*, while the text 'He suffered and was buried' (Example 11) has the dramatic rhetoric of a Continental Catholic Requiem. In the A major Service the same clause is marked by a striking modulation from D to A flat, and the secular ambience is underscored by an equally elaborate song accompaniment for the organ and the interjections of the *turba*-like chorus ('and was made man'). Likewise the depiction of Jesus's suffering, as the tonality 'darkens' to G flat, is deeply anguished, and the recovery to A flat (through the semitonal juxtaposition of E major and E flat) shows the hand of a master (Example 12).

Although progress may have been sluggish under Webber's stewardship, Stainer was not slow to fall in line with a movement strongly supported by Barnby and Macfarren for the promotion of oratorios and passions in churches and cathedrals, especially within the context of the liturgy. Macfarren had put forward the idea in his series of articles 'The Music of the English Church' in 1868,[85] but it was Barnby who took the principal initiative. During the 1860s Barnby developed the music at St Andrew's, Wells Street, with unique vigour (helped on by the enthusiasm of its Tractarian rector, Benjamin Webb), featuring elaborate choral services of Roman Catholic masses and motets and Gounod's *Messe Solonelle* (first given there in 1866); after moving to St Anne's, Soho, in 1871 he continued this practice with greater alacrity with weekly performances of Bach's *St John Passion* during Lent. Away from St Anne's, Barnby promoted other choral works with his own choir, and performed the *St Matthew Passion* at the Exeter Hall on 6 April 1870. Then, on 6 April 1871 (Maundy Thursday), the *Matthew Passion* was given again, but this time in a liturgical setting in Westminster Abbey with the combined choirs of the Abbey and local churches and a sermon delivered by Dean Stanley. Only the day after Stainer arrived at St Paul's, on 26 March 1872, he was asked by Barnby to accompany the recitatives (on harmonium or American organ) in the *Mat-thew Passion* on the Tuesday of Holy Week, again in Westminster Abbey. Stainer's acquaintance with Barnby proved enormously fruitful, for not only did Barnby invite him to act as organist for the Royal Albert Hall Choral Society (RAHCS)

---

[85] See G. A. Macfarren, 'The Music of the English Church', *Musical Times* 13 (February 1868) 279–83.

Example 12. Service in A: Nicene Creed: 'He suffered and was buried'

– which gave Stainer regular access to Willis's magnificently palatial organ, opened in July 1871 – but the very resource of Barnby's orchestra gave him the opportunity to promote oratorio in St Paul's. Stainer also became acquainted with Gounod, who, having retreated to London after the outbreak of the Franco-Prussian War, entered into musical life in London, and the two men participated together in

Gounod's 'Grand Choral Concerts' at the Albert Hall (which began in May 1872), Stainer performing and accompanying on the organ.

The first of Stainer's new oratorio initiatives at St Paul's was to perform a selection of movements from Mendelssohn's *St Paul* (commencing with St Paul's conversion and ending with the last chorus) at the cathedral's patronal festival on 25 January 1873 with his enlarged choir, singers from the Sunday Evening Special Choir and members of the RAHCS. It attracted a substantial congregation (including Barnby); 3,000 were expected but 8,000 turned up. With its success Stainer was granted permission to perform the *St Matthew Passion* on Tuesday of Holy Week.[86] The event caught the public imagination and the cathedral staff were utterly taken aback when close to 10,000 people attempted to squeeze into the building; many had to be turned away.

Another major event in the cathedral's calendar was the Festival of the Sons of the Clergy in May. In 1872 Stainer had accompanied the service on the organ (with Cooper), while William Winn conducted the combined choirs of St Paul's, the Chapel Royal, Westminster Abbey, St George's Windsor, Canterbury, Winchester and Eton College. The conservative programme of Smart in B flat, Gibbons' 'Hosanna to the Son of David' and Goss's 'Brother, thou art gone before us' itself marked an important watershed, for, the following year, in 1873, Stainer decided to revive the tradition of commissioning a new anthem or service setting with orchestral accompaniment.[87] On this occasion the orchestra performed the first two movements of Mendelssohn's *Lobgesang* as an opening voluntary and the choral part as an anthem.[88] The canticles were supplied by Stainer in a new setting of the Magnificat and Nunc dimittis in A. This fine, robust service, especially in its orchestral garb (which, regrettably, is now missing), proved a great favourite and was included in the 1874 festival (when it partnered Mendelssohn's overture to *Athalie* and the cantata *As pants the hart*) and in 1876 (when it appeared alongside a selection from *Elijah*).

These services stood as musical high points of the year and continued to receive enthusiastic reviews in the press, but other services also began to assume a higher profile; these included those given by the London Church Choir Association and the Gregorian Association, in which Stainer often participated as organist; and

---

[86] Frost (*Early Recollections of St Paul's Cathedral*, 40) has suggested that Stainer underwrote the costs for this event.

[87] The orchestra had always been a feature of the Festivals of the Sons of the Clergy until 1844 when it was suppressed by the Bishop of London, Dr Blomfield. Stainer's 'reinstatement' of the orchestra was greeted with considerable favour.

[88] Stainer often chose to conduct overtures by Mendelssohn and Spohr as opening 'orchestral' voluntaries for the Sons of the Clergy festivals, but he particularly favoured Sullivan's overture *In Memoriam*, which was used for many years.

there were also significant events such as the funeral of Sir Edwin Landseer (11 October 1873), and a substantial choral festival for the College of Organists on 20 October 1874 (with a choir of 500 and attended by a congregation of nearly 10,000),[89] conducted by John Limpus with Stainer at the organ. A similar event took place the following year on Cecilia's Day, this time conducted by Edmund Hart Turpin (the newly appointed Honorary Secretary of the College), which included the orchestrated version of Stainer in A as well as the first hearing of Purcell's Te Deum since 1829. Also worthy of mention was a massed Harvest Thanksgiving service at the Crystal Palace on 20 October 1875 in which Stainer drew a large choir of 2,000 singers from the London churches together with a substantial orchestra.

In removing to London, the Stainers found a home in Bloomsbury, at 7 Upper Montague Street, Russell Square, close to the British Museum. They remained there for the next three years until Barff and Martin removed to accommodation in the new choir school in early 1875. This vacated 1 Amen Court, close to the cathedral where the Stainer family subsequently set up home for four years before moving, in 1879, to 5 Amen Court where they resided for the remaining period of Stainer's appointment.[90] On 27 September 1872 Stainer's wife gave birth to their sixth child, Frederick Henry, at Grandpont House in Oxford; just over a year later, on 7 October 1873, a seventh child, William Edgar, was added to the family.

During this time Stainer's professional opportunities had begun to expand. He was appointed an examiner for the College of Organists between 1871 and 1873,[91] and also served on its council. As a virtuoso organist he performed Prout's Organ Concerto at the Crystal Palace on 19 October 1872, and, fifteen months later, on 24 January 1874, Gadsby's Organ Concerto at the same venue, in addition to appearing as an orchestral organist in Manns' performance of Mendelssohn's St Paul on 30 November 1872 and Handel's L'Allegro on 28 November 1874. This 'orchestral role' was one Stainer carefully cultivated, and in 1873 he was employed by Barnby as the organist for the RAHCS concerts in which, besides acting as a continuo player (in the eighteenth-century works), he was also expected to support the choral parts in more contemporary works. Much of the repertoire, at least those in the early history of the RAHCS, were popular favourites – Handel's Israel in Egypt, Judas Maccabeus and Messiah (the latter especially on Ash Wednesday and at Easter), Haydn's Creation, Mendelssohn's Lobgesang, St Paul and Elijah, Bach's

---

[89] C. W. Pearce, A Biographical Sketch of Edmund Hart Turpin (London: The Vincent Music Company, [1911]), 28.

[90] Frost, Early Recollections of St Paul's Cathedral, 60. See also Chapter Minutes, 7 June 1879, GB-Lsp.

[91] Pearce, Biographical Sketch of Edmund Hart Turpin, 27.

Christmas Oratorio and *St Matthew Passion* and Rossini's *Stabat Mater* – but new works were to follow, notably Sullivan's *The Light of the World* in March 1874.

His reputation as a theoretician and harmony teacher, generated by the two editions of *A Theory of Harmony*, led to the acceptance of a teaching position at the Crystal Palace Company's School of Art, Science and Literature (Ladies Division). 'I have been asked to take the Harmony class at the Crystal Palace (Art Department)', he wrote to his wife in September, 'and I think I shall accept it – as it will help off my <u>second Edition</u> – and also get me down to the Palace often – with a good excuse!! More about it when we meet.'[92] This appointment brought him rapidly into contact with other prominent performers and pedagogues in London, among them Ernst Pauer, Prout, Julius Benedict and Alberto Randegger, and this was enhanced by conspicuous social occasions such as William Sterndale Bennett's testimonial on 19 April 1872.

Stainer's influence in London's musical circles was also brought to bear on the appointment of Frederick Bridge to Westminster Abbey (after the retirement of James Turle), the appointment of Charles Sherwood Jekyll to the Chapel Royal (after George Cooper's death in 1876), and the publication of the revised edition of *Hymns Ancient & Modern* (1875). It also brought him closer to his old friend Sullivan, who introduced him to Arthur Duke Coleridge, one of the future founding-fathers of the Bach Choir. 'Are you disposed and have you time', Sullivan wrote in June 1872, 'to hear a Cantata of Bach, bits of Lohengrin, and other choice morsels tomorrow afternoon? If so, I am charged by an old and dear friend, one Arthur Coleridge by name, to invite you to his home at 4.30 tomorrow afternoon. He will be delighted to make your acquaintance and you will find many musical friends amongst others.'[93] Coleridge, a young lawyer, had cultivated an enthusiasm for Bach as a Cambridge undergraduate. There he had met the up-and-coming Stanford, and in London he came into contact with Otto Goldschmidt, an advocate of Bach's music since his student days at Leipzig. It was at Coleridge's and Goldschmidt's homes that informal performances of Bach's choral music, particularly of the Mass in B minor, nurtured the idea of forming a choir to perform the work in public. With a wide circle of musicians and friends – among them Stainer – Goldschmidt was able to form a choir of 150 singers and two landmark performances of the Mass in B minor – the very first hearing of the complete work in England – took place in London on 26 April and 8 May 1876. Stainer wrote many years later: 'I feel pretty sure that I am right about this being the first use in England of the long

---

[92] Letter from Stainer to Elizabeth Cecil Stainer, 24 September 1872, in private possession (MN).

[93] Letter from Sullivan to Stainer, 7 June 1872 [postmark], *US-NYpm*.

"Bach" trumpet, as I presided at the organ and the instruments were just below me
– a little to my right.'[94]

The combination of reforming work at St Paul's and his inclination towards
antiquarianism and theoretical scholarship, nurtured by his years at Oxford,
fuelled Stainer's zeal for a musical profession that was not only highly skilled and
properly trained but also enjoyed a reputation comparable with other professional
bodies, notably those of a scientific bent. In order to protect what he regarded as
a profession with well-defined principles of competence, discernment and public
standing he could be pugnaciously defensive of the responsibilities that university
degrees signified, as was shown in a furious exchange of public correspondence
with Thomas Lloyd Fowle, a local Winchester musician, with whom Stainer had
had brief contact in 1863:

> SIR, – I understand from the current number of the *Musical Times*, that the
> friends of Thomas Lloyd Fowle, MA and Mus.Doc., are endeavouring to
> obtain for him a pension to the Civil List of the Government. It is not my
> intention to say one word on the question of Mr Fowle's claims to such a
> substantial recognition, but I think as a preliminary step to any agitation in
> his favour, it is absolutely necessary for his own credit, that he should give
> a public explanation of the grounds on which he affixes *MA* and *Mus.Doc.*
> to his name.
>
> As one of the mere handful of men who hold both these honourable
> degrees, I consider no apology is needed for thus bringing this subject for-
> ward, and I believe in so doing I shall have the moral support of my brother
> musical graduates.
>
> I ask Mr Fowle then, to set all doubts at rest by stating in your next
> issue:
>
> 1. At what University he graduated?
> 2. How long he resided at his University?
> 3. How many examinations he has passed, and in what subjects?
> 4. By whom was he examined, and does he possess any "Testamur?"
> 5. Was he ever a BA and Mus.Bac.?
>
> If Mr Fowle's answers to these very simple questions are satisfactory, I
> will gladly apologize for having thus dragged him before the bar of public
> opinion.[95]

The letter's forthright accusations inevitably provoked an angry reply from Fowle

---

94 Letter from Stainer to Edwards, 13 November 1896, *GB-Lbl* Egerton 3092, fol. 22.
95 Letter from Stainer to the Editor of the *Musical Times* (February 1875), 22.

in which some of the old, festering resentment of Stainer's unchallenged appointment to St Paul's brusquely re-emerged:

SIR, – If I was to follow the advice tendered to me by members of the musical profession I should treat the letter of the above writer, in your last impression, with the contempt it deserves. Although I deny his right to catechise me in such an offensive manner, and which no *real gentleman* would have done, I do not desire to evade the subject to which he refers, and therefore will at once state that I will give a full and perfect answer, on certain conditions, and that it rests with you and him whether I shall do so or not. As I am Mr Stainer's senior in *years*, and certainly in *length* of musical reputation, no just and sane individual will deny me the right to put a few pertinent questions to him before I answer those he has put to me. I ask therefore:–

Firstly. How was it that he, an obtuse organist in the country (and called by a contemporary "the singing man at St Paul's") came to be quietly ensconced into the organ gallery of the Metropolitan Cathedral, *without competition*, and to the exclusion of men who had made their reputation before he was scarcely out of his teens?

Secondly. If the authorities at St Paul's had the right, and the bad taste to quietly place a former "singing man," *without competition*, as their organist, does Mr Stainer consider it a professional act towards eminent men to exclude them by *non-competition* – men such as Mr George Cooper, and other well-known players, and with whom in *fair competition* he could have had no chance of election.

Thirdly. I ask Mr Stainer whether he is not perfectly familiar with the University at which I took my degrees, and whether he is not bringing forward the subject out of petty and pitiful jealousy to try to do me an injury? I am afraid he has a very little mind, and as he refuses me my *just title*, I decline to give him his own.

Fourthly. I ask Mr Stainer whether he thinks it a *professional* act and the act of a *gentleman* to moot such a question in a *public* manner? If he does, permit me to inform him that the general opinion is (from letters I am receiving) that if he had been a real *gentleman*, and not actuated by the *malus animus*, he would, in doubting the *bonâ fide* nature of my degrees, have written to me *privately*.

Fifthly. I ask Mr Stainer whether he has not previously attacked me *anonymously* with reference to this subject, and whether he has not been in private correspondence, or in communication *in propria persona* with a printer in the neighbourhood of his residence, who so libelled me that an investigation was instituted by a clergyman and a barrister resulting in an

award wholly condemnatory of the said printer? I have a letter in my possession which, although not conclusive on the point, is extremely suspicious.[96]

Fowle was not without his supporters, and one critic raised the legitimate question that Stainer's triumphal claims for the British music degree were misplaced.
Stainer's reply was, however, immediate and claimed victory:

> SIR, – I have much pleasure in replying to Mr Fowle's queries, in the order
> in which they occur.
>
> 1. This question should have been addressed to the Dean and Chapter.
> 2. Yes.
> 3. I have not the smallest conception where, when, or how, Mr Fowle
>   became a *Doctor* and a *Master of Arts*. I am not jealous of Mr Fowle.
> 4. Yes. Titles publicly used are open to public criticism.
> 5. Certainly not. I know absolutely nothing of the printer mentioned by
>   Mr Fowle. I have never had any communication, signed or anonymous,
>   with any printer, person, paper or periodical, except the *Musical Times*
>   (in last number), on the subject of Mr Fowle's University status, or any-
>   thing else connected with him.
>
> He is quite at liberty to take any further steps he may deem advisable,
> with regard to any "suspicious" letter he possesses.
> I now claim the fulfilment of Mr Fowle's promise to answer *my* questions
> printed in your last issue.[97]

Fowle did reply again, but the editor of the *Musical Times* considered that his
rejoinder failed to address any of Stainer's further comments and refused to insert
it, though with the comment that Fowle intended to publicise the source of his
degree; this, it transpired, was a PhD from the University of Giessen.[98]

Of much more telling significance, however, in the quest for professional legitimacy was the forming of the Musical Association in 1874, in which Stainer played a
central role. Addressing members of the Association at the beginning of its twenty-
first session on 13 November 1894, Stainer recalled that the seeds of an idea for an
organisation devoted to the 'science' of music had been sown at Oxford:

> As most of you know, the initial idea of this Association was started in Oxford,
> in the house of the late Dr Corfe. During an interesting conversation with

---

[96] Letter from Fowle to the Editor of the *Musical Times* (April 1875), 55–6. See also
T. G. Barry's letter, 57.

[97] Letter from Stainer to the Editor of the *Musical Times* (April 1875), 57.

[98] See P. Horton, *Samuel Sebastian Wesley: A Life* (Oxford: Oxford University Press,
2004), 249, n. 152.

Dr Corfe and Dr Pole, I expressed a regret that musicians did not possess any organisation for encouraging and collecting information or papers on special subjects connected with our art. I was told I ought not to lose sight of such a scheme, and when I found myself settled in London I made the first attempt at establishing it by calling together a meeting, which was very influentially attended ...[99]

Stainer was almost certainly instrumental in planting the idea, though it was the eminent scientist William Spottiswoode who circulated a letter to the musical and scientific fraternities on 8 April 1874:

It has been suggested by several leading persons interested both in the theory and in the practice of Music, the formation of a Society similar in the main features of its organization to existing learned Societies would be a great public benefit.

Such a Musical Society might comprise among its members the foremost Musicians, theoretical as well as practical, of the day; the principal Patrons of the art; and also those scientific men whose researches have been directed to the subject of acoustics, and to kindred inquiries. Its periodical meetings might be devoted partly to the reading of papers upon the history, the principles and the criticism of music; partly to the illustration of such papers by actual performance; and partly to the exhibition and discussion of experiments relating to theory and construction of Musical Instruments, or to the principles and combination of musical sounds.[100]

From twenty-two names, nine people – John Tyndall, Sedley Taylor, Chappell, Grove, Hullah, Pole, Macfarren, Stainer and Spottiswoode – attended a first meeting at Spottiswoode's home at 50 Grosvenor Place in London on 16 April 1874. Among the group there was much optimism and willingness to see the initiative succeed, though Macfarren felt it his duty to point out that earlier attempts, such as the Musical Institute and the Musical Society of London with comparable, if not identical aims, had failed through lack of support. However, the group was undeterred, and the notion of the Society was proposed and seconded unanimously along with the suggestion, from Spottiswoode, that proceedings of meetings should be published. To draw up the Society's regulations, a steering committee was proposed consisting of five members – Chappell, Pole, Spottiswoode, Hullah and Stainer, Stainer agreeing to act as Honorary Secretary *pro tem.*

At the next meeting, on 22 April, which was chaired by Pole, it was agreed to

99 J. Stainer, 'Inaugural Address to the Twenty-First Session [of the Musical Association]', *Proceedings of the Musical Association* 21 (1894–5), xiii.

100 Musical Association Minute Book 1874–5, *GB-Lbl* Add. MS 71010.

write to other influential musicians, scientists and professionals – Charles K. Salaman, Manuel Garcia, Bosanquet, Alexander J. Ellis, Charles Wheatstone, Edward
Dannreuther, Helmore, Barnby, Goss – which gave rise to a third meeting in the
Board Room of the South Kensington Museum on 29 May. At this stage the Society was ready to have its first constitutional committee meetings, which took place
in June and July at Stainer's residence in Upper Montague Street.

At the meeting in July the committee agreed to put two provisional names
before its members – 'The Musical Society of Gt Britain' and 'The Musical Scientific Society' – but at the next meeting, in August at the residence of Salaman (a
former founder of the Musical Society of London who had taken over the responsibility of Honorary Secretary after Stainer had resigned due to work pressures),
the definitive title of 'Musical Association' ('for the investigation and discussion
of subjects connected with the Science and Art of Music') was established, and
Ouseley appointed as the Association's first president. By the time the first official
meeting took place, on Monday, 2 November 1874 at 4.30 p.m. in the Beethoven
Rooms at 27 Harley Street, Cavendish Square, the Association had a President, five
Vice-Presidents (Grove, Hullah, Macfarren, Spottiswoode and Tyndall), a committee, on which Stainer sat with eight others, and seventy-nine members.

On 5 April 1875, with Ellis in the chair, Stainer delivered the first of his five
papers to the Association. Just as *A Theory of Harmony* had been driven by a desire
for pragmatism and simplicity, 'On the Principles of Musical Notation' focused
on questions of clarity and practicality through a comparison of stave notation
and Tonic Sol-fa, in which Stainer attributed advantages to both systems, and
even suggested that different systems for vocal and instrumental music might be
desirable:

> Do we require one and the same system of notation for voices and instru-
> ments? I think not: for this reason: I believe that in ninety-nine cases out of
> every hundred, the first impulse of a singer is, when a vocal part is placed
> before him, to consider the *relations* of the sounds to the key-scale, and to
> each other. I am equally certain that an instrumentalist instinctively looks
> upon a note as representing a *locality*: if he is a pianist, it represents to him
> the position of a certain black or white key; if a violinist, the position his
> finger should take on a string.[101]

However, in concluding that the 'letter' system for voices and the 'stave' system for
instruments were well suited, and even advocating the publication of oratorio vocal
scores where the vocal parts were printed in Tonic Sol-fa and the accompaniment

---

[101] J. Stainer, 'On the Principles of Musical Notation', *Proceedings of the Musical
Association* 1 (1874–5), 102.

in stave notation (an opinion formed no doubt by his experience of the RAHCS, where many of the singers read from Sol-fa), he ultimately recognised, through musical examples, that the 'letter' system of Sol-fa was too limited for the notation of instrumental music, its limitations being especially exposed by the rhythmical and chromatic complexities of contemporary works. Nevertheless, Stainer remained a devotee of Sol-fa as an educational tool (he remained convinced of the value of Curwen's 'movable Doh' system – rather than Hullah's 'fixed Doh' – all his life), believing it to be a sound basis for the teaching of simple music and as preliminary system for those 'aspiring to reach the higher branches of the art.'[102] But, having concluded that the stave system presented greater potential for the music of contemporary composers, Stainer imparted one further possible notational method which could obviate the need for the present awkward system of accidentals: 'This can be easily done by using *round* notes only for naturals or normal sounds, *diamond* notes for sharpened sounds, *square* notes for flattened sounds. No other alteration need be made in the present system.'[103] According to Stainer, a version of the proposed system had been tried in both England and America 'with marked success', though like his *Theory of Harmony*, it never achieved any practical currency.

The institution of the Musical Association undoubtedly reflected a coalescing of interest in musical 'science' that had been latent in Britain for many years, but which now provided a focus and momentum which other initiatives had lacked. In the wake of the Association's foundation came the timely publication in early 1876 of *A Dictionary of Musical Terms* by Novello, edited by Stainer and his former Magdalen and now St Paul's colleague, Barrett,[104] a single volume which, besides superseding outdated efforts by Thompson (his *Dictionary of Music*) and J. A. Hamilton (his *Dictionary of 1,000 Musical Terms*), became for future decades a standard handbook for pedagogical institutions, especially the emerging Training Colleges, and which was published in several editions (the last of which Stainer, after Barrett's death in 1892, edited alone in 1898). The dictionary was aimed at both the musical student and the interested amateur; articles of moderate length not only attempted to explain a broad variety of terms in a straightforward, unelaborate manner, across a surprisingly ambitious spectrum – ranging from acoustics to musical forms, tonality, plainchant, copyright law, antiquarianism, notation, temperament, organology and human physiology – but also with a persuasive scientific earnestness that lent the study of music and its extensive reservoir of knowledge a new gravity of purpose and application.

[102] Ibid., 103.

[103] Ibid., 104.

[104] After being an Assistant Vicar Choral at St Paul's, Barrett was promoted to Vicar Choral in the spring of 1876 after Francis resigned for a fixed pension.

Stainer and Barrett provided a large proportion of the articles themselves, but for others they invited national experts to contribute. Among these was Stainer's colleague from St John's College, Oxford, R. H. M. Bosanquet, who had given one of the opening papers at the first session of the Musical Association on 'Temperament' (which, incidentally had referred to Stainer's *Theory of Harmony)* and a keen member of the organisation; John Francis Bulley (a one-time chorister at Magdalen and undergraduate at the college in the early 1860s), a prominent London barrister, provided articles on 'Licensing' and 'Copyright'. F. Champneys, a former pupil of S. S. Wesley in Winchester and brilliant natural scientist at Brasenose College, Oxford between 1866 and 1870, was regarded as the finest musician in the medical profession and, as a doctor at St Bartholomew's Hospital, provided articles on the 'Ear', 'Larynx' and 'Laryngoscope', as well as assistance with the physiology of the hand for 'Fingering'. A. E. Donkin, son of the late Savilian Professor of Astronomy at Oxford and himself a Fellow at Exeter College, wrote the article on 'Acoustics', while, along with Champneys and Bosanquet, another prominent member of the Musical Association, the phonetician and mathematician, A. J. Ellis, furnished an article on 'Duodene'. Other colleagues who assisted, from the world of music – W. Chappell ('Ballads', 'Greek Music' and old systems of 'Notation'), Thomas Helmore ('Plainchant'), Gadsby ('Form') and W. H. Monk ('Hymn Tunes') – all reflected the present juncture of Stainer's career in church music, *Hymns Ancient & Modern*, scholarship and the Musical Association, while his association with Hullah ('Nomenclature'), and more so William Gray McNaught ('Tonic Sol-fa'), lately a student at the Royal Academy and well known for his choir conducting at the Bow and Bromley Institute, would, within a few years, have a profound effect on the expansion of his professional horizons.

In the first four years of his appointment at St Paul's, Stainer was naturally pre-occupied with the practical considerations of organ-playing, weekly practices (for both the choir and Special Sunday Evening volunteers), and a more disciplined planning of the music. This, as has already been mentioned, soon provoked him into the production of works to suit both Chapter's liturgical reforms as well as his own insistence on the amelioration of standards. With a view to assisting George Martin, who had been employed as his assistant in 1876, and whose responsibility it was to train the boys, he edited and revised Richard Mann's *A Manual for Singing* (first published in 1866), a primer especially directed at the training of cathedral choristers. To meet the requirements of St Paul's more regular use of choral communion, he produced the *Choir Book of Office to Holy Communion* (which included Merbecke's service as well as a harmonised Confession and Lord's Prayer) and other important functional music, which included the now famous 'Sevenfold Amen', composed in October 1873, the Ferial Preces, Responses and Litany (published in 1886), the Preces and Responses with harmonised confession

(Tallis) as used at Ely (again published many years later in 1900), and a setting of the *Miserere* (Psalm 51), also written in 1873. Specifically for use in the Tuesday service of Passion week to precede the performance of the *St Matthew Passion*, this was a setting of the 'Tonus Regalis' (an adaptation of 'Tonus peregrinus') in which solo recitation from the priest was interspersed by variegated (often elaborately chromatic) versions for the choir, culminating in an ornate finale of imitative counterpoint and double-choir antiphony. He assisted, along with S. Flood Jones, Turle, the Rev. J. Troutbeck and Barnby, with the pointing of the *Cathedral Psalter*, a widely used publication which included some of Stainer's chants. This publication, which foreshadowed the *Cathedral Psalter Chant Book* (with the same editors), came with the ringing endorsements of the Deans of St Paul's and Westminster Abbey. This may have had some currency at St Paul's, but it was superseded by the publication in 1878 of the *St Paul's Cathedral Chant Book*, which signalled, essentially after Webber's retirement in 1876, a more properly conceived and well-ordered schedule of chants for psalms and canticles to which Stainer had grown accustomed at Magdalen.

Stainer's production of chant material was matched by a similar industry in the way of hymn tunes. Written in 1873, for the London Church Choirs Association, 'Rest', a fine tune, was one of sixteen tunes to be included in the revised edition of *Hymns Ancient & Modern*, though copyright difficulties, caused by Stainer giving copyright to the Choirs Association, led to severe difficulties for the chief editor, Sir Henry Baker.[105] Constructed almost exclusively on a three-note descending motive, 'Rest' is a particularly cogent example of how Stainer would studiously develop his melodic ideas within the genre of the hymn. This is not only evident from the ubiquity of the three-note motive (where even the platitude of the final cadence seems to take on motivic significance), but also in the musical 'enjambments' at the ends of lines two and three where the motive is chromatically extended to five notes (Example 13). Other carefully wrought tunes included 'Author of Life', a setting of John Wesley's famous communion text 'Vespers' for R. Hayes Robinson's evening hymn (which Parratt was to set so effectively some years later), 'Lux' for the morning hymn 'Light of Light! Enlighten me', 'St Francis Xavier' for Caswall's translation 'My God, I love Thee', 'The roseate hues', somewhat reminiscent of Dykes's manner of dividing the hymn into two contrasting metrical sections, and 'Sebaste', using Keble's famous translation from the Greek 'Hail, gladdening Light') in a setting characterised by the chant-like recitation of the first and second lines. The fifteen tunes composed for *Hymns Ancient & Modern* constituted the lion's share of Stainer's output in this genre between 1872 and 1876,

---

[105] See letters from R. Murray to Sir Henry Baker and Stainer to Sir Henry Baker, April–May 1875, Canterbury Press (Norwich).

Example 13. Hymn tune: 'Rest'

but he was commissioned to produce two tunes for *Song of Praise*, one for the *New Mitre Hymn Book*, one, 'A Child's Evensong', for *The Sunlight of Song*, a collection of hymns and moral songs profusely illustrated with engravings by the Brothers Dalziel, published in 1875, and 'Stella in oriente', a setting of W. J. Irons' carol 'Star of Heaven, new glory beaming', which appeared in Chope's *Carols for Use in Church* in 1877.

Between 1873 and 1876 Stainer produced six anthems. The most substantial of these was a setting of verses from Psalm 47 and Isaiah, 'O clap your hands', a multi-sectional anthem written for the Eleventh Annual Festival of the Richmond and Kingston Church Choral Association; it was later orchestrated with Stainer's permission by Battison Haynes. The strongest music lies in the sturdy opening and in the attractive, limpidly flowing semichorus ('They that wait upon the Lord') whose inventive use of imitation and effortless lyricism rivals that of 'How beautiful upon the mountain'. The closing fugue, by comparison, is somewhat mundane. In 1874 three anthems came from his pen. The first, an unpublished short anthem for solo tenor and choir, 'Rogate quae ad pacem sunt Hierusalem', written in March, was probably composed for the annual Convocation for the Province of Canterbury at St Paul's which was always given in Latin. For the short Easter anthem, 'They have taken away my Lord', the juxtaposition of the opening solo lament in G minor and the dramatic chorus in D major ('O Death, where is thy sting?') has a Handelian directness and simplicity (the contrasts of 'Since by man came death' from *Messiah* come to mind). The heart-rending circumstances under which this miniature essay was composed were explained in a letter by Elizabeth Stainer to J. S. Egerton some years later, after its completion at the end of December 1874:

> The little Anthem which has charmed you as it has many others was written on the night of Dec 30 74. In the early morning of that day our little Harry [Frederick Henry], a sweet curly headed boy was taken from us by Scarlet Fever – aged 2 years and 3 months.
>
> I was quite prostrate from grief and nursing and went early to bed. My husband sat up late, and the thoughts of a joyful resurrection suggested what you now see on paper. I naturally think it very lovely, but it has touched others very remarkably, and one or two letters from America we have which show what singular influence it has had.
>
> You now have its history. I do not think I ever told it before – as it is not a thing one mentions – but your letter draws it from me.
>
> With our kind regards and best wishes for your Easter day (we shall think of you doing the Anthem).[106]

Published not long before this affecting miniature was composed, the Christmas anthem, 'O Zion, that bringest good tidings', appeared as the first of many supplements to the *Musical Times*. It is cast in a simple ternary structure, the outer sections (setting the familiar text from Isaiah) drawing much of their classical 'minuet' character from Attwood. In marked contrast, however, the central section (setting two verses of text from the medieval hymn 'Of the Father's Love begotten') is a gentle 'Pastorale' with a simple repetitive, almost folk-like melody (Example 14) accompanied by the traditional Baroque timbres of oboe and flute stops on the organ. 'Hosanna in the highest', composed for Advent Sunday, dates from 1875. Clearly intending to ape the manner of a short cantata (more overtly after Mendelssohn rather than Bach), the bipartite anthem concludes with a chorale (setting the third verse of the Advent hymn 'O Heavenly Word, Eternal Light' compiled from the Latin) as a solemn apotheosis to the lyrical 'concerto' structure of the first section and its more declamatory closing paragraph, replete with more striking chromaticisms. 'I desired wisdom', a counterpart for Epiphany and written for the Sion College Choral Union festival service on 16 January 1877, follows a comparable path in concluding with a verse from 'Adeste Fideles' ('Sing choirs of angels'), the other constituent parts of its tripartite form – an opening penitential

---

[106] Letter from Elizabeth Stainer to J. S. Egerton, 13 March 1879, in private possession (JRS).

Example 14. Anthem: 'O Zion, that bringest good tidings' ('Pastorale' central section)

chorus which moves from F sharp minor to a more reconciled A major, and a Mendelssohn-inspired trio in F major for trebles – are more substantial as is the conspicuous role of the organ in the second section.

It is stated by Fellowes that 'after eighteen months in office [at St Paul's] he had a bad nervous breakdown. On the Isle of Wight, where he went for a rest, someone saw him looking desperately ill and thought he would not get over this breakdown.'[107] Eighteen months into Stainer's appointment would bring us to the last few months of 1873, at which point there is absolutely no evidence for Stainer's absence in any of the extant sources – there is nothing in either the minutes of Chapter, or the Saturday weekly chapter meetings, or in Frost or the press who, given their interest in the choral progress of the metropolitan cathedral, would surely have reported such an event. It is possible, however, that the 'breakdown' may have been confused with a serious accident that occurred while Stainer was playing tennis at Tenbury on Michaelmas Day (29 September) 1875, when a ball struck his good eye. For a while Stainer attempted to resume his duties at St Paul's but it was evident by October that things were not satisfactory, for Martin was taking Stainer's place at the organ,[108] while Fred Walker undertook

[107] Fellowes, 'Sir John Stainer', 7.
[108] See Weekly Chapter Minutes, 16 October 1875, GB-Lsp.

choir practices.[109] Through the season of Christmas Stainer attempted to fulfil his duties as best he could, and he was greatly touched by a presentation in the Chapter House on 30 December of an ivory and gold baton made by members of the Special Evening Service Choir 'upon his recovery from the serious accident which had for a short period incapacitated him from the performance of his professional duties'.[110] But by January 1876 his condition had not improved, and he was advised to take leave of absence, during which time Martin took control and Barnby was asked to conduct the *St Matthew Passion* on 11 April. On 2 February, as Elizabeth Stainer recorded in her diary, 'We left home in consequence of wishes and orders of the Dean of St Paul's, Canon Gregory and Mr Power, Occulist, that my husband should give his eye and his brain entire rest and change of scene, and with every hope that the sight would become strengthened and fit for work on our return.'[111]

Since their marriage the Stainers had developed a taste for travel and sightseeing, and had, since their days at Magdalen, spent time in Scotland and Wales, in wild places away from the hubbub. In 1876 they decided, probably for the first time, to look to the Continent for an extended 'tour', one that so whetted their appetite that they often took the opportunity to travel abroad whenever the chance presented itself. They travelled to Paris, where they spent much time visiting the city's churches and witnessing the desolation of the Tuileries and Hotel de Ville after the Franco-Prussian war; they also visited the opera, and Stainer called on Gounod at his home at 17 Rue de la Rochefoucauld. From Paris they moved on to Lyons and then Marseilles, where they took a boat to Algiers on 8 February. After ten days in Algeria they left for Malta before moving on to Sicily and Naples. From Naples they travelled to Rome, where they often visited St Peter's to hear the music and for Stainer to satisfy his curiosity as to the present choral standards. 'We went to St Peter's at 9.30 to hear High Mass', Elizabeth Stainer recalled, 'and came to the conclusion that the musical part of the service was greatly inferior to our own at St Paul's – only about 12 men sang, and the chanter was very much out of tune.'[112] For more than two weeks the couple resided in Rome before moving on, spending time in Siena, Florence (where they attended High Mass in the cathedral), Pisa, Leghorn, and Bologna, before arriving in Venice. But, in spite of alluring sights, Venice was cold and damp, and they soon felt compelled to travel on to Milan, whose climate they greatly preferred. On 27 April, having been away for three

---

109 After Martin's appointment it was clearly established that, while he undertook the training of the choristers, he, like Cooper before him 'would have nothing to do with the gentlemen of the Choir'. (See Frost, *Early Recollections of St Paul's Cathedral*, 60.)

110 *Musical Times* 17 (March 1876), 362.

111 Diary of Elizabeth Stainer, in private possession (JRS).

112 Ibid., 19 March 1876.

months, the Stainers began their return, through Turin, Switzerland (which they loved and where they returned in July 1879),[113] and then Paris, which they reached on 6 May, though on arriving in London Stainer desisted from conducting a selection from *Elijah* for the service for the Sons of the Clergy on 17 May, leaving the task to Walker.[114] He was, however, back in harness by 27 May, when he conducted Handel's *Dettingen Te Deum* (with Mendelssohn's accompaniments) on the safe return of the Prince of Wales from India.

During Stainer's absence Webber retired and the Dean requested that William Sparrow Simpson, a minor canon in the cathedral, become the new Succentor. It was an inspired choice. Sparrow Simpson was the epitome of the clerical scholar. He was a bibliophile, librarian and an indefatigable cataloguer of the St Paul's archives (a study of the volumes of the St Paul's library today bears witness to his extraordinary energy), but, most significant for Stainer, he was a good organiser, a keen musician and a good amateur pianist (with a wide knowledge of both sacred and secular music and an equally broad musical palette to match) who took a natural interest in the cohesion of the choir:

> This special gift showed itself constantly at the weekly rehearsals of the full choir. He always attended them, he himself read the roll-call, checked the attendance, and superintended the general arrangements ... Attracted and influenced by Dr Simpson's hard work, amiability, culture, and sense of justice, the members of the musical staff became bound together by a firm resolution to do their very best in their respective spheres.[115]

Years later, when Stainer was asked by Sparrow Simpson's son, W. J. Sparrow Simpson, to comment on the musical role the new Succentor had played in the cathedral, he was effusive in his tribute:

> The work of Dr Simpson as succentor of St Paul's Cathedral calls for more than a passing notice. When he succeeded the Rev T. Fynes-Webber, the musical condition of the Cathedral was still more or les unsettled, and it may safely be said that it required a hand at once firm and kind to secure that stability which alone could ensure the *future* of music in St Paul's. Had Dr Simpson been liable to fads and fancies, or had taken a narrow view of

---

[113] See the diary of Mrs Elizabeth Cecil Stainer, in private possession (JRS). During their holiday in 1879 the Stainers (together with Helen, Edith and Dean Church) also spent time in Strassburg, where they observed the rebuilding of the cathedral after the Franco-Prussian War.

[114] Frost, *Early Recollections of St Paul's Cathedral*, 64.

[115] W. J. Sparrow Simpson, *Memoir of the Rev. W. Sparrow Simpson* (London: Longmans, Green & Co., 1899), 72.

the function and position of cathedral music, my own humble efforts to provide St Paul's with a service worthy of its historical prestige and architectural grandeur would have been utterly fruitless. But Dr Simpson's views on cathedral music were both broad and eclectic. By broad, I mean that he did not pledge himself to introduce any special school of music to the exclusion of other schools; by eclectic, I mean that if any composition or work was in his belief capable of edifying worshippers, he adopted it, regardless of any suggestions thrown out by outsiders that the composer did not perhaps belong to the first rank. Hence it was that, within St Paul's could be heard music ranging from Redford to Sullivan, from the early part of the sixteenth century to the latter part of the nineteenth.[116]

In his eulogy of Sparrow Simpson, Stainer was, in effect, applauding an aesthetic standpoint which he himself had articulated publicly on two occasions at the Church Congresses, at Leeds in 1872, and at Brighton in 1874.[117] At Leeds Stainer had been noticeably voluble in his criticism of those succentors and organists who revealed 'a tendency to run into one groove, to become adherents and admirers of only one style or school of music'.[118] His reproach was aimed in many directions – to the stereotypical repertoire of eighteenth-century music at St Paul's, to 'old favourites', which, he contended, 'in nine cases out of ten [were], ... very poor specimens of music';[119] to the criticism of the press; to the polarisation of the 'Gregorianisers' who believed that plainchant and 'old' polyphony was the only pure ecclesiastical ideal for music; and to the acolytes of Crotch's tripartite aesthetic code (significant in that Ouseley, also a speaker directly before Stainer at the Congress, had devoted his paper to a veneration of those very principles). But, perhaps more radically, Stainer was inviting his audience to consider an entirely new evaluation of church music and its function:

It will be said, "It is easy enough to say, 'Select music new and old,' but what is meant by old? Do you include Gregorian tone and tunes under *old*, or eject them as obsolete?" It may be urged also, "If you include Gregorian music, you should, to be consistent, also have a little descant sometimes, and a little diaphony, with its perpetual succession of consecutive fifths and octaves." This objection cannot be satisfactorily answered until a definite test of the value of church music be found. What makes church music good

[116] Sparrow Simpson, *Memoir*, 66–7.
[117] Stainer's lecture at Sion College on 15 January 1874 (see *Life and Letters of John Bacchus Dykes*, 188) on 'the Ecclesiastical Style in Music', now missing, probably discussed the same principles.
[118] J. Stainer, 'Church Music', *Proceedings of the Church Congress* (Leeds, 1872), 334.
[119] Ibid., 335.

or bad? What criterion can we apply to it which will enable us to gauge its value? This is the test, the only test. *It must edify*.[120]

In rejection of Crotch's *dicta*, Stainer presented a different set of aesthetic categories: the *simple harmonic* in which he identified two sub-categories (one in which melody held sway over harmony which included harmonised accompaniment to Gregorian chant; the other where harmony was the predominant factor); the *contrapuntal* (which, Stainer, contended, possessed not only 'rare merits, but also some serious defects' in its potential obscuring of the text); the *dramatic* (a style he attributed largely to modern composers, though pointing out that Purcell and Humfrey were genuine contributors), in which he warned against excessive 'effect', constant key-change 'and a forced departure from musical form';[121] and, last, the *composite* style, entailing a combination of the previous three. With the last style in mind, he, not surprisingly, took the opportunity to proselytise the virtues of performing oratorios in church, particularly since this brought many of those secular (instrumental) advances of the nineteenth century within the confines of the cathedral. 'I assure you', he asserted, 'the Church will have no chance of success, till she knows how to produce the oratorio, the Passion music, the cantata, with all their proper instrumental accompaniments, within her precincts.'[122]

At Brighton in 1875, with the aid of choral examples, Stainer sought to reinforce his views with an historical narrative of church music through the ages, highlighting Tye's 'Laudate nomen Domini' (exhibiting a sparing use of imitation – 'just enough to give variety to its rhythm, not enough to mar its simplicity'), Palestrina's 'O bone Jesu' (though believing that a proper performance of this music, with its 'obsolete' modal scales was impossible without a specially trained group of singers), Leo's 'Tu es sacerdos', the music of both Handel and Bach, Mozart's 'Ave verum', Crotch's 'Holy, holy, holy', Goss's 'O Saviour of the World' (believed by Stainer to be among his finest works), Gounod's 'Jesu, our Lord' and Sullivan's 'We have heard with our ears', and at the same time denouncing the unsuitability of the seventeenth-century French style for cathedral music and the stultifying influence of Crotch at Oxford. From this emerged his recommendation to precentors of cathedrals: 'let your selection of music be a chronological series of works of art, giving no preference to new as against old, or old as against new; remember the catholicity of art, and draw freely from all wells.' It was the voice of a musical liberal who eschewed the nineteenth-century zeal for historicism and its search for a new 'purity'.

A man of catholic tastes, Stainer unequivocally rejected the more extreme Ecclesiologists who, like their European counterparts, the Cecilians, petitioned for

---

[120] Ibid.
[121] Ibid., 338.
[122] Ibid., 339.

a return to a 'true church music', away from the theatrical secularism of Romanticism.[123] This is evident in his general dislike of Thibaut's *Purity in Musical Art*, which was published in English translation by W. H. Gladstone in 1877, though, as the translator made it clear, his motives were designed to encourage a contemporary interest in 'old music':

> I fear you are not pleased with Thibaut.
>
> In whatever you say with regard to him pray bear in mind that his specific complaints refer to the state of things 50 years ago, and it is not contended that they are to any great extent applicable now. The revived interest in old music is, in my view, a justification rather than a refutation of Thibaut's argument – at least <u>post hoc</u>, if not <u>propter hoc</u>.
>
> I want the book to act as an encouragement to curiosity in old music, not as a censure on the existing state of things.[124]

In fact Stainer fully endorsed 'the revived interest in old music' (as his future antiquarian activities would affirm). He was undoubtedly engrossed by the music of Palestrina, whose music was enjoying a major renaissance in Europe, and he had always taken a keen interest in plainsong and the work of plainsong scholars;[125] yet, though he was undoubtedly aware of those elements of 'taste' appropriate to ecclesiastical music, his ultimate aim was to challenge those who sought morally or artistically to define (and thereby delimit) the 'true' nature of the church repertoire.

It is not known precisely whether Stainer's musical *Weltanschauung* had a major influence on Sparrow Simpson, but the new Succentor's views chimed remarkably happily with those of his organist, as is manifestly evident from the first of Sparrow Simpson's musical reports made biennially during his time in office:

---

[123] Though Stainer dissociated himself with the more extreme manifestations of the Ecclesiological movement, he nevertheless remained a Vice-President of the St Paul's Ecclesiological Society from 1879 until his death.

[124] Letter from W. H. Gladstone to Stainer, 17 November 1877, *GB-Lbl*. Stainer's copy of Thibaut survives with annotations (*GB-Lbl* Music.Misc. 7898a9).

[125] Stainer's practical interest in plainsong and plainsong scholarship is supported not only by his *Gregorian Tones* of 1867, his harmonisations of the Parisian Tones (*c.* 1869) and the *Miserere* (1873), but by his surviving copy (in private possession) of *Hymnarium Sarisburiense* published in 1851 (signed and dated '1874') which contains numerous annotations comparing versions of the hymns with Helmore's *Hymnal Noted* (1851–4) and the Sarum Hymnarium of 1555 in Magdalen College Library. He also went on to publish numerous practical fauxbourdon editions with organ accompaniment such as the *Canticles of Church Arranged to Gregorian Tones* (*c.* 1876–8) and his harmonisations of Merbecke.

Any one who will take the trouble to glance over the list of Composers' names, and, still more, who will read the list of works themselves, will see that the principle upon which the Music Bills have been constructed has been that of pure eclecticism. And this principle, as I conceive, needs no defence. I have yet to learn that any period of Church Music can claim to be regarded as the Augustan Age, or that any date can be fixed of which it may be said to the ecclesiastical musician, "Hitherto shalt thou come, but no further." Whatever is really good in Church music, of whatever age, by whatever composer, I claim as our rightful heritage. To restrict selection to the music of any particular age or country would be as wise an act, as to refuse to employ the railway or the electric telegraph, because they did not exist a century or two ago. Equally unwise would it be for a Succentor to limit himself to the ponderous volumes of Boyce and Arnold, or even to the copious writings of the Anthem composers of the eighteenth century.[126]

Even before Stainer had returned to London, Sparrow Simpson grasped the opportunity of having several pieces of Gounod sung (which included two pieces for which even Stainer pronounced reservations). This entailed concentrated bouts of application and note-learning to which both the men and boys were largely unaccustomed, but in the new regime, reinforced by Stainer's return, the choir took to its unfamiliar and exacting task with eagerness. Sparrow Simpson's reports were essentially directed at the press and public (they were sent to anyone who requested one, free of charge), but they also chronicled a sea-change of attitude towards the choir at St Paul's in which music at the metropolitan cathedral was rapidly assuming iconic status and becoming a choral model which other cathedral establishments were choosing to emulate. Sparrow Simpson was quick to credit Stainer with the choir's new *esprit de corps* and 'acknowledged in the handsomest terms the invaluable co-operation of ... the organist of the Cathedral, to whom is so largely due the credit for the marked improvement in the character of the music during the last few years.'[127] Stainer duly returned the compliment, and considered that 'without Dr Simpson's help, my work would have been an impossibility. He drew up, of course, all the lists of music to be sung, but he always submitted them to me for my approval, and was most anxious to receive any criticisms or listen to any hint.'[128]

Sparrow Simpson's tastes were indeed eclectic, and he was just as ready to embrace music of foreign climes as those from home. He did little to change the

---

[126] W. Sparrow Simpson, *A Year's Music in St Paul's Cathedral, Easter 1876 – Easter 1877* (London, 1877), 5.

[127] *Musical Times* 18 (March, 1877), 222.

[128] Sparrow Simpson, *Memoir*, 70–1.

repertoire left by Webber, but he was quick to expand in every direction. During Sparrow Simpson's first year a ten-week cycle of canticles was imposed; by 1883 this had become a cycle over sixteen weeks. The number of Communion services doubled after 1881; Morning Services increased from forty-five to fifty-seven, and Evening Services from fifty-five to seventy-nine.[129] Moreover, with the publication of the St Paul's Cathedral Chant Book in 1878, chants for the psalms enjoyed a more ordered exposition.

For the anthems Sparrow Simpson, with Stainer's assistance, had Chapter invest in large quantities of music which were bound into stout volumes. They drew heavily on Gounod, Spohr and Mendelssohn (whose works numbered, twenty-seven, thirty-one and sixty-seven by Sparrow Simpson's retirement in 1885).[130] There was, of course, music by Handel and Bach (whose music was still a relatively new sound to congregational ears), as well as Graun (his passion music), Haydn, Mozart and Schumann, and one could also hear movements from Brahms' A German Requiem and Spohr's Last Judgment, a work which became a third major fixture in the cathedral on the second Tuesday of Advent from 1878, sung without a conductor and with the orchestra represented by Stainer's presence at the organ. Indeed, Stainer's virtuoso realisation of Spohr's orchestra, especially in the 'Sinfonia' drew particular approbation from the critics, and, in many ways, symbolised his 'coming of age' and of the pre-eminence with which he was thereafter unswervingly regarded:

> and last, but by no means least, the accompaniments were played by Dr Stainer. Few of those present will easily forget his splendidly brilliant, and well-judged rendering of the Symphony in C minor, which forms such a grand introduction to the second part of the Oratorio. Our feeling at the close of this performance was that the Cathedral authorities, as well as those who usually attend St Paul's, might be not only satisfied but proud of both organ and organist.[131]

Goss's music, so much admired by Stainer, held its place, as did excerpts from Sterndale Bennett's Woman of Samaria, Attwood's well-known miniatures and Sullivan's anthems, especially sections from The Prodigal Son and The Light of the World. Much of the music from the volumes of Boyce and Arnold fell into disuse (in spite of calls for its inclusion by Elvey in 1877),[132] as did the music of Greene,

---

[129] Storey, 'The Music of St Paul's Cathedral, 51.

[130] Ibid., 50.

[131] Musical Times 20 (January 1879), 24. It is presumed that Stainer used his own arrangement of Spohr's Sinfonia arranged and published by Novello.

[132] See W. J. Gatens, Victorian Cathedral Music in Theory and Practice (Cambridge: Cambridge University Press, 1986), 64.

Wise, Blow and a good deal of Purcell. Like Stainer, Sparrow Simpson believed that much of the seventeenth- and eighteenth-century repertoire was ill-suited to the large spaces of cathedrals. Most loathed by Sparrow Simpson, however, was the species of archaic pastiche (for which Ouseley seems to have been a conspicuous culprit), as Stainer corroborated:

> He could not tolerate imitations: he held that a modern composer should write up to date; that he should not face about and turn his back on new possibilities in order to secure the commendation of those who dread the introduction of all that is new as an experiment so dangerous that it ought to be universally shunned. This attitude of Dr Simpson towards highly respectable sham old music caused him to exclude from the Cathedral lists nearly all the compositions of several comparatively recent writers who have borrowed old moulds wherein to cast their thoughts and then have posed as reformers.[133]

For the Sons of the Clergy, the revival of commissioning new canticles continued its momentum; services were either newly composed or newly orchestrated by Barnby, Eaton Faning, E. H. Thorne, Myles Birket Foster, and perhaps most propitiously by the young up-and-coming Stanford, whose B flat Service, issued by Novello in 1879 and first sung in the chapel of Trinity College, Cambridge, had rapidly come to the notice of cathedrals and churches in England and beyond. Stanford's Service in A – his one Evening Service expressly written for choir and orchestral accompaniment – was first sung at St Paul's on 12 May 1880 under Stainer's direction and soon joined its B flat counterpart in cathedral repertoires; both were regularly taken up at St Paul's by 1881.[134] Parry's Evening Service in D (known today as the 'Great' Service), composed in early 1881, was intended for Stanford at Trinity, but it was first sung at St Paul's on 19 February and 2 July 1882 before disappearing permanently from the list.[135] Among the new anthems were Schubert's *Song of Miriam*, Spohr's *God, Thou art great*, Hiller's *Psalm 125* and *A Song of Victory* (all for the Sons of the Clergy).

In December 1877 Chapter decided 'that a carol should be sung after Evensong

---

[133] Sparrow Simpson, *Memoir*, 70.

[134] See Storey, 'The Music of St Paul's Cathedral', 178.

[135] Parry's Service was also sung at Trinity in December 1882 but suffered the same fate, probably because it was performed from single manuscript parts, a manner of performance which was fast becoming outmoded with Novello's printed full octavo vocal scores. In fact, Parry's Service remained in manuscript until 1925, when it was posthumously published in a private edition by Emily Daymond for the St Paul's patronal festival in January 1925 and orchestrated by Charles Macpherson. The Service was eventually published in 1984.

before leaving the choir, during the Octave of Christmas: the words and music to be fixed by the Succentor and the organist'.[136] The music, in a specially published pamphlet of eight carols, was taken from Stainer's published carols, soon to be augmented by a third set in 1878. This collection, which brought the number of carols to seventy, included the usual complement of traditional items, though 'The Coventry Carol' and 'I saw three ships' are perhaps the only ones commonly sung today; the rest were contributed by Bridge, Monk, Prout, J. F. Barnett, Gadsby, Calkin, Brown and Martin, together with J. H. Hopkins' famous 'We three kings'. Most, though by no means all, of Stainer's anthems were included by Sparrow Simpson, notably 'Grieve not the Holy Spirit of God', 'I am Alpha and Omega' for Trinity-tide and 'Let the peace of God rule in your hearts'.

In 1877 Stainer produced two new settings of the Evening Canticles. The first, in 'chant form' was specially composed, as was the anthem 'I desired wisdom', for the festival of the Sion College Choral Union in St Paul's Cathedral on 16 January 1877. The second and arguably his finest setting of the Magnificat and Nunc dimittis, was written for the Fifth Annual Festival of the London Church Choir Association in St Paul's on 8 November 1877. This big-boned music was clearly conceived for a large body of singers, a grand organ and the generous acoustic of St Paul's.[137] One of the most memorable features of the Magnificat is the introduction for the organ alone. Here Stainer presents us with a forceful fanfare-like idea which is supported by an impressive tangential progression from D major (as V of G) to B flat (Example 15a). The thematic idea, which triumphally accompanies the first line of text, is later recapitulated and thereby helps to form the muscular frame of the Magnificat's structure. More important, however, to the organic cohesion of the movement is the precedent of the opening progression for Stainer evidently wished to integrate D major more fully as an 'opposing' tonality. At the point of 'genuflection' ('And Holy is His Name'), a juncture at which Stainer had already shown a propensity for striking key change (as in the A major Service), he modulates to D major (Example 15b). This time, however, D major is no longer purely an agent of tonal contrast and expressive colour; it is now part of a deeper level of structure and provides the means by which the recapitulation of the opening material can be enacted seamlessly. Moreover, D major is also used strategically to announce the gloria (Example 15c), whose bracing and theatrical fugue (note the climactic top B flat for sopranos as the final statement of the subject) is concluded by a majestic closing assertion of the fanfare (marked 'Tromba'), this time in B flat. D major also announces the more truncated gloria of the Nunc dimittis, and although it is not so prominent as a tonality, it nevertheless plays a significant role

---

136 Weekly Chapter Minutes, 1 December 1877, GB-Lsp.

137 Stainer later orchestrated the Evening Service in B flat, but this, like the score of the A major Evening Service, is now missing.

Example 15. Service in B flat: (a) Magnificat (opening progressions);   (b) 'And Holy is His Name' (D major);   (c) 'Glory be to the Father' (D major);   (d) Te Deum (opening)

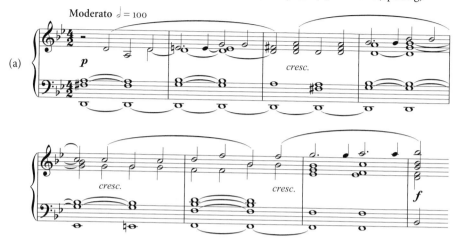

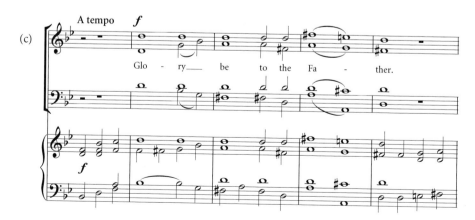

as V of G minor. In the Morning and Communion components of the Service in B flat, published later in 1884, this seminal relationship between B flat and D continued to be a major generative force in a more complex matrix of tonal links between the individual movements. B flat was naturally assigned to the Te Deum. However, the Benedictus, which had in past service settings also been couched in the tonic, was set in D major, while the Communion Service was cast in F major, flanking the Sanctus in A major.

Morning Service		Communion Service				Evening Service	
Te Deum	Benedictus	Credo	Sanctus	Benedictus & Agnus	Gloria	Magnificat	Nunc dimittis
B flat	D	F	A	F	F	B flat	B flat

Clearly, therefore, Stainer took the opportunity to infuse the entire service with the germane third-relationship presented in the Magnificat, and, as Temperley has compellingly argued, the predilection for third-related keys is carried to a point where the schemata closely emulates those of Schubert's sonatas and chamber works.[138] In fact not only do these third relationships exist at the architectonic level of individual movements but at other levels too. The Te Deum, a robust musical structure with well-defined paragraphs, conceived on a large scale, continues to develop the B flat–D axiom of the Magnificat. Indeed, from the outset, D as V of G minor, underpins the first line of text (Example 15d), and it is only after eighteen bars that the first cadence into B flat occurs (and even then it is immediately contradicted by a move back to D). A secondary tonal area, in F major, defines a

---

[138] N. Temperley, 'Ancient and Modern in the Work of John Stainer', in *Nineteenth-Century British Music Studies*, vol. 3, ed. P. Horton & B. Zon (Aldershot: Ashgate, 2003), 111.

new ternary paragraph ('Holy, holy, holy'). This, in turn, yields a restatement of B
flat and another ternary scheme ('Thou art the King of Glory'), and like the opening section it too has a strong inclination towards G (note especially the sole verse
'When Thou tookest upon Thee'). It is only with the closing fughetta ('Let me never
be confounded'), for much of its duration above an extended dominant pedal, that
B flat is unequivocally stated.[139] The Benedictus, in D major, also sets up a tonal
dialectic with its relative, B minor, though Stainer reserved the greatest pathos
for the central verse ('In holiness and righteousness') in B major. For the ternary
structure of the Credo, Stainer created a tonal scheme of F and D, but we are dramatically reminded of B flat in the fanfares ('And He shall come again with glory'),
where D major is unceremoniously juxtaposed with its flat submediant. The Gloria
also makes use of the same tonal scheme as the Credo, with an affecting central
section for solo quartet and chorus in D major. Of the shorter movements, the
Sanctus, in A major, stands as the furthest limit of the third-relationship schema,
and it is as if Stainer intended to emphasise this event by using it as the contrasting tonality in the subsequent Benedictus qui venit. After this 'apogee', A major is
relinquished and for the Agnus Dei, the principle tonal opposition is between F
and D minor.

Such a detailed scheme of tonal interactions abundantly reveals that Stainer was
attempting to bring an element of integration to his service in a manner which was
being practised essentially in secular instrumental music of the time. Moreover,
one also senses that there is a more strongly delineated sense of form to the movements of the B flat service than in early works in the genre. Of course, Stanford
would later explore these same principles of tonal integration in his own services
and extend the 'instrumental concept' where an organic process of thematic development, a cohesive network of cyclic interrelationships and a interdependence
between choir and organ would form a new symphonic style of church music. But
what is clear is that Stainer had already begun to explore these possibilities with
considerable fertility and would continue to do so in the later service music of his
Service in D for men's voices (see Chapter 6).

In the closing years of the 1870s the reputation of Stainer and the choir at St
Paul's began to increase markedly as the cathedral became a focus, as Gladstone
had hoped, for religion and ceremony in the capital. Westminster Abbey followed
suit in 1880 with an augmentation of their own boys and men, and the 'oratorio
fixtures', well established at St Paul's, were also emulated by Bridge's performances
of Bach's *Christmas Oratorio* and orchestral services on Ascension Day, in which

---

[139] In the alternative ending for small choirs, Stainer opted for a truncated reprise of
the opening material, providing us with a final, albeit fleeting encounter with D
(as V of G).

Stainer frequently participated as organist. The aberrant behaviour of the Vicars Choral, if we are to believe the Weekly Chapter minutes, perceptibly dissipated.

The only awkward moments were those created by dissenters protesting against what they perceived as pernicious ritualist practices. One such incident occurred during the singing of the anthem on Easter Eve, when a man stepped forward and over the cord usually drawn across the entrance to the choir. It was thought he would go into the choir to take a seat there, but he walked past the choir (who were singing the anthem from Stainer's *Daughter of Jairus*) and clergy, suddenly put on his hat, and jumped onto the altar, decorated with flowers for Easter, seized the cross and candlesticks and flung them violently to the ground. He was then apprehended by a group of men including some clergy and taken out of the cathedral 'vociferating at the top of his voice', and handed over to the police. Meanwhile the organist and choir went on with the anthem.[140]

The first wedding of the nineteenth century in the cathedral (a rare event since the 1750s) was that of the Lady Mayoress, Miss Ada Louisa White; it took place in August 1877. Stainer presided at the organ and was also present for a second wedding in April 1883 when Dean Church's daughter was married to the Rev. Francis Paget (the future Dean of Christ Church, Oxford). Liddon officiated. For this occasion he also composed a new anthem, 'There was marriage in Cana of Galilee', with an extensive and affecting treble duet, using Paget's words. On a sadder note, Goss died on 10 May 1880. His funeral took place at St Paul's five days later, the choir singing 'If we believe' as a gesture of tribute and respect. Stainer's own personal tribute was to provide an obituary for the *Musical Times*.

During his time at Oxford Stainer's bibliophile tendencies began to develop into a serious preoccupation, and, as numerous letters reveal, in London he became an inveterate visitor to bookshops and antiquarian dealers. Much of his energy was devoted to the gathering of seventeenth-, eighteenth- and nineteenth-century volumes of songs, especially English songs (his collection of carols being an important manifestation of this fascination) as numerous letters readily betray: 'I am much obliged to you for sending the books to me. One however is very imperfect and the other rather expensive. The copy of La Philomele Seraphique sold at a sale lately – only fetched 4/6 – but was resold for 10/6. Could you call here tomorrow evening or on Wednesday evening after your business is over?'[141] In addition to songs, Stainer nurtured a passion for bells and campanology – 'the beautiful art',[142] he once termed it – which inevitably led him to accumulate published texts on the subject, notably William Sottanstall's *Elements of Campanologia* (1867), Edmund

---

[140] *Daily Chronicle*, 26 March 1883.
[141] Letter from Stainer to unknown bookdealer, 18 April [c. 1880], in private possession.
[142] Letter from Stainer to J. E. Haworth, 9 February [1890], *GB-Lsp*.

Beckett Denison's *A Rudimentary Treatise on Clocks, Watches and Bells* (1868) and the Rev. H. T. Ellacombe's *Practical Remarks on Belfries and Ringers* (1871);[143] he was also a great admirer of the Belgian art of carillons. Indeed, such was his enthusiasm that he was invited to be a member of the Antient Society of College Youths, a society of bell ringers in existence since 1637 which numbered among its members – from all walks of life – many of the best change ringers in the country.

Curiously, St Paul's, unlike many of the city churches, such as St Mary-le-Bow, St Giles Cripplegate, St Botolph Bishopsgate, St Sepulchre's, St Bride's and St Dunstan's, lacked a proper ring of bells and chimes for striking the quarter-hours. The issue of acquiring them for the cathedral was raised incipiently in 1872, but more officially in 1875. Stainer was at the forefront of the campaign at the Mansion House meeting on 2 November 1875 to raise funds for the venture, and he served actively on the committee with the Dean of St Paul's, Gregory, Penrose and Sir Edmund Beckett Denison, regarded as an authority on bells and their casting. Dean Church argued that 'no church of its rank on this side of the Alps ... was so deficient in the matter of bells as St Paul's',[144] and the lacuna had been noticed on Thanksgiving Day in 1872, when there were no bells to greet the Queen on her arrival at the cathedral. Furthermore, the deficiency of St Paul's was also opportunely compared with Worcester Cathedral, which had recently acquired a new peal. Stainer suggested that the cathedral 'should have first a good English peal of bells, which would cost about £3,500 and with chiming apparatus £500 additional, and next, if money was forthcoming, that they should establish chimes at an expense of between £3,000 and £4,000 more',[145] a proposal which was subsequently adopted.

An appeal was directed towards the London Livery Companies, and by 1876 a ring of twelve bells had been underwritten with additional assistance from the Corporation of London, Baroness Burdett-Coutts and the Turners' Company, though the scheme of a Belgian style of chimes was abandoned.[146] The task of casting the bells was given to J. W. Taylor & Sons of Loughborough (who had cast the Worcester peal) and specifications were drawn up by Denison. The bells were duly cast and the task of ringing them given to the Antient Company of Youths, who tried them on 4 October 1878. The official opening took place on 1 November with a packed evensong and a large crowd outside ready to hear the first peal.

Before the official opening, controversy erupted through the intervention of the

---

143 See Appendix II of Stainer's *Catalogue of English Song Books* (London: Novello & Co., 1891), 105–7.

144 *The Times*, 3 November 1875.

145 Ibid.

146 £250 was contributed by Chapter, funds which were probably raised by the sale of the Panopticon organ. (See Chapter Minutes, 14 June 1873, *GB-Lsp*.)

Rev. H. R. Haweis, who claiming to have pleaded the cause of bells and carillons in England, pronounced that the bells were out of tune.[147] Denison leapt to the bells' defence and to their English (as opposed to Belgian) manufacturer,[148] and Stainer joined the fray, reluctantly, in November. Already in a letter to Liddon, he had refuted Haweis's reasoning:

> I do not think it necessary to reply to Mr Haweis. I could do nothing more than contradict him by saying that our bells <u>are</u> in tune; this would hardly edify the readers of the 'Times'. His theory about producing a 3–5–8 chord by tapping the bell at different points I believe to be utterly untenable on scientific grounds, especially as he claims to find a major <u>or</u> a minor 3rd. But I will explain what I mean fully when we meet.[149]

Yet Stainer did after all feel compelled to answer Haweis in *The Times* on 7 November.

> The only bell place where a bell should be struck is on the sound bow itself; if the bell is good it will generally show the existence of a third or other harmonious partials; if it is bad, inharmonic partials will abound and the "beats" will result in discord: Would Mr Haweis test a Stradivarius violin by bowing below the bridge? When properly tested on the sound-bow, there will be found a remarkable purity of tone throughout the St Paul's peal. All have a proper admixture of the "third". I confess that I am much surprised that Mr Haweis thinks our bells get sharper as they ascend. He says 11 is sharp with 12, 10 with 11, 8 with 9, 6 and 7 with 8; or rather this is what he should have said; in reality he turned the peal upside down, and rendered his letter well-nigh unintelligible to ringers, calling No. 12, No. 1, and so on.[150]

He was also keen to remind Haweis of his own experience of Belgian carillons, notably of S. Van Aerschodt's at Louvain, which he had personally tested. Haweis was not easily deterred, but a further letter elicited more vituperative replies from Beckett, Canon Richard Cattley (of Worcester Cathedral) and the Rev. Ellacombe; thereafter the matter was dropped.

With the successful installation of the peal of bells, Gregory, who had been energised by the city's support, strove to acquire a further bell for the cathedral, this time a substantial one commensurate with the size and status of the building. An appeal fund was launched in 1880 with money coming once again from the City Livery Companies. At first a bell of about ten tons was envisaged, though

---

[147] *The Times*, 29 October 1878.
[148] *The Times*, 31 October 1878.
[149] Letter from Stainer to Liddon, 4 November [1880], *GB-Okc*.
[150] Letter from Stainer to *The Times*, 7 November 1878.

The Times, evidently quickened by the reforming mindset of the St Paul's chapter, felt that this was too modest. 'It will leave London still far behind Olmütz and Vienna, to say nothing of the unquoted cases of Moscow and Novgorod. If we wish to know what a really big bell ought to be, it is from Moscow that we must take our example.'[151] An order for a 14–ton bell was placed, again, with John Taylor of Loughborough, and the bell was cast on 23 November 1881. With the evident public interest, and perhaps as a means of warding off criticism which the peal of bells had attracted, Stainer, whose attentiveness to the project took him to Loughborough to monitor progress, provided a letter of commentary to *The Times* on 9 December 1881. Besides the narrative of the casting itself, the letter was one of subtle propaganda; 'Great Paul', as it was dubbed, was now bigger than the original specifications, and it would be one of the largest bells in Europe:

> "Big Ben" sinks into comparative insignificance by the side of "Great Paul," now lying comfortably, mouth upwards, in the foundry of Mr Taylor, of Loughborough. She (for I fear "Great Paul," as a bell, must, like all other bells, be considered feminine) will take her rank among the six or eight heaviest bells in Europe. At present her position cannot accurately be assigned, as she has not yet passed the scales; but it will probably lie between the great bell of Olmütz, weighing 17 tons 18 cwt, and that of Vienna (cast in 1711), weighing 17 tons 14 cwt. Three furnaces, one of which was specially built for the purpose, poured out more than 20 tons of molten metal into the gigantic mould of "Great Paul," and after writing off 43 cwt as "overplus" and 8 cwt as "waste," this will leave 350 cwt actually in the mould, or a weight of 17½ tons.

The mould and bell were hoisted out of the pit on 29 November, when the considerable heat had dissipated. Much anxiety attended the breaking of the mould and clay. On 7 December, Stainer together with Penrose, tested it for the first time:

> The casting proved to be as smooth and delicate in surface and outline as if it had been a little "treble" of 5 cwt. I have to-day, in conjunction with Mr F. C. Penrose, been examining the bell and testing its tone. The "skin" of the casting showed no flaw of any kind whatever, and when the tone was produced by swinging a heavy ball of iron against the sound-bow a musical note boomed out which was impressive beyond description. ... The note is E flat, the upper partials B flat, E flat and G being just audible with the sonorous grand-tone. The general appearance of the bell is handsome, and all campanologists should, if able to get to Loughborough, take a walk round here, and also have an eye to the many valuable appliances which Mr Taylor has brought together for the perfecting of his art. The cost of the bell and

151 *The Times*, 16 November 1880.

hoisting it into its place will be about £3,000, a portion of which has already been contributed. It has been decided to use the bell for the first time on Easter Sunday next, when I shall be surprised if Londoners do not realize the fact that "Great Paul" is worthy alike of their ancient city and splendid cathedral.[152]

The bell, in fact, weighed 16 tons 14 cwt 2 qr 19 lbs. Stainer's hope that it would be ready for Easter Sunday proved too optimistic. 'Great Paul' was the largest bell in the country and none like it had ever been swung in Britain before. After experiments at Loughborough in March 1882, and a test ringing in the presence of Stainer, Cattley, Denison and Penrose, a decision was made to hang the bell in the south-west tower, behind the faces of the clock. The bell also had to be transported to London – an operation in itself – which, because of the problems by rail (entailing multiple loadings and unloadings), meant that it had to make the journey by road. It was conveyed on a specially strengthened boiler truck pulled by a steam traction-engine. It left Loughborough on 11 May 1882 and was accompanied along its journey, through Leicester, Northampton, Dunstable and St Alban's, by cheering crowds. It finally reached St Paul's on Monday 22 May. Hoisted into position by a team of Royal Engineers on 30 May, the bell was ready for ringing on 3 June, on which date a special dedication service was sung in the cathedral. After the service clergy and choir climbed the dome stairs and made their way along the south triforium gallery, where, below the stairs leading to the south-west tower's bell-chamber, Gregory performed the dedication. Stainer's final contribution to this auspicious episode in St Paul's reclamation was to provide an extensive and scholarly preface ('About Bells'), amounting to almost fifty pages of historical, scientific and practical detail, to accompany S. J. Mackie's book *Great Paul: from its Casting to its Dedication*, published later in 1882.

The role Stainer played in the acquisition and installation of the bells, and indeed of his defence of English bell-making, reflected the fact that by the late 1870s he had become something of a public figure, not only in church music but in Britain's wider musical fabric. His pre-eminence was expressed in various ways. The Royal Academy of Music made him an Honorary Fellow in 1877, as did the Tonic Sol-fa College after its inception in 1869; he was a Vice-President of the College of Organists, and he was invited, with Pole, to be an Examiner for London University's new musical degree in addition to the two years of examining work he did, at Macfarren's invitation, for the Cambridge Mus.Doc. degree. The Madrigal Society of London, in which he had participated since his days as a chorister, invited him to be their Musical Director in 1878 in succession to Otto Goldschmidt; he enjoyed a similar position with the London Male Voice Club which he held for thirteen years.[153] He was regularly seen at the major choral festivals for the Three Choirs and at Birmingham, where he was particularly encouraging to Parry with his First Symphony in 1882,[154] and was one of a major gathering of eminent British musicians brought together by Lady Folkestone (herself an able amateur musician) on 14 May 1880 at St James's Hall for a charitable performance of Haydn's 'Toy' Symphony, an event given further prestige by the presence of the Princess of Wales. According to Sullivan, he played the triangle, though a photograph taken at the time shows him holding some form of trumpet or horn.[155] He participated in musical deliberations at the Royal Society of Arts, and, after being elected a member of the Philharmonic Society in November 1880,[156] he was invited to appear as soloist in a Handel Organ Concerto. Because of other work pressures, he declined, but he did agree to act as a Director of the Society in 1882 and 1883 (even guaranteeing the sum of £25 towards the Philharmonic's concerts during the 1882–3 season) at a challenging time when the Society was being overshadowed by the whirlwind of Richter's orchestral concerts, where the Austrian's much higher standard of conducting and more ambitious attitude towards the programming of contemporary European works was seriously threatening the prestige of the Philharmonic's reputation.[157] Berger urged him to serve as a Director again in 1885, when the financial predicament of the Society was in the ascendant, but Stainer declined: 'I have been moving about "on duty" – so forgive my delay in writing. I really <u>must not</u> undertake the office of a Director of the Phil: Soc.ʸ. I am so pressed with work that I can scarcely keep pace with it; but thank you all the same for your kindness in suggesting it and offering to vote for me. I am delighted at the financial result of the concerts.'[158]

In 1880 he was invited to act as adjudicator for the Eisteddfod at Caernarvon, an experience that was intriguing as well as exacting:

All is going off well. But my whole day is occupied – the competitions take

---

[153] F. G. Edwards, 'John Stainer', *Musical Times* 39 (May 1901), 305.

[154] Diary of Hubert Parry, 1 September 1882, *GB-ShP*.

[155] A photograph of the time, signed on the back by all participants and dated 11 May 1880 (presumably from a prior rehearsal), lists the presence of the Countess of Folkestone, Stainer, Louis Engel, Julius Benedict, Jacques Blumenthal, Hugo Daubert, William Cusins, Wilhelm Ganz, Barnby, Charles Santley, Sullivan, J. F. Barnett, Charles Hallé, Manns, Carl Rosa, Frederick Cowen, Champneys, Randegger and Henry Leslie.

[156] See letter from Stainer to Stanley Lucas, 18 November 1880. See also Minutes of the Philharmonic Society, 4 December 1880, *GB-Lbl* Loan 84.3/2.

[157] Minutes of the Philharmonic Society, *GB-Lbl* Loan 84 MS 286.

[158] Letter from Stainer to Francesco Berger, 7 June 1885, *GB-Lbl* Loan 48.13/32, fol. 200.

the whole morning till 3 or 3.30 then a long concert begins at 5.30.!!! This morning at Gorsedd of the Bards held in the inside of the Castle I was dubbed a "Pencerdd" or Minstrel under the poetical name of Alaw'r Cyssegr (Musician of the Sanctuary)

The old man who presented me made a pretty speech. The chief bard stands on a large <u>stone</u> round which others form a druid circle. Lots of people were looking on and it was very pretty. I must be off so adieu.[159]

Impressed as he was with the role music played in Welsh society, he nevertheless felt that levels of expert teaching for outstanding talent were absent. As he said to Henry Leslie, who had invited him to stay after the Eisteddfod was over:

It is really very kind of you but I <u>must</u> get back – to do a little work before going to the Gloucester Festival. I hope you are taking a complete rest – it is a wonder to me that you can tear yourself away from Wales and anchor in London instead. I am much struck by the musical talent of the common people here – but there seems to be a sad want of some organisation for giving a <u>high</u> class of musical instruction to those with special gifts – and – the instrumental music (except brass bands!) is <u>below</u> the average.[160]

But perhaps one of the greatest honours Stainer received at this time was, on the recommendation of the Prince of Wales, to act as juror for the musical instrument category of the Paris Exhibition in June and July of 1878. 'I am at work here as a Juror of the Exhibition', he wrote home. 'I have the honor to represent England for Class XII – a great honor no doubt but a decided nuisance.'[161] Required to visit Paris on at least two occasions, he worked alongside a panel of judges (with distinguished French musical scholars such as Gustave Choucquet) in providing an adjudication for Class 13 of the exhibition, which consisted of no fewer than 488 entries.[162] The outright winner of the competition was Cavaillé-Coll for organs, and Stainer had the pleasure of visiting the organ builder to discuss the presence of one of his instruments at a concert of British choral and orchestral music on 17 July conducted by Sullivan. 'With regard to the organist', Cavaillé-Coll wrote, 'I am sorry that you are not able to play the organ on this occasion, but in your absence but I will point out for your attention and that of Mr Sulivan [sic] two of our best organists, that is Mr Widor, organist of St Sulphice or Mr Guilmant, organist of the Trinity. These I believe are the two of the most capable artists that Mr Sulivan

[159] Letter from Stainer to Elizabeth Randall Stainer, 26 August 1880, in private possession (JRS).

[160] Letter from Stainer to Henry Leslie, 27 August [1880], GB-Lcm.

[161] Letter from Stainer to Hume, 17 June [1878], in private possession.

[162] Stainer's signature can be seen with those of the other jurors at the end of the handwritten report, F-Pn NUMM-90424.

would endorse. However, as I would not wish to allow myself to prefer one or the other and that both would be delighted to put themselves at the disposal of Mr Sulivan, I would be obliged to tell you please to write a word to Mr Widor or Mr Guilmant to ask them to play the organ on the occasion of the festival on 17 July.'[163] For this work he, along with Sullivan, was awarded the Legion d'honneur by the French government.[164]

Stainer had further contact with Widor in 1882. The Prince of Wales had asked the French organist if, for the purposes of a festival in London to raise money for his hospital, he would compose a work for organ and orchestra in which Widor might also appear as soloist on the Willis organ in the Albert Hall. Arranging three movements from his organ symphonies (one and three from Symphony No. 6 in G minor, and the middle movement from Symphony No. 2 in D major), Widor produced his *Symphonie pour orgue et orchestre*, Op. 42. Premiered in Paris on 13 April 1882, the work came to London for its first English performance on 20 May in the Albert Hall, where Widor was accompanied by the Royal Amateur Orchestral Society before the royal court and a large audience. Stainer was present for this concert and was unexpectedly called upon to assist in the performance. From this experience he formed a mixed opinion of Widor's abilities as an executant:

> Widor might perhaps be put second to [Best] as a player on the manuals, but only in that one respect; he could not pedal like Best, and as to registration, he was not to be considered in relation to Best. When Widor came over to play at the Albert Hall, I took him up to the organ the afternoon before the concert. On seeing the stops, he at once said he would not attempt to deal with them; he would write on his music the qualities of tone he wanted, and I could work the stops for him. I did so at the concert next day, keeping as much out of sight as possible, and mostly using the pistons.[165]

Of course, Stainer was intimately acquainted with the Albert Hall organ and it undoubtedly confirmed his undying admiration for Willis's handiwork as an organ builder. Week in, week out, Stainer had experience of this with the instrument at St Paul's, but he was quick to recommend Willis to other churches and town halls either interested in refurbishment or new installations. One of these was at a St Paul's living, St Augustine and St Faith, Watling Street, where the boys and men of the cathedral would occasionally supplement the existing choir (usually for the Dedication Festival). The new Willis organ was officially opened on 30 January 1881, and at a special service on 4 February, which included Stainer's

[163] Letter from Cavaillé-Coll to Stainer, 25 June 1878, *GB-Lbl* Add. MS 62121.

[164] Stainer's medal is still retained in private possession (MN).

[165] J. M. Levien, *Impressions of W. T. Best* (London: Novello & Co., 1942), 29.

'O Zion, that bringest good tidings', the composer presided as organist. That same year, as a result of a request by Stainer to Chapter, St Paul's acquired a smaller, two-manual organ. Known as the 'Willis on Wheels' through its placement on a moveable platform,[166] it was probably intended to be mobile. But in reality the organ found a virtually permanent home in the North choir-aisle, where it was used to help the Celebrant at the High Altar stay in tune.[167] In fact, Stainer's endorsement of Willis and his company led some, among them a number of Willis's competitors, to question whether the St Paul's organist's unbridled praise was encouraged by other inducements. A firm, unequivocal rebuttal, in the form of a published letter, followed:

> Mr H WILLIS, being of the opinion that Dr. STAINER's own words will be sufficient refutation of the report to which he alludes, begs to call attention to the following letter, which he prints with the permission of the writer.

> DEAR MR WILLIS,
>
> A report is, I understand, being assiduously circulated to the affect that I have a pecuniary interest in your business, and that this is the real reason why I constantly profess such a high opinion of your skill and success as an Organ-builder. Some assert that I pocket large sums for "Commission," on all orders I send you; others go so far as to say that I positively have a "Share" in the firm.
>
> As a rule I think it is better to allow things of this kind to pass without notice; but, there are some special reasons at the present moment why this report should be publicly and emphatically denied. I shall be glad, therefore, if you will devise some means of letting our Clergy and Musicians know the true facts of the case, which are simply these: I have never received any money as commission or remuneration from you, or in any other shape or form, directly or indirectly; I have never received any presents from you of any kind whatever; I have no sort of pecuniary interest whatever in your business.
>
> I think I ought to take this opportunity of expressing my high sense of the good taste and gentlemanly feeling you have shewn during all our intercourse, in never *offering* me gifts or payment: and although my unwavering advocacy of your claim to be our leading organ-builder involves a considerable sacrifice of time, and makes me the object of frequent petty attacks from your rivals and their clients, I shall still remain your staunch

---

[166] Plumley & Niland, *A History of the Organs in St Paul's Cathedral*, 106–7.
[167] The 'Willis on wheels' was also used more extensively in 1883 when the main organ was cleaned.

supporter, knowing that you have contributed so largely by your natural talent and patient industry to the musical success of our Cathedral and Church Services, and to the Musical influence of our large Halls and Public Buildings.

> Believe me, dear Mr. Willis,
> Yours sincerely,
> JOHN STAINER[168]

Stainer retained his high opinion of Willis throughout his life, endorsing the work of Walker as a second choice. Both organ-builders, as he once told William Barclay Squire, were paragons of high quality in a world where churches often sought to restore their organs on price rather than superiority of workmanship:

> Please consider my note confidential, but pray advise your friend to go to Walker (in preference to the other man), his price may be higher, but his work is first rate and will last out twice the time of cheaper work. I place Walker as only second to Willis.
>
> It is curious that people rebel so, against a high price for the best quality of organ-building! If I asked a man whether he would have a watch at £2 from a Mr Jones or one which would cost £20 at Dent's, he would unhesitatingly choose the latter: but when men are offered a cheap organ, there seems to be an irrepressible temptation to buy it! I could tell many sad stories about cheap organs.[169]

As the regular organist for the RAHCS, Stainer was obliged to attend most of the weekly Monday evening rehearsals at the Albert Hall to accompany the choir. Writing in the 1930s, the blind organist Alfred Hollins attended on one memorable occasion:

> It was the custom then, as it is now, to rehearse every work with organ accompaniment. It requires great skill to arrange some of the bigger works for the organ, and even more to play them. [Harry] Balfour, a pupil of Stainer's, used often to attend the rehearsals, and once took me with him. … Stainer accompaniments were wonderfully fine. Hodge, a fellow pupil of Balfour's under Stainer, was deputy organist, and Balfour told me that Hodge could imitate Stainer's style so perfectly that it was hard to distinguish between master and pupil. The post of organist to the Society has always been a kind of apostolic succession. First was Stainer, the master. His pupil, Hodge, succeeded him,

---

[168] Letter from Stainer to Willis, 20 October 1879, *GB-Lsp* Dugdale 2127.
[169] Letter from Stainer to Barclay Squire, 11 July 1898, *GB-Lbl* Add. MS. 39680, fol. 140.

and was in turn succeeded by Balfour, who has been followed by one of his own pupils.[170]

Barnby's schedule of concerts was appreciably onerous. There might easily be up to nine or more concerts per season, including those organised at short notice. Badly needed holidays were often foregone because of this responsibility, as he explained to his wife:

> Although Sims Reeves did not appear last night – we really had a very fine performance of the Messiah. The Hall was very full; the lowest computation states that 8000 people were present.
>
> As to your delightful proposal that I should come to Ventnor – I am afraid it is no good hoping against hope. I shall have my hands quite full – preparing for the little performances of Jairus at Morrish's Institute – on the 18th of March and our Passion Service on the 23rd. On the 11th and 12th of March I have to be in Cambridge examining candidates for the Doctorate; and – On the 4th of March we produce Hiller's "Song of Victory" and Goetz "By the Waters of Babylon" at the Albert Hall. So you see my time is completely mapped out. I am very sorry as I am getting rather fagged – from extra work and scanty sleep. For the last five or six nights I have not slept more than about 4 hours.[171]

The new works by Hiller and Goetz (who was enjoying a purple period in London – Rosa was staging *The Taming of the Shrew* which Stainer also attended) were not easy for the chorus, and Barnby's inclusion of other novelties, ranging from Verdi's Requiem (which Verdi conducted in London for the first time on 15 May 1875 to a receptive though smaller audience than usual),[172] Macfarren's oratorios *Joseph* (1878) and *St John the Baptist* (1881), Sullivan's *The Martyr of Antioch* (1881), Gounod's *Redemption* (1882), encored by popular demand as at Birmingham the same year, to Berlioz's *Damnation of Faust* (1883) meant that Stainer's role, both as rehearsal and concert organist, was an extremely active one.

Novello, who had by now become Stainer's sole and loyal publisher, continued to issue a series of his anthems, a number of which were printed as supplements to the monthly editions of the *Musical Times*. This was the case with the somewhat Attwoodesque 'Leave us, neither forsake us' for Ascensiontide (1877), 'I am Alpha and Omega' (1878) and the somewhat more imaginative 'Ye shall dwell in the Land'

---

[170] A. Hollins, *A Blind Musician Looks Back: An Autobiography* (Edinburgh: William Blackwood & Sons, 1936), 152–3.

[171] Letter from Stainer to Elizabeth Randall Stainer, 12 February 1880, in private possession (JRS).

[172] Stainer's copy of Verdi's Requiem survives complete with markings from this performance and subsequent performances under Barnby; in private possession.

(also 1877) with its neo-Baroque concerto form in the first section and a second section ('Oh, blessed is that land of God') for treble solo and chorus which is more reminiscent of Goss's admixture of classicism and early romanticism. 'Grieve not the Holy Spirit of God', a full anthem (which can be sung *a cappella*) probably written in or around 1880, is also suggestive of Goss, though the transition between the paragraphs in minor and major modes ('and be ye kind') is much more typical of Stainer's predilection for chromaticism. This is also true of the first part of 'Let the peace of God rule in your hearts' (*c.* 1882) and is much more distinguished than its sturdy but dull fugue. The rather less interesting short anthem, 'Thus speaketh the Lord of Hosts' (also 1880), concluding with part of hymn text translated by James Russell Woodford, Bishop of Ely, also appeared in the *Musical Times* and was one of several anthems by Stainer added to Novello's lengthy series of vocal works published in Tonic Sol-fa notation.

The main focus of Stainer's composition at this time was, however, a first commission from the Three Choirs Festival of 1878 for a sacred cantata, an invitation which undoubtedly added to the prestige that had been gained at St Paul's. The text of *The Daughter of Jairus*, compiled by the composer (with help from his friend H. Joyce), was based on a variety of sources: three of the Gospels (Matthew, Mark and Luke) as well as extracts from Isaiah, Baruch, Wisdom, two letters of St Paul (Ephesians and Romans) and a hymn of Charles Wesley. Stainer's cantata, first performed on 14 September 1878 under the composer's baton (with a young Edward Elgar in the second violins), was first heard in the context of the final service, alongside Ouseley's Magnificat and Nunc dimittis in A, rather than in one of the concerts.

It appears that Stainer conceived the design and content of this short sacred cantata to accommodate the difficulties that were still haunting Worcester after its disastrous débâcle in 1875 when the Dean and Chapter declared that 'musical performances which are unconnected with any religious service, and to which admission is given only by purchased tickets, should no longer take place in the Cathedral.'[173] In fact it transpired that the Dean of Worcester's main objection was to the cathedral becoming a 'carpenter's shop' before and after the festival due to the erection of the platforms. Condemnation rained down from the national press, and as Anthony Boden has eloquently described, 'the "reformed" Festival [consisting of no oratorios, not even *Messiah*] of 1875 went ahead in an atmosphere of civic gloom and anger', without orchestra or soloists – only a series of ill-attended choral services. It was, arguably, the Three Choirs at its lowest ebb, and earned an epitaph from the *Birmingham Town Crier*.[174]

[173] See A. Boden, *Three Choirs: A History of the Festival* (Stroud: Alan Sutton, 1992), 72.

[174] Ibid., 75–6.

By 1878, after festivals had taken place at Hereford and Worcester in the intervening years, the Dean and Chapter wisely capitulated with the assurances that, with prayers before performances of sacred music in the cathedral, concerts could effectively be acts of worship. Even though some criticism suggested that Stainer's cantata should have merited a concert performance, the context of *The Daughter of Jairus*, within a service, seems to have had a powerful influence on its future, for it was to become an immensely popular work for about twenty years. Of an ideal length and moderate technical difficulty, it gained many of its hearings from performances in cathedrals and churches, invariably within the framework of the Anglican liturgy.

There were, of course, exceptions. Stainer presided at the organ when the cantata was sung by the Brixton Choral Society on 27 November 1878, and he participated in performances by numerous choral societies, notably (at the organ) for McNaught's choir at the Bow and Bromley Institute on 4 November 1882 and (as conductor) for the St Augustine Musical Society on 6 May 1886, at which he enjoyed an ovation. McNaught, who often directed the cantata, staged a much larger performance at the Albert Palace on 18 July 1885 with 1,300 singers from twenty-five choirs from in and around London. Stainer's pupil William Hodge, who played the organ, was sanctioned by Stainer soon after to arrange the work for piano and harmonium, a popular pragmatic combination promoted by another of Novello's series. But, for the most part, *The Daughter of Jairus* was a frequent ecclesiastical fixture. The year after Worcester it was the anthem for the Festival of the Sons of the Clergy at St Paul's (14 May 1879); it was often sung at St Augustine's and St Faith's, Watling Street; and Hodge invited his teacher to conduct performances at St Marylebone Parish Church in October 1886. Indeed, other London parish churches were eager to sing the cantata, and, with Stainer's proximity in the capital, were keen to invite him to participate or be present. By the 1890s it was less popular, but it still enjoyed a number of high profile performances, notably at King's College, Cambridge, under Mann in 1895.

The emotional disposition of *The Daughter of Jairus* is largely contemplative, and its most effective parts are invariably those of an introspective, non-dramatic bent. Though Stainer was by no means unaware of developing operatic styles – he was fully cognisant of Verdi, Wagner, Meyerbeer, Goetz and others – the outward affectation of theatrical rhetoric did not lie within his ken, and, consequently, those sections of the cantata that attempt to express a more dramatic sentiment were largely constrained by a rhythmical and gestural conservatism, though, significantly, this circumscribed language with its moderate technical demands made such choruses as 'Awake, thou that sleepest' enormously popular, especially with its executants. More successful, and within more familiar stylistic territory, are those lyrical meditations such as the Mendelssohnian tenor solo

'My hope is in the everlasting', replete with highly effective tonal divergences, and the euphonious ternary 'love' duet, 'Love divine! All Love excelling', pre-dating the composer's enduring hymn setting for the 1889 revision of *Hymns Ancient & Modern*.

Yet perhaps the most interesting and, arguably, striking part of *The Daughter of Jairus* is the overture, a rare example of Stainer in purely instrumental garb. The slow introduction (the lament material symbolising the death of the daughter) to the cantata (see Example 16a), with its immediate chromatic sidestep from C minor to the Neapolitan (D flat) is thoroughly reminiscent of Spohr, and this tonal shift remains an important motive for the opening theme of the sonata Allegro (Example 16b), an orchestral overture that, for its craftsmanship, rhythmic *élan* (surely Beethoven-inspired) and impressive *savoir faire*, deserves to be heard independently in its own right.

Stainer's national pre-eminence as a composer, organist and harmony scholar also led to an invitation to join the first staff of a new educational venture in London, the National Training School (NTSM), which after three years of managerial deliberation, finally opened its doors in May 1876. Stainer accepted the position as Professor of Organ on the Board of Professors (with Bridge as his assistant), a position which brought him into contact with other prominent musicians in London, among them Ernst Pauer (piano), Alberto Visetti (singing) and John Carrodus (violin). He taught at the institution for its short-lived, six-year span, teaching not only the organ but also harmony. Among his organ pupils were Walter Alcock, future organist of Salisbury Cathedral, Frederick Cliffe, Henry Balfour, William Hodge and Francis Cunningham Woods, and among the many harmony pupils that passed through his hands was the hugely talented pianist and composer Eugen D'Albert.

Success of the NTSM, as Giles Brightwell has eloquently summarised, 'hinged upon its ability to attract funding through subscriptions, government subsidy or by accepting fee-paying students'.[175] By 1878 discussion was active to amalgamate the Royal Academy of Music (RAM) and the NTSM, though in the end this proposal proved to be burdened with insuperable difficulties. It was necessary for the RAM to surrender its charter, and this it was unable to effect (requiring a unanimous consent which did not exist), so that by 1879 deliberations were forced to conclude, and a new project, for a Royal College of Music (RCM), under the aegis of the Prince of Wales, began to gather added momentum. It was proposed that the RCM, with sufficient funding, would open for the Easter Term of 1881, a time which would ideally suit the NTSM (whose subscriptions were due to expire and

---

[175] G. W. E. Brightwell, 'The National Training School for Music, 1873–1882: Catalyst or Cul-de-Sac?' (MA diss., Durham University, 1998), 69.

Example 16. Cantata: *The Daughter of Jairus*: (a) orchestral overture: introduction; (b) orchestral overture: opening of Allegro

was thus destined for closure). However, the negotiations for the RCM were still not concluded, and a Committee of Management at the NTSM was anxious that the institution was not forced to close before the RCM had even been properly constituted. Pending the establishment of a charter to the RCM, the NTSM, under the leadership of the Duke of Edinburgh, succeeded in acquiring enough subscriptions for one more year, until the NTSM closed in March 1882.

During these turbulent years, Stainer's administrative role at the NTSM increased. In 1880 he was promoted to Vice-Principal and, a year later, after the resignation of Sullivan (who wanted to concentrate on his career as a composer), he rose to Principal. Though Stainer undoubtedly saw his function as one of 'caretaker', he nevertheless took his responsibilities very seriously, both in his duties as a teacher – he directed a major concert for the institution in the Great Hall of the Society of Arts on 22 June 1880 (the choral class was conducted by Eaton Faning) – and as a moral leader. This demeanour was amply communicated by the lengthy address he delivered at the beginning of the institution's final year on 27 September 1881; it was subsequently published by Novello. The address concentrated on generic issues – the difference between amateurism and professionalism, the need for hard work, application and all-round musicianship, as well as the mission of the NTSM itself. (In this sense Stainer delivered something of a manifesto.) But perhaps more importantly, Stainer, conscious of the limitations of Britain's musical infrastructure to furnish its musicians with a full-time career, was anxious to leave the NTSM scholars in no doubt of the struggle they faced after leaving their studies:

Before many months have passed, the greater number of you will have left this school to take your place in the profession of music, as vocalists, solo instrumentalists, organists, orchestral players, and teachers generally. You will, I dare say all of you, find more or less difficulty in obtaining a sure footing at first, and I fear at times all be liable to a certain amount of disappointment. You will probably be obliged to undertake work which you know to be somewhat below your powers; the excellent solo violinist to play literally second fiddle among a score of others; the accomplished vocalist to sing for a small fee at provincial performances of oratorios with a wretched chorus and a wonderfully constituted band, between whose erratic pauses a mild harmonium struggles to be heard; the first-rate pianist to watch day by day little hands directed by little heads; the organist to discover that the total effect of half a dozen stops is not adequate to the interpretation of masterpieces. But I think I offer sound advice if I say, never despise the elementary work of your profession; something can always be learnt as to the principles of an art whilst teaching the lowest elements of its practice. Your young or backward pupils will thus train you to be good teachers; indeed, it is only from them that you can learn how to teach.[176]

Stainer trusted that these principles he so enthusiastically preached would soon be put in to practice. Before the NTSM closed its doors, however, he felt himself compelled to conjoin in a contentious public correspondence in the *Musical World*, initiated by 'An Amateur' who urged that, given the NTSM's 'failure', the new RCM scheme should be received with caution. Proud of the NTSM's achievements, Stainer swiftly leapt to its defence:

The real facts of the case, which I defy anyone to gather from "Amateur's" letter, are these: The National School of Music was founded for five years only, and merely as an experiment, while the Royal College was being brought into existence. At the end of the five years the Royal College was not ready; the founders of scholarships were then asked to renew the scholarships for another year, and they did so gladly with scarcely an exception. This year of renewal expires at Easter, and no further request of help is to be made to the founders. It does not require a very large amount of common sense to see that this sort of death, at the close of a definite period of successful work, is a very different thing to the death of failure and ignominy to which "Amateur" suggests that the National School of Music is about to succumb. ... If "Amateur" knew a little more about the working of the National

---

[176] J. Stainer, *An Address to the Scholars of the National Training School for Music* (London: Novello & Co., 1881), 19–20.

School he would find that it has in its short career sent forth a group of singers who are to be heard on every platform where high class music is to be found, violinists who are beginning to be highly valued as orchestral and solo players, organists who fill very high positions, and many teachers of music in "high schools" and other places of education. … Is this the failure of which so much is said?

In fact, Stainer aimed his criticism more forcefully at the RAM's opposition to the new RCM scheme and of the proposal to amalgamate both institutions, both of which attracted his full endorsement:[177]

> In conclusion, I will only say that I do think the public will rightly demand some explanation of the conduct of the Royal Academy of Music in setting itself in opposition to the splendid scheme of musical education now being matured; but I hope "Amateur" will not be angry if I say that he is evidently quite unequal to the task of defending his beloved institution in Tenterden Street [the RAM], and I shall be much surprised if the public will not at once see that the existence or non-existence of the National School of Music will not in the smallest degree influence the real struggle going on between the Royal Academy and the proposed Royal College. It is a mere ruse thus to point to the "moribund" National School as a justification of the lamentable action of the Royal Academy, or as a proof that the body has acted wisely in declining to form the nucleus of the Royal College. All who can get at facts know better.[178]

'Amateur' rejected Stainer's assertion that the NTSM was purely an experiment, claiming instead that the intention for the NTSM had been one of a lasting establishment. It was a view Stainer unequivocally and somewhat indignantly rejected:

> I cannot, however, in the smallest degree follow his argument that the National School was intended as a permanence and not as an experiment. Corporations and individuals were asked to subscribe for five years; does this mean for ever? I wonder "Amateur" would take the same poetic view of the length of this term if one of his friends were to borrow a large sum of money from him "for five years." It may be quite true that the promoters of the school hoped that a Government grant might be obtained for its support at the end of this period. But does "Amateur" seriously believe that our admirable professors are responsible for this compulsory stoppage?

---

[177] A further indication of Stainer's belief in the cause of the RCM was his attendance at the Manchester meeting on 12 December 1881, an event at which he delivered a supporting speech.

[178] Letter from Stainer to *Musical World* (21 January, 1882), 42–3.

I only wish we might have this question put to the test by being permitted to carry on the school on our own responsibility with free hands. I think I might safely prophesy, if this were done, that other schools and academies of music would soon be making much more genuine lamentations over our survival than they are now making over our death. Considering the high position of our Kensington teachers, and their close connection with many other important institutions for musical education, it certainly surprised me to find their six years' labour and anxiety described in an offhand way by an anonymous amateur as resulting in a "failure," and I do not think that he has any reason to complain of the tone of my former letter.[179]

Time healed Stainer's evident rancour against the RAM, and he was quick to remind his critics that he was himself a member of that august institution. Nevertheless, even after joining the Council of the newly instituted RCM in 1883, he continued to retain a lifelong wish that the RAM and RCM would join forces:

After I had been some time in London, I was asked to go and help in a school of music, founded at Kensington. There I found myself shoulder to shoulder with my old boy-friend Arthur Sullivan. I think now, perhaps, that I ought not to have added that to the work I already had on hand, but I could not help taking pleasure in that which I felt likely to be a new departure in the history of music in the country. That school was founded under very unfavourable circumstances, and I think it was put forward almost as a forlorn hope, with serious doubts as to whether it were possible or feasible. We had to sustain the brunt of very severe attacks from all quarters, from all hands. Some people thought that a school of music established under the wing of Royalty must necessarily be (what shall I say) humbug, if nothing else. Some said that no further school was wanted, we had better assist those already in existence. I think many of my brethren have lived to see that those opinions were, more or less, unreasonable. Perhaps this is hardly the place to say it, but I still hope to live to see a union between the Royal College and the Royal Academy of Music. I know there are very great difficulties in the way; I have looked into the matter, and I am well aware of their existence; but I am certain it would be, on the whole, of very great benefit to the nation.[180]

Yet, though the doors of the NTSM finally closed at Easter 1882, Stainer's contact with education was only briefly severed. That same year John Hullah, H. M. Inspector of Music in Schools and Training Colleges retired, and Anthony John Mundella, Liberal MP and head of the education department in Gladstone's second

[179] Ibid., 44.
[180] 'The Sir John Stainer Dinner', *Musical World* (4 August 1888), 610–11.

ministry (and whose daughter Stainer had taught at the NTSM), invited Stainer to take up the post. It was a difficult decision, not least because the post would mean weeks of exacting physical work and travel as well as time away from his work at St Paul's. Though there is no supporting documentary evidence, one may assume that the Dean and Chapter were willing to release Stainer for the time in which he needed to support the Ministry of Education, and it also clearly suggests that both Stainer and Chapter had full confidence in Martin to superintend the music in his absence. Stainer's willingness to undertake the post of H. M. Inspector was also motivated by his own social conscience. A Liberal, like Mundella, he was driven by a sense of social duty and a desire to build both on Forster's Education Act of 1870 and Mundella's Elementary Education Act of 1880; and, more importantly, he was keen to provide new momentum to the study of music in schools and training colleges already established by Hullah. Moreover, filled with the new idealism of Mundella's policies, which sought to broaden the school curriculum, Stainer was keen to grasp the opportunity to give new *gravitas* to music as an educational vehicle and to reform the rigid system of payment by exam results. In addition it was vital to establish a firm bedrock of trained competent teachers without whom his objectives had little chance of realisation. Such aspirations brought with them an enormous responsibility and the prospect of hard, physical and repetitive work. Yet, though increasingly exhausted by the drudgery that the appointment entailed, Stainer retained this position until his death, an indication undoubtedly of the social as well as cultural importance he attached to musical education and his mission to raise its profile in the eyes of government and the public.

V ❦ 1882–1888

H. M. Inspector of Schools
and *The Crucifixion*

Having accepted Mundella's invitation, Stainer and his wife spent July and part of August 1882 in Holland and Belgium, visiting Rotterdam, Antwerp, Amsterdam, The Hague and Brussels. A few weeks after his return he was asked by Grove to join the staff of the RCM, due to open its doors in 1883:

> I write to you by the express desire of the Prince of Wales to convey his hope that you will accept the Professorship of the Organ in the Royal College of Music, and thus aid in carrying on the excellent work with which you are so closely identified at the National Training School. The Prince hopes to open the College early in the spring.
>
> His Royal Highness knows what severe calls are made on your time and strength by your engagements at St Paul's and elsewhere; but he feels convinced that you will see the gravity of this fresh attempt to serve the interests of music in England, and will not refuse him the advantage of your well known devotion to the cause which both he and you have so much at heart. There will be plenty of room for your services in other departments also; but I hope you will agree to take the organ as your leading professorship.
>
> I need not add how sincerely delighted I shall be to receive your assent, and thus secure the prospect of having you for a Colleague.[1]

It was a most tempting offer, not least because Stainer had lent his full support to the Prince of Wales's venture. 'I should only have been too glad to be attached to the staff of the Royal College, as Sir George Grove asked me to be', he later admitted, 'if Mr Mundella … had not asked me to work under the educational department.'[2] But no doubt Stainer was also conscious of the additional time he would need to take away from St Paul's, and, given Chapter's co-operation (which we must presume in the absence of documentary evidence), he must have been loath to extend its generosity any further. In mitigation, however, Stainer's

---

[1] Letter from Grove to Stainer, 7 September 1882, in private possession (JRS).

[2] This is also confirmed in Grove's letter of appointment to Parratt (as Chief Professor of Organ) dated 13 February 1883 where he stated: 'I must say that Dr Stainer having accepted the appointment of Inspector of Schools under the Privy Council will not be able to take a Class in the College.' See *GB-Lcm*.

position on the RCM Council maintained for him an important link with higher musical instruction, all the more significant since one of the initial objectives of both the NTSM and RCM – and one in which Hullah had taken a keen interest before him – had been to prepare and train teachers for elementary and secondary schools.[3]

Mindful of his great expertise and experience at the NTSM, Grove was also keen to employ Stainer early on (in 1884 and 1885) as an examiner for the RCM examinations (with Manuel Garcia, Joachim, Goldschmidt, Barnby, Dannreuther and Ouseley) both politically to smooth the transition from one institution to the other and to lend prestige to the RCM's fresh public profile.[4] In 1880 Stainer was also appointed as the first Professor of Organ at the new Guildhall School of Music by its first principal, Thomas Weist-Hill, though it seems probable from the surviving records that, through scarcity of time, he was forced to give up this responsibility in or around 1882.[5]

Although Stainer was no longer at the vanguard of London's musical conservatories, he nevertheless retained strong pedagogical links with them through his continued editing and publishing of musical primers, a project undertaken since 1875 with a series of instruction manuals for Novello (a system not unlike that used by students at the Paris Conservatoire). Between 1875 and 1878 he oversaw the production of no fewer than thirteen primers, many of them authored by colleagues within the circles of the NTSM or the Musical Association. There were three important manuals from Ernst Pauer (*Pianoforte Musical Forms, Musical Forms* and *Elements of the Beautiful*), and individual manuals reflecting the specialisms of their contributors, notably Ellis's *Speech in Song*, Curwen's *Tonic Sol-fa*, Stone's *Scientific Basis of Music*, Helmore's *Plain Song*, Cummings' *The Rudiments of Music*, Prout's *Instrumentation*, Higgs' *Fugue*, Bridge's *Counterpoint* and two from Stainer himself – *Harmony*, a manual which gained a much wider circulation than his earlier theoretical treatise, and *The Organ*. The latter sold many thousands of copies,[6] and remained an important guide for beginners well into the twentieth century. Today its careful study provides us with a picture of organ technique that pertained for decades. Stainer, as he explained to one correspondent, believed

---

[3] See F. Hullah, *Life of John Hullah* (London: Longmans, Green & Co., 1886), 282–3.

[4] See letter from the President of the RCM Council to Stainer, 5 January 1885, in private possession (JRS).

[5] Prospectuses in a surviving scrapbook (*GB-Lma* CLA/056/AD/04/001) provide evidence that Stainer was Professor of Organ at the GSM for 1880 and 1881. There are no further GSM Prospectuses until 1887, where his name is absent.

[6] In a letter to Parry, dated 22 April [1890] (*GB-ShP*), Stainer explained that 'My primers sell at 2/- so get 2[d] per copy – but *50,000* of my "Harmony" have been sold and *30,000* of the "Organ"!!! So I have been well remunerated.'

that successful execution at the organ could only come with an initial thorough grounding on the piano:

> No one should be allowed to begin organ-playing until a sound training has been received in the art of "fingering", "the carriage of the hand" etc on the <u>pianoforte</u>. If the necessary foundation has not been laid out <u>before</u> organ-practice is commenced, the pupil will never make a really good organist.
>
> For students you <u>must</u> have an organ of 2 manuals at least, with full compass of pedals, and one independent pedal stop; but the instrument may be very small. The organ at the Training School where we taught our cleverest pupils had 2 stops on the Swell, 3 or 4 on the Great, 1 on the Pedals. And cost I think about £180, or £200.[7]

The organ primer was not only a seminal instruction manual on purely physical elements of technique, for it also put forward characteristic 'interventionist', not to say 'symphonic' recommendations for registration which Stainer provided for interpretation, particularly of fugue. This concept of performance practice remained highly prevalent in the organ world for years afterwards:

> In playing fugues or other pieces not calling forth the minuter details of expression, care must be taken that the general rendering is broad and dignified. The grandeur or beauty of fugue consists in the fact that it is constructed so as to be of constantly increasing interest from beginning to end. Several important considerations present themselves if this be borne in mind. First, the full power of the instrument should be judiciously reserved for the climax (probably the *stretto*); and although the enunciation of the subject should not be soft or weak, enough power should be kept in hand to enable the player to add to the strength of tone from time to time. It need hardly be pointed out that nothing but a most vicious taste could suggest the giving out of a fugue-subject on a *tuba mirabilis* or any other "fancy" stop.
>
> Next, it is certain that if the interest of a fugue is to go on increasing, the *episodes* (those portions of a fugue which do not actually include the working out of the subject) must not be severed from the context by being played on a different manual, or with a strongly contrasted quality of tone. The notion that a fugue is made more interesting by suddenly skipping from the Great organ in order to play an episode on the Swell Manual (with much pumping) cannot be too strongly condemned. Thus to cut a slice out of the middle of the work completely destroys its unity of purpose. It sometimes

---

[7] Letter from Stainer to Mr Thompson, 5 January [1884], *GB-RAM* McCann Collection.

may happen that the episodes require even greater power and vigour of style to keep them up to the level of the fugue.[8]

Other primers rapidly followed after 1878, including a volume on *Singing* by Randegger, Berthold Tours's *The Violin*, the Rev. Troutbeck's *Church Choir Training*, Bridge's *Double Counterpoint and Canon*, James Greenwood's *Lancashire Sol-fa*, the Belgian cellist Jules de Swert's *The Violoncello* and Stainer's own *Composition*, a volume intended for beginners and to be used in conjunction with the author's *Harmony* primer. To this Stainer and Barrett added a condensed version of the *Dictionary of Musical Terms* in 1880.

In addition to the primers, Stainer was invited by Grove to contribute articles, mainly on the organ, to the third volume of his *Dictionary of Music* due for publication in 1883. (The articles for the previous two volumes on this subject had been contributed by E. J. Hopkins.) Stainer wrote fourteen in all for volume 3 (including an article on 'Service' music), and also went on to write six more for volume 4, published in 1889 (which also included an article on 'Verse').

At much the same time as *Harmony* and *The Organ* were being written, Stainer was also occupied with a series of organological writings commissioned for *The Bible Educator*, by Edward Hayes Plumptre, Professor of Exegesis at King's College, London (and future Dean of Wells Cathedral) and one of the most prominent biblical scholars of his time. *The Bible Educator* was published in four volumes from 1874. Stainer was asked to contribute to Part II with articles on vocal and instrumental music of biblical times. Much of his work was drawn from the pioneering *Music of the Most Ancient Nations* published in London by the German scholar Carl Engel in 1864, and which focused principally on the musical culture of the Assyrians, Egyptians and Hebrews. For the philological parts of the book he had much help from the young Ernest Budge, the future orientalist, to whom Stainer gave much early encouragement.

Engel's organological work was symptomatic of a the new scientific wave of Darwinist (and Spencerian) thinking that was inhabiting nearly all areas of study and spawning new disciplines such as psychology and anthropology. In a similar way music was also finding itself subject to evolutionary scrutiny, and curiosity about the roots of musical thought and practice were gathering considerable momentum. 'It [music] has become so thoroughly a part of our existence that we rarely pause to consider to what an extent we are, as it were, enveloped in its sweet sounds, or how irremediable its loss would be to us. As a natural result of this', Stainer commented, 'much interest has of late years been shown in every research which might tend to throw some light on its early history.'[9] The philosophical

---

[8] J. Stainer, *The Organ* (London: Novello & Co., c. 1877), 85.

[9] J. Stainer, *Music of the Bible* (London: Novello & Co., 1879), ed. F. Galpin (1914), 1.

imperatives of Stainer's articles, inspired by the concepts of Darwin and Spencer, added much to the momentum of similar opinion espoused by *Grove's Dictionary* (in particular the generic articles of Parry), and would prove to be important not only in Stainer's future theoretical writings but also for a more general school of thought promulgated in Britain and especially in Oxford after Ouseley's death.

After publication in *The Bible Educator*, the articles were collated into book form and published by Novello as *The Music of the Bible*. A popular book, it went through two substantial editions before going out of print. Yet, conscious of scholarly advances in organology made by the mid-1890s, Stainer would not consent to any further reprinting. 'I won't allow Novello to reprint it', he told Arthur Mann, 'because, since I wrote it, so much new information has turned up on the subject of ancient instruments. I should like to rewrite it; but I am too hard-worked at present.'[10] After Stainer's death, however, agreement was given for the publication in 1914 of a revised version edited by the prominent organologist Francis Galpin.

Stainer's interest in musicological issues was also reflected in other pursuits and events. In 1876 he joined Cummings and others on the committee of the newly formed Purcell Society. With the Caxton Commemoration and Printing Exhibition in June 1877 he lent a number of his own precious first printed editions from his growing library collection (as did Cummings, who was himself another major bibliophile). With G. Phillips Bevan he contributed chapters concerned with the choir and organ to the *Handbook of the Cathedral of St Paul's* in 1882.

He also devoted as much time as was feasible to the Musical Association, which was enjoying a healthy membership. Between 1874, the date of the Association's inception, and 1878 he was able to attend an average of three sessions each season, and at those sessions he attended he was either in the chair, giving a paper on subject-matter of special interest to him, or supporting colleagues close to him. Sedley-Taylor's 'On a suggested simplification of the established pitch-notation' (7 December 1874) and Hullah's 'On musical nomenclature' (1 March 1875) chimed with the paper he gave on musical notation he gave a month later on 5 April 1875. Though he was undoubtedly interested in the content of their papers, he was also driven by personal regard to hear Ouseley's 'Considerations on the history of ecclesiastical music of Western Europe' (3 January 1876) and Pole's 'Philosophy of Harmony' (5 March 1877). On 7 January 1878 Stainer chaired his first meeting, with 'On the laws of musical expression, as formulated by M. Lussy in his "Traité de l'expression musicale" ' by John Spencer Curwen, and he was in the chair again in 1880 when Ouseley delivered a paper 'On the early Italian and Spanish treatises on counterpoint and harmony' (3 March 1879), material he undoubtedly recalled from his Tenbury days. He attended Eustace Brakespeare's 'Musical Aesthetics'

---

[10] Letter from Stainer to A. H. Mann, 31 January 1895, *GB-NWr*.

(2 February 1880), reflecting his growing interest in musical philosophy (on which he was widely read), and during the 1881–2 season he chaired Monk's 'The cultivation of church music' (5 December 1881) and took a lively interest in the discussion following Ouseley's 'On some Italian and Spanish treatises on music of the seventeenth century' (6 February 1882).

However, the surviving attendance books make it evident that from this time Stainer was unable to afford as much time for the Musical Association's sessions, and his visits declined, first of all to two sessions each year and, once his responsibilities to the Education Department at Whitehall began, sometimes to only one. These isolated attendances, once again, were largely dictated by specialist interest, notably Marmaduke Browne's 'Music in Elementary Schools' (31 October 1885), Ouseley's 'On the position of organs in churches' (1 February 1886) and John Spencer Curwen's 'The musical form of the hymn tune' (January 1887), the last two of which he chaired.

Perhaps the most significant paper among those that Stainer chaired for the Musical Association, however, was Parry's paper of 3 November 1884, 'On some bearings of the historical method upon music', in which the speaker more fully argued his theoretical and philosophical espousal of Darwinism seen through the prism of Herbert Spencer's social-Darwinist thought. Stainer had, to a considerable extent, already embraced this same thrust of philosophical thinking in his own paper 'The Principles of Musical Criticism', delivered to the Musical Association on 3 January 1881. This, combined with his allegiance to Mills' principles of Utilitarian Rationalism, is evident in one of his first major aesthetic declarations in that 'the principles of art-criticism are nothing more or less that the *consensus* of the fittest on the true characteristics of that which gives the highest order of pleasure in the best possible way.'[11] Yet he was also keen to establish a balance of critical understanding which, he felt, had been eroded by a present polarisation of principles, where one camp advocated 'scholastic criticism' while the other championed a complete emancipation from it, believing the 'non-technical experience' of music to be superior and untrammelled. 'Musical criticism', he asserted, 'is at the present moment oscillating between the two extremes of dogmatic conventionalism and unblushing nihilism. I think it is the duty of us all to try to steady it.'[12]

In search of his own equilibrium Stainer considered the essence of criticism to be the judgement of the relation between the composer's purpose and the work under scrutiny. In consequence, Stainer avowed, since the purpose of a work throws it into a distinct class of composition, we need to know what class of composition that is and how to measure the merit of the work as representative

[11] J. Stainer, 'The Principles of Musical Criticism' [3 January 1881], *Proceedings of the Musical Association* 7 (1880–1), 36.

[12] Ibid., 37.

of that class. Thus, we must know the point of time in which the work was composed with some relation to the actual development of that class at that time, *and
its merit when compared with contemporary efforts of the same kind.* There followed from these claims that merit could be assessed by the quality of conception
and treatment, a seemingly cumbersome division, Stainer suggested, but these, he
stressed, had been the very division that Mendelssohn had deployed to criticise
Hiller's Overture in D minor at Leipzig in 1837:

> I dislike nothing more than finding fault with a man's nature or talent; it
> only depresses and worries, and does no good; one cannot add a cubit to
> one's own stature; all striving and struggling are useless there, so one has to
> be silent about it, and let the responsibility rest with God. But in a case like
> the present, with your work, where all the themes, everything which is talent
> or inspiration (call it what you will), is good and beautiful and impressive,
> *and the development alone not good*, then I think it may not be passed over;
> there, I think blame can never be misplaced, – that is the point where one
> can improve ones-self and one's work. ... Don't go and tell me ... that your
> treatment is always as good as your invention; I don't think it is. ... The
> two overtures are certainly your best things, but *the more clearly you express
> yourself* the more one feels what is wanting, and what, in my opinion, you
> ought to remedy.[13]

Stainer believed that 'originality' was ultimately 'the stamp of individuality left
by a composer on his work', and more crucially that individuality was 'the special
emotional bias and intellectual bearing of a creative genius'.[14] This emphasis on
intellectual genius, allied with the criteria of 'conception' and 'treatment', was pro-
totypical of Parry's later watchwords of 'instinct and character', and more specifically of 'form and expression', so heavily accentuated in the primer, *A Summary
of Musical History*, that Parry later produced for Stainer in 1893, and the more
extensive *Art of Music* which he published the same year. At the conclusion of his
paper Stainer took pains to point out that, though the application and training of
the intellect formed a major part of a critical acumen, his acknowledgement of the
'non-technical' critic prompted him to admit that an allowance of purely emotional
response was vital for a healthy balance, and that 'the standard of merit in music
is, and ever will be, determined by the *consensus* of that body of educated listeners
and thinkers whose intellect and emotions are equally trained and refined, and
who are silently elected to a sort of "board of taste."'[15] At Oxford, Stainer would
return to this subject with greater eloquence.

[13] Ibid., 39–40.
[14] Ibid.
[15] Ibid., 46.

When Stainer assented to the appreciable task of leading musical education in England, Scotland and Wales, he already knew that he brought to his appointment little experience, theoretical knowledge (other than that of working with choristers) or methodological creed of teaching. By contrast, Hullah, influenced by the French philosopher Claude-Adrien Helvetius, by Ruskin and the educational reformer James Kay, had been intrinsically motivated by the democratic ideals of Christian Socialism and by the ideals of social emancipation that education could bring, particularly to the lower classes. In turn, music and singing, Hullah believed, could be a vital agent in the transformation of a human being's grasp of knowledge and of wider society. These principles he brought to his appointment as H. M. Inspector of Music in 1872, yet in the ten years he held office, his insistence on the dull teaching of musical theory proved to be a deterrent to pupil teachers, and the proliferation of numerous teaching methodologies – 'singing by ear', the 'Fixed-Doh' system (which Hullah advocated), Curwen's 'Moveable-Doh' system (which was increasingly preferred) and conventional staff notation – all added to a perceived fragmentation of the subject. This in turn militated against the sympathy of many training colleges who actively discouraged it from their curricula since it interfered with the teaching of other disciplines. Moreover, Hullah's position was, if anything, little more than titular. His task may have been to produce annual reports for the Whitehall Committee of Council on Education, but he was not expected to visit schools or colleges, a factor which effectively hamstrung his efforts *ab initio*. Progress was painfully slow, and Hullah himself was forced to admit: 'The little or no direct results in elementary schools of the teaching of music in training schools has led to a very widespread belief that this teaching is in a large number of instances, all but useless.'[16]

Yet, though Stainer brought little in the way of educational ideology to his appointment, his own personal prestige undoubtedly lent a new *gravitas* to musical education throughout Britain, and his presence, along with that of McNaught at the Conference on Education at the International Health Exhibition (in the first week of August 1884), raised the profile of music and music-teaching within the national debate. Similarly, the demand for Stainer's attendance, especially as adjudicator, at festivals and competitions – notably for the London School Board, musical festivals and bodies such as the National Temperance Association – meant that he was a household name to young and old alike; this was, as Bernarr Rainbow has suggested, also strengthened by the publication of *Instructions to Inspectors*, a new series of advisory circulars designed to engender a closer

---

[16] G. Cox, *A History of Music Education in England, 1872–1928* (Aldershot: Scolar Press, 1993), 30.

relationship with inspectors and schools, and Stanford's *The Song-Book for Schools* (1884).[17]

In the first of his annual reports to the Lords of the Committee of Council on Education, in 1883, Stainer immediately displayed his innate sense of pragmatism by appointing two more experienced and energetic assistant inspectors, William Gray McNaught and his lifelong colleague, William Barrett. (Barrett, along with the Rev. W. H. Bliss – whom Stainer had known through his association with Exeter College, Oxford – had acted as assistants to Hullah). The Tonic Sol-fa-ists were delighted:

> Dr Stainer has lost no time in proving the earnestness of his endeavour to do justice to the Tonic Sol-fa system in his new position as Inspector of Music in Training Colleges and Schools. The advantage of having a practical Sol-faist associated with him in the work is obvious, and we are glad that Dr Stainer has recognised it. … Our readers will, one and all, join in congratulating Mr McNaught upon his appointment. From a financial point of view neither he nor Dr Stainer are gainers; they are rather to be commiserated. But the possibilities of national work that lie before them are enough to stir the least generous mind. … We assure Dr Stainer of the hearty sympathy and best wishes of Tonic Sol-faists for the new *régime*.[18]

Stainer resolved early on that he would take responsibility for inspecting the colleges, while McNaught and Barrett would report on the elementary schools. The support of these motivated individuals was invaluable,[19] especially from McNaught, who was undoubtedly the most important expert figure in British musical education in the nineteenth and early twentieth centuries. With their advice and commitment, Stainer was able, by degrees, to rationalise Hullah's disjointed system. It would not be easy. Payment by results, which Stainer disliked, was not abolished immediately, but was phased out only gradually.

Moreover, there was pressure to abolish the teaching method of 'singing by ear' to which many, including Stanford, were outspokenly hostile, in favour of teaching musical literacy.[20] To achieve this, Stainer wanted to promote 'singing

---

[17] B. Rainbow, 'Inspectors of Music: An Introductory Note on the Nineteenth-Century Background', in *Sir Arthur Somervell on Music Education*, ed. G. Cox (Woodbridge: The Boydell Press, 2003), 5.

[18] 'Dr Stainer's New Régime', *The Tonic Sol-Fa Reporter* (February 1883), 31.

[19] William Henry Bliss, a distinguished Oxford scholar (not least in his knowledge of Bodleian and Vatican manuscripts), was relieved of his duties, largely because he was not familiar with the Tonic-Sol-fa system which Stainer considered a vital part of an inspector's armoury.

[20] See C. V. Stanford, *Studies and Memories* (London: Archibald Constable & Co.,

by note' using both systems of musical notation (Tonic Sol-fa, which now had broad currency, and staff notation). To this end, he and Mundella devised the New Code, whereby the original 1/- grant paid to schools for the satisfactory training of children in singing was halved to 6d where 'singing by ear' persisted, but was paid in full where 'singing by note' was pursued; yet even here Stainer had misgivings about abolishing 'singing by ear' altogether since it might disadvantage poorer schools from partaking in any form of musical practice:

> I am not prepared to advise that singing by ear should not count in receiving a share of the Government grant. The conditions under which the various schools exist differ considerably, and in some cases school teachers labour under very considerable difficulty with respect to giving systematic instruction in music. Singing by ear, like playing by ear, is not bad in itself. How often do we have to lament that a performer who can play or sing well is utterly lost without the notes before him. I frequently regret to find persons playing with their eyes glued on to the music before them, unable, as it were, to think for themselves for a single bar. Depend upon it, from those who know their music by heart, we get finer and more artistic performances than is the case with those whose memory has not been cultivated, and are unable to go on without the notes before them.[21]

At heart Stainer believed that music was a birthright for every child, and that singing, above all, engendered cultural cohesion and educational amelioration. The formation of choral societies had proved to be a major agency in the participation and appreciation of the great masters, a fact he emphasised in his contribution to the Conference on Education at the Health Exhibition on 8 August 1884. Indeed, he was proud of the nation's musical advances:

> The existence of such bodies as the Bach Choir, London Musical Society, Albert Hall Choir and Amateur Orchestral Society, show that our best men and women have become our best workers in music, and put their hands to the plough. This recent musical revival has now permeated our educational systems, and has at last reached our elementary schools. If any here present have heard the children of the London Board Schools singing in

1908), 43–60. Ten years earlier, in 1879, a petition of no fewer than 118 names had been sent to the Ministry of Education protesting against the promulgation of 'singing by ear' (see *Musical Times* 20 (March 1879), 82–3). R. B. Litchfield's article 'Tonic Sol-fa' for *Grove's Dictionary of Music and Musicians* also expressed opposition, which drew a vociferous protest from McNaught (see *Musical Times* 20 (July 1880), 360–1).

21 M. Browne, 'Music in Elementary Schools' [31 October 1885], *Proceedings of the Musical Association* 12 (1885–6), 21.

their thousands under the transept of the Crystal Palace, or in the Albert Hall, I shall be excused if I say that the progress of music in our elementary schools has simply been marvellous; I have been particularly struck with the absence of the old nasal twang, and also, with the presence of genuine musical sentiment which exhibited itself in the observance of the marks of expression. All these children can read from notes.[22]

In training colleges, staff notation still held the upper hand, but, aware of the popularity in many elementary schools of the Sol-fa system (where Stainer and McNaught particularly wanted to promote the 'Movable-Doh' method), Stainer wanted students to be conversant with both systems, and recommended that this take place in their second year of study. In advocating the teaching of Tonic Sol-fa, Stainer was in fact prepared to stand firm on a principle which attracted a good deal of antagonistic comment. Though he had assessed the limitations of the system some years earlier in his paper for the Musical Association, he nevertheless retained the conviction that for diatonic music, for the pitching of intervals and for ear training, Tonic Sol-fa was ideal as a preparatory method for more advanced work. It was a policy in which he and McNaught believed strongly, though neither liked Hullah's 'Fixed-Doh' system (which largely expected its subjects to have or develop perfect pitch) and felt that its continued presence in the classroom only served to confuse teachers and students alike. However, Macfarren, in his position as Principal of the RAM and Professor of Music at Cambridge, weighed in with a letter to Mundella denouncing the effectiveness of Tonic Sol-fa as a whole:

> I think the adoption of the system unjust, since imposing on the poor any expenditure of time and money which they can never turn to any practical account, and placing them at a disadvantage with the rich, who are able to read musical publications of all countries; whereas the use of this exceptional notation is confined to a sect in England and some of its colonies also.[23]

Macfarren's letter inevitably caused a furore in the corridors of Whitehall and amongst Tonic Sol-fa's most fervent advocates, but his words nevertheless high-lighted an important class distinction that had emerged with the increasing usage of Tonic Sol-fa in schools and its positive adoption by school boards, the most significant and substantial of which was the London School Board (LSB). This was a point amply made by the Rev. Marmaduke Browne of the Marylebone Division of the LSB in his paper for the Musical Association on 31 October 1885.[24] Tonic

---

[22] J. Stainer, 'Musical Education in Elementary Schools', *Health Exhibition Literature: Conference on Education*, vol. 13 (London: William Clowes, 1884), 396.

[23] Cox, *History of Music Education in England*, 56.

[24] See Browne, 'Music in Elementary Schools', 4–6.

Sol-fa was an ideal educational agent for teaching music to the less well off, and its utility was equally appreciated by those participating in choral societies such as the RAHCS, many of the recruits of which emanated from the lower classes.[25] Stainer undoubtedly realised this class association, but his Liberal passions kicked against what he perceived to be social prejudice. Indeed, in order to express his conviction in the system and its relationship to the more altruistic cause of universal education, he attended a public meeting of the Tonic Sol-fa-ists to lend his weight to the campaign:

> I am quite willing … to declare my belief in the system (Loud cheers). It is just because Tonic Sol-fa is capable of producing such good results with the "rather too young" and the "rather too old" … that it deserves such hearty support from everybody who takes any interest whatever in education. (Applause) … I am really ashamed of the great prejudice which some of my musical brethren show towards this movement … We shall all receive some day the blessings of countless thousands of little children who by this system can learn to sing, but who without it would be deprived of that enjoyment.[26]

It was a brave and politically aware response, but it did not put an end to opposition which persisted well into the twentieth century.

With the introduction of the New Code, Stainer hoped that some of the endemic problems experienced by teachers of music in colleges might be more properly addressed. Some of these were undoubtedly serious. The system of pupil-teachers, apprenticed to professional teachers for four or five years in school before, if possible, beginning their training at a college, were invariably educated at a minimum level and often arrived at college with almost no knowledge of music at all, thus creating a hopeless burden for college music instructors and anxiety for the college principals who were often disposed to jettison music from their curriculum altogether. Stainer had other recommendations. Where musical aptitude was clearly lacking in candidates, they should be strongly encouraged not to pursue music; instrumental music, which he had met on his travels, had little recognition and deserved more. Candidates generally looked for legitimacy in terms of their musical qualifications to other awarding bodies such as the Tonic Sol-fa College or the Society of Arts rather than to the state system; this was a lacuna which needed addressing by the introduction of graded certificates. There was presently no room within the inspection for part-singing which was vital for choir

25 By contrast, the Bach Choir, largely peopled by the more moneyed classes, used staff notation.

26 J. S. Curwen, *Replies to Recent Attacks on the Tonic Sol-fa System* (London: Tonic Sol-fa Agency, 1882), 10–11.

training, an element he wanted to see introduced as soon as possible. As a legacy from Hullah's time, students retained the view that musical paperwork was more important than practical work, a perception, given his conviction that practical work was a visible manifestation of the power of teachers as versatile musicians, he wanted to amend by awarding more marks for performance. Consistent with his views on teaching harmony and counterpoint to students of a more senior standing,[27] Stainer also recommended that the teaching of harmony to training college students be dropped, not because he did not regard it as vital, but, on the contrary, because it was too time-consuming, given the constraints of time, and because so many students considered it a kind of mechanical puzzle. As Stainer put it: 'Time bestowed on the study of harmony, if it only produces such a result as this, might as well be employed in learning to poise a plate on the point of a stick, or in tossing up three brass balls, provided, of course, that a certain number of marks were obtainable by such feats.'[28]

There was, in this first report, quite a lot for the Lords Committee to digest. Over the course of the year, of forty-eight colleges visited, Stainer inspected thirty-five, which entailed much travelling around the country, not just to the larger urban centres but to teacher-training colleges in Aberdeen, Bangor and Truro at more distant ends of the kingdom. It was enormously tiring work, and during the Christmas break of 1883 he had been forced, through ill health and advice from medical practitioners, to hand over marking of musical examination scripts to Barrett and McNaught. Stainer also requested clarification from Whitehall about how to handle the matter of elementary schools and what his role was to be. It was a question intended to probe, for though government was keen to promote universal education, it was nevertheless constrained by the availability of public funds. Stainer had two suggestions. Either the position of H. M. Inspector of Music was to be full-time (a proposal which would undoubtedly have forced Stainer to reconsider his position one way or the other), or the Inspector should be held in readiness to proceed to any part of the country where he and his assistants could be of use. Perhaps inevitably, given Stainer's own circumstances, he thought the second suggestion more practicable, but, if the government was serious about musical inspection in *schools*, then more funds needed to be made available to him for the purpose, especially for travel, since at present the Education Department asked its Inspector do his work for no remuneration whatsoever.

For the academic year 1885–6, Stainer increased his workload so that he was able to visit forty-one out of forty-three possible training colleges, a punishing

---

[27] J. Stainer, *An Address to the Scholars of the National Training School for Music* (London: Novello & Co., 1881), 11.

[28] J. Stainer, *Report of the Committee of Council on Education (England and Wales) with Appendix 1883–4*, GB-Lpro ED17/56, 596.

task which he performed again for 1886–7. From this he was able to give an almost comprehensive report. Three years in the job had taught him that, if improvements were to be observable, the Education Department needed to accept a long-term view of his work and that of his assistants; indeed he estimated ten to fifteen years before amelioration could be perceptible. Standards in training colleges, he confessed, would only improve if candidates arrived at the institutions with greater knowledge of the subject and he continued to advise music professors at the colleges to block entry to unpromising students. Yet, Stainer found some room for optimism. The number of marks he was now able to award for music had risen from thirty to fifty. At Southlands College he observed good second-year practice where each student had to show a lesson on 'singing' and 'teaching a new tune', a practice he recommended be taken up by the Board of Education even though it would triple the time for inspections. A number of colleges, such as those at Bangor, Battersea, Borough Road, Bristol, Carmarthen, Chelsea, Culham, Exeter, Homerton, Lincoln, Liverpool, Saltley, Swansea, Tottenham and Winchester gave evidence of successful choral classes; colleges such as Chelsea, Chester, Exeter and Cheltenham showed real potential for students becoming competent organists, and at Homerton College he praised the policy of bringing both sexes together for music-making. Finally Stainer could also report favourably about the standard of repertoire chosen by the students for their practicals. This had improved markedly from days when candidates invariably sang simple ballads or even music hall songs and passed them on to younger students. 'When he is compelled to listen to a small number of common-place ballads, presented with a persevering iteration', Stainer reported with some frustration, 'this portion of the examination is, to say the least, not the most enjoyable.'[29]

By the mid–1880s, Stainer sensed that the New Code was beginning to have its desired effect. Many elementary schools were taking the 1/- grant devised to encourage, above all, musical literacy. Even more positively, instrumental work was beginning to become common practice at some institutions such as Cheltenham, Culham and Westminster, while at Battersea, Durham and York, part-singing was supplemented by boys' voices. The proportion of candidates deficient in music, who wanted to enter colleges, was diminishing and practical musicianship was improving. Yet Stainer harboured caveats in several areas. The quality of music sung at schools was often of a poor standard and he exhorted composers of the highest rank to consider writing children's songs (a demand which was to spawn a vast repertoire of educational music published in both staff and Tonic Sol-fa notation). The expectation from some in the music profession that students at colleges

[29] J. Stainer, *Report of the Committee of Council on Education (England and Wales) with Appendix 1885–6*, GB-Lpro ED17/56, 473.

should emerge from their training as thorough musicians was too ambitious: they had a wide programme of subjects to study and many students knew little music and were starting from a base-line of low proficiency.[30] Moreover, there were simply not enough funds from government to examine the subject fully as Stainer made abundantly clear in 1885:

> It would be, of course, a great gain, musically speaking, if the examinations in music at Elementary Schools could be carried out throughout the whole country by skilled professional musicians. A scheme for this purpose was drawn up some time ago by Lord Charles Bruce, but its cost would have been (speaking from memory) about £20,000 a year; it was, therefore, like many other excellent schemes, shelved.[31]

In spite of the government's financial limitations, Stainer held tenaciously to his task. In 1888–9 he visited all the training colleges throughout the country, examining no fewer than 1,266 candidates. Moreover, to encourage progress, his general report was supplemented by a short report on each educational institution, a pattern he was to establish for the rest of his appointment.

The amount of time needed for his educational work meant that Stainer spent much time away from London, *incommunicado*, on trains and in hotels. Such a schedule, of a repetitive and monotonous nature, he summarised unceremoniously as 'on tramp', as is evident from many of the headings accompanying the letters he wrote during this period. An indication of the sheer physical exertion required was provided by Bridge, who, on occasion, stood in for his mentor:

> I have never done much work as a travelling examiner, such employment being for me very fatiguing. On one occasion when Sir John Stainer was incapacitated through illness, I accompanied the late Dr McNaught for a week on one of those whirlwind examination tours in which his soul delighted. The genial Doctor was Sir John Stainer's assistant, but I believe Sir John's physical make-up could not support the fierce bouts of "inspecting" that seemed to be the breath of life to McNaught. My week with him is a nightmare, in which processions of candidates come and go endlessly; in which we seem always to be boarding trains by the smallest margin of safety; in which night brings no rest, for we have to sit far into the small hours making up returns and preparing for the morrow; and generally the whole thing proceeds at breathless speed, and the problem emerges in all its stupendous proportions. I remember telling my companion that it really had

---

[30] Browne, 'Music in Elementary Schools', 16.
[31] Ibid., 16–17.

been the hardest week's work I had ever done, and I would not undertake his job for £5,000 a year.[32]

Yet Stainer insisted on retaining his position as organist for the RAHCS, and, though Martin, whose greater presence was noted by the press, directed at least three weekday services a week from the organ loft at St Paul's, Stainer was invariably there for the weekly practices, for both the cathedral and Sunday evening choirs and for the weekend and for those services adjacent to it. His reputation as an organist, moreover, was still supreme and he drew much approbation for his extemporisations before the service and the voluntaries after, a fact borne out by no less a figure than the Austrian conductor Hans Richter who, after a visit to St Paul's in May 1882, commented 'Stainer played the organ quite wonderfully.'[33] For Stainer and the RAHCS it was a fertile period in terms of new works. Besides the staple repertoire of Handel, Haydn, Mendelssohn and Bach's *St Matthew Passion*, less familiar works such as Bach's Mass in B minor, Beethoven's *Missa Solemnis* and Gounod's *Redemption* were more frequently sung, and there were a number of new works which Barnby introduced, among which were Mackenzie's *Rose of Sharon* (4 February 1885), Dvořák's *Stabat Mater* (13 March 1884) conducted by the composer, Gounod's *Mors et Vita* (26 February 1886), Sullivan's *Golden Legend* and Stanford's *The Revenge* (both 15 November 1886). Most of these performances were the first in London after their premieres at provincial festivals in Norwich and Leeds, but perhaps the most propitious events were the first two hearings in England of Wagner's *Parsifal* (on 10 and 15 November 1884), a work which made a deep impression on Stainer and which he would later wish to see at Bayreuth (at that time the only possible place to witness it, owing to Wagner's circumscription of staged performances of the work). In addition to the RAHCS, he was requested to stand in for an absent Goldschmidt as the conductor of the Bach Choir at St James's Hall on 1 February 1883 though the choir was under-rehearsed and did not sing well. In 1885, when Goldschmidt retired from the conductorship, Stainer was the choice of the choir committee to succeed him, but given Stainer's already exacting schedule, he declined and it was Stanford who was eventually appointed. There was also little time for Stainer to devote to performance on the organ other than at St Paul's. Yet as an advisor of the building or renovation of organs, he continued to be consulted. One of the most important of these consultations was for the new Willis organ at Canterbury Cathedral in 1886, a four-manual instrument of eighty-seven stops which included the organ-builder's new patent combination

---

32 J. F. Bridge, *A Westminster Pilgrim* (London: Novello & Co., Hutchinson & Co., 1918), 260.

33 See C. Fifield, *True Artist and True Friend: A Biography of Hans Richter* (Oxford: Oxford University Press, 1993), 193.

of pneumatic and electrical appliances (for which Willis received a Gold Medal at the Inventions Exhibition in 1885). At Mattins on 30 July the new instrument was dedicated, and at evensong in the afternoon (which also included the choirs of St Paul's, the Chapel Royal and Rochester), Stainer gave two recitals, one during the offertory, the other after the service. Similarly he gave guidance to the Duke of Sutherland in 1889 who proposed to install an organ by Willis in the gallery of Stafford House in London.

The combination of St Paul's organist and senior government appointee undoubtedly meant that Stainer was now one of Britain's most respected musical luminaries, and with a steady income nourished by healthy royalties, he could afford to send his sons to good schools and to university. The oldest, John Frederick Randall, attended Winchester before going up to Magdalen College, Oxford in 1885; Edward, who attended St Paul's School, followed his brother to Magdalen in 1888; Charles Lewis, educated at St Mark's School, Windsor, was an undergraduate at Christ Church, Oxford from 1889, and William Edgar, who was sent to Magdalen School, followed Charles Lewis to Christ Church in 1891. The two girls, Cecie and Ellie, would also pursue their own educations (in the spirit of their father's conviction of the merits of education for women) in Germany. Though he chose to resign his position as conductor of the London Male Voice Club in 1887 (who entertained him to a sumptuous farewell dinner at the Cannon Street Hotel on 14 December 1886), he was a frequent guest of musical societies and associations around London. In 1885, in recognition of his work, Durham University conferred on him the honorary degree of D.Mus., and, after a number of years as a Vice-President of the College of Organists, he accepted the position of President in 1887 and held it until 1890. A further indication of his esteem was shown by his election to the Athenaeum Club in 1887, proposed by William H. Milman (son of the former Dean of St Paul's) and Spottiswoode.[34]

Stainer was also naturally expected to fulfil official duties, not least attendance at a garden party at Buckingham Palace in July 1886, a description of which he provided for his proud mother-in-law:

> Perhaps you thought me rather unwise – to come back to London on purpose to be present at the garden party today, but I have been rewarded for my pains; it certainly was the most brilliant royal reception I ever saw. There

---

[34] Stainer was actually put up for membership of the Athenaeum Club on 30 November 1874. He was elected into membership as a Rule 2 member in January 1887, an honour in the gift of the General Committee, and his name was put forward by Sir Richard Rivington Holmes, the Royal Librarian. This enabled Stainer in effect to 'jump the queue' of the waiting list, which at that time was running at 18 years. In 1892 he became a member of the United University Club, which became his London base after he moved to Oxford.

were I believe about 4000 people present during the afternoon (4 to 7), but of course not <u>all present at once</u>. It may seem odd, but I have never really seen the Queen, although I have been in her (distant) presence at least a score of times; this afternoon she walked round the garden several times leaning on the arm of the Prince of Wales, and on her first "tour" passed within a few feet of me, looking wonderfully well and smiling from genuine pleasure at the beautiful sight of her hearty though respectful reception. An additional interest in the assemblage today was the presence of several of the French "exiles"; my four-wheeled cab followed an open carriage full of them in the court-yard. I was very much impressed with their easy and affable bearing. In addition to the "usual" band of the 2nd Life-Guards, we had at another corner of the gardens the Russian Choir, which sang charmingly, and in a third portion of the garden the band of the West Indian Regiment (– all niggers) in a curious uniform. I saw a great many people that I knew well and had some interesting "chats". When I left I got into a penny omnibus and came home; the swells who had come in carriages had some difficulty in finding them – many waited nearly an hour for them.[35]

Other official obligations included consultation from the Archbishop of Canterbury about honorary Lambeth doctorates for both Martin (1883) and Turpin (1889),[36] both of whom almost certainly received their degrees on the strength of Stainer's recommendation. As a friend of the politician and Prime Minister, William Ewart Gladstone (particularly since the time the Stainers had moved to London in 1872),[37] Stainer was consulted by Gladstone's Private Secretary, William Hamilton, on the matter of a bell for St Seiriol's Church, Penmaennawr, one of Gladstone's most beloved holiday retreats. St Seiriol's, designed very much in the Ecclesiological Gothic revivalist tradition by Alfred Waterhouse, was built at Gladstone's instigation in 1867 and latterly he wished to make a gift of a bell for the tower. For this he drew on Stainer's knowledge of bells from St Paul's. Writing to Hamilton in November 1884, Stainer was keen to establish the specifications:

Will you give me some idea of the amount the bell should cost? Single bells I think cost (including "cage" and necessary apparatus) about £8 per cwt.

35 Letter from Stainer to Elizabeth Randall, 10 July [1886], in private possession (JRS).

36 C. W. Pearce, *A Biographical Sketch of Edmund Hart Turpin* (London: The Vincent Music Company, [1911]), 55. In honour of Turpin's Lambeth doctorate a banquet attended by some 200 guests was given at the Holborn Restaurant on 22 January 1890. Stainer was in the chair.

37 See letter from Stainer to F. G. Edwards, [June 1898?], *GB-Lbl* Egerton 3092, fol. 42.

So a 1/2 ton bell would cost £80 and a 1 ton bell £160. I have no doubt a bell of 20 cwt could be placed in a tower 10 feet square. – but of course a bell of 7 or 8 cwt would be a handsome present & invite people to church from a long distance. As soon as I hear from you I will make enquiries – I have no doubt we can find a first-rate single bell ready-made.[38]

Bells were also a concern for Sullivan and the London premiere of *The Golden Legend* by the RAHCS, but this time it was a question of pitch compatibility and whether the Albert Hall organ could be used for the performance:

> I heartily congratulate you on your splendid success at Leeds.
>
> Your kind letter, asking me to come and hear the bells at Warner's reached me at Aberdeen or somewhere equally near the North Pole. All seem to say they were in excellent tune. But how about the high pitch of the Albert Hall? I am rather fidgetty about this. If much out of tune – it would seriously affect the result of the music, especially at the opening scene.
>
> Are the bells in town?
>
> Could you get them up to the Albert Hall and let us hear them with the organ? If they will not go with the organ – could you drop the organ altogether at the performance? and use the <u>Leeds</u> pitch?[39]

Interestingly, the whole question of musical pitch had, at the very time of the performance of *The Golden Legend*, exercised Stainer and many others in the musical profession, including the Society of Arts who consulted him on this controversial matter. In 1869, the Society of Arts, in its attempt to contribute to the debate, reported through a specially appointed committee that Britain should adopt the pitch established by the 'Congress of Physicists' in Stuttgart in 1834 to fix $A = 440$ and true $C = 528$. The recommendation had no real national effect and the matter was allowed to run until, under the aegis of the International Inventions and Music Exhibition in London (1885–6), a Conference on Musical Pitch was organised at St James's Hall in June 1885 on whose council Stainer served.[40] Led by the RAM (who were the sponsors of the meeting) and chaired by Macfarren, the meeting consisted of speeches given by Charles Santley (on behalf of singers), Stainer (representing the interests of organists), Goldschmidt, and two scientists, Ellis and Bosanquet.[41]

---

[38] Letter from Stainer to William Hamilton, 21 November [1884], *GB-Lbl* Add. MS 44488. As a result of Stainer's enquires, he recommended two bells from Taylor's of Loughborough (who had supplied the bells for St Paul's), one, already made at the foundry of 21 cwt, and the other, to be newly cast, of about 13 cwt.

[39] Letter from Stainer to Sullivan, 26 October [1886], *US-NYpl*.

[40] The Conference on Musical Pitch took place in the wake of Verdi's attempt to standardise pitch in Italy in 1884.

[41] See *The Times*, 22 June 1885.

A general consensus seemed to be the adoption of French pitch (A = 435 and C = 522), that is, at a lower level than was used by orchestras, brass bands, wind instruments and many organs. Serious concern for the decision to adopt French pitch, expressed not only by Stainer for organs throughout the country, but also for military bands and the expense it would entail to purchase new instruments, led to the request for the formation of a steering committee on which Stainer was invited to sit. Later that year he was approached by the Society of Arts in their bid to counteract the conference's decision, a stance he endorsed:

> I shall be very happy to serve on the Committee for promoting the general use of the Society of Arts pitch C = 528.
>
> I really believe that the failure of the effort made at the great meeting at St James Hall to secure a uniform pitch was entirely owing to the fact that the "French pitch" was proposed.
>
> I feel sure that the English nation will never adopt the French pitch – I hail with satisfaction, therefore, this effort to establish a "medium pitch" which I am confident would be accepted by orchestral and other players, by singers, by makers of instruments, and by military bands – the wood-wind instruments of which could be modified to a medium pitch at a comparatively small cost.[42]

However, realising that his desire to retain the *status quo* was unpopular, he informed the Society of Arts that he was withdrawing from the committee:

> I can see that I shall be in a glorious minority of 1 – if I join the committee on Musical Pitch; so I think I had better withdraw.
>
> Of course I shall not attempt in any way to throw obstacles in the way of the adoption of the French pitch; but I am absolutely certain the attempt to establish it will fail; we <u>cannot</u> ask the government to throw away as useless £100,000 worth of military instruments.
>
> On the other hand, a [*sic*] English National Pitch of C = 528 would be adopted by all our colonies, I am sure; and would I believe be some day adopted on the continent.[43]

In fact, by 1896, through the offices of Hipkins, Ellis and Pole, there was an attempt to establish a standard pitch at what was more or less equivalent to French *diapason normal* (A = 439), though later in the twentieth century, much as Stainer predicted, concert pitch once again rose to A = 440. Moreover, though Stainer withdrew from the committee on pitch, he remained on good terms with the Society of Arts

---

[42] Letter from Stainer to Henry Trueman Wood, 29 January [1886], *GB-Lsa*.
[43] Letter from Stainer to Henry Trueman Wood, 16 February [1886], *GB-Lsa*.

and acted as an examiner for the Society's practical musical examinations between 1879 and 1884, and, after the death in 1891 of Barrett (who had been responsible for setting the written examinations), he took over the responsibility for a year before handing it on in the first instance to Barnby and then to McNaught.

Although his work at St Paul's after 1882 was interrupted by his travels for the Ministry of Education, Stainer still remained an imposing presence at the cathedral (though he had undoubtedly to rely on the increased attendance of Martin to take services in his absence). Under Sparrow Simpson's Succentorship, music flourished as the Succentor's Reports for 1882–3 and 1884–5 abundantly testify. Sparrow Simpson's assiduousness as a librarian, scholar and musician meant that the choir library was no longer intended to be one of musical 'subsistence' but one of real musical value. With the support of Chapter, proper finance was devoted to the purchase of substantial amounts of music in the more modern format of vocal scores (the acquisition of single parts was consciously discontinued) in recognition that this facilitated rehearsals. Sets of octavo services and anthems were compiled, each comprising a series of forty volumes which included music for men's voices, settings of the Benedicite and the now little-used folio volumes of Boyce, Arnold, Croft, Greene, Hayes and Page. All were inspected twice a year for wear and tear, and if found to be deteriorating, they were mended under the watchful eye of the Succentor. Sparrow Simpson characteristically rejoiced at the introduction of additional new repertoire by Gounod (especially extracts from *The Redemption*), Dvořák, F. E. Gladstone, C. H. Lloyd, Bertram Luard Selby, A. C. Mackenzie, Rheinberger, Sullivan, John E. West and, of course, a number of Stainer's own anthems; moreover, as one of Stainer's fellow propagandists for the 'orchestral service', he trumpeted the success of the Patronal, Passion and Advent services (which continued to attract huge congregations and whose regularity had now established a tradition) and reiterated that 'I must again repeat that the credit for the success of our great musical Festivals is due not to the Succentor, but to Dr Stainer. At my desire, he has organised these grand services; every detail has been superintended by himself, in person, with what success all who have been present know.'[44] He was also delighted to announce that the cathedral had successfully commissioned new orchestrated services, by Prout, Calkin, Faning and Steggall almost every year since 1873, and the inclusion of carols was now a regular feature of the Christmas season.

Sparrow Simpson retired in 1885 and in his place the Rev. William Russell was appointed both as Succentor and as Master of the Choristers School (with the Rev. Henry Macnamara as his assistant). Russell, like his predecessor, maintained a healthy interest in the cathedral's musical welfare, but in his first report of 1885–7,

---

[44] W. Sparrow Simpson, *Succentor's Report* [no. 4], 1883–4, 7.

had the somewhat unenviable task of providing a memorial to the former chimeri-
cal Precentor, Charles Almeric Belli, appointed to his office in 1819. Effectively a
relic of a past era. Belli was something of legend to Chapter; his absence from the
cathedral meant that he was completely unknown to the Dean's Verger who had
subsequently refused him access to his stall.[45] Belli's replacement, Canon Henry
Scott Holland, a Residentiary Canon, was a new departure for Chapter and rudely
threw the anachronism of Belli's role into relief. Russell did his best:

> For although Mr Belli never took any active part in connection with the
> Services of the Cathedral (not having certainly been appointed with that
> idea), yet as having occupied the office of Precentor, and so having been
> *theoretically* [Russell's italics] responsible for the chief direction of the music,
> for upwards of half a century, a musical report would not be complete with-
> out making reference to his decease. But for the sake of strangers, who read
> this Report, it should be mentioned that it has long been customary at S.
> Paul's for the Precentor to delegate all his duties and responsibilities, in
> respect of the music, to the Succentor for the time being: and Mr Belli, in
> so accepting and holding office, was only acquiescing in an order of things
> which he found, and which probably had existed long before his time. And
> as, moreover, the office of Succentor is invariably associated with that of
> a Minor Canon – Minor Canons, of course, being chosen with a special
> regard to musical efficiency – perhaps this arrangement is not so unjustifi-
> able as at first sight it may appear.
>
> The appointment of a Canon Residentiary as Precentor is a new depar-
> ture; but (if, as a member of the Body to whom this Report is addressed, he
> will forgive its being said) in the person of the Rev. H. Scott Holland there
> is felt to be every reason for congratulation. For the new Precentor has a
> thorough appreciation of good Church music, and has already given proof
> of the interest he is likely to take in all persons and matters connected with
> the Choir. And whether or no he will be prepared ultimately to take upon
> himself the *actual* duties of his office, he may be relied upon for desiring or
> favouring no change, which will not evidently tend to promote the highest
> possible perfection in the musical Services of the Cathedral.[46]

The amount of new music added to the cathedral's repertoire as evidenced by the
report was, by Russell's admission, small by comparison with previous years. In
part this was probably due to Stainer's partial absence, but Russell was at pains
to point out that the list of anthems now numbered in the region of 500 pieces,

---

[45] G. L. Prestige, *St Paul's in its Glory* (London: SPCK, 1955), 10.
[46] W. Russell, *Succentor's Report* [no. 6], 1885–7, 3–4.

236   JOHN STAINER: A LIFE IN MUSIC

a more than manageable quantity for the choir to negotiate. And although this did
not preclude the addition of new works, he advised that the future musical regime
would exercise a more stringent form of selection:

> A great deal of new music is sent on trial, and that which is immediately
> or ultimately rejected may be divided into three classes: (1) music which is
> in itself considered insufficiently meritorious; (2) that which is considered
> inappropriate to the words, or (in the case of *Anthems*) the words of which
> are deemed unsuitable for use in Church; (3) music which, although good
> in itself, is not considered suitable for the particular conditions imposed by
> S. Paul's Cathedral, the acoustic properties of which are very peculiar. The
> fitness or unfitness of music in this latter respect can, for the most part, only
> be ascertained after some considerable trial, and thus it frequently happens
> that music which has been in use for some time is allowed ultimately to drop
> off the list.[47]

But perhaps the most notable modification to the repertoire, for which Russell was
largely responsible, was the introduction of Gregorian chants (using Helmore's
Gregorian Psalter) for the psalms during the services for men's voices. The Succentor considered that not only was the performance of traditional Anglican chant
unsatisfactory in its ATTB form, but that the absence of Gregorian chant in the
cathedral needed to be remedied. It was a decision received unenthusiastically
by the men,[48] and Russell clearly felt that Stainer, who happily acquiesced to the
innovation, revealed little understanding of the beauties of plainchant by performing it in measured form (akin to the Ratisbon tradition he preferred) with organ
accompaniment, rather than in a free unmetrical style.[49]

During the 1880s the St Paul's choir enjoyed a period of stability and development perhaps unknown in its history. The choristers now numbered forty, and the
firm foundation of the choir school provided a bedrock for music to prosper and
for the sense of 'community' to strengthen. Indeed, such was this sense of collective spirit that the cathedral instituted an annual dinner for 'Old Boys' at the Holborn Restaurant, the first of which took place on 8 January 1887 which was chaired
by Stainer and supported by Gadsby. There were still some difficulties to overcome.
In 1881 Stainer encountered problems with recruiting enough suitably competent
choirboys,[50] and the previous year he had had to cope with a measles outbreak

---

[47] Ibid., 5.
[48] See W. A. Frost, *Early Recollections of St Paul's Cathedral: A Piece of Autobiography*
(London: Simpkin, Marshall, Hamilton, Kent & Co., 1925), 78.
[49] W. Russell, *St Paul's under Dean Church and his Associates* (London: Francis Griffiths, 1922), 84.
[50] See Weekly Chapter Minutes, 14 and 21 May 1881, *GB-Lsp*.

which removed some boys from their duties.[51] But the most serious occurrence of this kind was an epidemic of scarlet fever in September 1885 when the entire contingent of choristers was absent. This necessitated a whole month of music for men's voices alone which persuaded Chapter to institute, in the summer of 1886, a month's leave for the entire choir school, an arrangement which later extended to periods at Easter and Christmas after 1896. The acquisition of new services for ATTB became an imperative and undoubtedly helped to galvanise Russell's decision to institute the singing of plainchant.

St Paul's also increasingly became the focus of state occasions, memorial services, funerals and large-scale church events. This included the funeral of the controversial Commissioner to South Africa, Sir Bartle Frere on 5 June 1884, a memorial service for General Gordon on 13 March 1885 attended by the Princess of Wales, the enthronement of Bishop Temple on 8 April 1885, and the re-interment (in the grave of Boyce) of a former organist of St Paul's, Maurice Greene, on 18 May 1888. This removal of Greene's remains became imperative owing to the planned demolition of St Olave Jewry in 1888, a Wren church close to the long and winding Ironmonger Way, Cheapside. Through the offices of Cummings and Stainer it was arranged: 'You will be glad to hear', Stainer finally proclaimed to his friend, 'that the Dean and Chapter have given permission to me to apply for the remains of Dr Greene and will place them in or near Attwood's grave.'[52] But the grandest services of the decade were reserved for 1887, the year of the Queen's Golden Jubilee. For the Sons of the Clergy in May, Stainer composed one of his most ambitious anthems since his time at Magdalen, 'Lord, Thou art God' (though very much a *pièce d'occasion* with its incorporation of the National Anthem at the close) and hoped that it might partner a specially commissioned setting of the canticles by Sullivan, but in the end Sullivan was unable to oblige:

> It is a bitter disappointment to me that I am unable to get the Magnificat and Nunc Dimittis which I promised you for the Festival of the Sons of the Clergy ready in time for that occasion. I have been working at it since I returned from Berlin, but all my efforts are weak and unworthy of the object. I have certainly not been idle, but I have failed to produce any kind of result satisfactory to myself. I worked up to the last hour, hoping against hope, and that is why I have delayed making this communication to you.
>
> You cannot be so vexed as I am myself.[53]

In the end Stainer was compelled to use Martin's Service in C, though Sullivan was

---

[51] See letter from Stainer to Mrs Stainer, 19 February [1880], in private possession (JRS).

[52] Letter from Stainer to Cummings, 17 October [1887], *GB-En* MS 3071.

[53] Letter from Sullivan to Stainer, 4 May 1887, *US-NYpm*.

represented by his *In Memoriam* overture at the opening of the service. On 21 June 1887 the official national Jubilee Service took place at Westminster Abbey under Bridge's direction with a choir constituted from the Abbey, St Paul's and many of the London churches who sang from galleries built in the bays on either side of the organ. Payment for the St Paul's boys who participated was passed onto the choir school: 'The boys' fees will probably be turned into special school-prizes', Stainer wrote to Flood-Jones, the Precentor at the Abbey, 'as it is against our custom to let the <u>boys themselves</u> be paid.'[54] Two days later, St Paul's staged its own major Jubilee service compiled by Liddon. Stainer conducted a choir of 300 voices and an orchestra of sixty in a service which included Handel's *Dettingen Te Deum* and his own anthem composed for the occasion, 'Let every soul be subject to the higher powers', based on a text from Romans and Psalm 118 and concluding with verses from a hymn by Godfrey Thring for choir and congregation. One further gesture Stainer made to the Queen on her Jubilee, of a slighter nature, was the madrigal 'The Triumph of Victoria'. An archaic setting in five parts of the composer's own text, the madrigal was first sung at a summer concert at Keble College on 16 June 1887 under the direction of Charles Harford Lloyd. Its publication the same year drew a generally favourable review from the *Musical Times* with the accompanying comment that Stainer had more or less assumed the role of national 'Composer Laureate', though this unofficial role would soon pass to Parry in the 1890s.

It is an indication of the demands that Stainer's Inspectorship brought that his creative life at St Paul's suffered a noticeable decline after 1884. The early 1880s had witnessed a steady flow of anthems and service music (including the Morning and Communion components of his Service in B flat), and in 1883 he completed his largest work, an oratorio for the Gloucester Three Choirs Festival, *St Mary Magdalen*, to a libretto by the twenty-four-year-old Rev. W. J. Sparrow Simpson, a high churchman, son of the Succentor of St Paul's and a recent graduate of Trinity College, Cambridge. Three years earlier, Stainer had in fact turned down a commission from Gloucester owing to pressure of work but after the closure of the NTSM he was able to find time to undertake a more ambitious canvas than *The Daughter of Jairus*.

St Mary Magdalen was constructed in three scenes, 'The Magdalen in the house of Simon', 'The Magdalen by the Cross', and 'The Magdalen at the Tomb' (St John), using for its main framework the well known texts from the Gospels of Saints Luke, Mark and John. Sparrow Simpson and Stainer nevertheless drew freely on a wide range of other literature, from the letters of Paul, Job, the Song of Solomon, and the Latin Hymn 'Pone luctum, Magdalena', as well as poetry by Sparrow Simpson himself who was evidently keen to promote the 'High Church' interpretation of

---

[54] Letter from Stainer to Flood-Jones, 8 July [1887], *GB-Lwa*.

Mary Magdalen by means of extolling the 'ancient opinion of the Church', its early teachers, the writers of the *Acta Sanctorum* and prominent contemporary scholars such as Lightfoot and Pusey. Perhaps one of the most striking parts of the oratorio is the opening 'Overture with Recitative'. Here Stainer chose to interrupt his sonata scheme after the exposition – one full of surprising harmonic boldness reminds one more of Schumann than of Spohr – with a short narrative interjection from the solo bass in the tonic minor (F minor). A dialogue between soloist and orchestra ensues which effectively constitutes a developmental phase before the recapitulation, cleverly veiled by Stainer's handling of tangential progressions, gets under way. The overture is also framed by a slower prelude and (short) postlude in which a seminal idea (Example 17a) is introduced and which inhabits many of the contours of the oratorio's thematic material. This can be observed in the first idea of the Allegro (Example 17b), but characteristics of its distinctive shape, notably the rising sixth interval, are detectable in later movements. This is particularly so in the recitative material of Scene I and in the preludial material of the chorus 'For none of us liveth to himself', but one can also feel it strongly projected across the first two parts of the oratorio, especially in the solemnity of the opening to Scene II (Example 17c). Stainer's choral writing is largely uncomplicated but highly effective at its best. The reflective ternary movement, 'Come, ye sin-defiled and weary', projects Stainer's well-established predilection for hymn- or chorale-like textures,

Example 17. Oratorio: *St Mary Magdalen*: (a) orchestral overture (with recit.): seminal motive; (b) orchestral overture (with recit.): opening of Allegro; (c) Opening of Scene II

this time in the form of a pastoral, enhanced by his penchant for contrasting verses a third part (A flat – E – A flat) and for a deft handling of chromatic progressions (note the detour in the final verse from F minor to G flat and then to C flat) in which recovery to the tonic is managed with masterly adroitness. A similar affinity is also present in 'Rest in peace' at the close of Scene II. It was this treatment of chromatic harmony which many of the reviewers attributed to Wagner. Certainly Stainer's assimilation of chromaticism was intense and there is much that is comparable with the range of harmonic experimentation in Wagner's earlier operas, notably with *Lohengrin*, but in reality the matrix of Stainer's style, his method of voice-leading and his organisation of tonal relationships belongs more to an assimilation of Spohr filtered through Schumann and Gounod, whose own use of *leitmotiv* did not extend to the ethos of Wagner's later manner of 'developing variation'. Reviewing the work for the *Tonic Sol-fa Reporter*, McNaught drew special attention to this aspect of the work (not least because its chromatic elements were a challenge to the Tonic Sol-fa notation), above all in the extended final movement for soloists and chorus ('Magdalena, past is wailing'), again based on the rhetorical device of a chorale, which is built on a tonal structure of thirds underpinning the scheme of five strophes:

> Commencing with a long section in the key of D [strophe 1], modulating to D♯ – treated enharmonically as E flat – there follows another long section mostly in the key of B [strophe 2], leading to D [strophe 3]. From this key a series of modulations lead to B flat [strophe 4], in which key the long section formerly in the key of B is repeated, and again made to lead to D [strophe 5], and in this key the music is closed.[55]

The creative harmonic dimension of *St Mary Magdalen* reminds us that Stainer was a master in this area of composition (a fact borne out by the later songs). There is also much of merit in the melodic fertility of the oratorio which, as McNaught noted, is treated with much greater freedom than in *The Daughter of Jairus*. Working within these confines, Stainer exuded confidence and appositeness, but in a work the length of an oratorio, this propensity for spiritual reflection is not sufficient to sustain the 'drama' and those moments of *anagnorisis* and *peripiteia*, principally in the final scene, are not conveyed with sufficient vividness by the *turba*-style choruses (for example 'He is not here') or the rhythmical restraint of the declamation.

Stainer conducted the performance of his oratorio at Gloucester on 5 September 1883. Its reception was mixed; though some critics noted that he had attempted his

---

55 W. G. McNaught, 'The Gloucester Festival and Dr Stainer's St Mary Magdalen', *The Tonic Sol-Fa Reporter* (October 1883), 165.

most ambitious work to date, they heard a style of choral music that was to some extent outmoded, and Hueffer, while appreciating the more contemporary direction of the composer's musical language, described it as 'Capellmeistermusik'.[56] Although the work was destined to have a further performance at the 1891 Hereford Festival (again under Stainer's direction) and at the Sheffield Choral Union in 1893, it was to find much greater appeal among smaller choral societies and church choirs, notably those who wished to perform it in parish churches. The first London performance was undertaken by McNaught and his Bow and Bromley Institute Choir on 30 October 1883. Stainer presided at the organ and was given a standing ovation afterwards. By popular request a repeat performance, though only with organ, was given on 10 November. In 1885, Stainer included extracts as the anthem for the Festival of the Sons of the Clergy on 20 May, and for the Dedication Festival of St Peter's, Eaton Square in July he appeared as organist under William de Manby Sergison. Indeed the oratorio retained a modicum of popularity, especially in its arrangement made by Hodge for piano and harmonium, but with the advent of *The Crucifixion*, with its more appealing material and economic practicalities, interest in *St Mary Magdalen* clearly waned until, in the 1890s, it fell into neglect.

The Crucifixion, called deliberately by Stainer 'A Meditation on the Sacred Passion of the Holy Redeemer' aimed to be an emotional reflection on the theology of the events leading to Christ's crucifixion and not a dramatic oratorio or cantata. Indeed W. J. Sparrow Simpson, to whom Stainer turned once again for his text, clearly intended to explore Christ the man in all his vulnerability and desolation rather than as a theatrical protagonist, a fact accentuated by the lack of violence, weeping or the thunder of God's wrath. Stainer conceived his work for his former pupil, William Hodge, its dedicatee, who was organist at St Marylebone Parish Church. Since 1882, when the Rev. W. Barker, a passionate Ecclesiologist, had arrived at the church, changes in the building's décor had been extensive. Major alterations such as the removal of the upper galleries had brought more light into the church, not only exposing the the full length of the stain-glass windows but also enhancing the marble of the new pulpit and mosaic floors and many other decorative details full of symbolic theological references. More important from a musical point of view, however, was the creation of a chancel replete with mahogany choir stalls and capacity for a numerous choir of in excess of thirty choristers and a dozen or more men. Such a choir, close to Stainer's heart in terms of its size and expressive power (to which he had become accustomed at St Paul's), was an apt instrument to lead a substantial congregation who filled the church every Sunday.

---

[56] *The Times*, 6 September 1883.

The Crucifixion was first sung under Hodge at the series of special Lenten Thursday services at St Marylebone Parish Church on 24 February 1887 and was repeated at three further services on 10 and 24 March and 8 April; Gounod's *Redemption* was sung on the intervening Thursday evenings (on 3, 17 and 31 March), a significant juxtaposition in the eyes of several critics who noted an affinity of style. Yet Stainer's work did not derive from the large-scale oratorical structure or gestures Gounod conceived for Birmingham. Quite conversely, his work was designed to be performable by relatively modest resources. In an age where the battle had been won to incorporate larger choral works, such as oratorios and passions, into the Anglican liturgy – one which had been spearheaded by Stainer himself – *The Crucifixion* revealed Stainer's 'democratic' aspirations for parish church choirs to enjoy the same form of experience and occasion, yet without the expense of an orchestra or the challenging technical difficulties of, for example, Bach's choral writing or the highly demanding task of performing Bach's orchestral accompaniments in reduction for organ. All of these elements are more simply realised: the choral parts, predominantly though not exclusively homophonic, are uncomplicated and the organ part, though requiring a competent performer, is thoroughly idiomatic for a late nineteenth-century romantic English organ of moderate dimension. By contrast, the two solo parts call for a more professional or at least semi-professional disposition in terms of their expressive and technical range. Stainer was, of course, conscious of the link between his work and the Lutheran Passion in the way he wished to follow the traditional pattern of biblical prose narrative (conveyed in the solo and choral recitatives) and poetry which meditates on each aspect of the passion story. Moreover, the entire narrative itself is punctuated by a series of Anglican hymns – an entirely 'national' substitute for the chorale – for congregational participation which, in their turn, attempt to explore and distil those quintessential tenets of Anglican (and particularly Anglo-Catholic) theology.

After the 'performances' at St Marylebone, *The Crucifixion* was an immediate triumph as well as a major commercial success for Novello. It was performed throughout the Anglican communion around the world and Stainer took much delight from hearing of performances by small choirs in remote parts of Australia and the West Indies. 'Perhaps you might encourage music in Queensland', he reminded Edwards at the *Musical Times*, 'by noticing this performance of "The Crucifixion" in Toowoomba, under the direction of Mr Stanley Hobson.'[57] In fact, so popular did *The Crucifixion* become, that it became a household work known by millions of people even in the face of subsequent excoriating invective, and, over a century later, it still lives on as favourite work among choirs throughout

---

[57] Letter from Stainer to Edwards, 15 June 1898, *GB-Lbl* Egerton 3092.

the English-speaking world for its balance of pragmatism, pure romanticism and religious sentiment.

The appeal of *The Crucifixion* was also undoubtedly enhanced by Stainer's well-crafted structure. Deftly simple, classical designs served, as they had done in his many previous anthems, to convey a message of considerable immediacy. There is, for instance, a deeply felt melancholy in the opening strophic number 'The Agony' which, replete with choral refrain, portrays the genuinely pathetic figure of Christ in Gethsemane, and the masterly choral centrepiece of the work, the unaccompanied anthem 'God so loved the world' (the only choral movement founded on a biblical text), makes use of a simple ternary design, aping the simple Baroque tonal shift to the mediant minor at the end of the central section before the recapitulation. More complex, though no less direct, is the 'Processional to Calvary', an extended structure in which two themes, a march in A minor and a more Gounodesque song are introduced in a substantial ternary introduction for the organ alone. The chorus emerges part way through the recapitulation of the march theme to which they provide a counterpoint 'Fling wide the gates'. Almost elusively this material moves to the forefront of the structure, this time rooted in C major, though subtly we still hear references to the original march in the guise of consequent musical phrases ('He has come from above, in His power and love'). The solo tenor's through-composed trio section, so characteristic of its composer, explores third-related tonalities, embarking from A flat, passing through B and D major, before returning to the march in A minor. The other principal choral section, 'The Appeal of the Crucified', also begins with march material in C minor, but it is counterbalanced by the Old-Testament entreaty, 'Is it nothing to you, all ye that pass by?', from the first chapter of Lamentations based on a motive (Vb – vib – Vb) presented in the previous recitative for bass (though hinted at much earlier – see the tenor solo's passage 'Past evil, and evil to be' in the Processional to Calvary). This 'questioning' material continues to be insistent, and its presence becomes ever more conspicuous within the context of the richer diatonic texture of the supplication 'O come unto Me' as a flat submediant within G major. Simplicity, as in 'The Agony' for bass and chorus, also inhabits the solo numbers, though for the tenor aria 'The Majesty of the Divine Humiliation' ('King ever glorious') and the Duet ('So Thou liftest Thy Divine Petition') Stainer's style is overtly more Continental, reminiscent of Gounod in the former and Schumann in the latter, and there are moments – especially the emotional crux 'So Thou pleadest' (Example 18a) – when it is possible to hear a palpable link with Elgar's earliest musical essays for the church, such as 'Ave verum', 'Ave Maria', and 'Ave Maris Stella', written, as it would happen, in the same year.[58]

---

[58] We also know that Elgar noted a resemblance of his anthem 'Ave verum' to the duet

Example 18. *The Crucifixion*: (a) 'So thou pleadest'; (b) 'God so loved the world' (opening); (c) 'God so loved the world' (conclusion); (d) Hymn: 'All for Jesus'

Probably the most enduring part of *The Crucifixion* has been 'God so loved the world' and, thanks to Novello's publication of it as a separate number, it is frequently sung as a freestanding piece, though its impact gains much from the bass arioso which precedes it. Perhaps most telling is Stainer's harmonic adroitness, notably the dissonance that gently accentuates 'God *so* loved the world' (Example 18b), but other touches such as the subdominant inflection ('believeth in Him'), the charged suspensions of the climax ('everlasting') and the reworking of the opening material in the coda (Example 18c) all contribute to a miniature of profound emotion and, on Stainer's part, deep religious conviction. Only second to the anthem,

'Love Divine, all love's excelling' from *The Daughter of Jairus* with which he was well acquainted; see J. Butt, 'Elgar's Church and Organ Music', in *The Cambridge Companion to Elgar*, ed. D. Grimley & J. Rushton (Cambridge: Cambridge University Press, 2004), 114.

however, in terms of popularity come the series of six hymns. Arguably the finest of these is the first, 'Cross of Jesus', a robust melody full of passing modulation and effective sequence, but there is a similar magnificent sweep of melody to the last hymn, 'All for Jesus', where Stainer's characteristic use of motivic cells is cleverly manipulated within the bright and transforming backdrop of E major (Example 18d). 'I adore Thee' is distinguished by its oblique opening progression (IIIb–V–vi) made increasingly more fervent by its repetition in the mediant, and 'Jesus, the Crucified' derives its expressive power from its chromatic if not its melodic interest. Perhaps least distinctive is 'Holy Jesu, by Thy Passion', though even in this tune Stainer provides a telling unison refrain that, with its monotone, seems to invoke the style of a plainchant recitation.

By the end of 1887 Stainer was clearly experiencing considerable physical strain. At the heart of the problem was the recurring weakness of his sight which had remained a delicate part of his physiognomy since the accident of 1875, an affliction aggravated by inadequate light of the gas lamps in the St Paul's organ loft; and, so Russell informs us, Stainer found the accompaniment of Spohr's *Last Judgment* increasingly strenuous, and it was this that 'ultimately ... seemed to bring to a head his determination to retire.'[59] By January 1888, Stainer finally concluded, with advice from his doctors and friends, that to continue in his present circumstances was impossible, and so tendered his resignation to Gregory and Chapter:

Dear Canon Gregory,

I beg to place in the hands of the Dean and Chapter my resignation of the posts of Organist and Vicar Choral of St Paul's. The resignation to date from June 25th. In doing so I cannot but express my deep sense of the kindness and consideration which I have received during my tenure of office, and I feel thankful that I have had the privilege of devoting 16 years of my life to the great work being done by St Paul's.

I shall sever myself from the close ties which bind me to St Paul's with sincere regret; but the delicate state of my eyesight and the gradual falling off of my general health compel me to take the step.

May God's blessing rest upon you all and prosper your work.[60]

Chapter reluctantly accepted, but, at the same, moved quickly to effect further reforms. Stainer's replacement, Martin, would now not only be responsible for the organ but also for the training of the boys, the additional work being rewarded by an increase of salary to £500 and a house in Amen Court (with rates and taxes paid

[59] Russell, *St Paul's under Dean Church*, 53.
[60] Letter from Stainer to Canon Gregory, 27 January 1888, Chapter Minutes, *GB-Lsp*.

by Chapter).[61] The position of Assistant Organist, to which Hodge was appointed, would be paid a salary of £100 and a 'suitable person' at £70 a year, who proved to be W. A. Frost, would be appointed to assist Martin with the training of the boys.

Although his resignation dated from 25 June 1888, Stainer in fact played his last service at the cathedral on the morning of 4 May. Having received testimonials from the Special Evening Choir and the Cathedral Choir, he was honoured by a full choir dinner at the Albion Tavern on 22 June. That same month the announcement was made that he and Charles Hallé were to be honoured with knighthoods. Stainer, who was evidently deeply touched by the public accolade, considered it not only recognition of his own work but that of his profession and attributed the recommendation to his old friend Liddon:

> Although I am not supposed to know, yet I <u>do</u> know that I am indebted to you entirely for the "honor" I have lately received on retiring from St Paul's.
>
> Please accept my warmest thanks for this act of kindness, which not only honors me but the whole of my professional brethren. It will always be a comfort to me to know that my work at St Paul's gave <u>you</u> satisfaction.[62]

Liddon denied any involvement, for more likely the proposal for the honour came from Gladstone who was one of the principal proponents of a banquet to pay tribute to the St Paul's organist. On 17 July Stainer was knighted with Hallé at Windsor Castle. The same evening, at the Hotel Metropole, a substantial proportion of the most prominent members of Britain's musical profession attended a dinner in Stainer's honour, chaired by Lord Herschell; it was a mark of homage rarely repeated and one that verified the universal respect that Stainer commanded. He was heard to pay tribute to the Dean and Chapter of St Paul's, to Sullivan and the former NTSM, to the RCM and RAM (whom he hoped might still join forces), and to the Ministry of Education. Sullivan replied and concluded with the following tribute to his old friend:

> Sir John Stainer may perhaps have asked himself why this latest honour has been conferred upon him. Now his modesty (which is really one of his most striking characteristics) may have made him shrink from acknowledging the true reason. I have no such scruples. I will tell you. It is because he is a great master on the king of instruments; it is because he is a profound, eager student; it is because he is a zealous and enthusiastic teacher; it is because

---

[61] In this regard, Martin assumed the role of Cathedral Organist with which we are largely familiar today.

[62] Letter from Stainer to Liddon, 25 July [1888], *GB-Okc*.

he is a composer of power and imagination, and it is because he is a man of blameless honour.[63]

With his resignation from St Paul's, Stainer resolved also to give up his role as organist for the RAHCS and musical director of the Madrigal Society, but agreed to continue his commitment to education. Such decisions were intended to make a clean break with the pressures of London's musical life for the tranquillity of Oxford where, as he explained to Henry Trueman Wood, he hoped to find a 'haven of rest' in their new home in South Parks Road.[64]

---

[63] 'The Sir John Stainer Dinner', *Musical World* (4 August 1888), 612.
[64] Letter from Stainer to H. T. Wood, 21 June [1888], *GB-Lsa*.

'Love Divine, All Loves Excelling':
Oxford (2)

WITHOUT the major tie of services and practices at St Paul's, the unremitting pressure of work on Stainer's daily existence was lifted. The house in Oxford was comfortably situated, close to the university and the Bodleian, and, though he was still called away for college inspections – in 1889 he visited thirty-eight of the forty-three teacher-training institutions – there was more time to devote to composition, scholarship, the publication of the ever expanding series of Novello primers and the third edition of the *Dictionary of Musical Terms*. There was also more freedom for him and his wife (and his children if they chose to accompany them) to visit the Continent for relaxation. Mentone, a favourite resort for the British (as reflected in the many British-named hotels there),[1] especially during the winter months, was often favoured by Stainer, who found the warmer climes more conducive to his declining health. In 1889, however, he chose to visit southern Germany, first to hear *Parsifal* at Bayreuth, and then to witness the famous Domspatzen in Regensburg (Ratisbon), renowned for its singing of polyphony, plainchant and its role in the Cecilian movement (notably with scholars such as Haberl and Proske). Indeed Stainer much admired the Ratisbon edition of plainchant and retained a scepticism about the new hegemony of performance doctrine that was now being promulgated by Solesmes:

> But as one gets old one gets cynical; I remember the clergy of Malines dictated to all the Gregorian world; they were overthrown and superseded by those of Ratisbon; at present the monks of Solesmes are getting the mastery over Ratisbon, so I presume the next generation will see the overthrow of the present dogmatic Benedictines of Solesmes! I prophecy that the next régime will be a dynasty at Rome. You will see.[2]

On 1 March 1889 the death of his old friend and colleague W. H. Monk was announced, and just over a month later came the sad news of Ouseley's death on 6 April in Hereford. One of Ouseley's greatest concerns before his death had

---

[1] See J. Pemble, *The Mediterranean Passion: Victorians and Edwardians in the South* (Oxford: Clarendon Press, 1987), 44.

[2] Letter from Stainer to F. G. Edwards, 22 October 1898, *GB-Lbl* Egerton 3092, fol. 53.

been the welfare and continuance of his foundation at Tenbury, which had never been properly endowed and had largely relied on regular subventions from its founder. Without Ouseley the income of St Michael's was severely reduced and the foundation found itself in a major financial crisis. An appeal for funds was launched to raise an endowment of £10,000, and both Oxford and Tenbury inaugurated a memorial fund for Ouseley, initiatives to which Stainer enthusiastically lent his financial support as well as serving on the memorial committee chaired by Alfred Littleton. But Stainer was moved to pay his fullest tribute to Ouseley in 'The character and influence of the late Sir Frederick Ouseley', a well-balanced paper for a meeting of the Musical Association on 2 December 1889, assessing both the strengths and weaknesses of his former mentor.

With Ouseley's death the Oxford Professorship lay vacant, and speculation naturally ensued about who might succeed him. Stainer's name, of course, was widely discussed and many considered him the natural choice:

> If such a man be appointed, it would not be rash to prophesy a brilliant future for the Oxford School of Music. The names of many eminent musicians are spoken of as candidates. There can be no doubt that if Sir John Stainer were appointed, his acceptance of the office would give the highest possible satisfaction in all quarters. He possesses all the qualifications necessary, and would command the confidence of musicians and of all interested in music throughout the world.[3]

As an Oxford resident he was now ideally placed (even though the position was non-resident), but, given his failing health and poor sight, there was doubt about whether he wanted this additional responsibility having so recently retired from St Paul's. Moreover, there were those in Oxford, among them C. H. Lloyd, organist of Christ Church Cathedral, and the historian, Henry Pelham, who were urging Parry to stand, no doubt to complement the recent appointment of Stanford at Cambridge. Indeed, Stanford was also keen to see his RCM colleague step into Ouseley's shoes, and wrote to Francis Palgrave, Professor of Modern Poetry at Oxford, to give his influential opinion:

Strictly Private

My dear Palgrave,

> I cannot resist writing you a line, as I see you are one of the board of Arts at Oxford, asking you in the interests of all that is right and proper in music to forward Hubert Parry's interests (for the sake of Oxford) in the matter of the Professorship of Music. I know he will do nothing himself because of

---

[3] *Musical Times* 30 (May 1889), 272.

his loyalty to his old friendship for Stainer: and I also have the very highest regard for Stainer: but all the same the world 50 years hence won't understand Stainer having been made Professor, when Parry was there to be made it. Anymore than they would understand if Beethoven and Spohr were candidates, the selection of Spohr in preference to Beethoven.

That is perhaps a high flight of comparison, but it fairly represents the comparative value.

I of course have no business to meddle or say a word: and if I did I should do more harm than good. But one like yourself can do a great deal. So don't mention me, but please do what you can. The post is one of the blue ribbons of the musical profession, and it ought to go to one of our greatest men, especially as he is through and through an Oxford man.[4]

But, as Stanford anticipated, Parry would not betray the loyalty he retained to his old Oxford friend, and wrote to him in April urging him to accept the post if offered to him 'as the only man who had a chance of doing any good', and with the proposition that he (Parry) would be delighted to assist him as Choragus. Stainer, however, held off his decision to apply for over a month, and Parry, not wishing to be seen to disregard the support of his friends, sent a copy of his application to Lloyd.[5] By pure chance, Parry and Stainer happened to meet on Gloucester station, where Stainer informed his younger colleague that his eyes were much improved and that he would be willing to accept the chair: 'In the circumstances Parry decided that it would be both ungenerous and impolitic to stand against him. A contest might result in splitting the vote and bringing in an undesirable candidate.'[6] As it transpired, twenty-four applicants were considered for the professorship, though there seemed little doubt that no one but Stainer would carry the day. Official news of his appointment was announced in the *Oxford University Gazette* on 18 June 1889; Ouseley's ancient wish had finally been realised.

Initially Stainer had major ambitions of transforming music at Oxford into an educational edifice that aspired to a much broader range of musical attainment than was possible with the *status quo*. Recognised as a part of the Oxford Liberal set – one that was now in the ascendant – he was expected to bring his reforming zeal to a degree which, in the light of Stanford's meteoric reforms at Cambridge, had advanced only moderately since Ouseley instituted his changes in the early 1860s. Indeed, Hadow mentioned that Stainer, with his experience at

---

4 Letter from Stanford to Francis Palgrave, 27 April 1889, *GB-Lbm* Add. MS 45741, fol. 209.

5 J. C. Dibble, *C. Hubert H. Parry: His Life and Music* (Oxford: Clarendon Press, 1992), 282–3.

6 C. L. Graves, *Hubert Parry: His Life and Works* (London: Macmillan & Co., 1926), vol. 2, 15.

the NTSM and as H. M. Inspector, entertained the notion of a conservatoire in Oxford, though the proposal that practical tuition might be introduced (which Stanford had partially achieved through the employment of Richard Gompertz as a resident violinist) proved to be well beyond what could realistically be achieved.[7] Nevertheless, Stainer sought to give music in Oxford a prominence, status and respect which it had hitherto never enjoyed.

He had, fortunately, arrived back in Oxford after another period of considerable reform to the ancient universities generated by the 1877 Commission. Rules on celibate fellowships had been relaxed, the religious tests were abolished (through the Universities Tests Act of 1871), the number of clergymen fellows was, in spite of High Church opposition, diminishing rapidly (indeed, the Commission no longer saw fellowships as existing purely for the interest of the Church), and a more organised, secularly based system of education for undergraduates was taking shape through the formation of Boards of Studies, advocated by W. W. Jackson and H. Pelham.[8] A major consequence of this development was the publication of public lectures by university professors who, with the Commission's blessing, were encouraged to appoint readers to assist with teaching and tuition.[9] Moreover, a full reading list was published,[10] and Stainer, encouraged by this new pedagogical spirit, took it upon himself to provide a short manual, *A Few Words to Candidates for the degree of Mus. Bac. Oxon.* in 1892 to advise prospective students of the university's expectations.

Stainer took full advantage of this opportunity to develop a teaching staff at the music faculty by appointing Henry Hadow (Worcester College), Lloyd (Christ Church), John Varley Roberts (Parratt's successor at Magdalen), Taylor (New College), Francis Cunningham-Woods (Exeter), the J. H. Mee (Worcester and Coryphaeus) and the physicist, Frederick John Jervis-Smith (Trinity), while Parry,

---

[7] See Hadow archives, 12 May 1889, *GB-Owc*. See also J. Dibble, *Charles Villiers Stanford: Man and Musician* (Oxford: Oxford University Press, 2002), 102.

[8] A. J. Engel, *From Clergyman to Don: The Rise of the Academic Profession in Nineteenth-Century Oxford* (Oxford: Clarendon Press, 1983), 168–70.

[9] Ibid., 173.

[10] Recommended texts for students for the Mus.Bac. (many of them from the list of Novello Primers) were Ouseley's *Treatise on Harmony*, harmony manuals by Macfarren and Stainer, and counterpoint manuals by Cherubini, Ouseley and Bridge. For the D.Mus. Stainer recommended Bridge's *Double Counterpoint*, Higgs's *Fugue*, instrumentation manuals by Berlioz and Prout, histories of music by Burney, Hawkins and Naumann, Hullah's *History of Modern Music* and *Transition Period of Musical History*, Ouseley's *Treatise on Form* and Parry's article on 'Form' in *Grove*. For the study of acoustics, Helmholtz's *Sensations of Tone*, Pole's *Philosophy of Music*, Stone's *Scientific Basis of Music* and Sedley Taylor's *Sound and Music* were stipulated.

based in London, lectured and examined degrees in his capacity as Choragus. As Heather Professor of Music, Stainer was obliged to deliver one lecture each term; these took place in the Sheldonian Theatre, illustrated by singers and instrumentalists. The rest were given by Parry (whose presence as a lecturer ceased after 1892) and Hadow, who provided a substantial number on music of the Classical and Romantic eras. In the first two years there were only five lectures, three by Stainer and two by Parry, but after 1890 the number of lectures increased to six or even seven lectures as other scholars were invited to speak. Lloyd, Woods, Percy Buck and Frederick Iliffe gave individual lectures, and Stainer, who, retaining his fascination for ethnic musics, invited outside scholars such as Francis Taylor Piggott (one time constitutional advisor to the Prime Minister of Japan, Hirobumi) to speak on Japanese music (1892–3), Rabbi Francis Cohen on musical traditions of the synagogue (1893–4), and the well-known Slavophile, W. J. Birkbeck on music of the Russian liturgy (1894–5).[11]

J. H. Mee, in his role as Coryphaeus (one soon to be abolished), conducted what was called the 'Professor's Choir' in all choral illustrations for Stainer's lectures. This body was constituted of various singers around the university, but irregular attendance and the number of singers – Stainer always preferred a larger body to a small one – often left him feeling anxious. Arthur Mann, whose chapel choir and choral society Stainer much admired, offered his help for the lectures, but Stainer clearly feared that bringing singers from Cambridge would be politically embarrassing:

> You are very good to bring us help, but I verily believe I should be "stoned to death" if I were to suggest such a thing! No! I must wait a little longer: perhaps more voices may offer. We have a very good Society 250 strong in Oxford, but my lectures are illustrated by a distinct body called the "Professor's Choir" which only musters about 70 or 80.
>
> If I can find time I certainly will accept your kind offer of singing a service or a madrigal: it is too tempting! At present I feel more like a merchant's clerk than a musician; nearly the whole of my time is occupied in an uninteresting routine of business letters! Best thanks all the same.[12]

Parry's lectures were, to a large extent, characterised by his strong affinity for Spencerian philosophy and his view of history as 'progress', but his lectures also revealed his particular interest in music of the seventeenth century, in early Italian vocal music, opera, the music of Cavalieri, Monteverdi, Cavalli and Carissimi,

---

[11] All these scholars duly gave papers for the Musical Association: Birkbeck on 14 April 1891, Piggott on 12 April 1892, and Cohen (with Stainer in the chair) on 13 June 1893.

[12] Letter from Stainer to A. H. Mann, 20 July 1891, *GB-NWr*.

Lully, Purcell and English viol music. The last topic brought Parry's former RCM pupil Arnold Dolmetsch to Oxford, as he recalled:

> Met Stainer at station and he brought up a bus to take down Dolmetsch and his folk and their instruments. Lunch at Stainers and a deal of talking which exhausted me utterly, and by the time I got to the [Sheldonian] Theatre I was quite unfit to say a word. But I got through somehow and Dolmetsch gave the audience a very complete dose of old viol music. Too much contrapuntal stuff, and too little damn music. His daughter played Christopher Simpsons last 'division' wonderfully well.'[13]

The subjects of Stainer's lectures were even more wide-ranging than those of Parry, and reflected the Oxford Professor's impressive catholicity of interest and enthusiasms. Among them were old favourites. His veneration of Mendelssohn was enshrined in two lectures on *Elijah* and *St Paul*, of Handel with a lecture on *Messiah* (for which he drew on material collected by Mann, an ardent collector of Handelian memoribilia, at Cambridge), and Mozart on his Requiem. His love of carols gave rise to a lecture on 19 November 1890 in which a discussion on different types of carol 'genres' (Carols of the Shepherds, Dialogues on the Nativity, Localisation of the Christmas Story, Summons to Native Townships, Cradle Songs, Reflective Carols, Epiphany Carols and Feasting Carols) was based on his recent publication of *Twelve Old Carols, English and Foreign* for Novello.

Enthralled by the genre of song, hymn and carol, Stainer had spent much of his life assiduously collecting editions of English song books. Such was the extent of his library that, in May 1891 he decided to publish a catalogue for private circulation with Novello in the hope that it would 'prove a useful instalment towards a Bibliography of Song-Books' and remind scholars that the literature of this subject was immensely wide. The volume was compiled with the assistance of J. F. R., Cecie and Charles Lewis Stainer, and listed hundreds of valuable publications in addition to appendices of 'Popular Songs of Various Nations, Carols, Dances and Dancing' and 'Bells and Ringing'.[14] His passion for song manifested itself in a number of different ways in his Oxford lectures. On the generic questions of melody he delivered a lecture on 'Influences which affect melodic form' (November 1895), and on the general relationship between song forms and dance forms his lecture 'Song and Dance' on 29 November 1893 had a strong practical dimension in that it involved both choral and orchestral illustrations performed by members of the university.

---

[13] Diary of Hubert Parry, 26 November 1891, *GB-Shp*.

[14] Stainer continued to add to this portion of his library after 1891; the present writer owns a copy presented by Stainer to the Cambridge University Musical Club which shows further autograph annotations of additional volumes.

He was also a keen advocate of song composers. His second lecture, on 27 February 1890, was devoted entirely to Schumann's songs, with illustrations provided by a gifted RCM student, Mary Maude Paget, daughter of the celebrated surgeon Sir James Paget. She was evidently a favourite of Stainer's for she was often prevailed upon to sing at his lectures. In a lecture on composers' styles seen through the prism of settings of the same lyric (which included seven settings of Goethe's 'Kennst du das Land' and Heine's 'Du bist wie eine Blume' on 6 May 1891) she was asked to perform, and for his lecture on Purcell (marking the composer's bicentenary) on 19 November 1895 she sang 'Fairest Isle', among other vocal numbers. For his lecture on 'Song-writers of the Classical period' he chose as his principal examples pieces by Cavalli, Alessandro Scarlatti, Gasparini, d'Astorga, Durante and Galuppi which were later published as *Six Italian Songs, arrangements of Italian seventeenth- and eighteenth-century songs and arias* with English words adapted by Stainer himself. Paget sang the illustrations from the proofs:

> You are most kind. I am sure the Italian songs could not be in better hands for a thoroughly musicianlike rendering.
>
> I send today a set of printers proofs of all the six songs. I thought you might like to make the acquaintance of all of them, although I only want you to sing three. The two which have Violin obbligato are Non dar più pene (Scarlatti) and Fier destin (Gasparini) so these will naturally fall to your lot.
>
> I suppose Miss Bué had better sing Dolce Amoir (Cavalli) – otherwise you will have 3 songs consecutively! Now I want you to select the one you like best from Danza fanciulla (Durante) and La bella pastorella (Galuppi) and let me know. The "Danza fanciulla" goes at a great pace and is very bright and spirited. I selected Galuppi's Pastorella as a good specimen of the innumerable songs of its type, which our ancestors were so fond of. Astorga's song is really very beautiful, and if you fall in love with it and do not mind 3 songs consecutively – you can sing that instead of Durante or Galuppi. Only, I shall be glad to know soon. You can keep the proofs until I send you a proper copy.
>
> I am yours gratefully
> John Stainer
>
> I may ask you to sing one or two tiny scraps by Monteverde, as early specimens of opera songs.[15]

Stainer's interest in the seventeenth- and eighteenth-century songs also extended to the lute and consort song ('Lute, Viol and Voice' in November 1892),

---

[15] Letter from Stainer to Mary Maude Paget, 15 October 1896, *GB-Lam* McCann Collection.

and his fascination for the music of Gibbons, Byrd, Morley and other English composers of this period reflected a profound love he retained from his days at Tenbury in the music of the Renaissance. Given the massive revival of Palestrina's sacred music on the Continent, particularly among the Cecilians, and the growth of new editions by scholars such as Haberl, it is little surprise that Stainer devoted one whole lecture to Palestrina's *Missa Aeterna Christi munera* (1893). Other lectures on early topics followed. During the academic years 1895–9 he delivered lectures on Morley's *Plaine and Easie Introduction to Practicall Musicke*, Christopher Tye's mass *Euge bone* (which he described to Barclay Squire as 'quite a revelation'),[16] Hans Leo Hassler, the 'Madrigals of the Gallo-Belgian School' (in which he included illustrations by Jannequin, Sermisy, Verdelot and Jacotin taken from sources consulted in the Bodleian Library), and of perhaps greatest consequence, the secular compositions of Dufay.

Stainer's lecture on Dufay, given during the summer of 1896, arose essentially from his friendship with the Bodleian Librarian, Edward Williams Byron Nicholson, who had been appointed after the death of H. O. Coxe in 1881, having been librarian at the London Institution since 1873. Nicholson had brought major reforms to the Bodleian, including extensions to its premises, new rules for cataloguing, a considerable expansion of its books and an enlargement of staff. Nicholson was a man of wide interests which included comparative philology, classical literature and Celtic antiquity. In connection with the latter, he took a practical interest in song texts. In December 1894 Nicholson sent a simple Welsh air (with an accompaniment by Barrett) to Stainer for his scrutiny. Stainer was much taken with it:

> I think the song is exceedingly pretty and I should like to keep my eye on it for publication amongst Novello's School Songs unless you would like to see it turned out in a more ambitious form. I think Barrett's accompaniment is not quite simple enough to suit the sort of "national" character of the song. If you will allow me I will try my hand at a suitable accomp[t] – you can destroy my effort if you don't like it. … I think it might run the length and breadth of the land if introduced into schools. Barrett had quite overlooked the beautiful harmonic sequence which commences at bar 13.[17]

In October 1895 the two men were working on several Welsh airs. In setting the Welsh Stainer was bemused about stress and syllable: 'I find I have not the least idea how to divide the Welsh words into syllables. Would you kindly write them

---

[16] Letter from Stainer to Barclay Squire, 10 March 1896, *GB-Lbl* Add. MS 39680, fol. 128.

[17] Letter from Stainer to E. W. B. Nicholson, 21 December 1894, *GB-Ob* Eng. Misc. e.63, fols. 2–3.

under the music and return it to me?'[18] And writing from the office of the *School Music Review*, where he had consulted his colleagues on the airs, he added: 'I have been ... talking over your song "dear mountains." I don't know much about Welsh airs, but the folk here seem to think your tune would remind people of the "Ash Grove." Is that so? If you know any Welsh musicians, you might ask him if there is any real likeness or whether it is merely the relation of style and rhythm.'[19]

This collaboration engendered a close rapport between the two men, and Stainer was keen to support Nicholson during his reforms. These had excited controversy and opposition, not least from the Bodleian's senior sub-librarian, Falconer Madan, an acolyte of Coxe, and a detractor of what he perceived as Nicholson's inadequate scholarly abilities. Nicholson, sensitive to criticism, always reacted strongly; this brought much stress to his job, as well as numerous enemies. 'I am always sorry to see you so worried about your work', Stainer wrote sympathetically. '*Do please* try my plan of being perfectly pliant and submissive for a year or two. If you do this I feel confident that certain folks won't give up teazing you. ... Do try it, and make yourself perfectly "hardened" inwardly to the results.'[20]

But undoubtedly the most important product of the friendship with Nicholson was Stainer's introduction to the catalogue of manuscripts in the Bodleian, principally because Nicholson was interested in publishing a facsimile collection under the title *Early Bodleian Music*.[21] This must have been by the end of the summer of 1894, for Stainer informed Arthur Mann at Cambridge that he was unable to compose an eight-part service for King's College because he was so absorbed with the Bodleian's musical treasures:

> How I should like to write an 8–part service for you! but where is the time to come from? I and two of my children are preparing a big 2 Vol work:- Vol. I, over a hundred facsimiles of Bodleian music dating from AD 1225 to AD 1400. Vol. II a transcription of all the music! Of course it will only appeal to students and antiquarians – but to them it will be deeply interesting. I am also super-vising for the said 2 children "Dufay and his contemporaries" a collection of 50 compositions between AD 1400 – & 1440! from the Canonici M.S.[22]

In the first instance it was Charles Lewis Stainer who examined the indices of

---

[18] Letter from Stainer to Nicholson, 14 October 1895, *GB-Ob* Eng. Misc.e.63, fol. 13.

[19] Letter from Stainer to Nicholson, 22 October 1895, *GB-Ob* Eng. Misc.e.63, fols. 15–16.

[20] Letter from Stainer to Nicholson, 7 December 1896, *GB-Ob* Eng. Misc.e.63, fol. 98.

[21] D. Fallows, *Oxford, Bodleian Library MS. Canon. Misc. 213* (Chicago: University of Chicago Press, 1995), 1.

[22] Letter from Stainer to Mann, 28 September 1894, *GB-NWr*.

the Bodleian catalogue. After he came upon the Canonici manuscript (MS. Cano-nici misc. 213) through Coxe's inventory published in 1854, it was soon decided that a publication of selected pieces from this source warranted a separate volume.[23] Nicholson had actually glanced at Canonici misc. 213 in 1887, but at that time had not grasped the importance and rarity of the fifteenth-century Continental secular music that it contained.[24] It is an indication of Stainer's scholarly awareness that, when he came to scrutinise the Canonici manuscript, he immediately understood its significance through his knowledge of Continental scholarship. It is clear that he knew Kiesewetter's *Geschichte der europaeisch-abendlaendischen oder unsrer heutigen Musik* (1834) and, co-authored with Fétis, *Verhandelingen over de Vraag* (1829), but of later scholarly work he boasted considerable familiarity. This is evident from the paper he delivered to the Musical Association on 12 Novem-ber 1895 entitled 'A Fifteenth Century MS. Book of Vocal Music in the Bodleian Library, Oxford', in which we know that he drew on a range of European sources, such as Coussemaker's *Scriptorum de musica medii aevi novam seriem a Gerber-tina alteram collegit nuncque primum* (1864), and his paper *Les harmonistes du quatorzième siècle* (written, though unfinished, in 1869), Jules Houdoy's *Histoire artistique de la cathédrale de Cambrai* (1880), E. Vander Straeten's *La musique aux Pays-Bas* (1878), Ambros's *Geschichte der Musik* (1862), Fétis's *Histoire générale de la musique* (1869), Gevaert's *Les origines du chant liturgique de l'église Latine* (1890), Guiseppe Liseo's *Una stanza del Petrarca musicata da Guillaume Du Fay* (1893), and, perhaps of greatest importance, Haberl's substantial monograph in *Bausteine für Musikgeschichte* (Vol. 1) on Dufay, published in Leipzig in 1885. It is clear too that he had developed a working knowledge of important treatises (such as those by Johannes de Muris, Ciconia and Tinctoris) and primary sources, especially in Italy.[25]

What is also evident, however, is the extraordinary energy that Nicholson and John, J. F. R. and Cecie Stainer showed in their work on the manuscript before Stainer gave his paper in November. It was J. F. R. and Cecie Stainer who made

[23] See J. F. R. Stainer's preface in *Early Bodleian Music*, vol. 1 (London: Novello & Co., 1901). Though C. L. Stainer appears not to have participated in further study of Canonici 213, he went on to become a distinguished gentleman scholar, particu-larly of English seventeenth-century literature.

[24] The Canonici manuscripts, so titled because they had belonged to one Matteo Luigi Canonici, a Venetian Jesuit who died in 1805, had been purchased by the Bodleian in 1817. Canonici, as Nicholson later argued, acquired these manuscripts from Giacomo Soranzo, though this is now disputed by Fallows.

[25] It is not clear whether Stainer also new Hugo Riemann's *Sechs bisher nicht gedruckte dreistimmige Chansons (für Tenor, Diskant, und Kontratenor) von Gilles Binchois c. 1425* (Wiesbaden, 1892), though it is evident that his work was known by the publication of *Dufay and his contemporaries* in 1898 (see p. 15).

the transcriptions – preliminary work (of the separate voice parts) still survives, chiefly in the hand of J. F. R. Stainer, of twenty-four Dufay songs dated between 24 August and 24 September 1895.[26] As Fallows reminds us, though all the Dufay songs were in unfamiliar notation, they were put into score with an impressive quality and accuracy.[27]

Stainer's paper mentioned no fewer than twenty-eight songs by Dufay and listed all the other composers contained in the manuscript. Clearly enthused by his material, Stainer attempted to provide an historical context for the songs, not only in terms of the individual composers, their lives and employment, but also in the hope that the music of John Dunstable (whose absence from Canonici was remarked by both Stainer and his son), would become an important focus of national attention.[28] Stainer also provided an explanation of the manuscript's notation, the first seven pages written in the old 'black' notation and the rest in the 'white or open note' notation (now described as 'void').[29] He also gave numerous examples of cadences, the system of *musica ficta* and the nature of the open fifths at cadences, though much of this, as Temperley has remarked, was largely governed by his understanding of contemporary harmony and tonality.[30] 'It was quite natural and logical', he wrote, 'that composers of this early period should close with a simple fifth, without a third. The argument which produced *organum*, or the movement in octaves, fifths, and fourths, was this: these intervals are perfect; how can one improve perfection? Why should I spoil my perfect concord by adding imperfect intervals?'[31]

[26] See *GB-Ob* Add. MS 43736. This manuscript also contains fair copies of Dufay songs which were not included in the *Dufay* volume but which were evidently prepared for engraving.

[27] Fallows, *MS. Canon. Misc. 213*, 1.

[28] Such was Stainer's interest in Dunstable that he enquired to Barclay Squire at the British Library about the possibility of transcribing facsimiles: 'Is it true that you have a lot of facsimiles or working copies of Dunstable's works? If you should at any time want assistance (I know how you are pressed with work) I am sure my son John (who lives at 8 Furnivals Inn) would gladly help to score them. He has developed great skill and correctness at it.' (See *GB-Lbl* MS. 39680, fol. 126.)

[29] For a commentary on these notational differences in the manuscript, see Fallows, *MS. Canon. Misc. 213*, 6.

[30] N. Temperley, 'Ancient and Modern in the Work of Sir John Stainer', in *Nineteenth-Century British Music Studies*, vol. 3, ed. P. Horton & B. Zon (Aldershot: Ashgate, 2003), 107.

[31] J. Stainer, 'A Fifteenth Century MS. Book of Vocal Music in the Bodleian Library, Oxford' [12 November 1895], *Proceedings of the Musical Association* 22 (1895–6), 15.

A striking element of Stainer's paper, and one that is palpable even now, is the novelty of Dufay's music to his audience and the fact that he was, to some degree, anxious as to its reception. In a world where consecutive fifths were still a grammatical taboo, the position of Dufay and the music of the early fifteenth century was perceived largely in teleogical terms, as 'primitive' and part of a Darwinist historical model of 'musical babyhood' (to use Parry's term). Indeed, Stainer himself clearly understood it as music which 'cleared the ground for, and helped to lay the foundations of that splendid fabric of pure polyphonic vocal music which, two centuries later, stood revealed in its beauty and grandeur.'[32] He felt the need to prepare his listeners for the experience of hearing this music for the first time. 'Dufay not only uses bare fifths in cadences and elsewhere', he explained, 'but he evidently had a genuine liking for what we call "consecutive fifths." He sometimes writes them boldly, but he generally indulges his taste for them by crossing the parts.'[33] Drawing attention to these unfamiliar sounds and methods, Stainer primed his audience for an aural event almost entirely foreign to them. He had been somewhat confounded by the provision of live musical examples. 'It would have been a hopeless task to try and find three or four good singers who were sufficiently advanced philologists to sing the old French words', he expounded; 'it would require a vocal quartet of Max Müllers!'[34] Instead, with the theory that the songs would have been performed on 'an early form of viol', four examples, printed copies of which were distributed to the Musical Association members and guests, were played on three or four violas by players from the RCM. 'On listening to Dufay', he beseeched his listeners, 'his archaisms and crudities may at first tempt you to laugh. But as the music proceeds I think your interest will be thoroughly roused, and, if I am not mistaken, you will leave this room giving in your hearts honour to this great man.'[35]

Three years after Stainer's paper for the Musical Association, he, his son and daughter, and Nicholson published *Dufay and His Contemporaries* with Novello. Parry, who had attended the paper in 1895, described Stainer's work as a 'revelation', and made much of the 'gap in musical history which required to be filled up between Dunstable and the late Netherlander before the process of evolution could be verified'.[36] Other European scholars were quick to notice the volume. Stainer suspected that Henri Expert, author of *Les maîtres musiciens de la renaissance française* was privy to his work: 'I suspect Mons. Henri Expert has been reading our Dufay. I have just received the last number of his edition of old French

[32] Ibid., 18.
[33] Ibid., 15.
[34] Ibid., 18.
[35] Ibid.
[36] Ibid., 22.

masters and he (*for the first time*) bursts out into a disquisition on musica ficta and its relation to the Tritone! giving some of my examples but in the C clef.'[37] Johannes Wolf made an extensive review in the *Sammelbände der Internationalen Musik-Gesellschaft*,[38] Robert Eitner wrote a short review in the *Monatshefte für Musikgeschichte*,[39] and Guido Adler, editor of *Denkmäler der Tonkunst in Öster-reich*, paid tribute to Stainer in his latest volume:

> I presume you have seen the recently issued volume of the "Denkmäler der Tonkunst in Österreich" which contains the celebrated Trent coll.[ection] (6 MSS) so full of Dunstable's works. If you have not provided for a notice of it in your next, would you like one? My son or daughter (both good German scholars) would do it satisfactorily I think. In the preface, Dr Adler, the Editor, pays sweet compliments to our "Dufay".[40]

As part of Novello's commercial plan to give the volume added prestige, a copy was presented to the King of the Belgians. 'I suppose we must wait for an acknowledge-ment from the King of the Belgians before we announce that he has accepted a copy', Stainer wrote to Edwards; 'but he is a cultured man, and Cambrai is a part of his kingdom.'[41]

In preparing the *Dufay* volume, Nicholson provided an introductory essay on the provenance and condition of the Canonici manuscript; J. F. R. and Cecie Stainer furnished an historical chapter; J. F. R. Stainer produced an essay on men-surable music (material which he was to use later for a Musical Association paper 'The Notation of Mensurable Music' on 12 June 1900); and Stainer himself pro-vided an analytical essay on elements of style and method. A letter to Edwards, written on holiday in France from the Hôtel du Cap, Antibes, shortly before the volume was published, reveals his satisfaction in the project, the realisation of its intrinsic musical value, and of the new questions it posed to musical historians and scholars:

> I had not time to pursue our conversation about the consecutive 5ths in the works of Dufay and his contemporaries. But I want to tell you <u>in confi-dence</u>, and before the Book is out, that these consecutives open up a most interesting historical fact, not hitherto suspected, namely that Organum and

37 Postcard from Stainer to Edwards, 7 July 1899, *GB-Lbl* Egerton 3092, fol. 83 .

38 J. Wolf, 'Dufay und seine Zeit', *Sammelbände der Internationalen Musik-Gesell-schaft*, 1 (1899–1900), 150–63, 330.

39 R. Eitner, *Monatshefte der Musikgeschichte*, 31 (1899), 63–4.

40 Letter from Stainer to Edwards, 22 June 1900, *GB-Lbl* Egerton 3092, fol. 101. Cecie Stainer's article, 'The Trent Codices', for the *Musical Times*, effectively provided a review of Adler's volume.

41 Letter from Stainer to Edwards, 14 July [1899], *GB-Lbl* Egerton 3092, fol. 84.

Diaphony (movement in 4ths and 5ths) must have held complete control over the music of church and <u>people</u> for a couple of centuries at least. All historians touch lightly on Diaphony, as if it were a mere <u>passing phase</u> of musical evolution, whereas, our book will prove that up to the very threshold of modern music consecutive triads were <u>loved</u>. If you heard the Dufay examples at the Mus. Ass^{n.} played on 3 violas, or on 4, you must have been struck with a certain weird charm when the old man crosses the parts in order to obtain the 5ths in which he and his hearers <u>delighted</u>.

I shall of course bring out this fact in the musical dissertation which I shall add to my son's learned historical and critical Preface. You will be interested to know that the large volume of manuscripts from Bodleian MSS (A.D. 1200–1400) brings out this equally strongly, and many other things of even greater interest.

Thus "Dufay and his contemporaries" will be sufficiently exhaustive to set at rest for ever all questions as to what sort of music was considered best and most beautiful between 1400 and 1440. No one need take the trouble to produce more specimens or go over the same ground! No small matter to have achieved such results![42]

Stainer did indeed express these views in the preface to the second part of a double-volume publication *Early Bodleian Music*, which contained facsimiles (Vol.1) and transcriptions (Vol. 2) of much of the rest of the Bodleian's early 'Sacred and Secular Songs', from a range of sources, written between *c.* 1185 and *c.* 1505. This publication meant that a substantial portion of the scheme Nicholson had originally envisaged was brought to fruition. J. F. R. and Cecie Stainer once again provided the transcriptions under Stainer's editorship. However, as his son pointed out in his postscript, Stainer did not live to complete his critique, though he did provide pencil notes about some of the areas on which intended to expound.[43] With Stainer's death in March 1901, the momentum of Nicholson's project was lost for a time, and it was only in 1913 that the final volume, *Introduction to the Study of Some of the Oldest Latin Musical Manuscripts in the Bodleian Library, Oxford*, solely edited by Nicholson, was brought before the public. Had Stainer lived, he would almost certainly have co-edited the entire publication, but what he left, albeit unfinished, in terms of a scholarly legacy, was remarkable. As Fallows has stated, Stainer 'revolutionised the study of fifteenth-century music' after his paper for the Musical Association, and the 'epoch-making' publication of *Dufay* was one of the 'earliest of the grand editions of fifteenth-century music that continued with the early volumes of the Austrian *Denkmäler* series',

---

[42] Letter from Stainer to Edwards, 11 January 1898, *GB-Lbl* Egerton 3092, fol. 34.

[43] See *Early Bodleian Music*, vol. 2, ed. J. Stainer (London: Novello & Co., 1901), xii.

its only precessor being Barbieri's *Cancionero musical de los siglos XV y XVI* of 1890.[44]

Excluding Stainer's Dufay lecture at Oxford in 1896 (which was disseminated under the aegis of the Musical Association), only three of Stainer's Oxford lectures were published, and none of them reflects his scholarly interests in antiquity. However, these published writings provide an insight into two other sides of his multi-faceted interests and broad experience. 'Music in its Relation to the Intellect and the Emotions', given at the Sheldonian Theatre on 8 June 1892, revealed his enthusiasm for broader aesthetic questions. His discussion of sound and reception, which drew heavily on Helmholtz's *Die Lehre von den Tonempfindungen als physiologische Grundlage für die Theorie der Musik* (1863) and Pole's English summary *The Philosophy of Music* (1879), formed the beginnings of an exposé of how evolutionism in the Brahms–Wagner axis of the late nineteenth century was venerated as the apogee of musical creativity.

Stainer believed that 'no aiming at good art by the creator, no criticism of music by its hearer, no separation of good and bad can take place, until creator and hearer have on some common ground passed judgment on certain questions which are not within the scope of mere intellect, but are within the realm of taste'.[45] It is in connection with this point, rehearsed in 'The Principles of Musical Criticism', that he examined the 'sentiment of the Beautiful' as 'an operation [which commences] where the explanation of the intelligence ends'.[46] He showed himself to be well read in the philosophical writings of Kant, Hegel, Holmes-Forbes, Spencer, Sully, Gurney, Herbarth, Hanslick and Véron. He fully concurred with Hegel in believing that music was the most subjective of the all arts, and, rejecting the notion of *objective* art, he believed that 'there can be no emotion where there is no sentiment of the Beautiful; no sentiment of the Beautiful without an operation of the Intellect; no operation of the Intellect without Sensations of Sound'.[47] Stainer accepted Kant's view (read in Max Müller's translation of the *Critique of Pure Reason*) that critical judgment of the beautiful under rational principles would only be empirical, and 'could never serve as definite *a priori* rules for our judgment in matters of taste'.[48] Yet in the last part of his paper he attempted to articulate a rationale for the 'Intellect' and the 'Apprehension of the Beautiful' by way of establishing abstract instrumental music, and more specifically *symphonic* music, as the 'most advanced walk of art'. A full comprehension of symphonic music required the

---

44 Fallows, *MS. Canon. Misc. 213*, 2.

45 J. Stainer, *Music in its Relation to the Intellect and the Emotions* (London: Novello & Co., 1892), 19.

46 Ibid., 20.

47 Ibid., 24.

48 Ibid., 31.

possession of 'technical acquirements' and the application of the intellect (here he and Edmund Gurney markedly diverged), but Stainer wanted to steer a course between the 'intellectualists' and the 'emotionalists' (the one claiming the art purely as cerebral territory, the other denying necessity of 'rules and regulations') by creating an 'ideal hearer', though he clearly admitted to favouring the 'intelligent non-emotionalist' rather than the 'untrained emotionalist', since the latter he considered would have little or nothing to offer. The crux of Stainer's lecture was his pleading for a new generation of 'intelligent hearers', for in them, he contended, lay the future of an educated musical public. Moreover, he appealed to his public to reject the beguiling genres of programme music, for, he argued, deep emotion can only arise where 'the beauty of pure music is grasped and felt by an intellect musically trained'.[49]

At the heart of his musical philosophy, however, lay his conviction in the principles of 'social Darwinism' and the theory that man's biological progress was mirrored by a similar process in the arts and ethics. It was a view which ultimately endorsed the supremacy of symphonic music, in all its formal involution and abstractness, as the highest achievement of the composer and the aspiration of the sophisticated listener. In this he was at one with Parry (whose book *The Art of Music* appeared the following year) and Hadow (whose *Studies in Modern Music* were published in 1892 and 1894) as an admirer of Herbert Spencer, an allegiance which characterised what Frank Howes described as 'an Oxford school of criticism'.[50] 'May not our own great living philosopher [Spencer]', Stainer concluded his lecture, 'be also a true prophet when, having approached music purely from the side of the scientific analyst, he says: Music is "a language of feelings which may ultimately enable men vividly and completely to impress on each other the emotions they experience from moment to moment." '[51]

For his inaugural lecture at Oxford on 13 November 1889, published by the university printers, Stainer chose to examine musical progress in England as a major issue, in part to give a balanced view of where ground was being made, but also as a means of inculcating, indeed encouraging, change in the perception of music as a university discipline. In the opening paragraphs of 'The Present State of Music in England', he paid tribute to his predecessor, Ouseley, for the broad range of subjects on which he had lectured. But at the same time, in describing his former master's 'old type of discourse', there was undoubtedly the sentiment that time had moved on and the world of Ouseley's university was altogether outmoded. At the age of forty-nine Stainer had witnessed huge changes in the role of music in England and

---

49 Ibid., 60–1.

50 F. Howes, *The English Musical Renaissance* (London: Secker & Warburg, 1966), 355.

51 Stainer, *Music in its Relation to the Intellect and the Emotions*, 63.

the various major debates that had developed on the subjects of education, church music, concert life and opera. These were the principal foci of his assessment, considered, he hoped, with unbiased faculties, treading a central course between the 'two opposite schools': one that continued to assert that England was not a musical nation, and never would be; the other determined to gainsay this claim by avowing that England had always been musical in spite of foreign prejudice.

The first object of scrutiny was opera, a genre in which Stainer had participated little except as a keen spectator. Here he expressed a number of interesting views. Like Macfarren (who had died in 1887), he guarded against an excessive worship of Handel, an influence which had been injurious on English music; yet he maintained that, though Italian opera no longer enjoyed European supremacy, its traditions of voice-training should be not be ignored in favour of 'the melodic progressions of the modern German school'.[52] Nevertheless, Stainer greatly admired the operatic progressivism of Wagner, in spite of the distrust with which the composer was still regarded in some national quarters:

> It is perhaps too early to gauge the exact position of Wagner in the world of art, or to prophesy the extent of his influence on the music of the future. Indeed, it is difficult to obtain a calm judgment of his merits at the present time. It would be folly to ignore the fact that many admirable musicians and astute musical critics view his innovations with suspicion, and are not attracted by the rich flow of novelty in his later works. On the other hand, I think it clearly impossible to place the composer of Lohengrin, Tannhäuser, and Die Meistersinger, in any but the first rank.[53]

Stainer's approbation of Wagner stemmed of course from his visit to Bayreuth only weeks before his lecture, but he had almost certainly attended performances of Wagner's operas at Drury Lane under Hans Richter and the first English performances by Barnby and the RAHCS of Parsifal in 1884 (as organist), and read Franz Hueffer's writings, notably in Half a Century of Music in England.

With 'the temporary gap between the ejected Italian Opera and the not yet acclimatized German Opera',[54] Stainer perceived an important opportunity for native composers such as Stanford, Mackenzie and Goring Thomas to forge a place for English opera, since during the decade of the 1880s, they had produced several operas for Carl Rosa (which, presumably, Stainer had also attended). These performances had also thrown into relief other pressing issues. Rosa's operas were sung in English, a vital element, Stainer believed, in the establishment of a national school of opera:

[52] J. Stainer, The Present State of Music in England (Oxford: Horace Hart, 1889), 7.
[53] Ibid., 6.
[54] Ibid., 7.

It is perfectly certain that no real progress will be made towards a national school of opera until we English are accustomed to listen to our own language with the same respect we give to the Italian or German. I could never understand why such an expression as 'Good morning, sir,' should strike hearers as nothing short of comic if set to music in an English opera, whereas, 'Noble sir, I salute you,' sung in Italian to the most extraordinary roulades up and down the gamut, is listened to as if it were quite the most natural way in which a page would address a gentleman.[55]

The time of Stainer's lecture reflected an important discourse which had recently taken place in Britain's capital city. The Corporation of London had been approached, largely through Stanford's initiative, to see if a major subvention for the establishment of a national opera building could be raised. This event provoked a further germane debate about financial support and whether state funds, or those from local government, should provide pecuniary assistance for such a venture, rather than leave it to the more unpredictable fate of the commercial market. As is plain from his lecture, Stainer clearly supported Stanford's initiative: 'Are we still to allow the Carl Rosa Company to be a private speculation, carried on by a limited-liability company? We ought, I think, to make great efforts to carry out to its logical end this work so nobly initiated by a sympathising foreigner.'[56] The outcome of the opera initiative, however, was negative, though it did not prevent Stanford from resuscitating the debate in 1898 by approaching the new London County Council. To the petition that was raised, Stainer was an enthusiastic signatory, though, in the end, he, like the many other supporters of the scheme, would be disappointed by the LCC's refusal to take up the mantle.

Stainer naturally held many convictions on the role of church music in English musical life and how it differed from Continental developments, notably in the Roman church. He was particularly conscious of how historical events, since the Reformation in England, had helped to shape a particularly national form of music, and how little known it was to the foreigner who was scarcely acquainted with the Anglican liturgy. He was sensitive to the perennial criticism of 'outsiders' who complained of 'the want of thematic development in our movements',[57] but was quick to leap to the defence of Anglican composers who were compelled by their environment and the contemporary demands of clergy and congregation to write short pieces. Indeed, that same year, Stainer had himself acknowledged (however reluctantly) the demand for brevity in acting as co-editor with Russell in

---

55 Ibid., 8.
56 Ibid., 10.
57 Ibid., 11.

Novello's *A Series of Short and Easy Anthems adapted to the Seasons of the Church, and suitable for Introits.*

These exigencies aside, however, Stainer recognised that church music was passing through a crisis. With the progress of secular music, particularly in the opera and concert hall, there was pressure within the church to limit the advance in musical expression in sacred musical works, a trend characterised by 'restoring older types, and retracing steps'.[58] Such a debate was present in England, but on the Continent he pointed to the Cecilians for the rapid ejection of symphonic masses, public singers and the presence of orchestras from the Roman liturgy in favour of ritual music from the sixteenth- and seventeenth-century or contemporary imitations devoid of the 'modern style'. Stainer warned against such a trend in Anglican music. 'Any attempt', he advised, 'to force our modern church composers to become mere imitators of a bygone style will be disastrous to art.'[59] In fact Stainer was keen to highlight the very opposite trend that was becoming fashionable in cathedrals and large churches – that of the introduction of orchestras into special services – 'was one of the most encouraging signs of our times'.[60] Moreover, though Stainer enthusiastically advocated the musical superiority of boys as church-singers, he was nevertheless sad to see the Roman trend of ridding their choirs of women singers,[61] just as the Anglican church was beginning to show signs of encouraging them to participate on a more active level.

Stainer's evaluation of concert music and festivals was essentially positive, and he rejoiced in the improvement of standards and quantity, though he was cautious about the merits of provincial festivals which temporarily imported professional musicians to the limited benefit of the town or city. 'We shall never be a musical nation', he presaged, 'until our largest and wealthiest towns possess their own complete orchestras, choral societies, and opera company, capable of giving good performances of masterpieces of all kinds, and carefully nurturing all local talent.'[62] Moreover, he counselled against the monopolisation of festivals by a small number of star singers. This could only be ameliorated by giving young talent, from the conservatoires, proper experience.

---

[58] Ibid., 14.

[59] Ibid.

[60] Ibid., 15.

[61] This had been a steady characteristic of Cecilianism and the Roman Church throughout the nineteenth century, reaching its apogee in 1903 with the papal declaration *In motu proprio*, which encouraged the exclusion of women from church choirs. See J. Dibble, 'Musical Trends and the Western Church: A Collision of the 'Ancient' and Modern', in *World Christianities, c. 1815–c. 1914*, ed. S. Gilley & B. Stanley, The Cambridge History of Christianity 8 (Cambridge: Cambridge University Press, 2006), 127.

[62] Stainer, *The Present State of Music in England*, 18–19.

In this regard, he rejoiced that music was now a serious component of the nation's musical fabric. With the New Code more and more children were 'singing by note', and, out of 34,000 elementary schools in England and Wales, only eighty-two did not teach music at all. In the universities Stainer was full of praise for the advances effected by Stanford at Cambridge, and he acknowledged the work of Lloyd, Mee, Roberts, Taylor and John Farmer in their work for the Oxford Musical Club and Musical Union, though he lamented the manner in which college musical societies had fragmented the choral possibilities of performing large-scale oratorios. As a member of the Council of the RCM, an institution still only six years old at this point, he spoke warmly of its progress, and though he did not refer to his underlying desire to see the amalgamation of the RCM and RAM, he applauded their collaboration in the venture of the newly inaugurated Associated Board.

Above all, though, Stainer still detected an air of condescension from abroad, especially from the German newspapers, who referred to English musical events 'with a lofty sense of our unfortunate mediocrity as if we were extorted by pity rather than engendered by admiration.' It was clearly an attitude he found distasteful, and, in part, he blamed the English public for perceiving music as a foreign commodity. In later years he expressed this frustration on a number of occasions:

> You might suggest that English composers ought to appear more often in programmes of organ recitals. I often read them and find <u>very often</u> a whole programme without a single English name! Audiences are partly to blame; a foreigner always gets careful attention; an Englishman is discounted before heard.
>
> My boy J. F. R. S. gives a useful hint to those who wish to impress the British public with their knowledge of foreign musicians. The list might be indefinitely increased.
>
> Yours truly
> John Stainer
>
> <u>turn over</u>
>
> [on back page of letter:]
>
> 1. Chevalier Dupont
> 2. Henri Adroit
> 3. Walter von Papagei
> 4. Georg von Mauerschwalbe
> 5. Kohlerücken-Kleidermacher
> 6. Hans von Farbenbeizer
> 7. M. Galetas
> 8. Chevalier de la Riposte

1. Bridge
2. Henry Smart
3. Parratt (Parrot)
4. Martin
5. Coleridge (Coal-ridge) Taylor
6. John Stainer
7. Garrett
8. Parry[63]

To a former female Guildhall piano student, he offered similar jaded advice:

I congratulate you very sincerely on the press-notices, they are most gratifying; but I do hope they will soon cease to patronize you as being "promising"
"undeveloped" "feminine"!!! But you must put up with this sort of remark,
because, you are fighting rather an uphill battle, you are English, and have
been trained by English. Both are serious offences! and but few critics *dare*
to give unqualified praise to anyone guilty of both.[64]

For his last lecture at Oxford, on 5 May 1899, Stainer revisited many of the
categories he had explored ten years earlier in 'The Influence of Fashion on the
Art of Music'.[65] This lecture attempted to reassess the influences of Wagner and
Brahms (whose music Stainer acknowledged was now widely appreciated), but
it also warned against the over-complication of song accompaniment, lamented
over the demise of the glee-club as a valuable form of social interaction, praised
the 'modern school' of hymn-writers (notably Dykes and S. S. Wesley) for their
congruity of melody to words, and exulted at the dying fashion of singing hymns
at a rapid pace even if, as Stainer understood well, this had been a 'reaction from
the tedious drawl of Tate and Brady's New Version, which was to be heard in most
of our churches when I was a child.'[66]

Stainer announced the resignation of his position in May 1899. His health was
still declining and, while he agreed to continue in his role as Inspector of Education for music (perhaps against his better judgement, for in 1898 he was compelled to take leave from it), he harboured a longing to withdraw further from
the public gaze which the Professorship necessitated. Quite early on in his Professorship Stainer had felt compelled to act when the University of Trinity College,
Toronto (UTCT), decided to give degrees *in absentia* through an agency set up in
the United Kingdom and the USA. Led by Stainer, a substantial group of prominent musicians in Britain presented 'memorials' to the colonial secretary, Lord

[63] Letter from Stainer to Edwards, 23 August 1900, *GB-Lbl* Egerton 3092, fol. 107.

[64] Letter from Stainer to Miss Payne, 14 May 1899, in private possession (MN).

[65] For a full text, see *Musical Times* 40 (July 1899), 458–61.

[66] Ibid., 469.

Knutsford, in 1890, criticising not only the *in absentia* nature of UTCT's degrees but also its failure to stipulate literary tests for matriculation. With the help of Thomas Southgate, editor of the *Musical Standard*, and other influential figures in national newspapers and music journals, Stainer appealed mainly to public opinion to protect what he understood to be 'national intellectual property'. The Provost of UTCT, C. W. E. Body, made a special voyage to England to plead the university's case but he failed to make headway, and in early 1891 it was decided to discontinue its agencies in London and New York. Through strident collective opposition and an appeal to public opinion, the work of UCTC ceased, but, at Stainer's instigation, it provoked the inauguration of the Union of Graduates in Music in 1893 in order to focus the power of degree-giving institutions as well as the collective opinion of those holding music degrees. Stainer chaired the Union for two years, as was constitutionally agreed, before resigning in favour of Stanford.

National ownership of music degrees was a subject close to Stainer's heart and one that he had clearly cherished since his Oxford days. He had been influential in the setting up of the London University degrees with Bridge, and in 1890 had assisted Philip Armes in the establishment of degrees at Durham University (where he was the first external examiner), an institution which had honoured him with a D.Mus. in 1885 and, no doubt in recognition of his work for the university, a D.C.L. in 1895. Surviving evidence from Parry's diaries suggests that Stainer found the arduous work of examining Oxford B.Mus. and D.Mus exercises, year in, year out, excessively tiring.

With the exception of Hadow and Parry, Stainer was mistrustful of his musical colleagues in the university, especially Mee, Farmer and Walker. In May Parry recorded that he had 'dined with the Stainers and heard a bitter screed by the Professor on the state of Oxford music. He said he never would have come to Oxford if he had known what a nest of hornets it was.'[67] This diatribe seems to have stemmed from what he perceived as his colleagues' 'systematic "scheming" and ill will to him'.[68] He clearly cherished his old friendship with Parry, and staunchly supported his appointment as successor to Grove at the RCM towards the end of 1894:

> As regards the RCM I <u>do</u> hope all is going straight: it will be nothing short of a national calamity if it falls into other hands than yours. I hear that my letter was read to the meeting, and the suggestion approved of: no doubt it would have occurred to the members in any case, but I thought it wise not to risk it. I am really <u>anxious</u> about the result.[69]

[67] Diary of Hubert Parry, 3 May 1899, *GB-ShP*.
[68] Ibid., 7 November 1899.
[69] Letter from Stainer to Parry, 14 November 1894, *GB-ShP*.

But he distrusted Varley Roberts's 'blarney' and clearly failed to conceal a 'fiendish hatred' for Parratt at RCM Council meetings,[70] whose examination questions set for the Oxford degrees he equally disliked:

"Below this melody write a 2nd T[reble]. Alt. Ten. and Bass, each part must enter separately"

I have tried to work this, but the melody does not at all lend itself to a pretty or interesting entry of each part separately.

Here is another:-

"Below this counterpoint write a canto fermo"

rather like asking a man to walk on his head! I cannot conceive that any man would excogitate a counterpoint <u>without reference to any subject!</u> and then set to work to discover a subject to fit it! He might select a Figure-form which he would like to predominate in a Fugue, but that's quite another thing.[71]

Stainer had managed to reconcile the rivalry of the Oxford Philharmonic and Choral Societies who decided, for their mutual benefit, to merge in 1890, but he had himself to be reconciled over the formation of the new Oxford Bach Choir in 1896.[72] There was also a lingering acrimony between university musical organisations, as he reported to Edwards:

Mind you do not get into a muddle about the Musical <u>Club</u> and the Musical <u>Union</u>.

The Musical <u>Club</u> is the one which Parry helped to found, for the purpose of letting young men hear the best possible performance of chamber music etc and <u>now</u> it includes Orchestral concerts also.

The Musical <u>Union</u> was a <u>schism</u> from the Club, of men (Dons and Undergraduates) who thought that the <u>men themselves</u> should learn to perform, instead of paying professionals.

The schism has given rise to a certain amount of ill-feeling between the two societies. (In confidence.) Mr Heberden (Principal of Brasenose Coll), Mr Hadow and Dr C. H. Lloyd are the ruling spirits of the parent <u>Club</u>, while Dr Mee is the very life-blood of the Musical <u>Union</u>. Both are prosperous, pay their way, and have invested capital.[73]

Yet the biggest controversy in Oxford was ultimately reserved for the musical

---

[70] Letter from Grove to Edith Oldham, 26 October 1890, *GB-Lcm*.

[71] Letter from Stainer to Parry, 14 April 1899, *GB-ShP*.

[72] See letter from Hadow to his mother, 8 March 1896, *GB-Owc*.

[73] Letter from Stainer to Edwards, 6 June 1898, *GB-Lbl* MS Egerton 3092, fol. 40.

degree itself. After Stanford's major reforms at Cambridge in 1893, which made residence of nine terms (and the appendage of a proper teaching curriculum) obligatory to qualify for the B.Mus. degree, it was inevitable that there would be a similar challenge to the non-residential status of the Oxford Mus.Bac. degree. Although an attempt had been made in 1870 to require music candidates to take the Oxford B.A. before entering for the Mus.Bac. (it had been, nevertheless, thoroughly defeated),[74] the notion of a more rounded and integrated music student had not gone away, and, after Stanford's reforms, the matter became increasingly more controversial. By 1898 it was being hotly debated. Hadow, in favour of residence, thereby giving the Oxford music degree a proper status (which had been Stanford's goal at Cambridge) in the university, had gained the support of an impressive battery of influential figures, namely Parry, Stanford, Oakeley, Lloyd, Harwood, Buck and Parratt, as well as ecclesiastical figures such as Troutbeck and Fellowes, Fuller Maitland of *The Times* and J. S. Curwen of the Tonic Sol-fa College.

Stainer, however, was implacably against it, but demurred from publicly voicing his antagonism:

> But it will be a <u>terrible</u> blow to the profession to lose this privilege of taking degrees without residence. I suppose you know we have had it for <u>400 years</u> at least! In fact there is <u>no record</u> of a musician being asked or made to reside. If the B.A.s kept away, the case would be different, but, as you know, they come to us in considerable numbers, so practically, the "resident" v "non-resident" systems are actually going on together <u>now</u> with genuine success. What a pity to rob all English musicians simply because our <u>ancient</u> system (called contemptuously the "present" system) does not <u>match</u> civil law and medicine!
>
> I also regret the proposal on another ground, it will be in dead opposition to the spirit of <u>University Extension</u>. The other day Congregation and Convocation passed by a large majority a Statute to allow men passing two years in Reading, Sheffield, Nottingham etc to take B.A. with <u>one year's residence in Oxford less</u> than other men(!) namely at the end of their second Oxford year!!!
>
> Also, Oxford and Cambridge musical degrees are simply a part of the history of English Music! Think of Tye, Morley, Bull, Kirby, Dowland, Weelkes, Hilton, Ravenscroft, Gibbons, Child, Blow, Croft, Greene, Arne, Boyce, Callcott, Bishop, Horsley, S. S. Wesley, Garrett, and a score more, all of whom, were graduates of Oxf. or Camb. and <u>not one of whom</u> could have resided for 3 years <u>and</u> have taken B. A.

---

[74] See S. Wollenberg, *Music at Oxford in the Eighteenth and Nineteenth Centuries* (Oxford: Oxford University Press, 2001), 110.

Look at the good men now living who were non-residents – Armes (Durham), Arnold (Winchester), Bennett (Lincoln), Monk (Truro), Bridge (Westminster), Crowe (Ripon), Creser (Roy. Chap.), Hiles (Manchester), Pyne (d°), Keeton (Peterborough), Martin (S. Paul's), Pole (engineer), Steggall, Sweeting (S. John's Camb.), Wood (Exeter), and oddly enough I owe everything to non-residence. I took my Mus.Bac. <u>when Ouseley's organist</u>, and returned to Tenbury afterwards; but my Mus.Bac. degree got me among the elected candidates for Magd: – the rest you know. If this statute is passed, I shall be placed in a very awkward position indeed. But I am too proud to oppose it; I shall write to Grove and protest on behalf of my profession, and then, await the result. My successor will have an easy time if it passes, – probably 6 or 8 men at each examination, – this is calculating on a large <u>increase</u> of B.A. cand^tes; but without any special increase about 3 or 4 will take the Mus.Bac. degree in a year.

I leave you to form your own opinion.[75]

Parratt lent his weight behind reform, but Stainer was not to be pacified. 'I hope you will think twice before you give your approval to this scheme for depriving musicians of their immemorial privilege (? right) to come up here for degrees without 3 years residence', he pleaded to Parratt. 'The more I think of it, the less I like it. But, as I told you before, it would be far better than the Cambridge scheme, and would make *our* degree more valuable musically and educationally than that of our neighbour.'[76]

In the end it was Bridge, Stainer's old protégé, who mobilised opposition to Hadow's initiative. Bridge's objection, which Stainer, Prout and Southgate shared, was that many candidates for the music degrees were already individuals working for a living and could not afford the time to be resident for three years; degrees, henceforth, would be limited to 'amateurs of wealth and leisure'.[77] Moreover, Bridge argued, Oxford did not have in place a proper teaching facility to make residence beneficial. The outcome of Bridge's lobbying (and that of Prout, who also made his opposition clear at a meeting of the Union of Graduates in October 1898) was a rejection of the proposal by the Hebdomadal Council, with whom the decision finally rested.[78] The disappointment of Hadow and his supporters was considerable, and was most apparent in the furious exchange of correspondences between Stanford and Bridge in *The Times*. Parry, too, was bitterly aggrieved: 'I am

---

75 Letter from Stainer to Parratt, 5 August 1898, *GB-Bco*.
76 Letter from Stainer to Parratt, 2 September 1898, *GB-Bco*.
77 See Wollenberg, *Music at Oxford in the Eighteenth and Nineteenth Centuries*, 112n.
78 See J. F. Bridge, *A Westminster Pilgrim* (London: Novello & Co., Hutchinson & Co., 1918), 261–3.

always trying to bring the tests and questions up to date as much as possible, and we will go on doing that. But you will never prevent "scugs" and mechanic and plodding duffers getting degrees as long as exams and technique are the only tests required.[79]

Such a public show of differences and animosity may well have accelerated Stainer's desire to resign, but he was in actual fact also putting into practice a principle and belief that all Heather Professors of Music at Oxford should only maintain their appointment for ten years. Stainer succeeded in having this matter brought to a vote by the Hebdomadal Council in 1899, but out of 460 members of Congregation only twenty-six members came to vote. Thirteen voted in favour, thirteen against, so the motion was lost.

Though he was disappointed by the university's display of apathy, his parting gesture was to try to secure Parry as his successor. Rumours and whispers abounded in the press and the university about the matter, as Stainer explained to Edwards:

Some amusing remarks on the vacant Oxford Professorship of Music have appeared in the daily papers, evidently from the pens of men who feel bound to say something, but who know absolutely nothing about Oxford methods of procedure. One contemporary said "It is to be hoped that Sir Hubert Parry will allow himself to be nominated, etc." As a matter of fact no nomination is possible, the Board of Electors consists of the Vice-Chancellor, the two Proctors, the Heads of New College, Christchurch, Magdalen, and St John's, and the Savilian Professors, about nine in all, who will receive applications and elect at their discretion. It is not in their power to offer the post to anybody, and if Sir Hubert Parry or any other musician desires to hold it, he must ask for it. Another contemporary said that if Sir Hubert Parry did not stand there would be a "contested election" (!) at which "every Graduate would have a vote"(!). This last suggestion is quite alarming; it would be almost impossible to arrive at the exact number of the Graduates of Oxford, but certainly there would be no difficulty in getting 20,000 of them together. The idea of this black-robed army of graduates appearing suddenly in Oxford to record their votes for Beethoven-Brown is simply appalling. But worse still; in the event of a "contested election" between 10,000 adherents of Beethoven-Brown and 10,000 supporters of Jomelli-Jones what terrible results might follow! – a free fight in the High; graduates' eyes poked out by the sudden application of the sharp corners of caps; desperate attempts at strangulation by twisting the sleeves of their gown tightly round each other's throats, etc etc. May the Spirit of Harmony save Oxford

[79] Graves, *Hubert Parry*, vol. 2, 12.

from such a regrettable discord! The duties of the Professor are by no means light; he has to wade carefully through every exercise sent in, he is an ex-officio examiner in music, he is responsible for the proper carrying out of the examinations which take place twice a year, and the preparation of the papers, he must deliver three public lectures in each year, and of course, he has to deal with a really large amount of correspondence with candidates and would-be candidates to whom the plainest printed information seems to be quite unintelligible. He has also to present men for their Degrees, but this can be performed by a deputy (M.A.) nominated by him. The stipend is about £125 per annum, a small additional fee being granted for his work at each examination.[80]

Hadow also strongly supported Parry's nomination and, probably like Stainer, he had fears that Mee might be in the running: 'Of course I want Hubert Parry and am going to work all I know to get him. But my old enemy J H Mee is certain to put up and one never knows how irrational an Electoral board can be.'[81] In June 1899 Parry was honoured by the university with the degree of DCL, and afterwards he, Stainer and Hadow enjoyed a lively party at the Deanery of Christ Church (where they had been joined by the Duke of York, Cecil Rhodes and Lord Kitchener). Here no doubt, the subject of the Professorship was discussed. Later that year Stainer stood over Parry 'like a gaoler' while he signed his application for the Professorship;[82] it was confirmed on 30 November much to Stainer's satisfaction. Conscious, however, that Parry would bring an entirely new ambience to the Oxford degree, he wrote to King: 'I want you to *suppress* my little pamphlet "a few words of advice" or whatever it is called. In the first place I am no longer Professor, and next, which is more important, the *style* of the examinations here may rapidly change under "new management". Will you kindly see to this?'[83]

With Stainer's resignation at Oxford, the Education Department at Whitehall, among them McNaught, wondered whether Stainer might also resign his Inspectorship, but no such gesture materialised, such was Stainer's commitment to this part of his life's mission. After his resignation from St Paul's, he continued to undertake the punishing schedule of visits (usually visiting up to forty of the forty-three teacher training institutions), but after Barrett's death in 1891 McNaught's assistance became increasingly significant, until, in early 1901, Edwards joined the staff (by which time the number of institutions had grown to over sixty). Edwards had construed that Stainer had been responsible for his appointment, but Stainer

---

[80] Letter from Stainer to Edwards, [May 1891], *GB-Lbl* Egerton 3092.

[81] Letter from Hadow to his mother, 7 May 1899, *GB-Owc*.

[82] Diary of Hubert Parry, 9 November 1899, *GB-ShP*.

[83] Letter from Stainer to Henry King, 18 November 1899, *GB-Lsp*.

assured him, in spite of the political 'fall out', that the idea had been McNaught's: 'Don't thank me, (1) because Dr McNaught first suggested your appointment, (2) I consider myself lucky in having you as a confrere. But oh! I say! won't you catch it from the Curwen crew! They will ignore your peculiar fitness for the work and will only see in you one more "hanger on" to the firm of Novello & Co!'[84]

As Stainer's New Code became currency in elementary schools after 1885 (it was later modified in both 1893 and in 1901, shortly after Stainer's death), musical literacy in both staff notation and Tonic Sol-fa gained added impetus, as did the national affinity for singing in parts. Standard elements of this literacy were fully established through Stainer's role as Inspector, namely voice and ear training, the ability to sing a tune, to reproduce rhythm, a combination of the two, and the cultivation of a song repertoire. Hence, emphasis was placed increasingly on educational value rather than Hullah's more socialistic aims. Such was the interest generated by the improvement of music teaching in schools and colleges that Novello undertook the publication of a monthly periodical, the *School Music Review*, under McNaught's editorship from 1892. This proved to be a focus for the discussion of methodology, the official registration of music teachers as part of the Registration of Teachers Act (which Stainer opposed),[85] the annual government reports by Stainer and McNaught as well as the publication of a number of school songs by Stainer himself, intended both to contribute to a growing repertoire of 'tasteful' songs for children (away from trashy drawing-room ballads, which he loathed) and as encouragement for his composer colleagues (notably Stanford and Parry, who in time also produced pieces for the periodical). Stainer also expressed his reservations concerning folk song, whose prevalence was growing during the 1890s, with publications by Sabine Baring-Gould, Lucy Broadwood, Fuller Maitland, Stanford (who had expressed an unbridled desire to see the teaching of folk songs in his 1889 paper for the London School Boards) and Barrett. Stainer showed his support for the folk-song initiative by both accepting one of four positions of vice president of the Folk Song Society (the other three were held by Parry, Stanford and Mackenzie) and attending the Society's first public meeting on 2 February 1899 (where Parry gave the inaugural address), but he did not consider the folk song an ideal educational agency, owing principally to the wide range of the melodies for children's voices. After Stainer's death, however, educational stress on folk song, through the promotion by Somervell of the *National Song Book*, would grow substantially as educational method became

---

[84] Letter from Stainer to Edwards, 28 January 1901, *GB-Lbl* Egerton 3092.

[85] In consideration of the Registration Bill being put before parliament, Stainer sat on the RCM sub-committee with Lord Charles Bruce, Lord Thring, Grove, Goldschmidt and Morley. Stainer opposed the Act on the grounds that it undermined the status and qualification of the music degree.

inextricably entwined with cultural nationalism and the significance of 'national' music.[86]

A further educationally related movement that Stainer publicly supported was the promotion of competitive festivals as a means of raising standards. He had had past experience of adjudicating at the Eisteddfod, and had watched closely while J. S. Curwen had founded the Stratford Festival in 1882. After retiring from St Paul's he (with McNaught) regularly adjudicated the Annual Vocal Music Competition for the London School Board, an event which brought together a number of selected choirs from London's elementary schools. The festival was always strongly supported by the public, though it also attracted its critics, among them Bernard Shaw, who, with his socialist inclinations, was entirely antagonistic to the Darwinist-inspired competitive element:

> The competition, like all competitions, was more or less a humbug, the Elcho shield going eventually to the conductor who had trained his choir single-heartedly in the art of getting the highest marks, which is not the same thing as the art of choral singing. His pupils performed with remarkable vigour and decision, and were the only ones who really succeeded in reading the "sight test" all through; but Mr Casserley's choir from the Great College-street School shewed more artistic sensibility; and Mr Longhurst's boys from Bellenden Road were not further behind than all choirs of one sex alone are inevitably behind mixed choirs, both in quality of tone, in which the difference is enormous, and in the address with which girls pull boys out of difficulties, and boys girls, according to their special aptitudes.[87]

Nevertheless, although Shaw disliked the competitive spirit, he understood the value of the annual meetings as a demonstration of how public taxes were being used. 'Why should newspapers send their musical critics', he complained, 'to write useless notices of the five thousandth repetition of Home, Sweet Home, by Madame Patti, at a purely commercial concert, whilst ignoring the music that is paid for daily by public money, and only submitted to public judgment once a twelvemonth?'[88] In the main, the London School Board Competition was the only one that Stainer chose to adjudicate, but he did relent in June 1897 to address the audience (and give out prizes) at the Westmorland Festival. 'It is I̲', he wrote to the

[86] See G. Cox, *A History of Music Education in England* (Aldershot: Scolar Press, 1993), 63–81.

[87] B. Shaw, 'The Board School Competition', *The World*, 30 November 1892, in *Shaw's Music*, vol. 2: *1890–93*, ed. D. H. Laurence (London: The Bodley Head, 1981), 750–1.

[88] B. Shaw, 'A State Concert – New Style', *Daily Chronicle*, 14 November 1895, in *Shaw's Music*, vol. 3: *1893–1950*, ed. D. H. Laurence (London: The Bodley Head, 1981), 358.

pioneering Mary Wakefield, 'who ought to be grateful, for I really enjoyed my visit to Kendal very much. The enthusiasm and good feeling which you inspire are past praise!'[89] And knowing the quality of the choirs at the Morecambe Festival, he agreed to adjudicate their meeting in May 1900 where one of the test pieces was his own recently composed madrigal 'Room for Flora's Queen', written for Queen Victoria's 80th birthday.

Although Stainer's removal to Oxford in 1889 meant severing his practical ties with church music, he nevertheless retained a deep interest in preserving its values. His inaugural Oxford lecture expressed the hope that while cathedrals and churches continued to provide the resources for musicians at special services, younger composers would still look to the church for inspiration.[90] It was an aspiration he repeated in his Presidential Address to a party of American musicians at a meeting of the Musical Association on 16 July 1895:

> I cannot refrain from saying a few words about a branch of music in which my whole life has been passed, and to which I have devoted my best energies – I mean Church Music. We English church-musicians know no greater compliment, no higher reward for our labours, than to see our names appearing on the music lists of your churches and places of worship. We are most anxious that you should receive from us and carry on in its integrity the pure traditions of this branch of sacred art, so peculiarly national to us, but also so essentially a need of English-speaking races. I feel it to be my duty here to plead for preservation and culture of the anthem; a form of composition whose existence in England is at present seriously jeopardized by a strong wave of congregationalism. I can see no reason why a trained choir and a hearty congregation should not both find room for the exercises of their religious worship and musical gifts in the same building; but this moderate and common-sense view does not satisfy congregational agitators; they desire to expel all trained musicians from our churches. If the anthem should lose its hold in England, I pray you to make it your adopted child. You are too sensible to imagine that it is merely an ingenious contrivance for "showing off" trained voices; you know that it has in itself the power of teaching impressively, and bringing home to the inmost heart the highest truths of religion.[91]

Stainer's defence of the English anthem and the survival of trained church

---

[89] Letter from Stainer to Mary Wakefield, 24 May 1897, *GB-Lam* McCann Collection.

[90] Stainer, *The Present State of Music in England* , 15.

[91] J. Stainer, 'Address of Welcome [to visiting American musicians]', *Proceedings of the Musical Association* 21 (1894–5), 151.

choirs had been voiced the previous year in a somewhat outspoken paper at the Church Congress in Exeter, not least as a rebuttal to H. C. Shuttleworth's *The Place of Music in Public Worship* published in 1892. Here Stainer articulated the difficulties experienced in parish worship, where half-trained or wholly untrained choirs attempted music that was far too technically strenuous for them, resulting in irritable clergy and a bored congregation who, wincing at the cacophony, demanded simpler congregational music. But unfortunately the congregational lobby extended further than this, by demanding participation in each and every act of musical worship. 'I have quite failed to discover any artistic, historical, or ecclesiastical grounds for this sort of universal claim', Stainer complained, 'to hum or howl in *any* portion of our Church services.'[92] 'Why', he exhorted, 'should it be supposed that bad singing is good enough for church use?'[93] And in defence of having a trained choir, even in the humblest parish churches, he pointed to other church ornaments and architecture and questioned the abolition of these should the utilitarian view of worship prevail.

This more extreme congregational sentiment threatened those very tenets of Stainer's artistic sensibilities to which he was bound to react; but he was equally antagonistic towards the papers given by Parry and Stanford at the Church Congress in London in 1899.[94] Parry had complained of the commercial object of music publishers, and asserted that 'the services of the Church are exploited wholesale for the mere gathering in of royalties by professional makers of cheap twaddle to assist in the demoralization of Church musical taste.'[95] Given Stainer's tireless contribution to Novello's catalogue of parish music, this was too near the bone:

> I really do not think Parry's address worthy of comment. I think the wisest course to pursue would be to print it, and make no reference whatever to it in any part of the paper.
>
> If I criticized it, I should certainly shew up its worthlessness. But I fear my hand would be traced! I don't know why, but my leaderettes have more than once been laid to my charge.
>
> He might be much annoyed at any adverse criticism and revenge himself on Novello & Co. – but that paragraph about "gathering in of royalties by professional makers of cheap twaddle" is really unworthy of a man in Parry's

---

[92] J. Stainer, 'Music, Considered in its Effect upon and Connexion with, the Worship of the Church', *Proceedings of the Church Congress* (Exeter, 1894), 532.

[93] Ibid., 533.

[94] Stainer had been invited to give a paper at the same session, but had declined on the grounds of giving up public and semi-public appearances (see letter from Stainer to Fellowes, 15 September 1899, *GB-Ooc*).

[95] C. H. H. Parry, 'The Essentials of Church Music', *Proceedings of the Church Congress* (1899), 419.

position! If you <u>cannot</u> make up your mind to let the thing pass <u>without any comment</u>, I will write a "slightly sarcastic" notice of it for you. But I seriously believe it should be printed and – <u>ignored</u>.[96]

Furthermore, given his harmonious and entirely constructive experience with Sparrow Simpson at St Paul's, Stainer could not accept Stanford's proposition that musically uneducated cathedral and college Precentors should defer to the expertise of their organist colleagues: 'Stanford's quiet and calm hint that Precentors should hand over their functions to "experts" that is, students of the R.C.M., when they get a cathedral organistship, is really too cheeky!'[97]

During the late 1880s and throughout the 1890s Stainer remained one of Novello's most favoured composers, and his output of anthems, service music and other liturgical material continued unabated. With Russell of St Paul's, he published the *Cathedral Prayer Book* in 1891, and contributed to the *Church of America Altar Book* (1896). With his old Magdalen friend Lewis Tuckwell, Rector of Standlake, he edited the *Church Choir Chant Book* (published in 1899) as one of several liturgical publications, which included the *Holy Communion Office* (John Merbecke) and the *Order for the Burial of the Dead* (both 1898). He also superintended the *Manual of Plainsong* edited by H. B. Briggs and W. H. Frere, though, in deference to the expertise of Briggs and Frere (who, between them, had been responsible for several substantial publications under the aegis of the Plainsong and Medieval Music Society during the 1890s), he was reluctant to have his name connected with the publication:

Will Mr Littleton ask Mr Briggs if a copy of all the proofs of the Gregorian Psalter may be sent to Mr Frere? Also it will be advisable to ask Mr Frere if his name may appear on the title-page, with that of Mr Briggs. Mr Frere's name will mean a very general use of the book, and he might not care to give much of his valuable time to looking over proofs, if his name is not to be mentioned. I have definitely decided that my name must not appear on it. Please tell Mr Littleton that I think these details of much importance, and I should like the matter settled at once. It will be advisable to tell both Mr Briggs and Mr Frere that my name will not appear. Have you remarked that those Psalters (Gregorian) sell the best which come from clerical Editors? the musician taking a back seat? Briggs is 1/2 Parson. You must not think that I am always going to be as busy with composition as I am at present: I am only clearing up. I still owe a Madrigal to Mr Benson for his Choir, and a glee or partsong to the Oxford Gleemen. Also, I have to write two or more

[96] Letter from Stainer to Edwards, 10 November 1899, *GB-Lbl* Egerton 3092.
[97] Letter from Stainer to Edwards, 21 October 1899, *GB-Lbl* Egerton 3092.

Organ-pieces to complete the second set of 12. If I get through these I shall kick up my heels, and shall <u>idle</u> like an old horse turned out to grass.[98]

In terms of service music he reconstructed a Magnificat and Nunc dimittis in E minor by Daniel Purcell (who had been organist at Magdalen College between 1688 and 1695) from the autograph organ part (the voice parts being lost) preserved in the library at Magdalen. For churches with an Anglo-Catholic bent,[99] he added two settings each of the Benedictus qui venit and Agnus Dei (one elaborate, the other simple) to his Services in E flat and A (1899). He was particularly proud of the first of his two settings of the Benedictus in A, as he told King:

> I think my <u>No. 1</u> Benedictus for the A service is on an original model. Instead of separating the Benedictus and Hosanna I have made a <u>few</u> of the throng begin to <u>murmur</u> Hosanna while others are still singing Benedictus; you will notice that the cry "Hosanna" is gradually caught up, and increases excitement and intensity till the whole multitude <u>shout</u> "Hosanna" at the top of their voices! I am very sorry the S Paul's Choir cannot use it, they would sing it so splendidly.[100]

The following year the Morning and Communion components of the Service for Men's Voices in D, written with the choir of St Paul's in mind, were published. 'I am hard at work at another "unprofitable" undertaking – as far as Novello & Co are concerned', he informed King. 'At the end of next week you will receive a Te deum and Bened. for <u>Mens Voices</u> to complete my Service in D. Communion Service

---

[98] Letter from Stainer to Henry King, 25 October 1899, *GB-Lsp*. The *Manual of Plain-song* was in fact an attempt to revise Helmore's *The Psalter Noted*. The task was entrusted to Stainer, who immediately sought the collaboration of Briggs and Frere. At Stainer's death in 1901 a substantial part of the proofs had reached Novello and he had also discussed the matter of organ accompaniments and harmonisations with W. G. A. Shebbeare. The volume was published in 1902, by which time Briggs had also died.

[99] Ritualist churches such as the Anglo-Catholic Margaret Chapel became increasingly courageous in their choral innovations of the communion service at the end of the nineteenth century, and introduced the unauthorised Benedictus after the Sanctus and the Agnus Dei during the communion of the clergy; see N. Temperley, *The Music of the English Parish Church* (Cambridge: Cambridge University Press, 1979), vol. 1, 294–5. By the end of the century there was a notable commercial demand for such addditions to service settings.

[100] Letter from Stainer to Henry King, 19 January 1899, *GB-Lsp*. The mention of St Paul's refers to the fact that the cathedral did not permit the singing of the 'Benedictus qui venit' as part of choral communion until well into the twentieth century.

shall follow. I want it to be set up at once so that it can be used <u>this summer</u> while the boys are away. (July and August).'[101]

The music of Stainer's Morning and Communion Service in D shows a marked conceptual advance on the less sophisticated Evening Service of 1873 and, as a result of this disparity of years, the service as a whole lacks the stylistic consistency of his other complete services. Although the constituent parts do not reveal the same network of key relationships which Stainer worked so carefully into the Service B flat – most of the principal movements are in D major, with the Benedictus and Sanctus placed in A – there is nevertheless a more complex process of thematic interrelationships, a greater sense of symphonic development, a more intricate approach to form and a far richer harmonic palette. This can be observed in numerous contexts. The opening material of the Te Deum (also heard in the Gloria) is now germane to the entire structure (Example 19a); no longer is it simply used for the purpose of thematic reprise, but as a form of symphonic adhesive which, subject to recomposition, helps bind together much of the musical continuum. This is emphatically manifested in the recurrence of the opening material in E minor ('Thou art the King'), the 'false reprise' in the dominant ('Day by day we magnify Thee') and the final section, where the sequential rising phrases of the original material are distilled into a series of euphonious rising scales of D. Furthermore, Stainer places greater weight on the secondary tonality of E which occupies the central part of the structure. Here the principal framing material, derived from the second episode ('Holy, holy, holy'), is in E major, which Stainer continues to rework until we hear it in an emotionally charged prayer (Example 19b), fortified by the 'close harmony' of six parts ('We therefore pray Thee'). The structural involution of these later movements is also paralleled by Stainer's heightened sense of drama. Of all Stainer's expressions of musical 'genuflection', the enharmonic shift from the half-close of F sharp minor at the end of the first episode to the hushed 6/4 of F at the beginning of the second is particularly inspired; similarly the introduction of a bass verse in F sharp minor ('Vouchsafe, O Lord'), at the point of introspective reflection just before the conclusion, has a pathos worthy of S. S. Wesley. Other moments, such as the sudden excursion to C major in the Benedictus ('To give light to them that sit in darkness') and the ensuing progressions to the dominant of E are positively theatrical, as are passages in the Credo such as the declamatory 'Came down from heaven', the aria-like verse that follows, replete with organ obbligato (Example 20), the highly chromatic

---

[101] Letter from Stainer to Henry King, 10 May 1900, *GB-Lsp*. These additions to Stainer's Service for Men's Voices were probably motivated by the increased need for such service music after Chapter decided in 1896 to add periods of complete closure of the choir school at Easter and Christmas to the month's holiday in the summer already granted by Chapter in 1886 (see Chapter 5).

Example 19. Service in D for Men's Voices: Te Deum:
(a) opening idea); (b) secondary idea in E major

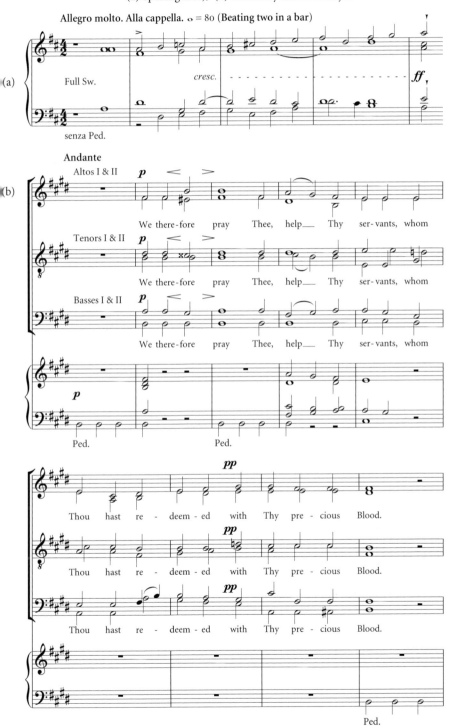

Example 20 Service in D for Men's Voices: Nicene Creed: verse for solo tenor

depiction of the resurrection and the substantial double fugue that ends the movement.

Text	Thematic Material	Key
We praise Thee O God	A	D major
Holy, holy, holy	B	F major
The glorious company of the Apostles	C	A minor
The Father of an infinite Majesty	B′	E major
Thou art the King of Glory, O Christ	A′	E minor
When Thou tookest upon Thee (verse)	D	E minor
We therefore pray Thee	B″	E major
Day by day we magnify Thee	A″	A major
Vouchsafe, O Lord, to keep us this day	D	F♯ minor
O Lord, in Thee, have I trusted	A‴	D major

A further setting of the Communion Service, for six-part unaccompanied choir, was also written specially for St Paul's. It was conceived as a deliberately archaic 'exercise'. 'I have written a Communion Service', he told Martin, 'for you and your choir in 6 parts – to be sung <u>without accompt</u>. ... I should like our young disciples of Wagner & Brahms who want to turn dramatic sound-pictures out of our Cathedrals to know that the old art of close imitation is not dead yet!'[102] Stainer was not confident about its appeal:

> I send with this a Kyrie, Credo, Sanctus & Gloria in 6 parts to be sung <u>unaccompanied</u>. I have written it specially for St Paul's where it will no doubt be sung. But probably no other choir will care about it; so I cannot ask Novellos to take it even as a gift. I want you therefore to send me an estimate of the cost of publishing it.
>
> 1. In type with Pf acc^{pt}
> 2. In type <u>without</u> accomp^t. 3 scores of 6 lines on each page
> 3. Engraved 8vo with Pf part
> 4. Engraved (3 scores on a page <u>without</u> Pf part)
> 5. Engraved on larger plates (size of albums (or even a little larger) <u>without</u> Pf part[)]
>
> I am not at all anxious to have any accomp^t as it will be absolutely spoiled if accompanied on the organ in church.[103]

[102] Letter from Stainer to Martin, quoted in Sotheby's catalogue, 21 May 1999, in private possession[?].

[103] Letter from Stainer to Henry King, 1 January 1901, GB-Lsp.

In fact Stainer even contemplated the notion of having individual vocal parts printed. 'I should also like to know the cost of <u>separate vocal parts</u> (engraved) <u>folio</u>, as I can give Sir George Martin a M.S. <u>score</u> to conduct from. ... I often think the old Cathedral manuscript books had a useful function. I am sorry they have entirely disappeared. This unaccompanied service of mine is a case in point; only 6 alto, 6 Tenor, 6 Bass & 20 treble copies will be wanted, even for S Paul's.'[104] Littleton, however, agreed to publish the service without Stainer's financial sub-vention. As a work, the Communion Service in C is unequal, the Sanctus being a weaker inspiration than the other three movements. The two extended parts – the Credo and Gloria – are, however, much stronger in concept, and are fine, if neglected examples of nineteenth-century English cathedral music in the *stile antico*. The Credo is especially well composed in its use of a 'motto' idea ('I believe in one God') which pervades many of the contrasting imitative and homophonic episodes, and there is much inventive and illustrative counterpoint (e.g. 'And the third day He rose again') which, with the richer texture of six parts, often gives rise to vibrant dissonance and sonorous textures. Added to which, Stainer's deft handling of the modal idiom often spawns progressions of an unusual and striking nature.

One other piece of note, written at the request of Parratt for *Choral Songs for Queen Victoria*, a publication written for the queen's 80th birthday and designed to ape the Elizabethan *Triumphs of Oriana*, was the madrigal 'Flora's Queen'. Par-ratt offered Stainer texts by the President of Magdalen, Herbert Warren, and by Lord Crewe, but he turned down both: 'I am sure it is quite possible to have words which are <u>too good</u> for music. All you sent me (the President's and Lord Crewe's) were charming as <u>poetry</u> but quite unmanageable.'[105] Instead, J. F. R. Stainer provided the text for the madrigal, which was performed before the monarch at Windsor Castle by Parratt's Windsor and Eton Madrigal Society (and as the com-petition piece at the Morecambe Festival in 1900). Stainer's contribution to the thirteen madrigals published by Macmillan was something of a *tour de force*. Set for six voices, the madrigal was cast in several stylistically contrasting sections, the first two, lively and dance-like with complementary quadruple and triple metres, the third, a studious Baroque fugue with a *cantus firmus* acclamation ('Long live Victoria'), and the last, based on the *cantus firmus* material, a vigorous polyphonic coda. 'At the close of my M.S.,' he told Parratt, 'I am afraid I poached on Gibbons' preserves. If I find it is so, I must alter the passage slightly.'[106] Stainer was also adamant that the piece must be performed at a vigorous pace, as he told Henry Littleton at Novello:

[104] Letter from Stainer to Henry King, 3 January 1901, *GB-Lsp*.
[105] Letter from Stainer to Parratt, 15 June 1899, *GB-Bco*.
[106] Ibid.

My son says he saw my madrigal (Flora's Queen) in the programme of the W.M.S.?

I hope they sang it well and that it was not taken too slowly!

I have marked it to be beaten <u>2 in a bar</u>, at rather a smart pace, but conductors of madrigals seemed unable to shake off the old   1   2   3   4 !!![107]

jog jog jog jog

A highly effective *pièce d'occasion*, the madrigal is a remarkable fusion of the old and new, and with the lively 'Cupid look about thee', a ballett written in 1900 for Henry Wilsdon and the Oxford Gleemen, these two secular miniatures reveal that the fifty-nine-year-old man had not lost any of that contrapuntal verve or romantic fervour that had produced the prodigious eight madrigals of his youth.

Of Stainer's anthems composed between 1888 and 1900, only three were multisectional. 'Lo! Summer comes again' (for harvest), dedicated to his friend, the Rev. F. H. Hichens of Canterbury, was probably intended for a special service. A larger ternary structure dominates the anthem whose central 'trio' ('Each month we sow or reap') is attractive for its melodic material and tonal treatment, though the closing fugue is, like numerous other examples in Stainer's anthems, somewhat lacklustre. More reminiscent of the emotionalism of *The Crucifixion* was 'And Jacob was left alone', written in 1894 for two solo basses and tenor (taking on distinct roles of the 'Narrator', 'The Angel' and 'Jacob') and chorus. The exchange between the 'dramatis personae' in all three solo sections gives the piece, unique in Stainer's output of anthems, the sense of a 'mini-drama', albeit of a more reflective disposition (this paradigm is also reproduced to a lesser extent in the short biblical 'scene', 'Two blind men sitting by the way side', of 1895). Moreover, Stainer assigns to the solo paragraphs a more agonised and poignant chromaticism which contrasts markedly with the expressive, languid diatonicism of the first and last choruses ('Come, O Thou Traveller' and "Tis Love! 'tis Love!'), while the shorter central chorus, neo-Baroque in demeanour, functions as a tonal transition. This is a beautifully crafted anthem, now much neglected, but reveals Stainer's consummate gift for tonal structure and the achieving of maximum effect within liturgical constraints:

Soli	*Chorus*	*Soli*	*Chorus*	*Soli*	*Chorus*
C minor	G major	C minor → V of G	G minor/ G major → E minor	E minor (ending on V)	E flat major
'And Jacob was left alone'	'Come, O Thou Traveller'	'And he said unto him'	'In vain Thou strugglest'	'And Jacob asked Him'	' 'Tis Love! 'tis Love'

[107] Letter from Stainer to Henry Littleton, 7 March 1900, *GB-Lsp*.

The third extended anthem was 'Thou, Lord, in the beginning', written in 1899 for Septuagesima or the Feast of St John the Apostle and Evangelist. Its texts were drawn from Psalm 102, the Book of Revelation and J. M. Neale's translation of a stanza and Doxology from the Latin hymn *Urbs beata*. Though less consistently striking in terms of its material, this anthem none the less has some powerfully affecting moments, not least the transition from C major at the opening to the hushed beauty of E major at the vision of the 'holy city, new Jerusalem', which is further enhanced by the antiphony between choir and solo treble. Similarly the contrast between the second choral recitative for basses in A minor, and the tender, Goss-like verses of the solo quartet and chorus ('And God shall wipe away all tears from their eyes') in the major, is deeply moving.

Stainer's remaining anthems from this period are all characterised essentially by their concision, brevity and modest technical demands, factors commercially endorsed by Novello who reproduced many of them as supplements for the *Musical Times*. A number of these works – 'The hallowed day hath shined upon us' (1888), 'Behold, two blind men' (1895), the Christmas anthem 'It came upon a midnight clear' (1899) – are either based on a hymn text or conclude with stanzas from a hymn, giving the impression of a miniature cantata. 'Day of wrath (Dies Irae)', described as a 'hymn-anthem' was an ambitious projection of eighteen verses incorporating numerous harmonic and choral variations of a sturdy melody in G minor composed by Stainer for the *Church of England Hymnal* in 1894. (Stanford was to emulate this in 'St Patrick's Breastplate'.) Three other works – *The Story of the Cross* (1893) interspersed by organ 'meditations', *The Story of the Advent of Jesus* (1900), written for St Mary's Mission Church, Springbourne by the Rev. E. W. Leachman, and *At the Manger* (1901) – exploited a 'narrative' model of hymns, while the *Seven Greater Antiphons* (1896), short anthems (or introits), were conceived for 'Special Advent Services' where hymns or addresses could be introduced between each.

Yet perhaps most impressive among this neglected series of pieces are the short full anthems. Here, Stainer once again looked back to the expressive paradigm of Goss as is evident in the simple homophony of 'Behold, God is my helper' and 'Blessed is the man' (both 1896); but of a more poignant and emotional disposition are the two anthems composed in 1900, 'O Bountiful Jesu' and 'O Saving Victim'. Based on a prayer found in a primer of 1553, 'O Bountiful Jesu', which may be sung unaccompanied, has a devotional power and simplicity to match the striking imagery of the text, and, as if to accentuate the prayerful supplication of the anthem, Stainer builds in his own repetitions of the opening words in the outer sections of the ternary structure. The opening twenty-eight bars have much in common with 'God so loved the world'. Modulation is handled with a legerdemain and subtle variation, gently underpinning (but not overtly 'painting') the devotional beauty of the sixteenth-century language. Moments of intensity, such as the Schubertian 'shift' to E flat major at the beginning of the central paragraph ('Thou hast created us of nothing') and the chromatic climax ('sin, death and hell') are classically restrained while the recovery from E flat (to the dominant of G) is masterfully enacted through use of sequence. A similar slight of hand is also revealed in the reprise, where Stainer includes telling yet unobtrusive imitation between the treble and tenor voices.[108] A comparable technique is evident in 'O Saving Victim', whose most spiritually emotional passage (bars 17–20) is the approach to the reprise where Stainer's concentration of uncomplicated imitation, chromaticism, and tonal obliquity (note the half-close on V of C sharp minor and its conversion to a first inversion of E major to expedite the reharmonised restatement) are positively epigrammatic (Example 21). As Temperley has commented, this species of anthem had a special appeal to parish congregations who looked not for intellectual inspiration in their church music but spiritual edification 'all of which call for a high degree of predictability, but also a high level of art'.[109]

After the publication of the revised edition of *Hymns Ancient & Modern* in 1875, Stainer had devoted comparatively little attention to the composition of hymns until the publication of *The Crucifixion* in 1887. After this date, however, and especially after retirement from St Paul's, his productivity in the genre burgeoned, a flurry of activity which mirrored the prolixity of hymn-book publications during the late 1880s and 1890s. The beauty, shape, craft and involution of Stainer's hymn tunes written for *The Crucifixion* reveal a creative mind that believed not only in the imperative of lyrical simplicity for the purposes of congregational use but also in a simplicity that also concealed a more complex, autonomous art coupled with spiritual emotionalism, values indeed cherished by the Tractarians. Yet, Stainer admitted, though these factors were vital, the success of a hymn tune finally had to be judged by its metaphysical effect on the religious mind: 'The true estimate of a hymn-tune cannot be found by principles of abstract criticism, or by any internal evidence that it exhibits an artist's handicraft. There is something, indefinable and intangible, which can render a hymn-tune, not only a winning musical melody, but also a most powerful evangeliser.'[110] Similarly, he held that poetry for hymns was in itself a distinct and separate art form which uplifts 'the heart and emotions as if by some hidden magic. Alas for the day if such a spiritual influence should ever be lightly set aside in order to make room for words and music intended to teach the higher laws of poetry and a cold respectability in music.'[111] In this regard Stainer

---

[108] For further discussion of this anthem, see Temperley, 'Ancient and Modern in the Work of John Stainer', 115–18.

[109] Ibid., 118.

[110] J. Stainer, *Hymn Tunes* (London: Novello & Co., 1900), iii.

[111] Ibid., iv.

Example 21. Anthem: 'O Saving Victim' (transition to reprise)

venerated Dykes, and to a lesser extent, W. H. Monk, as the supreme models of the nineteenth-century hymn, and drew inspiration from their example. Indeed, Stainer was a confessed devotee of Dykes in spite of the increasingly harsh invective that was being hurled against him.[112] 'I myself was carefully trained to despise Dykes', he acknowledged to Edwards in November 1899, 'but his beautiful tunes rapidly converted me to themselves and to him.'[113]

The hymn-books to which Stainer contributed were both many and varied. Among them were the *Congregational Church Hymnal* (edited by E. J. Hopkins), Edward Oxenford's *Holy Gladness* (whose hymns later found their way into the *Day School Hymnal*), the revised *Church of England Hymnal* (edited by Mann), the *Congregation Mission Hymnal* (edited by Barnby) and the *Westminster Abbey Hymn Book*. For Steggall's supplement for *Hymns Ancient & Modern* in 1889 he produced eight new tunes, among them the sadly neglected 'Stolia Regia', the Passion tune 'Woodlynn', and two Dykes-inspired items, the wedding hymn 'Matrimony' to Keble's text 'The voice that breath'd o'er Eden' and the enduringly popular 'Love divine' to Charles Wesley's well-known lyric. Both of these tunes exhibit a characteristically affecting intensity of chromaticism in the third line of their four-line stanzas. For the third edition of the *Hymnal Companion*, a hymn book originally published in 1870 and adopted by a substantial number of Anglican churches, Stainer was asked to 'assist' Charles Vincent (Organist of Christ Church, Hampstead) and D. J. Wood (Organist of Exeter Cathedral) in a major revision. For this volume he contributed five tunes, among them a beautiful setting of Charlotte Elliot's 'Just as I am' (though not quite matching the striking melodic arc of A. H. Brown's 'Saffron Walden') and the thoroughly Dykesian 'Oxford'.

Yet, in spite of his profound enthusiasm for the genre, Stainer had not enjoyed the privilege of editing a hymn book, at a time when so many of his colleagues – Sullivan, Barnby, Monk, Hopkins and Mann – had been invited by editorial committees, regardless of their denomination, to lend prestige to their publications. 'I shall never edit one!' he impatiently exclaimed to Mann in 1894,[114] but within two years a joint committee of the Presbyterian churches of Scotland and Ireland asked if he would act as editor for a new hymnal which would not only contain over 600

---

[112] Ibid. Stainer was here referring essentially to the new didactic policy that was being directed towards the composition of hymns by a new generation of composers and critics who favoured a new diatonic simplicity in stark contrast to the chromatic richness and High Victorian emotionalism of which Dykes, the greatest of all Tractarian hymn composers, was the epitome. Such a policy, didactic in its aim to 'educate' congregations towards a higher taste, was ultimately unsuccessful, as the failure of the 1904 edition of *Hymns Ancient & Modern* amply demonstrated.

[113] Letter from Stainer to Edwards, 6 November 1899, *GB-Lbl* Egerton 3092, fol. 95.

[114] Letter from Stainer to Mann, 12 February 1894, *GB-NWr*.

hymns but also canticles, doxologies, the Creed and other liturgical components set to music. In fact Stainer was faced with the challenge of amalgamating four older Presbyterian hymnals edited by Smart, Hopkins, Pearce and Barnby, but at the same time excising unwanted material and adding a substantial amount of new music. To this end he was keen to broaden the musical horizons of a conservative religious community suspicious of change. 'The Scotch have had 3 or 4 different books in use for many years, and this Joint Hymnal is merely a "rolling them together"; consequently there are some <u>wretched</u> hymns and tunes which <u>cannot</u> be turned out because they are so "dear to many."! But I have managed to get included some fine and little known German chorales. If I had been asked to edit <u>de novo</u> many things would not have appeared at all.'[115] More significantly, Stainer was able to promote and encourage the work of younger church musicians: 'As regards inviting new compositions – you must have observed how many of my generation have passed away – Barnby, Elvey (rather older) and others. We must look out for rising young men', he urged the hymnal's chief editor, W. Cowan.[116] And though many of Stainer's contemporaries were included – Sullivan, Bridge, Lloyd, Faning, Parry and Martin, the number of emerging names – Somervell, Cunningham Woods, Alcock, Buck and Mann – was conspicuous, as were the fifteen new tunes that Stainer contributed himself. The *Church Hymnary*, as it was called (though Stainer always referred to it as his 'Scotch book') was published in 1898, with a Tonic Sol-fa version provided by McNaught; the project had been a happy affair, made the more satisfying by the sole responsibility given to Stainer by the Committee. 'On the whole I could not have had a better Committee', he confided to Edwards, 'and am glad I was not saddled with a lot of self-willed and teazy professional musicians! All this private.'[117]

In 1894 the idea of publishing Stainer's complete hymns (a scheme perhaps encouraged by Barnby's *Original Tunes to Popular Hymns* of 1869 and S. S. Wesley's *The European Psalmist* of 1872) had been discussed with Henry King, a Vicar-Choral at St Paul's and an employee of Novello. The idea was certainly planted by the beginning of 1895, but work began slowly, revising old tunes, altering what he perceived as 'cribs' from other music (a habit of which he had a morbid dread), and composing new tunes, especially those of the 'processional' kind. 'I hope the book is now really progressing', he wrote anxiously to King, 'because I am sure there will be, very soon, a lot of weak imitations of my new form of Processionals and I should like *mine* to get into the field before the shams.'[118] *Hymn Tunes*,

[115] Letter from Stainer to Parry, 10 January 1898, *GB-ShP*.
[116] Letter from Stainer to Cowan, 22 April 1897, *GB-En*.
[117] Letter from Stainer to Edwards, 5 March 1899.
[118] Letter from Stainer to Henry King, 21 June 1900, *GB-Lsp*. Such was the fashion for publishing complete collections of hymns that, during the compilation of *Hymn*

consisting of no fewer than 158 items, was published in August 1900, late enough to accommodate his tune 'Omnium Dominatur', written in aid of the Transvaal War Fund; the first copy, which survives, was inscribed to his wife. For Stainer it was a repository of deeply personal significance, for the volume not only 'narrated' a lifetime's contribution to a genre, but it articulated many of the convictions he held as a church musician, his role as a servant of the church, and of his sacred task as intercessor between Creator and congregation. 'I cannot hope', he concluded, 'that many of this collection are destined to enjoy a long existence; but I can honestly say, that if any single one of my tunes should for a few centuries float along the ever-gathering stream of sacred song, even unlabelled with my name, I shall not have lived in vain.'[119]

Stainer's return to Oxford witnessed not only the rejuvenation of hymn composition but also of songs and organ works. In 1892 Novello published his *Seven Songs*, 'affectionately inscribed to Cecie and Ellie'. Written for a range of voices, all seven drew their literary sources from German poetry, with one of the songs, 'Quand je te vois comme une fleur' using a translation by Jules Bué from Heine's 'Du bist wie eine Blume' (a text which, significantly, Stainer had used for his comparison of song-settings in his Oxford lecture in May 1891).[120] Stainer paid tribute to the French *mélodie* in 'Quand je te vois', a delightful through-composed lyric in D flat redolent of Gounod, and showing true slight-of-hand in the effortless detour through the flat submediant and Neapolitan in the penultimate line of text. The remaining six songs, all set in German (with English alternatives, in different keys, provided in Stainer's own translations), reveal the composer's admiration, knowledge and thorough assimilation of the German *Lieder* tradition, particularly of his beloved Schubert and Schumann. 'Das ferne Land' (J. H. Voss), a simple strophic design, is one of several musical aphorisms in which the composer still finds room for the development of detail at deeper structural levels. The D flat of the minor subdominant, heard first in the brief preludial statement (Example 22a), is subsumed within the augmented-sixth harmony that pervades the first three lines of text, and it is then beautifully integrated into the coda's striking progression (Example 22b). The Schubertian 'Das ferne Land' is complemented by the Schumannesque 'Der Rosenstrauch' (E. Ferrand), another strophic aphorism.

Tunes, Stainer was asked to assist with an indentical project for the hymn tunes of J. B. Dykes. All of Dykes's tunes were submitted to Stainer for retention or rejection (see letter from Stainer to Henry King, 12 August 1899, *GB-Lsp*); the volume was published by Novello in 1902.

119 Stainer, *Hymn Tunes*, v.
120 Jules Bué taught French at Magdalen College. His son Henri was responsible for the first French translation of Lewis Carroll's *Alice's Adventures in Wonderland* in 1869.

Example 22. Seven Songs: (a) 'Das ferne Land' (opening); (b) 'Das ferne Land' (conclusion); (c) 'Der Rosenstrauch' (conclusion); (d) 'Poesie' (opening)

Here Stainer makes telling use of a pregnant dominant pedal and its 'interrupted' resolution to the submediant to convey the passing of time, and of its passions and pain, reserving, once again, those most pointed progressions for the melancholy refrain 'Die Jahre vergehen' in which the minor subdominant and diminished seventh harmonies lend great solemnity to the cadence (Example 22c). Rückert's 'Das Meer der Hoffnung' inspired Stainer to a more turbulent, texturally astringent setting in C minor (note the acerbic progressions of the opening) in which

considerable demands are made from the pianist. Set in the darker territory of F sharp minor, 'Poesie' (Justinius Kerner), arguably the finest and most adventurous song of the collection, owes much to Schumann in the arresting nature of the oblique opening progressions and the poignant appoggiaturas (Example 22d), but Stainer's own brand of harmonic imagination is surely implicit in the ethereal Neapolitan harmony of the second line of the first verse, and even more so in the extraordinary divergence to C major in the second verse, where the masterly recovery, through a series of upward semitonal shifts to the dominant of F sharp, aids the affecting, wordless coda for the piano alone. The vivacious 'An Leukon' (J. W. L. Gleim) is thoroughly Schubertian (of *Die schöne Müllerin* vintage), but for the final song, 'Daheim' (J. G. Fischer), an imaginative through-composed structure, Stainer looked to Schumannesque fantasy for his emotional contrasts of mood, a feature most conspicuous in the slow central 'interlude' in the flat submediant (a tonal move subtly anticipated, incidentally, in the opening progression of the song) and the broad affirmation of the final vocal statement.

The vast market for parish church music, especially the short easy anthem, also encouraged a similar demand for organ music suitable for parish organists, a niche in which Stainer and his Oxford colleague, Cunningham Woods, led the way editorially with an extensive series of volumes called *The Village Organist*. This was an immensely popular publication, and new volumes of short, varied pieces, appropriate for all seasons of the church year, were constantly being prepared by the two men during the 1890s.

In 1897, however, Stainer published *Six Pieces* for the organ (some of which were composed during his tour to Spain and his stay at Mentone), which were intended for performers of higher technical accomplishment and for an organ of a minimum of three manuals. Moreover, these compositions were not only intended for proficient players but also works in which Stainer himself exercised a more earnest, cerebral creativity. The 'Andante' in A flat, for example, is a skilfully crafted Schubertian sonata movement in which the second subject appears in two third-related keys – E major and C major – before reverting to the more traditionally classical dominant of E flat. This admixture of thematic material and tonal change also effectively represents both second subject and development for Stainer proceeds to his recapitulation without further treatment. The rhetoric of a Bachian chorale prelude characterises the 'Prelude' in C, whose understated abridged sonata design is as much about the alternation of 'trio' textures (first subject) and contrasting strains of a chorale melody (second subject). Of perhaps less interest is the 'Fughetta', a fugal exercise in 'Minuet' style, though this, like several of the pieces in this collection, notably the 'Impromptu' and pianistic 'Rêverie', is redolent of Schumann's fusion of the old and new in his pieces for pedal piano (works Stainer knew well from his time at Magdalen). The 'Adagio (ma non troppo)' in E flat is another sonata movement, but this time the material and the polyphonic disposition of the parts are strongly suggestive of a slow movement of a string quintet. Once again, Stainer's tonal treatment in this movement steers a course between traditional Classical precepts (tonic and dominant) and the continued presence of a third tonality, G, which persistently pervades the important structural junctures in both the exposition and development. Though 'On a bass' makes clear reference to the Baroque chaconne, the older form is ultimately a pretext for a set of more romantically conceived variations. This tendency becomes increasingly more prominent with the antiphonal exchanges between the manuals in Variation 3; Variation 4 is a Schumannesque character piece; Variation 5, a 'rêverie', divides the bass between the right hand and pedals; Variation 6 is a 'trio' in which the two manuals are in strict canon; Variation 7 adapts an augmented bass to a 'Recit. ad lib.' while the final variation, an attractive fugue, restores the bass figure at the climactic restatement of the tonic (G minor) in the final twelve bars.

Novello were clearly pleased with Stainer's collection, and he promptly set to work on a further set of six pieces written in Mentone and Florence during the months of January and February 1898. More complex than the first set, these pieces are essentially more idiomatic of a large-scale, late nineteenth-century romantic organ, such as the one familiar to Stainer at St Paul's. The three slower movements which begin the set were, Stainer remarked, 'the type of the extempore voluntaries

I used so often to play before service at S. Paul's,[121] and he retained a special pride in the originality of the 'Praeludium Pastorale (Super Gamut Descendens)' based on a descending series of pedal points through two octaves of the scale. Certainly the fantasy-like process of modulation, particular to extemporary voluntaries, is conspicuous in the 'Andante pathétique' and 'A Church Prelude', especially the latter, which has the sense of a grand arc-like structure, reminiscent of S. S. Wesley's larger organ works. By contrast, the last three pieces have a more classical discipline. The 'Introduction and Fughetta' is a substantial movement, beginning with an imaginative sonata movement juxtaposing the rhetoric of a slow march as first subject with a chorale as second. The 'Fughetta', to all intents a full-blown fugue, resembles those somewhat dour, studious movements of Merkel and Rheinberger, though the fugue subject, based acerbically on two opening tritones, gives the piece a surprisingly abrasive edge, an impression reinforced by extensive use of this characteristic in the closing stages. The 'Finale alla Marcia' is less thematically interesting (albeit more ambitious than the *Jubilant March* published in 1879), though it is partially redeemed by the two trios, one an attractive scherzando, the other a broad melody more suggestive of Parry's muscular diatonicism. But most spacious and challenging of the entire set of pieces is the 'Fantasia', a chorale fantasia, in which Stainer attempts to outdo both Bach and Mendelssohn in terms of contrapuntal dexterity and which pre-dates those major Bach-inspired essays of Parry written during the First World War. Cast in three broad sections, the first is based on an athletic fugal subject (which has concealed within it the bones of the opening strain of the later chorale) and a hymn-like melody (one a countersubject to the other). The second section introduces the six strains of the chorale melody, in A flat major, in the guise of a pastoral chorale prelude, though this soon yields to a return of C major in a second fugue, stretto in treatment and based initially on the first strain of the chorale. But by degrees Stainer introduces further components of the melody as the fugue dissolves into romantic fantasy and, as a result of the added momentum and intensity of the quasi-extemporisation, the movement reaches its inevitable climax with a majestic reprise of the chorale in the tonic.

In the knowledge that his schedule at Oxford and the responsibilities of the Education Inspectorship would absorb a substantial portion of his time, Stainer initially made a point of declining invitations to speak at functions as he explained to Edwards:

> I am much gratified by the kind expression of your wish that I should address your association of choirs, but I have to draw a "hard and fast" line and excuse myself from all such invitations (of which I receive many – I have declined <u>four</u> this week).

[121] Letter from Stainer to Edwards, 23 August 1900, *GB-Lbl* Egerton 3092, fol. 107.

I have not the time – I am much pressed with work, though of a different sort to what I had in London.[122]

The principle proved, however, to be more difficult to enforce in practice, and the many requests he received from professional and amateur bodies for his advice and leadership meant that his time in Oxford was constantly disrupted by visits to London and other parts of the country. In Oxford he had hoped to enjoy a modest degree of private life, reflected in his desire to play his humble part as churchwarden at St Cross Church.

It was, none the less, a vain hope, for neither the city nor the university could ignore the prestigious presence in their midst. Magdalen College conferred an Honorary Fellowship on him in 1892, the first time such an honour had been bestowed on a musician. He was sketched by Leslie Ward, otherwise know as 'Spy', for *Vanity Fair* (dated 9 August 1891); Holman Hunt included him in his painting *May Morning on Magdalen Tower*, first exhibited at the Grosvenor Gallery in the same year;[123] he was painted by G. E. Moira in his doctoral robes;[124] and in October 1896 Stainer went to Bushey, the studio of Hubert von Herkomer, to have his portrait done.[125] When Gladstone visited Oxford in 1890 Warren turned to Stainer, who was well known to the Liberal leader (then in opposition), to swell the members of his breakfast party: 'Mr Gladstone is coming to breakfast with us here on Thursday morning next. Will you come and help us to entertain him. I daresay you may be meeting him elsewhere, but if you will come and meet him here in your own college, it will I believe add to his pleasure and it will certainly add very much to ours.'[126] Considered 'a friend of the family', Stainer later attended Gladstone's funeral in Westminster Abbey in May 1898; 'I travelled from Aberdeen (500 miles) on the night of Friday', he informed Edwards, 'to attend the funeral on Saturday and returned to Glasgow (350 miles) the same night!'[127]

After retirement from the Professorship in 1899, it is evident that Stainer was destined to take a more active role in politics, for he was selected by the Liberal

---

[122] Letter from Stainer to Edwards, 19 July 1892, *GB-Lbl* Egerton 3092, fol. 8.

[123] The picture, completed in 1890, licentiously brought together onto one canvas three of Magdalen's directors of music, Stainer, Parratt and Varley Roberts, as well as Bloxam, Bramley, Warren the President, and W. E. Sherwood, headmaster of Magdalen School; and among the models for the choristers was Stainer's youngest son, William Edgar. It can be viewed at the Lady Lever Art Gallery, Port Sunlight.

[124] The Moira portrait survives at Magdalen College, and presently hangs in the Song School.

[125] The portrait is housed at St Paul's Cathedral.

[126] Letter from Warren to Stainer, 3 February 1890, *GB-Lbl* MS 62121, fol. 54.

[127] Letter from Stainer to Edwards, [n.d. June 1898?], *GB-Lbl* MS Egerton 3092, fol. 42.

Party for the City of Oxford as their candidate for the next election – sadly, a contest he did not live to see. Paul Victor Mendelssohn Benecke, Mendelssohn's grandson, and a young fellow at Magdalen, explained:

> Throughout his life Stainer, in addition to being a distinguished musician, was a good citizen, and he took the liveliest interest in social and political questions. His Inaugural Lecture contained references to many topics which have no direct relation to music and they will be found to represent serious and independent thought on matters that were in their time important and in some cases highly controversial. Shortly before his death he was adopted as the Liberal candidate for Parliament, and it was thought that he had a better chance of winning the seat for the City of Oxford than any Liberal candidate has had for a long time, in days when there were never more than two candidates.[128]

Stainer was consulted over organs for the town halls in Hove and in Oxford, both of which were built by Willis, and he took a keen interest in the chimes of the various Oxford colleges, as is demonstrated by a letter to the wife of the Rev. Spencer George Wigram, curate of St Paul's, Oxford, between 1881 and 1891:

> We have not any distinctive <u>Oxford</u> chimes like the Cambridge chimes (now more generally known as the Westminster chimes) which are attached to Great St Mary's in Cambridge.

The chimes of St Mary's here are very poor

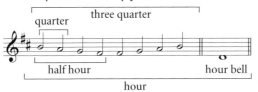

<u>These</u> are the Magdalen chimes:-

---

[128] See P. V. M. Benecke, 'Some Remarks Suggested by Laurie Magnus's Book "Herbert Warren at Magdalen" ' (unpublished typescript, *c.* 1941–4), *GB-Omc*, 156–7.

New College are quite as pretty, if not prettier:[129]

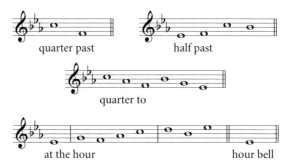

quarter past   half past

quarter to

at the hour   hour bell

But when St Martin's Church in Oxford was demolished in 1896, leaving only the now iconic Carfax Tower still standing, Stainer had the opportunity to remedy the lacuna by composing a set of 'Oxford chimes' for the new clock donated by Randall Higgins of Burcote House.

Even more than Oxford, London continued to claim much of Stainer's professional attention. He kept close contacts with St Paul's, attending dinners for the 'Old Boys' and the Evening Service Choir (though in later years he was often unable to attend the latter owing to winter holidays abroad), but his special relationship with the cathedral was marked by a dinner hosted by the Dean (who was now Gregory) and Chapter on 12 July 1899 to celebrate the 50th anniversary of Stainer's admittance as a chorister to the choir. His role as a father-figure in church music was acknowledged in various ways. For its first year he agreed to act as President for the new Church Orchestral Society, formed in 1894, whose aim was to support and promulgate the contribution of orchestral services to musical worship by the provision of a regular orchestra drawn from the Society. He also accepted the largely titular roles of President to the Plainsong and Medieval Music Society, and late in his life, the London Gregorian Association (in 1900).

From 1891 Stainer acted on an advisory panel to the Archbishop of Canterbury for the Lambeth D.Mus. Grove had initially been consulted on the constitution of this panel and suggested that it might consist of the Professors of Music at Oxford and Cambridge, as well as Parratt from Windsor.[130] Stanford declined, and Grove was then asked to join the panel, whose role was to determine particular criteria for the Lambeth honour. Stainer, who had seen such figures as Martin and Turpin successfully recommended for the degree, had distinct views on the matter, and was reticent about circumscribing too rigorously the grounds for awarding the degree:

[129] Letter from Stainer to Mrs Wigram, 23 August 1891, Pusey House, Oxford, Dalby and Wigram Papers, DAL 5/11/1.

[130] See letter from Grove to Archbishop Benson, 9 November 1891, GB-Llp.

I hope your Grace will allow me to suggest that it would be in my humble opinion unadvisable to make this Degree <u>only</u> attainable by very proficient musicians. A large number of men are made D. C. L. by our Universities merely as a compliment – certainly not on the legal knowledge of the recipients – and I cannot see why your Grace's degree should not sometimes stand on the same footing. For example – cathedral organists who are recommended to your Grace by their Dean and Chapter I should <u>always</u> regard as fit recipients – whether they are good composers or not – and whether they hold a Mus.Bac degree or not. Also – if my successor (in the future) as "Inspector of Music to the Education Department" holds no degree – I think his <u>position</u> would justify your Grace in granting the Degree. I may perhaps someday beg as a favor that my <u>Assistant Inspector</u> Mr W. G. McNaught (– an excellent musician and valuable educationalist) may receive this honor although he is not known as a <u>composer</u>. My fear is that your Assessors might gradually assume the functions of a board of Examiners, and thus rob the degree of its complimentary or "honoris causâ" character.

No doubt you are teased by applicants but nevertheless I really think it is better that the conditions of obtaining the degree <u>should be left in their present somewhat indefinite shape</u> rather than that such a definite code of requirements should be formulated as might lead musicians to suppose that they had almost a <u>right</u> to receive it – provided that satisfied your examiners. This would be quite disastrous – <u>I</u> think.[131]

McNaught received the Lambeth D. Mus. at Stainer's recommendation in 1896, but, on the whole, the panel advised against many of the candidates. Stainer appears to have relinquished his position after about 1896, but he continued to support supplicants for the degree, including Charles Frederick South of Salisbury Cathedral, a one-time organ student of George Cooper and former organist of St Augustine-with-St-Faith's (under the shadow of St Paul's):

I hear on all sides of the beauty of your musical services, Mr South seems not only to have raised them to a high standard but to have maintained them at this level. If I am correctly informed about this, do you not think it would be a nice compliment to him if you were to obtain for him the degree of Mus.Doc. from the Archbishop? Quite recently the organist of Hereford has received the honor, and I have little doubt that a direct appeal from you, supported by your Chapter would be favorably considered by his Grace.

---

[131] Letter from Stainer to Archbishop Benson, 14 November 1891, *GB-Llp*.

If any musical "god-fathers" are required, I would gladly be one, and there would be no difficulty whatever in getting others.[132]

Parratt, whose antipathy to Stainer was well known, begged to differ:

> I think the testimony of Mr South's fitness should be more varied and more direct. You will notice that Sir John Stainer does not speak from personal knowledge and the rather cold concurrence of the Dean is not sufficient to establish the claim. The Dean also does not mention his Chapter. I have some acquaintance with Mr South and I found him a talented but rather weak person. He could not stand in the same position as Dr Sinclair, who has conducted large festivals with conspicuous success and has lately been appointed to the important post of chorus-master to the Birmingham Festival Chorus. Sir John Stainer's recommendation is as valuable as any to be found in England but here he speaks from hearsay. Without doubt the evidence of fitness must be further supported.[133]

Archbishop Temple evidently required further evidence, for Stainer's reply was more forthright, and set out his belief that the Lambeth degree should seek to reward hard-working, successful cathedral organists for their service to the church and to church music:

> The Dean of Salisbury has forwarded to me the kind reply of His Grace, communicated by you. I hasten to remove a false impression which my letter to the Dean has produced.
>
> When I said that I had heard on all sides that the services in Salisbury were so beautiful, I merely meant that my own opinion as to their beauty and reverence is backed up <u>by all who hear them</u>. I have <u>frequently</u> attended them, and have always been deeply impressed with them. Owing to Mr South's ability and hard work I have no hesitation in saying that Salisbury is setting a noble example to other cathedrals.
>
> If I had known that the Dean would forward my letter to His Grace, I should have mentioned my attendance at his services, but as he <u>knows</u> I have often been amongst the congregation, it was clearly unnecessary to tell <u>him</u> so.
>
> Of course Mr South is ignorant of my having begged his Dean and Chapter to appeal to His Grace, and if His Grace will confer the well-deserved honor of "Mus.Doc." on him I believe he will be as much surprised as gratified.

---

[132] Letter from Stainer to the Dean of Salisbury, 5 November 1900, *GB-Llp*.
[133] Letter from Parratt to Archbishop Temple, 22 November 1900, *GB-Llp*.

I think it would be a great encouragement to Cathedral organists to know that steady conscientious work for the church might sometimes be rewarded by a Degree. I was exceedingly pleased when His Grace conferred this distinction on the Organist of Hereford recently [George Robertson Sinclair].[134]

Stainer also lent his influence to a new initiative begun in 1897 to establish a movement dedicated to the establishment of new standards in church music. The movement was given its preliminary momentum by Percy Buck, Organist at Wells Cathedral, and Edmund Fellowes, Precentor of Bristol. At first Buck wished to exclude Stainer from the preliminary discussions (on the grounds, so Fellowes suggests, that his music was outdated), but Fellowes, who was close to Stainer, did not feel he could participate any further unless his old Oxford mentor was invited.[135] Stainer was intrigued by the new scheme and chaired the first exploratory meeting at the Royal College of Music on 2 December 1897 along with Parry, Stanford, F. J. Read, Basil Harwood, Hadow, Fellowes and Buck. From there the organisation, the Church Music Society, began to develop, albeit slowly. Stainer was unable to attend many of the meetings since it conflicted with his government inspection work, but he did voice his opinion about the formation of a sub-committee to determine those anthems that should remain in the cathedral repertoire. He wrote to Hadow:

> If a temperate explanatory letter were to be sent with such a list, to all our Cath[l] organists and precentors I think it would receive their serious consideration. As we are an entirely self-constituted body I think we ought not to venture on more than this – at all events at present.
>
> You know my opinion as to early (post-Reformation) settings of Canticles; I am sure a good many musicians will agree with me that they were the experiments (and not very successful experiments) of our English composers, the question of "Services" might well be left untouched.[136]

Stainer's proposal was adopted within wider terms of reference which included a broad survey of music sung in cathedral and collegiate establishments throughout the United Kingdom. He could not be persuaded to continue his membership of the committee after September 1899, but he clearly agreed to sign a letter together with Parry and Stanford, inviting all organists and precentors to a conference

---

[134] Letter from Stainer to Archbishop Temple, 28 November 1900, *GB-Llp*.

[135] See E. H. Fellowes, *Memoirs of an Amateur Musician* (London: Methuen & Co., 1946), 83.

[136] Letter from Stainer to Hadow, 13 March 1898, *GB-Ooc*.

at the Royal College in January 1900 to discuss the tabulated form of data collected.[137]

Stainer's senior position within the establishment of British music made it inevitable that he would be invited to sit on committees and lead several of the nation's principal musical societies and bodies. He continued to take an active role in the governance of the RCM as a prominent member of Council, and remained closely associated with the College of Organists, distributing the Fellowship diplomas to successful candidates in July 1896. After joining the Musicians' Company in 1878 (the Worshipful Company of Musicians), he acted as both warden and master on several occasions and he played a prominent role in the proceedings of the Incorporated Society of Musicians, presiding at three of their annual conferences, in London (1893), where he delivered an address 'Technique and Sentiment in Music', in Dublin (1895), where he gave a further lecture 'Does Music Train the Mind?', and again in London (1898). He was also a member of the Royal Society of Musicians, but he allowed his subscription to lapse: 'For several years I have dropped my subscription to the "R. Soc. of Mus[ns]." because it seems so often to close its hand when most needed. It is however admirably managed by most conscientious men.'[138] An invitation came from the Duke of Edinburgh to serve on the committee (along with Grove, Cusins, Hipkins, Henry Irving, J. C. O'Dowd, Stanford and Mackenzie) of the British section for the Musical and Dramatic Exhibition to be held in Vienna in 1892; in 1893 he was invited to be a judge of the music exhibits for the Chicago Exhibition, but declined because of the short notice; and with Grove, Mackenzie, Parratt, Cowen and Randegger, he sat on the concert committee in 1895 for the Imperial Institute. He continued to sit on the editorial committee of the Purcell Society, whose fortunes had been revived after 1887 by the work of Cummings and Barclay Squire. At the Purcell bicentenary celebrations in London, on 20 November 1895, he attended the historic performance at the Lyceum Theatre of *Dido and Aeneas* by the RCM students under Stanford's direction. The following day, exactly 200 years after Purcell's death, Stainer was at Westminster Abbey to join in the procession and wreath-laying at Purcell's grave, and shared the direction of choir and orchestra with Bridge; in the evening, at the Albert Hall, he heard Parry's new work written for the Leeds Festival, *Invocation to Music*, sung by the Royal Choral Society. His position as vice-president of the Folk Song Society has already been mentioned.

The publication of Novello's primers continued unabated, but as the pressures of maintaining the series increased, Stainer insisted that Parry take the upper hand as senior editor. The series was by this time huge, and by 1899 included Hadow's

---

[137] See letter (signed by Stainer, Parry and Stanford), *GB-Ooc*, and the tabulation of data, *GB-Ob* Tenbury MS 1482.

[138] Letter from Stainer to Edwards, 30 June 1896, *GB-Lbl* Egerton 3092, fol. 15.

Sonata Form, Dannreuther's ground-breaking two volumes of *Musical Ornamentation*, Cummings' *Biographical Dictionary of Musicians*, Hipkins' *History of the Pianoforte*, George Martin's *The Art of Training Choir Boys*, Pauer's *A Dictionary of Pianists and Composers for the Piano* and a proposal from John West to publish a dictionary of cathedral organists.

> I have often thought that a book of the "History of English Organists" with plenty of portraits would be a "hit", because it would practically be a history of English music, if properly done; I mean, if the share each man took in musical events, a list of his compositions, when, where, and how performed, (this would bring in Cathedral and Church Services, Theatres, Vauxhall, etc etc), and such information – were to be got together. But I am rather doubtful whether a book of reference to men in their alphabetical order would appeal to a large class; and I should not like to pass it for the Primer Series without Sir Hubert Parry's approval.[139]

West's idea was, however, thoroughly approved by all parties and it was published in 1899. Stainer also contributed his *Choral Society Vocalisations* in 1895, and Cecie Stainer, like her brother J. F. R. Stainer, no mean scholar, published her *Dictionary of Violin Makers* the following year. He also lent weight to other scholarly aspirations, notably that of Grove, who wanted to publish facsimile editions of Beethoven's works. In writing a supportive letter to *The Times* he revealed his own fascination for musical philology and the editing process:

> Sir, – I have not the least doubt that the appeal of Sir George Grove for help to obtain facsimile productions of the manuscripts of Beethoven will receive the hearty support of all professional musicians. But there exists probably amongst your readers a large class of lovers of music and those interested in the art who do not fully realize the importance of the proposal. If there is some truth in the fact that men show the chief outlines of their character in their ordinary handwriting, it may certainly be affirmed with greater truth that composers unconsciously depict their artistic aims and instincts when they throw their thoughts on to music-paper, under the strong emotional force of creative genius. The autograph of a great musical work brings a student into the very presence of the composer, face to face. He feels that he is almost watching the process of the art; and it is impossible to overrate the enormous amount of instruction which he may gain by studying every slight alteration or addition, every note or mark inserted or cut out, even errors made by a palpable slip of the pen. It may be said that Beethoven's works have been so admirably edited within the last few years that there is no need

[139] Letter from Stainer to John West, 21 July 1898, *GB-Lbl* MS. 63846, fol. 5.

for such a costly production as that suggested by Sir George Grove. But it must be remembered that the manuscripts of Beethoven, especially those of the symphonies, present difficulties to an editor which he is not likely to meet elsewhere. An editor of J. S. Bach may find himself confronted with several early copies, or even autographs, of the same composition varying considerably in details of more or less importance, but his labour is chiefly limited to a chronological arrangement of the materials before him; he rarely has to decide on the actual autheticity of a passage. It is quite otherwise in the case of Beethoven; in certain well-known passages in his symphonies we are not quite sure to this day whether we are playing the right notes! ... if Sir George Grove's scheme is carried out, it is more than probable that valuable opinions will be gathered froma large mass of practical and thoughtful musicians, whose <u>consensus</u> will enforce emendations which no individual would dare to propose. I shall be grateful, therefore, if you will allow me in your columns to beg all true lovers of music to assist Sir George Grove in this project.[140]

After Ouseley's death in 1889 Stainer was elected President of the Musical Association, and in accepting this position, he was in London at least once every season, usually in the role of chairman. The papers he chaired were exceptionally broad. Of a more traditional nature was Prout's paper on 'Fugal Structure' (14 June 1892) and Edwards' on 'Mendelssohn's Organ Sonatas', but among the more exploratory were Rabbi Cohen's on the 'Ancient Musical Traditions of the Synagogue' (13 June 1893), Higgs's on 'Samuel Wesley' (12 June 1894), Hadow's 'Formalism in Music' (14 December 1895), Towry Piper's on 'Violins and Violin Manufacture' (14 March 1897), Joseph Goddard's 'Philosophy of the Higher Beauty of Music' (14 November 1899) and McNaught's 'The Psychology of Sight-singing' (12 December 1899). And besides Stainer's landmark paper on Dufay, he delivered a further important and lengthy paper, 'On the Musical Introductions found in Certain Metrical Psalters', on 13 November 1900, in which he drew attention to the importance of the musical preface and its relationship to the systems of notation and performance of Protestant congregational music particularly in the sixteenth and seventeenth centuries, drawing on English, French and German examples from the early publications of Thomas Sternhold, Davantes, Vallete, John Day, Mareschal, Lardenois and Gobert. This and the double volume of *Bodleian Music* were to be his last pieces of published scholarship.

It becomes clear from the broad array of activities and responsibilities that were Stainer's during the 1890s that his workload was no less considerable than at St Paul's, though he perhaps enjoyed the greater luxury of organising much of his

---

[140] Letter from Stainer to the Editor of *The Times*, 23 September 1891.

own itinerary without the stipulations of services and practices which his former cathedral employment had imposed. A common escape from his heavy schedule (which invariably involved paying McNaught additional funds to undertake his work, or other assistants such as Bridge or Charles Vincent, as well as giving his Oxford lectures in November, May and June) was to make extended tours to the Continent with a concluding 'rest' on the Riviera (usually at Mentone) over a three-month period between the end of November and the following March. In this way, at the end of 1891, Stainer and his wife visited Athens and Constantinople with Cecie and Ellie. At the end of 1895 they journeyed to Egypt, visiting Alexandria and Cairo, and took a steamer down the Nile to Luxor, Karnak and the Valley of the Kings before returning through Rome and Genoa to Mentone. According to Elizabeth Stainer's diary it was a memorable holiday, saddened only by the news of the deaths of Lord Leighton and Barnby. Similarly the couple spent two months in Spain at the end of 1896 and the beginning of 1897, including on their tour Burgos, Madrid, the Alhambra and Barcelona before returning to the Riviera via Marseilles. At the end of 1898 (a year which had brought the sadness of his brother William's death), Stainer and his wife spent time in Florence and Mentone. By 1899 a marked decline in Stainer's health made future visits to the Riviera in early 1899 and 1900 vital in the restoration of his physical constitution. 'Thanks for your letter and good wishes', he wrote to King in January 1899; 'I am feeling better, but am still far from well and am not at all hopeful of ever being "as I was before." '[141] Further holidays were also arranged closer to home, notably to the Isle of Wight, Sidmouth, and a five-week stay in Swanage (during the summer of 1899) while the house in Oxford was redecorated.

After retiring from the Oxford chair, Stainer reasonably hoped that he could begin to slow down, a sentiment he communicated in a letter written at the end of 1900: 'I am gradually giving up all professional work, but I find much to interest me in antiquarian research amongst the old music in the Bodleian. Feeling, both in mind and body, that my work in life is nearing its close, your good words are all the more gratifying.'[142] Though 1900 had witnessed the publication of his *Hymn Tunes*, a nostalgic summer visit to Tenbury, and the intriguing experience of hearing Elgar's *Dream of Gerontius* in rehearsal at Birmingham,[143] the year had brought much sadness. In early January news of the death of his old friend Edwin George Monk (formerly organist of York Minster) was announced. 'I am sorry to hear of Dr Monk's death', he wrote to King, 'but I knew he was gradually sinking. He has at least been allowed to die in peace and quietness, it seems to me that

---

[141] Letter from Stainer to Henry King, 19 January 1899, *GB-Lsp*.
[142] Letter from Stainer to Mr Buckley, 19 December 1900, *GB-Bp*.
[143] *Birmingham Gazette*, 1 October 1900.

I shall not enjoy a similar luxury.'[144] In June he was one of a large party of friends and dignitaries to attend the funeral of Mrs Gladstone at Westminster Abbey, but more tragic was the death of Dean Church's daughter, for whose wedding he had once played at St Paul's. 'I am in low spirits', he wrote to Edwards, 'having just returned from the funeral of the wife of the Dean of Christchurch who was Dean Church's eldest daughter and a dear friend to our whole household. Only aged 43! less than a week ill! Six children left. It is too sad! And tomorrow, again a[t] the grave's side! I am to be one of the pall-bearers!'[145] Stainer's final comment referred to the funeral of his old friend, Sullivan, who, aged only fifty-eight, was buried in St Paul's on 27 November.

In January 1901 the Stainers once again set out on another Italian tour, staying first in Cannes and Mentone before moving on to Florence, Bologna, Verona and Venice. Having stopped off in Verona at the Hotel de Londres, they took in a visit to the ancient amphitheatre in the morning of Palm Sunday, 31 March. After lunch Stainer retired to his room while his wife attended the English church. On her return she found him shivering and complaining of severe pains in his chest. Death came shortly after from a fatal heart attack. Stainer's coffin reached Oxford on Good Friday, and, at the family's request, was placed in the church of St Cross. The funeral took place on Saturday 6 April at the church, where the choir of Magdalen College, under Varley Roberts's direction, sang Croft's *Burial Sentences* and Spohr's anthem 'Blessed are the Departed'; the burial followed in Holywell Cemetery. Special carriages were assigned to the 1.45 train from Paddington to accommodate the large crowd of friends and colleagues who came to pay their respects; yet the service and the demeanour of the occasion was, as Parry described, 'very quiet and unpretentious …, just such as he would have liked.'[146]

There were many tributes to Stainer in the months and years that followed, perhaps the most notable being Canon Newbolt's from the pulpit in St Paul's on Easter Day. A year to the day after Stainer's death, a memorial stained glass window was placed in St Cross Church gifted by Lady Stainer, who in 1905 also presented Magdalen College with a monument placed on the west wall, designed by G. F. Bodley with an inscription by Herbert Warren. A memorial was also unveiled by Canon Scott Holland at St Paul's Cathedral on 16 December 1903 with a design by H. A. Pegram on the theme of 'I saw the Lord', while at Tenbury three years later a memorial brass, given by J. F. R. Stainer, was placed in the church (bearing a quotation from George Herbert's poem 'Employment'). Lady Stainer, who was

---

[144] Letter from Stainer to Henry King, 8 January 1900, *GB-Lsp.*
[145] Letter from Stainer to Edwards, 26 November 1900, *GB-Lbl* MS Egerton 3092, fol. 118.
[146] Diary of Hubert Parry, *GB-ShP.*

in mourning for a year,[147] was stunned by the unexpected death of her husband, but, as she explained to Francesco Berger of the Philharmonic Society, Stainer had lived in trepidation of an infirm old age:

> Will you convey to the Directors of the Philharmonic Society my most grateful thanks for their kind expression of condolence with me, and for their assurance of grief at the loss of their friend and colleague. To yourself personally I would also add a word of sincere appreciation of your kind and warmhearted sympathy.
>
> It is so comforting to know how everybody loved him who had once come within his influence.
>
> From all parts of the world come assurances that he had won all hearts. To me his loss is immeasurable, but I am thankful that he has been spared long illness and the weariness of old age, which he always dreaded – and also that he has not to bear this terrible heart-ache.[148]

With the sudden absence of a Chief Inspector of Music, the Ministry of Education needed to appoint a replacement. It was generally expected that McNaught would fill the post. However, as Rainbow has made clear, the view of Robert Morant, the Permanent Secretary of the newly formed Board of Education, was that the new Inspector required a broader cultural purview of music than would be forthcoming from those engaged only in elementary education, as this would be vital for the implementation of the 1902 Education Act which involved the secondary and technical sectors. For this reason McNaught was passed over, and Arthur Somervell, a completely inexperienced and untried teacher, was appointed and a new philosophy of music education was introduced which stressed the link between music and moral values and the development of music within the school curriculum as the agency of acculturation rather than purely as a means of technical proficiency. McNaught, having learned of Somervell's appointment, summarily resigned, feeling that he was unable to work under a man of so little experience. Until his death in 1928 he lived as a freelance writer and lecturer on musical education, and continued to act as editor of the *School Music Review*.

Stainer's voluminous library, one of the finest of its kind in the country, was bequeathed to J. F. R. Stainer, who would agree to lend occasional volumes to trustworthy applicants. One such request was addressed to Lady Stainer by Arthur Mann during the dark days of the First World War, while J. F. R. and Charles Stainer were in uniform:

[147] Lady Stainer died on 6 September 1916 at South Parks Road. The funeral took place on 9 September at Holywell Cemetery.
[148] Letter from Lady Stainer to Francesco Berger, 20 May 1901, *GB-Lbl* Loan 48.13/32, fol. 197.

I found the book you name, and wrote at once to Jack [J. F. R. Stainer] for permission to lend it to you, as all my dear husband's books belong to him. His reply is "It is often on my conscience that the books in the Library are not put to better use, and as far as I am concerned, any responsible person is welcome to borrow them for study or research. By all means let Dr Mann have the book" – So here it is, and I hope it may prove of use – Please return it to me here. I am so glad you use dear John's music – That anthem "Grieve not" was always one of my special favourites. I heard at the Cathedral here "I saw the Lord" last week, but do not often have a chance of hearing his music now. Yesterday was his birthday and he would have been 75 – I am so thankful he escaped the horrors of this dreadful war. Jack is in the East Surrey 11th Battalion now quartered at Colchester. Charles, who lives with me is 1st Lieutenant O[xford] & B[erkshire] Lt Infantry 4th Battalion here. It is all very disquieting at my age, and my friends are constantly losing dear sons on foreign service. I hope you and Mrs Mann have nobody very dear to you at the front.[149]

Lady Stainer died on 6 September 1916; she was buried alongside her husband. By then four of her children, J. F. R., Ellie (whose marriage ended by separation), Edward (who married Bridge's daughter Rosalind Flora in Westminster Abbey on 1 June 1907) and Charles were married; Cecie remained a spinster, William Edgar a bachelor. In 1932 the valuable library of songbooks was sold for £520 to the American collector Walter N. H. Harding of Chicago. Here the collection remained until Harding's death in 1973, when it was bequeathed in its entirety to the Bodleian, where it now resides. A further part of the library, sold in 1934, has been dispersed.

Though Stainer died a highly respected man, time has judged him harshly. Ernest Walker, writing in 1907, grudgingly acknowledged a strength of invention in 'I saw the Lord', but was unabashedly dismissive of what he deemed a 'tide of sentimentalism' running through the Victorian era, and in grouping Stainer with Barnby and Dykes, he disparaged the 'cheaply sugary harmony and palsied part-writing' of these figures as a blight on the history of English music. With evident relief he declared that future historians would look back on this period 'with the reverse of pride'.[150] Fellowes, emulating Walker, was equally disdainful of Stainer's 'easy prettiness', and somewhat lazily hid behind a popular criticism of all things Mendelssohnian, surely symptomatic of a generation overreactive against a century which symbolised his adoration.[151] Frank Howes was no kinder. He damned

---

[149] Letter from Lady Stainer to Mann, 7 June 1915, *GB-NWr.*

[150] E. Walker, *A History of Music in England* (Oxford: Clarendon Press, 1907), 308.

[151] E. Fellowes, *English Cathedral Music from Edward VI to Edward VII* (London: Methuen & Co., 1941), 222, *passim.*

Stainer with faint praise by admitting to his 'creditable scholarship when he held the Oxford chair',[152] and had little compunction in scorning *The Crucifixion* as 'banal and sentimental',[153] while Long, in *The Music of the English Church*, went as far as to describe the same work as 'squalid music' coupled with a chastisement of those who deigned even to perform it.[154]

Contemporary criticism has been less excoriating, but a general trend has been to praise Stainer's achievements elsewhere at the expense of his abilities as a composer. Benecke recalled that Stainer was himself openly critical of his own work:

> Of his compositions he was in the habit of speaking in a somewhat deprecia-
> tory way as though it were a mistake to take them too seriously. It ought not
> to be inferred from this (any more than from a somewhat similar habit of
> Sir Hubert Parry) that he did not put into them the best work of which he
> was capable; they were mostly concerned with religious words or intended
> to be used in connection with Church Services, and he would certainly not
> have regarded it as fitting that he should do otherwise. It was due rather to
> self-criticism and to the consciousness that he had not succeeded in reach-
> ing the very high standard at which he aimed.[155]

Fellowes recounted in print, on three different occasions, Stainer's hypercriti-
cism of his church music, though in each case inconsistencies emerged. In 1941, for example, reference was made to Stainer's 'earlier anthems' as being 'too easily written', and 'in response to pressure put on him in early days by the clergy and others, who assured him that they were "just the thing they wanted." '[156] In 1946, in his autobiography, the version was put slightly differently. This time the reference was to Stainer's regret 'that much of his church music had been published, for he realized in later days that it no longer gave him satisfaction, and he feared that it might create a misleading impression of his standard of taste in years to come.'[157] And in 1951 Fellowes claimed that Stainer 'regretted ever having published most of his compositions ... he was then a poor man and gave way to demand ...'[158] Temperley has rightly indicated that Stainer was ultimately referring to his early anthems,[159] works written in an older style redolent of the mid-nineteenth century

[152] Howes, *The English Musical Renaissance*, 288.

[153] Ibid., 158.

[154] K. R. Long, *The Music of the English Church* (London: Hodder & Stoughton, 1971), 364–5.

[155] Benecke, 'Some Remarks', 156.

[156] Fellowes, *English Cathedral Music*, 224.

[157] Fellowes, *Memoirs of an Amateur Musician*, 85.

[158] E. Fellowes, 'Sir John Stainer', *English Church Music* 21/1 (1951), 7.

[159] Temperley, 'Ancient and Modern in the Work of Sir John Stainer', 114.

which now seemed thoroughly outmoded in the context of the post-Wagnerian generation of Parry, Stanford and Elgar. Yet, significantly, it was precisely (and ironically) these works which elicited more positive criticism from his detractors.

As Temperley has stressed, it was the stylistic boundaries of a technically unde-manding, 'edifying' style of his maturity, with its concomitant challenges, that educed the most fruitful qualities of Stainer's talent, qualities that could produce the enduring meditative intensity of *The Crucifixion*, so aptly designed for parish use, anthems such as 'And Jacob was left alone', 'O bountiful Jesu' and 'O saving victim', and the deeply affecting 'High Victorian' sentiment of hymn tunes such as 'Rest', 'St Francis Xaver' and 'Love divine'. The precision of the later music should not, however, detract from the prodigiousness of 'I saw the Lord' (which, com-posed at 18, reminds us of just how technically assured Stainer was as a young man), 'Awake, awake' (with its exquisite verse 'How beautiful upon the mountain'), the contrapuntal dexterity of 'Drop down, ye heavens, from above', 'They were lovely and pleasant in their lives', and 'Lead, kindly light'. These works show a real invention for both chromatic and diatonic harmony, fertile structure and fecund melody comparable with the work of S. S. Wesley, while the small corpus of secu-lar works – the *Eight Madrigals*, the *Seven Songs* and 'Flora's Queen' – are fastidious gems which deserve greater exposure.

That we should remember Stainer as a capable composer, and as a figure who occupies an important place in both the canon of nineteenth-century English com-posers and the evolution of a distinctively 'English' musical parlance, is beyond question. But, more importantly, Stainer's music, its style, range, pragmatism and philosophy, warrants a full and comprehensive understanding of the man as polymath and reformer, conservative and liberal, practical musician and scholar. Beginning his musical life as a chorister and organist, Stainer gained a perspective of the music profession that was an intrinsically *practical* one. From a humble background, he had little option but to work his way up both the professional and social ladders, and this he achieved through pure ability and industry, self-belief, and the grasping of vital opportunities as they presented themselves. Through Ouseley he gained entry to the 'gentlemanly' class through his apprenticeship at Tenbury and his degree at Oxford, though sheer flair as an organist determined his appointment at Magdalen in spite of his tender years. 'Head-hunted' by the Dean and Chapter of St Paul's, he fought doggedly to establish major structural and organisational reforms at a foundation seemingly resigned to its atrophic fate. In securing a bright future for music at St Paul's, he instigated a model for other cathedral choirs throughout the nation, and, with the catalyst of Sparrow Simpson, spearheaded a new wave of musical repertoire and performance initiatives which drew congregations to London's metropolitan cathedral in their thousands. All this he accomplished through personal appeal, his ability to lead, a persuasive charm, an astute commercial mind (he benefited greatly from the expansion of Novello's cheap editions) and a good measure of Victorian optimism that standards could, and *must*, improve. To this, one must add that unusual and somewhat individual Gladstonian factor of the conservative churchman, profoundly influenced by the values, discipline and ritual of the Oxford Movement (itself a potential break on reform, especially in the ancient universities), yet driven by a Liberal social conscience that looked to educate, ameliorate and edify.

The result of this significant amalgamation was a man resolute to preserve at all costs those high standards of singing, performance, deportment and that sense of mystery engendered by sacred music quintessential to the vision of the High Anglican service (a factor, which, incidentally, spawned new creative developments in liturgical thinking, not least with the 'orchestral' service), yet at the same time looking to bring this aspiration of the 'cathedral style' closer to parish choral worship, or in the secular domain, to the children of elementary schools and the trainee teacher. To this end, of course, Stainer was motivated by the larger issues of political debate, but, like Gladstone, he was prompted by a deep religious conviction from which he never wavered, notwithstanding his allegiance to Darwinian and Spencerian notions of evolution. Addressing his colleagues at the Annual Dinner of the College of Organists on 29 April 1889, he declared:

> We have one great reward … and that reward is the opportunity of making at some time or other contributions, however small, to sacred music. I was one Sunday walking at some sea-side place and on turning a corner I heard a number of school children singing a hymn that I had composed. I thought to myself: I want no higher reward than that for all my work, and I think, gentlemen, if any of you contribute a single hymn or chant, however small, to the service of God, this contribution in itself is the highest reward you can have. I can only tell you that I would not exchange it for the very highest monument in Westminster Abbey.[160]

This fascinating chemistry of the traditional and progressive was equally reflected in the fusion of styles which Stainer embraced. He was, as a composer of church music, instinctively a Classicist, profoundly influenced by the models of Goss and Attwood, who looked to Mozart as a guiding star. This is evident in the finely honed structures, the regular periodicity of his phraseology (at times a potential weakness, especially in his handling of the fugal process) and the roots of his melodic gift. Yet Stainer was no slave to his Classical heritage, and he unequivocally rejected the regressive views of his mentor Ouseley and the aesthetic *dicta* of Crotch. He welcomed into the ecclesiastical environment the Romanticism of

---

[160] *The College of Organists 25th Annual Report 1888–9*, 33.

Mendelssohn and the chromatic ruminations of Spohr, the more adventurous key schemes of Schubert, and the contemporary harmonic vocabularies of Schumann and Gounod, at a time when a zeal for 'pure' church music (in the form of plain-chant and Renaissance polyphony) was considered *de rigueur* in Cecilian Europe and among the Ecclesiologists. He also remained unapologetic in his admiration for Dykes's hymnody at a time when fashion was beginning to expurgate his 'High Victorian' tunes from new hymnals. Time has shown, with the recognition of Dykes as one of the greatest of all hymnodists, that Stainer's veneration was well founded. Furthermore, we should not ignore Stainer's part in the Bach Revival. Fortunate to be alive at its inception, he retained a love for Bach's choral and key-board music which manifested itself later in his public recitals as an organist, his initial involvement with the Bach Choir, and his publicly acclaimed annual serv-ices of the *St Matthew Passion* at St Paul's.

Stainer may have rejected the aesthetic views of Ouseley, but he drew much from his mentor in other ways. Through Ouseley's teaching, he developed an extraordinary contrapuntal facility, a skill which, once assimilated, could, and was, used with creative originality (as is evident in 'I saw the Lord' and the opening pages of 'Drop down, ye heavens'), and his love of the madrigal repertoire, nour-ished by his years at Tenbury, having sunk below consciousness, emerged in excit-ing Romantic utterances which, at their best, largely surpassed the paradigms of Pearsall. Finally Stainer gleaned from Ouseley (perhaps inevitably, since he had at his fingertips one of the greatest private manuscript collections in England) an intense respect for scholarship, musical history and the enriching power of musi-cal 'science'. The editions of *Dufay* and *Bodleian Music* are an impressive testament to Stainer's pioneering courage as a scholar (and to the editorial abilities of his two eldest children), as is the rationalist thinking of his much neglected *Theory of Harmony*, but it is perhaps the legacy of the Royal Musical Association that was his most enduring and visionary initiative.

Stainer may be fairly termed the epitome of the Victorian composer. He was born three years after Queen Victoria acceded to the throne (and in the year of her marriage to Prince Albert) and died only ten weeks after her death. Until recently such a description, with its entrenched prejudices, would have led to a curt dis-missal of him, but a reappraisal of all things Victorian demands that we reassess the role of John Stainer. As a man of energy, conviction, vision, passion and academic vigour (and one that greatly benefited from Oxford's Liberal intellectual milieu) he was a towering figure in the Victorian musical world, and, while he could not boast the higher profiles of Sullivan, Parry or Stanford, his contribution to the larger fabric of Britain's music – in the Anglican cathedral and parish church, the Anglican hymn, the Christmas carol, education, the science of bells, musicology and the nation's musical institutions – was substantial and lasting. Moreover, in an age where anti-Victorian prejudices are themselves now completely outdated, the range and beauty of Stainer's achievements require more urgent revisiting to appreciate their individuality, sincerity and germane role.

ॐ

> Well, it is gone at last, the palace of music I reared;
>> Gone! and the good tears start, the praises that come too slow;
> For one is assured at first, one scarce can say that he feared,
>> That he even gave it a thought, the gone thing was to go.
> Never to be again! But many more of the kind
>> As good, nay, better, perchance: is this your comfort to me?
> To me, who must be saved because I cling with my mind
>> To the same, same self, same love, same God: ay, what was, shall be.

[from *Abt Vogler* by Robert Browning, quoted at the unveiling
of the Stainer memorial at St Paul's on 16 December 1903]

Stainer's Works

Manuscript sources are listed where they exist.

CHURCH MUSIC

Oratorios and Cantatas

'Praise the Lord, O my soul' (Bible). Mus.Bac. exercise. SATB soli + SATB chorus + orchestra. 1858. First performed 9 June 1859, Sheldonian Theatre, Oxford. Unpublished. Autograph *GB-Ob*.

Gideon (Bible). Oratorio. Mus.D exercise. SATB soli + SATB chorus + orchestra. 1865. First performed (though not in full) 8 November 1865, Sheldonian Theatre, Oxford. Published 1865? Autograph *GB-Ob* (vocal score only); autograph full score of overture in private possession (MN).

The Daughter of Jairus (Bible: text selected by Stainer and H. Joyce). Cantata. STB soli + SATB chorus + orchestra. 1878. First performed 14 September 1878, Worcester (Three Choirs) Festival. Published 1879. Autograph in private possession (JRS).

St Mary Magdalen (text compiled and written by W. J. Sparrow Simpson). Oratorio. SATB soli + SATB chorus + orchestra. 1883. First performed 5 September 1883, Gloucester (Three Choirs) Festival. Published 1884. Autograph of full score in private possession (MN); copy of full score in *GB-Lcm*.

The Crucifixion (text compiled and written by W. J. Sparrow Simpson). Passion oratorio. TB soli + SATB chorus + organ. 1887. Dedicated to W. Hodge and the choir of Marylebone Church. First performed 24 February 1887, Marylebone Parish Church. Published 1887. Autograph in private possession (JRS).

Anthems

Published by Novello unless otherwise stated.
Autograph manuscripts are missing unless otherwise stated.

'I saw the Lord' (Isaiah, vi, 1–4). Anthem for Trinity Sunday. Double choir + SATB verse. 1858. Published (i) Novello 1865; (ii) Ouseley's *A Collection of Anthems for Certain Seasons and Festivals*, vol. 2, 1866. Autograph *GB-Ob*.

'The righteous live for evermore' (Wisdom, v, 15–16). SATB + SATB verse. 1858. Published 1858.

'The morning stars sang together' (Job, xxxviii, 7; Luke, ii, 11; Isaiah, lxvi, 10–12). Anthem for Christmas Day. SATB. 1858. Dedicated to George Cooper. Published (i) Ouseley's *A Collection of Anthems for Certain Seasons and Festivals* vol. 1, 1861; (ii) Novello 1873.

'The Lord is in His holy temple' (Habakkuk, ii, 20). Anthem for the feast of the Purification. SSATB. 1861? Published (i) in Ouseley's *A Collection of Anthems for Certain Seasons and Festivals* (1861); (ii) Novello 1901.

'For a small moment have I forsaken Thee' (Isaiah, liv, 7, 8, 10). SATB + SATB verse. 1862. Dedicated to Dr C. W. Corfe. Published 1895. Copy of MS (in copyist's hand), Tenbury collection, *GB-Ob*.

'Deliver me, O Lord' (Psalm cxliii, 9–11). Short anthem for general use. SATB. 1863. Published (i) 1863 in *Parochial Anthems by the Cathedral Composers of 1863*, ed. Fowle, T. Lloyd (Winchester); (ii) Novello 1901.

'They were lovely and pleasant in their lives' (2 Samuel, i, 23; Wisdom, iii, 5–6; Ecclesiasticus, xxiv, 24). Anthem for the feast of St Simon and St Jude. SATB + SATB verse + BB duet. 1861? Published (i) Ouseley's *A Collection of Anthems for Certain Seasons and Festivals* (1866); (ii) Novello 1901.

'Drop down, ye heavens, from above' (Isaiah, xlv, 8; Luke, i, 28, 31–3; Psalm xlv, 2). Anthem for the feast of the Annunciation. SATB + SATB verse + S solo. 1866. Published (i) in Ouseley's *A Collection of Anthems for Certain Seasons and Festivals*, vol. II (1866); (ii) Novello 1901.

'Sing a song of praise' (Ecclesiasticus, xxxix, 19; v, 14–15; ii, 11, 1). SATB chorus + semichorus. 1867. Composed for 4th Annual Festival of the associated choirs of the Archdeaconry of Worcester, St Lawrence Church, Evesham. Dedicated to Rev. W. Rayson (Sacrist of Worcester Cathedral and honorary secretary for the Worcester Choral Association). Published (i) 1867; (ii) York Series, York (*c*.1920).

'Lead, kindly light' (J. H. Newman). SATB + S (or T) solo. 1868. Dedicated to H. A. B. Wilson. Published 1868.

'Awake, awake; put on thy strength' (Isaiah, iii, 1–2, 7–10). SATB + SATB semichorus. 1871. Dedicated to Rev. J. R. G. Taylor (Hereford). Published (i) 1871; (ii) *MT* lix (1918) supplement. Autograph in private possession (JRS).

'What are these?' (Revelation, vii, 13–17). Dedication anthem. SATB. 1871? Composed for the Dedication Festival of All Saints' Church, Lathbury, Buckinghamshire. Published 1871?

'O clap your hands' (Psalm xlvii, vv. 1–2; Isaiah, xl, 31; xxvi, 4). SATB chorus + semichorus, with orchestral accompaniment by Battison Haynes. 1873. Composed for the Eleventh Annual Festival of the Richmond and Kingston Church Choral Association. Dedicated to Capt. Malton. Published 1873. Autograph in private possession (JRS).

'Rogate quae ad pacem sunt Hierusalem' (in Latin). T solo + SATB chorus. Dated 3 March 187[4?]. Unpublished. Autograph *GB-Lsp*.

'O Zion that bringest good tidings' (Isaiah, xl, 9; part of hymn 'Of the Father's love begotten'). Anthem for Christmas. SATB. 1874. Dedicated to Rev. Dr Sparrow Simpson. Published (i) 1874; (ii) *MT* xvi no. 381 (1874).

'They have taken away my Lord' (John, xx, 13, 15, 16; Corinthians, xv, 55, 57). Anthem for Easter. SATB. 1874. Dedicated to Rev. Dr Troutbeck. Published (i) 1875; (ii) *MT* xvi no. 381 (1875). Autograph in private possession (JRS).

'Hosanna in the highest' (Luke, xxi, 9; Isaiah, lxiii, 1–4; part of hymn?). Anthem for Advent Sunday. SATB. 1875. Published (i) 1875; (ii) *MT* xvii no. 392 (1875).

'I desired wisdom' (Ecclesiasticus, li, 13–15; iv, 14; Matthew, ii, 1, 2, 9, 10; verse from 'Adeste fideles'). Anthem for Epiphany. SATB + trio for three trebles. Published 1876.

'Leave us not, neither forsake us' (Psalm xxvii, 11; Psalm xvi, 12; Acts, i, 11; Psalm lxviii, 18). Anthem for use at Ascensiontide. SATB. 1877. Published (i) 1877; (2) *MT* xviii no. 410 (1877).

'Ye shall dwell in the land' (Ezekiel, xxxvi, 28, 30, 34–5; Psalm cxxxvi, 1; hymn by Chatterton Dix). Anthem for harvest. SATB + Tr (or T) and B soli, with orchestral accompaniment. 1877. Published (i) 1877; (ii) *MT* xviii no. 414 (1877). Autograph in private possession (JRS).

'I am Alpha and Omega' (Revelation, i, 8; Sanctus). Anthem for Trinity-tide. SATB + S (or T) solo. 1878. Published (i) 1878; (ii) *MT* xix no. 423 (1878). Autograph in private possession (MN).

'Grieve not the Holy Spirit' (Ephesians, iv, 30–2). SATB soli verse + chorus. 1880. Published [n.d.]. Autograph, dated 22–3 Oct 1880, in private possession (MN).

'Thus speaketh the Lord of hosts' (Zechariah, vi, 12–13; part of a hymn translated by James Russell Woodford, Bishop of Ely). Anthem for Christmas. SATB. 1880. Published (i) 1880; (ii) *MT* xxi no. 453 (1880). Autograph in private possession (JRS).

'Let the peace of God rule your hearts' (Colossians, iii, 15–17). SATB + S (or T) solo. *c.*1882. Published [n.d.]. Autograph in private possession (MN).

'And all the people saw thunderings' (Exodus, xx, 18–19; hymn by John Keble, 'When God of old'; 1 John, iv, 7, 12). Anthem for Whitsuntide (or general use). SATB + duet for tenor (or treble) soli + recitative for T or B solo. Published 1883. Composed for the London Church Choir Festival.

'There was marriage in Cana of Galilee' (John, ii, 1–2; hymn by Francis Paget). Wedding anthem. SATB + B solo + duet for S (or T) soli. 1883. Composed for the wedding of Mrs Paget and the Dean of Christ Church, Oxford, 28 March 1883. Published [n.d.]. Autograph in private possession (MN).

'Let every soul be subject' (Romans, xiii, 1; Psalm cxviii, 1–5, 19; two verses of a hymn [which?]). Coronation anthem. SATB + S and T soli. 1887. Composed for the Golden Jubilee of Queen Victoria. Published (i) 1887; (ii) *MT* xxviii no. 527 (1887). Autograph in private possession (JRS).

'Lord, Thou art God' (1 Chronicles, xvii, 26–7; 2 Samuel, xxii, 2–4; Kings, viii, 57, 60; a versicle and response from the office of matins (or evensong); verse 1 of National Anthem). SATB + T solo + orchestral accompaniment. 1887. Composed for the Festival of the Sons of the Clergy, May 1887. Published (i) 1887; (ii) one movement in *MT* ('The Lord our God be with us') liv no. 843 (1913). Autograph full score *Lbm* MS 50782; autograph vocal score in private possession (MN).

'Lo! Summer comes again' (Dean of Wells Cathedral). Anthem for harvest (or general use). SATB and semichorus. *c.*1888. Dedicated to the Rev F. H. Hichens. Published [n.d.].

'The hallowed day hath shined' ('an ancient Office and part of a hymn by the Very Rev E. B. Plumptre'). Christmas anthem. SATB + tenor solo. 1888. Published (i) 1888; (ii) *MT* xxix no. 550 (1888).

'Honour the Lord with thy substance' (Proverbs, iii, 9–10, 19–20; Deuteronomy, xxxiii, 27–9). Harvest anthem. SATB + T and B soli. 1892. Published 1892.

'There was silence in Bethlehem's fields' (Chatterton Dix). Christmas anthem. SATB. 1893. Published (i) 1894; (ii) *MT* xxxv no. 622 (1894); (iii) unison arrangement, New York, 1893.

'And Jacob was left alone' (Genesis, xxxii; part of a hymn by Charles Wesley). SATB + BB (Narrator and The Angel) and T (Jacob) soli. 1894. Published 1894.

'Behold, two blind men' (Matthew, xx, 30; two verses of the hymn 'O lift the veil'). SATB + STB soli. 1895. Composed for the Gregorian Festival, 1895. Published 1895. Autograph in private possession (JRS).

'Let not thine hand be stretched' (Ecclesiasticus, iv, 31; vii, 35; xviii, 25). Anthem for Hospital Sunday 'or any other occasion of almsgiving to the poor'. SATB + S (or T) solo. 1895. Published (i) 1895; (ii) *MT* vol. xxxvi no. 628 (1895).

'Mercy and truth are met together' (Psalm lxxxv, 10–11; 'and from the Offices of the Greek Church'). Christmas anthem. SATB + S solo. 1895. Published (i) 1895; (ii) *MT* vol. xxxvi no. 633 (1895).

'Behold, God is my helper' (Psalm liv, 4, 6). Short anthem for general use. SATB. *c.*1896. Published (i) 1896?; (ii) 1926.

'Blessed is the man' (James, i, 12). Short anthem for general use. SATB. *c.*1896. Published (i) 1896?; (ii) 1926.

Seven Greater Antiphons: 'O Wisdom'; 'O Lord and Ruler'; 'O Root of Jesse'; 'O Key of David'; 'O Dayspring'; 'O King and Desire'; 'O Emmanuel'. SATB. 1896. Published 1896.

'It came upon a midnight clear' (hymn by the Rev E. H. Sears). Christmas anthem. SATB + B solo. 1899. Published (i) 1899; (ii) *MT* vol. xl no. 681 (1899). Autograph *GB-Lsp*.

'Thou Lord in the beginning' (Psalm cii, 25–7; Revelation, xxi, 1–4; a stanza and doxology from 'Urbs beata'). Anthem for Setuagesima, St John, or general use. SATB + solo quartet + S solo. 1899. Published 1899. Autograph *GB-Lsp*.

'Day of wrath' (Thomas of Celano, trans. Rev. W. J. Irons). SATB + solo quartet. 1900. Published 1900.

'O Bountiful Jesu' (from a prayer in the primer 'set forth by the order of King Edward VI in 1553'). SATB. 1900. Published (i) 1900; (ii) *MT* xli no. 684 (1900).

'O Saving Victim' (St Thomas Aquinas). Short anthem or introit. SATB + solo quartet. 1900. Published 1900. Autograph *GB-Lsp*.

Service Settings

'Magdalen' Service in A. SATB + organ. 1866? Unpublished. Autograph (and copy) in private possession (JRS).

Set No. 1 in E flat. SATB + organ.

> Evening Service. *c.*1870. Published [n.d.]. Autograph in private possession (JRS).
> Morning Service. *c.*1874. Published [n.d.].
> Holy Communion Office. *c.*1874. Published [n.d.].
> Benedictus and Agnus Dei (No. 1; for festival use). 1899. Published 1899.
> Benedictus and Agnus Dei (No. 2). 1899. Published 1899.

Set 2 in A (and D). SATB + organ.

> Evening Service. 1873. Composed for the Festival of the Sons of the Clergy.
>   Published [n.d.]. Autograph (vocal score) in private possession (JRS);
>   orchestration by Stainer missing.
> Morning Service. 1877? Published [n.d.]. Autograph in private possession (JRS).
> Holy Communion Office (sometimes referred to as the Communion Service in D).
>   1877? Published [n.d.]. Autograph in private possession (JRS).
> Benedictus and Agnus Dei (No. 1; for festival use). 1899. Published 1899.
> Benedictus and Agnus Dei (No. 2). 1899. Published 1899.
>
> An orchestration of the Sanctus and and Gloria from the office of Holy Communion was made by Sir George Martin for the Coronation of Edward VII in 1902.

Set 3 in B flat. SATB + organ.

> Evening Service. 1877. Composed for the Fifth Annual Festival of the London
>   Church Choir Association. Published [n.d.]. Orchestration by Stainer missing.
> Morning Service. 1884? Published 1884.
> Holy Communion Office (sometimes referred to as the Communion Service in F).
>   1884? Published 1884.

Service in D major. ATTB + organ.

> Evening Service. 1873. Composed for the choir of St Paul's Cathedral. Published 1898.
> Morning Service. 1898–1900. Published 1900.
> Holy Communion Office. 1898–1900. Published 1900. Autograph *GB-Lsp*.

Other Service Music

Music for the Communion Service

Service of Holy Communion in C. SSATBB *a cappella*. 1900–1. 'composed expressly for the choir of St Paul's Cathedral'. Published 1901. Autograph *GB-Lsp* and in private possession (see Sotheby's catalogue 21 May 1999, 133)?

'Kyrie eleison'. SATB? 1899. Published? [A contribution, No. 3, to a set of 4.] Autograph *GB-Lsp*.

Service of Holy Communion in A. ATTB + organ. 1900. Published 1900. Autograph *GB-Lsp*.

Kyrie in A flat. n.d. Autograph *GB-Lsp*.

Kyrie in D flat with 10th Commandment. 1899. Autograph *GB-Lsp*.

Music for the Service of Matins

Morning Service in C. SATB + organ (though mostly unison for congregation). Te Deum, *c*.1870. Published [n.d.].

Morning Service in G. SATB + organ (for congregational use). Te Deum, 1877? Published 1893.

Morning Service in A flat (in chant form). SATB + organ. Te Deum, 1877? Published 1899.

Morning Service in D (in chant form). SATB + organ. Benedicite, 1877? Published 1894. Autograph? *GB-Lsp*.

Morning Service in F major (in chant form). SATB + organ. Benedicite, chants by Stainer and B. Blaxland, 1877? Published 1896.

Morning Service in G (in chant form). SATB + organ. Benedicite, chants by Stainer and J. Turle, 1877? Published (i) 1915; (ii) *MT* vol. lvi no. 864 (1915).

Music for Evensong

Evening Service in E. SATB + organ. 1870. Published 1870.

Evening Service in D and F. SATB + organ (in chant form). 1877? Published 1894.

Evening Service in F. SATB + organ. 1877. Composed for the Third Festival of the Sion College Choral Union in St Paul's Cathedral, 16 January 1877. Published 1895.

Miscellaneous Works

Sevenfold Amen. SATB unaccompanied [A major]. 1873. Published 1873. (i) Arr. Hugh Blair for 3 treble voices + optional organ. Published 1909. (ii) Arr. G. J. Bennett for ATTB. Published 1909. Autograph of orchestration n.d. in private possession (MN).

Nicene Creed (Unison). *c*.1874. Published 1875.

Miserere (Psalm li). Unaccompanied. 1873. Published 1894.

Twelve Sacred Songs for Children (illustrated in the original publication of *Holy Gladness*), unison songs (with the exception of No. 1, which is a duet) with organ or piano accompaniment, words by Edward Oxenford. *c*.1875. Published 1889. 1. Listening angels; 2. Morning hymn; 3. Hour by hour; 4. The beautiful land; 5. The Crown is waiting; 6. The Cross of life; 7. We will praise Thee; 8. Sabbath bells; 9. The Good Shepherd; 10. The Haven of Glory; 11. The golden shore; 12. Evensong.

Fourfold Amen. SATB unaccompanied. Published 1909.

'Stars, that on your wondrous way' (Stainer?). Hymn for children. Published *School Music Review* (June 1892).

'A Child's Evensong'. Published *School Music Review* (August 1897).

Hymn Tunes

A collection of Stainer's hymn tunes, written between 1867 and 1900, was assembled and published in one volume by Novello in 1900. A volume containing autograph correspondence between Stainer and King survives in St Paul's Cathedral Library. Those in italics signify hymns tunes not included in the volume of 1900. Autographs of those tunes asterisked can be found in the copy donated by Henry King to the Library of St Paul's Cathedral.

No. First line	Author	Name of tune	Metre	Source of tune	Date
Now once more we greet Thee	*S. Childs Clarke*				*n.d.*
O God, our Hope, our Strength, our King	*Mrs Alexander*				*n.d.*
19 O come and bless us, ere the day	H. A. Martin	Vespers	8484D	Nottinghamshire Choral Union Festival Book	n.d.
Hail the day that sees Him rise				*Hymns for the Church of England, ed. Steggall*	*1865?*
44 Jesu, the very thought of Thee	trans. E. Caswall	Sudeley	CM	Supplemental Hymn & Tune Book 3	1867
		Emmanuel		*Hymns A&M 1868*	1868
		Nativitas		*Hymns A&M 1868*	1868
84 I need Thee, precious Jesus	Frederick Whitfield	Magdalena	7676D	Hymns A&M 186	1868
86 Gracious Spirit, Holy Ghost	Chr. Wordsworth	Charity	7775	Hymns A&M 210	1868
153 Heavenly Father, send Thy blessing	Chr. Wordsworth	Iona	8787D	Hymns A&M 338	1868
101 For the fount of life eternal	Damiani, trans. J. Dayman	Damiani	15 15 15	Sarum Hymnal 320	1869
30 Day of wrath	Thomas of Celano, trans. W. J. Irons	Dies Judicii	888	Supplemental Hymn & Tune Book 71	1869
17 Now when the dusky shades of night	W. T. Copeland & others	Dawn	11 10 11 10	Hymnary 53 [first pub. 1872]	1870
15 Come, my soul, thou must be waking	Canitz, trans. H. J. Buckoil	Matins	847847	Hymnary 59 (first pub. 1872)	1870
36 Wake all music's magic powers	trans. H. R. Bramley	Christmas Day	Carol	Novello's Carols 27	1870
48 O Jesu Christ, if sin there be	E. Caswall	The Haven	DCM	Hymnary 224	1870
77 O wondrous love, that rends in twain	H. Kynaston	Wondrous Love	LM	Hymnary 33	1870
28 Day of wrath, O dreadful day	A. P. Stanley	Celano	Six 7s	Hymnary 107 (first pub. 1872)	1870
71 Come, Holy Dove	R. Wilton	Columba Sancta*	4 7 10 11		1871
106 Are thy toils and woes increasing (and Setting)	J. M. Neale	Crux beata	88663	Hymnary 38	1872

No. First line	Author	Name of tune	Metre	Source of tune	Date
125 The Saints of God! Their conflict past	Archbishop Maclagan	Rest	Six 8s	Hymns A&M 428	1873
110 Jesu, Gentlest Saviour	F. W. Faber	Eucharisticus	6565	Hymns A&M 324	1874
141 Christ, Who once amongst us	W. St Hill Bourne	Pastor bonus	6565D	Hymns A&M 333	1874
111 Author of Life Divine	J. Wesley	Author of Life	666688	Hymns A&M 319	1874
128 Awake, awake, O Zion	B. Gough	Jerusalem	7676D	New Mitre Hymnal 45	1874
25 Holy Father, cheer our way	R. Hayes Robinson	Vesper	7775	Hymns A&M 22	1874
16 Light of Life, enlighten me	trans. C. Winkworth	Lux	787877	Song of Praise 403	1874
68 O Christ, our joy, gone up on high	D. T. Morgan	Ascendit	886886	Hymns A&M 145	1874
58 My God, I love Thee	trans. E. Caswall	St Francis Xavier	CM	Hymns A&M 106	1874
80 The roseate hues of early dawn	C. F. Alexander	The roseate hues	DCM	Hymns A&M 229	1874
23 And now this holy day	E. Harland	Harland	Eight 6s	Song of Praise 407	1874
85 There is a blessed home	H. W. Baker	The Blessed Home	Eight 6s	Hymns A&M 230	1874
55 Weary of earth, and laden with my sin	S. J. Stone	St Cyprian	Four 10s	Hymns A&M 252	1874
51 Good it is to keep the fast	trans. H. W. Baker	Jejunia	Four 7s	Hymns A&M 89	1874
21 Hail, gladdening Light	J. Keble, from the Greek	Sebaste	Irregular	Hymns A&M 18	1874
90 We saw Thee not when Thou didst tread	J. H. Gurney & others	Credo	Six 8s	Hymns A&M 174	1874
46 Lord Jesus, think on me	Rev A. W. Chatfield	St Paul's	SM	Hymns A&M 185	1874
5 Forward! be our watchword	H. Alford	Watchword	6 5 12 lines	Song of Praise 515	1875
154 From the heaven above us	Anon.	A Child's Evensong	6565D	Sunlight of Song	1875
147 There's a Friend for little children	A. Midlane	In memoriam	86767676	Hymns A&M 337	1875
91 On the Fount of life eternal	trans. E. Caswall	Ad perennis vitae fontem*	878777	Richmond District Choral Association	1875
45 Star of Heaven, new glory beaming	W. J. Irons	Stella in oriente	8787D	Chope's Carols 83	1875
7 Shout the praises of the Lord	S. B. King	Raise the Song	Seven 7s	London Church Choir Association Festival, St Paul's, 4 Nov 1875	1875
67 Forty days on earth	C. F. Hernaman	Gazing upward	757577	Child's Book of Praise 9	1879
33 Sing with joy, 'tis Christmas morn	C. F. Hernaman	Christmas Morn	Four 7s	Child's Book of Praise 2	1879
	Two tunes			National Temperance League	1880

No. First line	Author	Name of tune	Metre	Source of tune	Date
2 Is thy soul athirst for God	W. J. Irons	The Athanasian Creed	7676D	Iron's Psalms & Hymns	1883
64 Christ our Paschal Lamb is slain	B. P. Bouverie	St Paul	7774	Service for Children	1883
64 Jesu, God's Incarnate (2) Son	T. B. Pollock	St Paul (Pt. 2)	7776	Service for Children	1883
59 Hail, Thou Head, so bruised and torn	trans. E. Charles & G. Thring	Aletta	77775D		1885
115 Raise high the notes of exultation	Schöner, trans. F. E. Cox	Angelina*	989888	Church of England Hymnal 239 [written for marriage of Sir Reginald Dyke Roland at Temple Coombe, 1885]	1885
35 Now join we all with holy mirth	Hy. Blunt	Holy mirth	Carol	Novello's Carols 95	1885
133 God, the all-terrible	H. F. Chorley	Sabaoth	11 10 11 9	Congregational Church Hymnal 659	1887
50 When the weary, seeking rest	H. Bonar	Jaazaniah	7575757588	Congregational Church Hymnal 537	1887
127 In royal robes of splendour	trans. J. Mason	Stola regia	7676D	Hymns A&M 620	1887
148 Kind Shepherd, see Thy little lamb	H. P. Hawkins	Kind Shepherd	8684	Home Hymn Book 246	1887
54 Cross of Jesus	W. J. Sparrow Simpson	Cross of Jesus	8787	The Crucifixion 5	1887
92 All for Jesus	W. J. Sparrow Simpson	All for Jesus	8787	The Crucifixion 20	1887
61 Holy Jesu, by Thy Passion	W. J. Sparrow Simpson	Plead for me	878777	The Crucifixion 10	1887
132 Sons of labour, dear to Jesus	S. R. Hole	Sons of labour	8787D	Hymns A&M 584 [written for the Church of England Working Men's Society]	1887
98 I adore Thee, I adore Thee	W. J. Sparrow Simpson	Adoration	87887	The Crucifixion 15	1887
14 Thee, God Almighty	S. Childs Clark	Rex Regum	DCM	Dr Stephenson's Children's Home Jubilee Festival	1887
63 Jesus, the Crucified, pleads for me	W. J. Sparrow Simpson	Etiam pro nobis	Irregular	The Crucifixion 13	1887
12 Uplift your hearts, exult as ye sing	S. Childs Clarke	Sursum Corda*	99559 with ref.	'Eastertide, a Service of Song'	1887?
62 My Lord, Master, at Thy feet adoring	Bridaine, trans. T. B. Pollock	Woodlynn	11 10 11 10	Hymns A&M 494	1888
6 The God of Abraham praise	T. Olivers	Covenant	6684D	Hymns A&M 601	1888
118 The Voice that breath'd o'er Eden	J. Keble	Matrimony	7676	Hymns A&M 350	1888

No. First line	Author	Name of tune	Metre	Source of tune	Date
78 Redeemed, restored, forgiven	H. W. Baker	Redeemed	7676D	Hymns A&M 632	1888
149 Up in heaven	C. F. Alexander	Up in heaven	87775	Hymns A&M 565	1888
Eternal Wisdom, God's Incarnate Son	W. J. Frere?			Hymn for Hockerill College, Bishop's Stortford	1889
146 Thou, gracious Lord, our Shepherd art	E. Oxenford	The Good Shepherd	86 12 lines	Day School Hymn Book 41 [from *Holy Gladness*]	1889
156 There is a land where all is bright	E. Oxenford	The Beautiful Land	8686D	Novello's School Songs 136 [from *Holy Gladness*]	1889
155 We, O Lord, are little pilgrims	E. Oxenford	The Golden Shore	87 12 lines	Day School Hymn Book 42 [from *Holy Gladness*]	1889
97 Love Divine, all loves excelling	C. Wesley	Love Divine	8787	Hymns A&M 520	1889
150 Hour by hour, O gracious Lord	E. Oxenford	Hour by hour	Twelve 7s	Day School Hymn Book 35 [from *Holy Gladness*]	1889
103 Breast the wave, Christian	J. Stammers	Breast the wave, Christian	10 10 11 11	Hymnal Companion 358	1890
56 Thou knowest, Lord	J. L. Borthwick	Dominus misericordiae	11 10 11 10 10 10	Congregational Mission Hymnal 145	1890
107 Ten thousand times ten thousand (in C)	A. Alford	Jerusalem Coelestis	7686D	Congregational Mission Hymnal 288	1890
108 Ten thousand times ten thousand (in B♭)	A. Alford	Jerusalem Coelestis	7686D		1890
89 Just as I am	Charlotte Elliott	Just as I am	8886	Hymnal Companion 159	1890
130 Blessed and Holy Three	S. Childs Clarke	Oblations	DSM	Thorverton Offertory Hymnal	1890
94 Weary and sad, a wanderer from Thee	J. S. B. Monsell	Lynton	Four 10s	Congregational Mission Hymnal 142	1890
144 Buds and blossoms	J. Napleton	Offerings of Flowers	Four 7s	Flower Service (b)	1890
82 Jesu, Thy blood and righteousness	trans. J. Wesley	Oxford	LM	Hymnal Companion 288	1890
88 Thou hidden love of God, whose height	Tersteegen, trans. J. Wesley	Verborgne Gottesliebe	Six 8s	Quiver, Feb. 1890	1890
70 Come, Holy Spirit, come	D. A. Thrupp	Veni	SM	Hymnal Companion 466	1890
60 Bound upon the accursed tree	H. H. Milman	Crucifixion	Ten 7s	Hymnal Companion 194	1890
38 O Holy Star! O lovely Star	Shapcott Wensley	O Holy Star	Carol	Novello's Carols 83	1892
39 Now over the snow-white meadows	Shapcott Wensley	Sweet Christmas Bells	Carol	Novello's Carols 94	1892
40 There was silence in Bethlehem's fields	W. C. Dix	There was slience	Carol	Novello's Carols 210	1893

No. First line	Author	Name of tune	Metre	Source of tune	Date
42 See, amid the winter's snow	E. Caswall	Christmas Dawn	Carol	Christmas Service of Song	1893
100 O for the peace which floweth as a river	J. Crewdson	A little while	11 10 11 10	Church of England Hymnal 76	1894
27 Come, gracious Saviour	Charles D. Bell	Come, gracious Saviour	11 10 11 10 5 4 5 6	Church of England Hymnal 66	1894
137 We plough the fields and scatter	M. Claudius trans. J. M. Campbell	Harvest Offerings*	767676766684	Harvest Fest Book	1894
65 Christ the Lord is risen today	Ch. Wesley	Paschale Gaudium	7777 Hallelujah	Church of England Hymnal 132	1894
120 Now the labourer's task is o'er	John Ellerton	In Manus Tuas	777788	Church of England Hymnal 247	1894
31 Day of wrath	Thomas of Celano trans. W. J. Irons	Day of Wrath	888	Church of England Hymnal 77	1894
37 It was the quiet evening	W. C. Dix	The Golden Crown	Carol	Novello's Carols 219	1894
53 Saviour, when in dust to Thee	Robert Grant	Crux salutifera	Eight 7s	Church of England Hymnal 96	1894
76 Let me be with Thee where Thou art	Charlotte Elliott	Where Thou art	LM	Church of England Hymnal 351	1894
87 For the beauty of the earth	F. S. Pierpoint	Gratius agimus	Six 7s	Church of England Hymnal 477	1894
96 Father I know	Anna L. Waring	Self-sacrifice*	868686	Day School Hymn Bk 55	1895
		Soumission		Day School Hymn Book	1896
		Consolation		Day School Hymn Book	1896
		Piété		Day School Hymn Book	1896
119 Sleep on, beloved	S. Doudney	Vale, vale	10 10 10 2	Day School Hymn Book 28	1896
4 Come, O come, in pious lays	G. Wither	Te Deum laudamus	Ten 7s	Day School Hymn Book 51	1896
114 How doest Thou come to me	W. C. Dix	St Faith*	6464D	Children's Supplement 54	1897
142 All things bright and beautiful	C. F. Alexander	God in Nature*	7676D	Westminster Abbey Hymn Book 403	1897
158 Beauteous are the flowers of earth	W. C. Dix	Children's Offerings	775D	Children's Supplement 107	1897
145 Holy Blessed Trinity	S. Childs Clarke	Seasons*	7776	Flower Service (a)	1897
131 Holy Offerings, rich and rare	J. S. B. Monsell	Holy Offerings*	77778888	Rugby Hymn Book 177	1897
18 Through the day Thy love hast spared us	T. Kelly	Repose	878777	Westminster Abbey Hymn Book 29	1897
79 Father, whate'er	Anne Steele	Patience*	CM	Westminster Abbey Hymn Book 319	1897
24 Abide with me	H. F. Lyte	Mane mecum*	Four 10s		1897
34 O what must that home have been like	W. C. Dix	Nazareth	LM	Children's Supplement 19	1897

No. First line	Author	Name of tune	Metre	Source of tune	Date
83 O Thou, Who hast at Thy command	T. Cotterill	Obedience* (in canon)	LM	Westminster Abbey Hymn Book 331 (Canon)	1897
113 Jesu, we worship Thee, true God	W. C. Dix	Adoremus*	LM	Children's Supplement 52	1897
47 Thou say'st "Take up thy cross"	F. T. Palgrave	Following*	SM	Westminster Abbey Hymn Book 356	1897
99 Beloved, let us love	H. Bonar	Grandpont	10.10	Church Hymnary 245	1898
95 Show pity, Lord	D. Thomas	Tenbury	4646D	Church Hymnary 180	1898
22 When evening shadows gather	J. F. Swift	Protection	7676D	Church Monthly, Jan 1898	1898
157 Joybells are sounding sweetly	Unknown	Joybells	7676D and ref.	Church Hymnary 612	1898
123 Gentle Shepherd, Thou hast stilled	trans. C. Winkworth	Gathered in*	787877	Merbecke's Burial Service 3	1898
20 The sun declines o'er land and sea	R. Walmsley	Gloaming	8484D	Church Hymnary 360	1898
151 Jesus, tender Shepherd, hear me	Mary L. Duncan	Evening Prayer	8787	Church Hymnary 601	1898
152 Shall we gather at the river	Robert Lowry	River of life	8787 and ref.	Church Hymnary 594	1898
109 Whither, pilgrims, are you going?	F. J. Van Alstyne	Pilgrim Band	8787887	Church Hymnary 580	1898
140 Gentle Jesu, meek and mild	Ch. Wesley	Simplicity	Four 7s	Church Hymnary 554	1898
143 Saviour, teach me day by day	Jane E. Leeson	St Benedict	Four 7s	Church Hymnary 570	1898
49 Jesus, and it shall ever be	J. Grigg and B. Francia	Totland	LM	Church Hymnary 248	1898
81 O Thou to Whom in ancient time	J. Pierpont	Per recte et retro	LM	Church Hymnary 381	1898
121 Now lay we calmly in the grave	M. Weisse, trans. C. Winkworth	Mors et vita	LM	Church Hymnary 326	1898
52 Go to dark Gethsemane	J. Montgomery	Venit Hora	Six 7s	Church Hymnary 55	1898
72 Creator Spirit	trans. J. Dryden	Creator Spiritus	Six 8s	Church Hymnary 137	1898
69 Breathe on me, breath of God	Edwin Hatch	Veni, Spiritus	SM	Church Hymnary 146	1898
157 Joy bells are sounding sweetly	John Stainer?	Joy Bells	7676 x 3	Church Hymnary 612	1898
32 Lord God Almighty, the darkness around Thee	Horace Smith	Jam fulget oriens*	11 10 11 10		1899
66 Roll back the stone	Horace Smith	Surrexit*	14 13 14 13	New College Hymnal 86	1899
102 There is a singing in the homeland	F. Brook	Homeland	15 14 15 14	Church Mission Hymn Book 163	1899

No. First line	Author	Name of tune	Metre	Source of tune	Date
75 Oh, prasie the Lord of heaven	Horace Smith	Laudate Dominum Coelorum*	7676		1899
136 For the sunshine and the rain	J. Crewdson	Studland	77776	Baptist Hymnal 637	1899
135 Let God arise and lead forth those	A. C. Ainger	Exsurgat Deus*	8484	Novello's Hymns	1899
122 When the spark of life is waning	T. Dale	Weep not for Me*	84848884	Church Monthly, Jan 1900	1899
138 Praise, O praise the Lord of harvest	J. Hamilton	Swanage	8583	Baptist Hymnal 634	1899
29 Lo, He comes with clouds descending	J. Cennick, C. Wesley & M. Madan	Venturus est*	878787	Song of Praise 403	1899
129 Like a mighty man rejoicing	A. C. Ainger	Exivit sonus eorum*	8787D	SPG Bicentenary	1899
3 On, brothers, on to the better land	S. Childs Clarke	On, brothers, on!*	99979898 and ref.		1899
41 The Child Jesus in the Garden	J. Stainer	The Child Jesus in the garden*	Carol	Novello's Carols 286	1899
73 Thou who did'st move through formless night	Horace Smith	Spiritus vivificans*	CM		1899
124 God's faithful soldiers rest in peace	A. P. Purey-Cust	Faithful unto death*	CM		1899
74 Lord, it is good for us that we be here	W. J. Sparrow Simpson	Transfiguration*	Four 10s		1899
104 Sweet is the solemn voice that calls	H. F. Lyte	Where brethren meet*	LM		1899
139 Lord Jesus, Who, while here on earth	A. P. Purey-Cust	Whom Thou lovest*	LM		1899
112 Come ye yourselves apart	M. B. Whiting	Apart with me	Six 10s	Church Mission Hymn Book 207	1899
1 Rejoice, ye pure in heart	E. H. Plumptre	Deum videbunt*	SM		1899
116 O God of grace, Whose light is everlasting	Ella M. Gordon	Love is of God*	11 10 11 10		1900
117 Now is the earth with God's glory rejoicing	Ella M. Gordon	Go forth with joy*	11 10 11 10		1900
10 Day-star on high	J. F. R. Stainer	Scientia salutis*	11 11 11 15 D	[words written to fit the tune!]	1900
9 We are come to Zion	A. B. Donaldson	From strength to strength*	6565D	Truro Festival	1900
13 Put on thy strength, O Zion	S. Childs Clarke	Surge, O Zion*	7676D		1900
43 Across the sky	J. Hamilton	New Year's Eve*	8787887		1900
105 Are thy toils and woes increasing	J. M. Neale	Per Crucem Tuam*	88663		1900

No. First line	Author	Name of tune	Metre	Source of tune	Date
57 Lord, Thine Apostle heard Thee sigh	W. J. Sparrow Simpson	Non Te negabo*	888		1900
11 This is the day which the Lord hath made	W. J. Sparrow Simpson	Haec est dies	9999 and ref.		1900
8 To Zion, stately pile	S. Childs Clarke	Coelestis Curia*	Eight 6s		1900
134 Father forgive	S. Reynolds Hole	Omnium Dominatur*	Four 10s	Novello's Hymns [written in aid of the Transvaal War Fund]	1900
93 Teach us, O Lord, to see Thy will	A. P. Purey-Cust	Fiat voluntas Tua*	LM		1900
126 Dear Lord, Whose grave	W. J. Sparrow Simpson	St Peter and St John*	LM		1900
26 The Story of the Advent of Jesus	E. W. Leachman	In majestate	SM		1900
The Lamb of God				Church Hymns, ed. C. H. Lloyd 1903	1900?
Jesus reigns in glory	T. Harvey Rabone	Burslem		Church Hymns 1903?	1900?

Appendix [to Stainer's Collected Hymns]
(Melodies adapted and harmonised by John Stainer)

First line	Name of Tune	No.
All blessing, honour, glory, might	Stantes ante thronum	9
Come, Holy Ghost, our souls inspire	Veni, Creator Spiritus	14
Jesu, to Thy table led	St Kerrian	12
Jesu, Lover of my soul	Jesu, Refugium meum	4
Jesus! Name of wondrous love	Nomen Domini	2
Jesus, still lead on	Arnstadt	1
Now may He Who from the dead	Deus Pacis	7
O come, O come Immanuel	Veni, Immanuel	11
O Saviour, I have nought to plead	Amor Dei	6
Of the Father's love begotten	Corde natus	10
Rock of Ages, cleft for me	Rock of Ages	3
Saviour, like a shepherd lead us	St Sebald	5
To Thee, O Comforter Divine	Leipsic	8
Where high the heavenly temple stands	St Andrew	13

Unknown date

Vespers

Now once more we greet Thee. Composed for the children of the Royal Albert Orphan Asylum.

O God, our Hope, our Strength, our King. Composed for the children of the Royal Albert Orphan Asylum.

Pastor Bonus. GB-Lcm MS 7789a.

In memoriam. GB-Lcm MS 7789b.

Zz. GB-Lcm MS 7789c.

Behold, the Lamb of God (pub. 1903)

At home with Christ (pub. 1905)

The Boys and Girls of England Hymn (pub. 1913)

We'll sing and praise our God (pub. 1930)

Carols

The date of the first publication of *Christmas Carols, New and Old* was first advertised in the *Musical Times* in December 1867. The first publication in which Stainer collaborated with the Rev. Henry Ramsden Bramley (also of Magdalen College, Oxford) consisted of 20 carols, published by Novello.

1. God rest you merry, Gentlemen (words & music: traditional)
2. The Manger Throne (words: W. C. Dix; music: C. Steggall)
3. A Virgin unspotted (words & music: traditional)
4. Come, ye lofty (words: Rev. Archer Gurney; music: G. J. Elvey)
5. Come, tune your heart (words: trans. from the German by F. E. Cox; music: F. A. G. Ouseley)
6. The first nowell (words & music: traditional)
7. Jesu, hail! (words: trans. from the Latin by Bramley; music: J. Stainer) [This carol was sung by the Magdalen Vagabonds in 1865]
8. Good Christian men, rejoice (words: Rev. J. M. Neale; music: Old German)
9. Sleep, holy babe (words: Rev E. Caswall; music: Rev J. B. Dykes)
10. Good King Wenceslas (words: Rev J. M. Neale; music: Helmore's Christmas Carols)
11. When I view the mother holding (words: trans. from the Latin by Bramley; music: J. Barnby)
12. The seven joys of Mary (words & music: traditional)
13. On the Birthday of the Lord (words: trans. from the Latin by Rev. R. F. Littledale; music: J. B. Dykes)
14. What child is this? (words: W. C. Dix; music: Old English)
15. Glorious, beauteous, golden-bright (words: Anna M. E. Nichols; music: Maria Tiddeman)
16. Waken, Christian children (words: Rev. S. C. Hamerton; music: Rev. S. C. Hamerton)
17. A child this day is born (words & music: traditional)
18. Carol for Christmas Eve (words: Bramley; music: F. A. G. Ouseley)
19. When Christ was born (words: Harleian MS; music: Arthur H. Brown)
20. Christmas Morning Hymn (words: Rev C. J. Black; music: J. Barnby)

The first series was hugely succesful which persuaded Novello and Routledge to issue a 'Second Series' in 1871 of 42 carols, adding 22 carols to the original 20, with illustrations engraved by the Brother Dalziel:

21. A Carol for Christmas Eve (words & music: traditional)
22. Jesus in the Manger (words: trans. from the Latin by Bramley; music: H. Smart)
23. The Holly and the Ivy (words: traditional; music: Old French)
24. The Waits' Song (words & music: traditional)
25. The Virgin and Child (words: Old English; music: C. Steggall)
26. The Incarnation (words: Bramley; music: traditional)
27. Christmas Day (words: trans. from the Latin by Bramley; music: J. Stainer)
28. The Cherry Tree Carol (words & music: traditional)
29. God's dear Son (words & music: traditional)
30. Hymn for Christmas Day (words: E. Caswall; music: J. Goss)

31. The Babe of Bethlehem (words & music: traditional)

32. In Bethlehem, that noble place (words: Old English; music: F. A. G. Ouseley)

33. A Cradle-Song of the Blessed Virgin (words: trans. from the Latin by Bramley; music: J. Barnby)

34. Christmas Song (words: W. Bright; music: J. B. Dykes)

35. Jacob's Ladder (words & music: traditional)

36. The Story of the Shepherd (words: trans. from the Spanish of Gongora by Archdeacon Churton; music: J. Barnby)

37. The Wassail Song (words & music: traditional)

38. In terra pax (words: Mrs Alderson; music: J. B. Dykes)

39. Dives and Lazarus (words & music: traditional)

40. From far away (words: W. Morris; music: J. B. Dykes)

41. Carol for Christmas Day (words: W. Austin, c.1630; music: A. Sullivan)

42. The Child Jesus in the Garden (words and music: J. Stainer)

The second series was equally successful which led to a third series, published by Novello c.1878, when another 28 carols were added, bringing the final total to 70 carols.

43. What soul-inspiring music (words: imitation of the original by Bramley; music: Old Béarnaise carol, harmonised J. Stainer)

44. In the country nigh Jerusalem (words: K. Bartlett; music: G. Hine)

45. We three kings of Orient are (words and music: J. H. Hopkins)

46. Emmanuel, God with us (words: J. Chatterton Dix; music: H. Gadsby)

47. New Prince, new pomp (words: R. Southwell; music: C. Steggall)

48. A babe is born (words: 15th century; music: ancient melody, harmonised J. Stainer)

49. Come let us all sweet carols sing (words: Besançon carol trans. Bramley; music: F. Champneys)

50. Let music break on this blest morn (words: G. Dickinson; music: J. B. Calkin)

51. Carol for New Year's Day (words: Ashmolean Library; music: A. H. Brown)

52. The Angel Gabriel (words: traditional; music: traditional Devonshire, harmonised J. Stainer)

53. The shepherds amazed (words: 'A Good Christmas Box; music: A. H. Brown)

54. Noel! Noel! (words: traditional (London); music: ancient melody, harmonised J. Stainer)

55. I sing the birth was born tonight (words: Ben Jonson?; music: G. C. Martin)

56. Christmas Night (words: 'A Good Christmas Box'; music: A. H. Brown)

57. The Christmas celebration (words: A. Gurney; music: E. Prout)

58. Arise, and hail the Sacred Day (words: 'A Good Christmas Box (Dudley 1847); music: A. H. Brown)

59. The holy well (words: traditional Derby; music: traditional, harmonised J. Stainer)

60. The angel and the shepherds (words: Bramley, from the Towneley Mysteries; music: E. H. Thorne)

61. The Coventry Carol (words: Coventry Mysteries; music: ancient melody, adapted and harmonised J Stainer)

62. The Morning Star (words: American; music: J. F. Bridge)

63. The shepherds went their hasty way (words: S. T. Coleridge; music J. F. Barnett)
64. I saw three ships (words: traditional; music; traditional Derbyshire, harmonised J. Stainer)
65. Mountains, bow your heads majestic (words: Stoke-upon-Tern Hymn-Book; music: W. H. Cummings)
66. Luther's carol (words: M. Luther trans. Bramley, based on an old Scottish version; music: J. Higgs)
67. The boy's dream (words: traditional; music: W. H. Monk)
68. Legends of the infancy (words: E. L. Hervey; music: J. F. Bridge)
69. The black decree (words & music: traditional)
70. For Christmas Day (words: Bishop Hall 1597; music: traditional)

Twelve Old Carols, English and Foreign, Novello, 1890. [This publication formed the basis of Stainer's lecture on the subject at Oxford in November 1890.]

1. Besançon carol	7. Gascon carol
2. Tyrolese carol	8. Carol of the Basse-Normandie
3. Poitou carol	9. Flemish carol
4. Arpajon carol	10. The Golden carol
5. Carol of the birds	11. English (1661)
6. Carol of the flowers	12. English (1661)

Plainchant-related settings

Unison with accompaniment (fauxbourdon and organ)

Canticles of Church arranged to Gregorian Tones, series 1–4 (*c.*1876–8). Also published separately at a later date.

Te Deum, first set (1895)
Te Deum, second and third sets (1896)
Te Deum, fourth set (1895)
Benedictus, first and second sets (1895)
Benedictus, third set (1896)
Benedictus, fourth set (1897)
Magnificat and Nunc dimittis, first, second and third sets (1896)
Magnificat and Nunc dimittis, fourth set (1895)

Gregorian Tones with their Endings Harmonised in Various Ways, being the Accompanying Harmonies to the Merton Psalter (1867)

Magnificat (arranged to 1st Parisian tone), n.d., *c.*1869

Nunc dimittis (arranged to 2nd Parisian tone), n.d., *c.*1869

Magnificat (arranged to St Saviour's tone) (n.d.) (1870s?)

Ambrosian Te Deum (after Merbecke) n.d.

Holy Communion Office (John Merbecke, arr. with organ accompaniment) (1898)

Lord's Prayer (Merbecke) (1895)

Athanasian Creed (with organ accompaniment) (1882)

Preces, Responses and Litany (used in St Paul's) (Ferial) SATB, 1873 (1886)

Versicles and Responses with harmonised confession as used at St Paul's Cathedral, ATTB (1899)

Preces and Responses with harmonised confession (Tallis) (used at Ely), SATB, 1873 (1900)

Arrangements or Editions of Sacred Music

T. Tallis, Te Deum (a5), copied from MS 1001 (at *GB-Och*), 1860. Autograph *GB-Lsp*.

J. S. Bach, *St Matthew Passion* abridged with English translation, 1873, vocal score. Published ?

J. S. Bach, chorus, 'Come unto me' from *St Matthew Passion*, double choir and organ, adapted to new text, St Matthew, xi, vv.28–30, n.d.

F. Schubert, song, 'The Lord is my Shepherd', SATB with organ (1898)

W. Hayes, anthem, 'Save Lord, and hear us', n.d.

W. Croft, anthem, 'Sing praises to the Lord', n.d

D. Purcell, Magnificat and Nunc dimittis in E minor (1900)

Mendelssohn, hymn, 'All blessing, Honour, Glory, Might' (1901)

J. G. Naumann, 'Dresden' Amen, SSATB (1904)

Editions

Liturgy, Other Service Material and Canticles

A Choir Book of Office to Holy Communion (1874)

Jubilee: A Service of Praise and Thanksgiving for the Times (1887)

The Story of the Cross (1893). See also *Musical Times* xxxv (1894). Autograph *GB-Lsp*.

A Christmas Service of Song (1894)

[with W. Russell], *Cathedral Prayer Book* (1891). Autograph *GB-Lsp*.

Order for the Burial of the Dead (1898)

The Story of the Advent of Jesus (E. W. Leachman) (1900)

At the Manger, A Litany of the Incarnation (1901)

Hymnals

[with C. Vincent] *The Hymnal Companion* (1890)

The Church Hymnary (for the Church of Scotland) (1898)

Psalters

[with L. S. Tuckwell], *Magdalen Psalter* (1868)

[with S. Flood Jones, Turle, Barnby, and J. Troutbeck], *The Cathedral Psalter*, *c*.1874; 2nd edn 1875 (many later editions)

St Paul's Cathedral Chant Book (1878)

[with S. Flood Jones, J. Turle, J. Troutbeck and J. Barnby], *The Cathedral Psalter Chant Book* (n.d.)

[with L. S. Tuckwell], *Church Choir Chant Book* (1899)

Plainchant

Church of America Altar Book (1896)

Manual of Plainsong, ed. H. B. Briggs and W. H. Frere (overseen by Stainer) (1902)

Other

R. Schumann, *The Luck of Edenhall* (*Das Glück von Edenhall*) (*c*.1866)

A Theory of Harmony (1871; 2nd edn 1872; 3rd edn *c*.1875)

Christmas Carols New and Old (see Carols) (1867–78)

[with W. Rayson and J. Troutbeck], *Words of Anthems* (1875)

The Village Organist, ed. F. Cunningham Woods and J. Stainer (1897)

[with J. F. R. Stainer and C. Stainer], *Dufay and his contemporaries* (1898)

Early Bodleian Music (1901)

Educational Primers

The Organ (London: Novello & Co., *c.* 1877)
Harmony (*c.* 1878)
Composition (*c.* 1879)
Choral Society Vocalisation (*c.* 1895)
A Dictionary of Music Terms with W. A. Barrett 1876; rev. 1879 and (without Barrett)
1898.

Work as General Editor (with C. Hubert H. Parry)

E. Pauer, *The Pianoforte*
W. H. Cummings, *The Rudiments of Music*
King Hall, *The Harmonium*
A. Randegger, *Singing*
A. J. Ellis, *Speech in Song*
E. Pauer, *Musical Forms*
J. F. Bridge, *Counterpoint*
J. Higgs, *Fugue*
W. H. Stone, *Scientific Basis of Music*
J. F. Bridge, *Double Counterpoint*
J. Troutbeck, *Church Choir Training*
T. Helmore, *Plain Song*
E. Prout, *Instrumentation*
E. Pauer, *The Elements of the Beautiful in Music*
B. Tours, *The Violin*
J. Curwen, *Tonic Sol-Fa*
J. Greenwood, *Lancashire Sol-Fa*
J. de Swert, *The Violoncello*
J. Greenwood, *Two-part Exercises*
F. Taylor, *Double Scales*
M. Lussy, *Musical Expression*
F. Marshall, *Solfeggi*
J. F. Bridge, *Organ Accompaniment*
H. Brett, *The Cornet*
Ritter, *Musical Dictation*, Parts I & II
J. Higgs, *Modulation*
A. C. White, *Double Bass*
F. J. Sawyer, *Extemporisation*
H. A. Harding, *Analysis of Form*
A. W. Marchant, *500 Fugue Subjects and Answers*
T. Ridley Prentice, *Hand Gymnastics*
E. Dannreuther, *Musical Ornamentation*, Parts I & II
J. Warriner, *Transposition*
G. C. Martin, *The Art of Training Choir Boys*
W. H. Cummings, *Biographical Dictionary of Musicians*
G. Saunders, *Examples in Strict Counterpoint*
C. H. H. Parry, *Summary of Musical History*
J. F. Bridge, *Musical Gestures*
J. F. Bridge, *Rudiments in Rhyme*
R. Dunstan, *Basses and Melodies*

F. Berger, *First Steps at the Pianoforte*

E. Pauer, *A Dictionary of Pianists and Composers for the Pianoforte*

B. W. Horner,*Organ Pedal Technique*

J. E. Vernham, *Twelve Trios by Albrechtsberger*

A. J. Hipkins, *History of the Pianoforte*

F. Taylor, *Scales and Arpeggios*

W. H. Hadow, *Sonata Form*

C. Stainer, *A Dictionary of Violin Makers*

F. Iliffe, *Analysis of Bach's 48 Preludes and Fugues*

SECULAR SONGS, PARTSONGS & MADRIGALS

Solo Songs

All with piano accompaniment

'When all the world is young lad'. Contralto/baritone. 1863? [watermark 1863]. *GB-Lcm* MS 7788.

'To sigh, yet feel no pain' (anon.). Soprano. 1865. Dedicated to Eliza Randall. Unpublished. Autograph in private possession (JRS).

'Maid of my love, sweet Genevieve'. Soprano. n.d. GB-*Lcm* MS 7785.

'O that we too were maying'. Mezzo-soprano. n.d. GB-*Lcm* MS 7786 [copyist's hand].

'Rest (A Sketch)'. Contralto. n.d. GB-*Lcm* MS 7787.

'Insufficiency' (Mrs H. Browning). Tenor. 1869. Dedicated to Walter Goolden.

'Loyal death' (P. S. Worsley). Bass/baritone. 1870? Dedicated to J. Swire.

'Jilted' (W. A. Barrett). Soprano/tenor. 1870? Dedicated to T. M. Everett. Performed at Magdalen, 1870.

'My little pet' (W. A. Barrett). Soprano/tenor. 1870? Dedicated to Miss Clara Findeisen.

'Unbeloved' (Gerald Massey). Bass. 1871? Dedicated to Frank Pownall. Autograph in private possession (JRS).

'My Maker and My King' (Dr Watts). Soprano. 1873. Dedicated to Mrs W. Margetson.

'Slumber Song' (trans. from Körner). Soprano with cello *ad. lib.* 1873. Dedicated to Miss Mary Stewart.

Seven Songs. Mezzo-soprano, contralto, or baritone, in both German and English (with the exception of No. 6): 1. 'Das ferne Land' (J. Heinrich Voss); 2. 'Der Rosentrauch (E. Ferrand); 3. 'Das Meer der Hoffnung (F. Rückert); 4. 'Poesie' (J. Kerner); 5. 'An Leukon' (J. W. Ludwig Gleim); 6. 'Quand je te vois comme une fleur' (Heine trans. J. Bué); 7. 'Daheim' (J. G. Fischer). 1892. 'Affectionately inscribed to Cecie and Ellie'. Published Novello 1892.

Unison songs

'To a violet' (source of words unknown). 1892. Published in *School Music Review* (August 1892).

'A soldier's life' (John Stainer) from *Six Unison Action Songs*). n.d.

'If turn'd topsi-turvy you'll find I can go'. Dated 27 March 1894. Unpublished. Autograph in private possession.

Four melodies by E. W. B. Nicholson with accompaniments by J. Stainer (Novello: London, 1894).

Madrigals and Partsongs

Partsong: 'Daylight now hath fled'. c.1862. Unpublished. Now missing.

Eight Madrigals (composed by John Stainer B.A. and Mus.Bac., Organist to the University and Magdalen College). Published c.1865.

1. 'Encouragement to a Lover' ('Why so pale and wan fond lover?') (Sir John Suckling). Ballett, a6. Performed at Magdalen, 1865. See also Tenbury 945–54, No. 33 (partbooks).
2. 'Disappointment' ('Ye Shepherds give ear to my lay') (Shenstone). a6. Performed at Magdalen, 1864.
3. 'The Castle by the sea' ('Hast thou seen that lordly castle?') (Longfellow, from the German of Uhland). a10 (two choirs a5).
4. 'The Queen of May' ('Upon a time I chanc'd to walk') (anon.). Ballett, a6. Performed at Magdalen, 1863 and 1866. See Tenbury Vols. 945–54, No. 20 (partbooks). Also published Novello (1906).
5. 'The frozen heart' ('I freeze and nothing dwels In me but snow and ysicles') (Herrick). a5. Performed twice at Magdalen, 1865.
6. 'Love's servile lot' ('Love's mistress is of many minds') (Robert Southwell). a6. See Tenbury 945–54, No. 67 (partbooks).
7. 'Dry your sweet cheek' ('Dry your sweet cheek long drown'd with sorrow's raine') (Herrick). a8.
8. 'Love not me for comely grace' ('Love not me for comely grace') (anon.). a5.

'Like as a ship that through the ocean wide' (E. Spenser). Madrigal a8. 1865. Composed for the Bristol Madrigal Society. Autograph in private possession (JRS).

'Floreat Magdalena' . TTBB. n.d. [c.1865]. *GB-Omc* MS 993.

'Bind my brows' (T. Moore from Anacreon). Glee. ATTB (1879).

'The desert island' (J. Stainer). Catch. ATTBB (1880).

'The Triumph of Victoria' (J. Stainer). Madrigal. SSATB (1887).

'Flora's Queen' (A. Benson). Madrigal. SSATBB (1899). Composed for *Choral Songs for Queen Victoria*, ed. A. Benson and W. Parratt. Autograph in private possession (JRS).

'Cupid look about thee'. Ballett. ATTB (1900)

'I prythee send me back my heart' (Henry Hughes 1650). Glee. ATTB (1904)

'Prithee, why so pale?' (anon.). Madrigal. SSATBB (1906)

Arrangements

Six Italian Songs, arrangements of Italian seventeenth- and eighteenth-century songs and arias; adapted English words by John Stainer for mezzo-soprano (1896): 1. 'Dolce amor' (Cavalli); 2. 'Non dar più pene (A. Scarlatti); 3. 'Fier destin' (Gasparini); 4. 'Limmago tua vezzosa' (Baron d'Astorga); 5. 'Danza fanciulla' (Durante); 6. 'La pastorella' (Galuppi). Nos. 2 and 3 also published as *Two Italian Songs* with accompaniment for piano and violin obbligato.

The School Round Book, 100 rounds canons and catches: words ed. J. Powell Metcalfe; music ed. John Stainer.

Standard English Songs, Book 1, edited, revised and the words partly rewritten by W. A. Barrett, the accompaniments arranged by Stainer, Martin, Gadsby, Caldicott, Horner, Barnby and the editor. Nos. 8 ('Tell me dearest what is love', Robert Jones) and 16 ('The Contented Farmer', Henry Carey) were arranged by Stainer. n.d. Augener.

INSTRUMENTAL MUSIC

String Quartet. n.d. [before 1869]. Dedicated to W. F. Donkin. Unpublished. Autograph in private possession (JRS).

Arrangements for Organ. 1869–72. Published in five sections (1869–72):

1. (a) Beethoven: Andante from the String Quintet in E flat, Op. 4
   (b) Handel: Minuetto in B flat
   (b) Handel: Allegro and 2 variations in B flat

2. (a) Mozart: Andante in B flat (from a piano duet)
   (b) Handel: Overture [in C minor/major] to *Semele*

3. (a) Haydn: Introduction and Allegro from Symphony in D (London Symphony No. 104)
   (b) Schubert: Andante molto in G minor (from Piano Sonata Op. 122)

4. (a) Spohr: Sinfonia to *Last Judgement*
   (b) Eybler: Kyrie eleison [from Mass No. 1 in E flat]

5. (a) Schumann: Adagio expressivo [from the Second Symphony]
   (b) Beethoven: Cavatina (Adagio molto expressive) [from Quartet No. 13]
   (c) Abel: Andante [work not specified] in F
   (d) Schubert: Andante [from Piano Sonata No. 3 Op. 120]

Agnes Zimmerman: March [in D minor]. Arranged for the organ by John Stainer. 1869 (*c*.1869).

Jubilant March. Organ. 1879? (1879). Autograph in private possession (JRS).

'A Song of Praise'. In *The Village Organist*, Book 1 No. 9, ed. F. Cunningham Woods and J. Stainer (1897).

'Procession to Calvary' from *The Crucifixion*. In *The Village Organist*, Book 44 No. 6, ed. F. Cunningham Woods and J. Stainer (1897).

Six Pieces for the Organ (1897): 1. Andante; 2. Prelude and Fughetta; 3. Adagio (ma non troppo); 4. On a bass; 5. Impromptu; 6. Reverie.

Twelve Pieces for the Organ. 1898–9? (1900) [i.e. Book II of Six Pieces] 7. Andante pathétique (Florence 1898); 8. Praeludium Pastorale (*super gamut descendens*) (Oxford 1898); 9. A Church Prelude (Mentone Jan. 1898); 10. Introduction and Fughetta (Mentone Jan. 1898); 11. Fantasia; 12. Finale alla marcia.

LITERARY WORKS

Books

A Theory of Harmony Founded on the Tempered Scale (1871) [dedicated to Prof. Müller]

[with W. A. Barrett] *A Dictionary of Musical Terms* (1876); rev. J. Stainer 1898; also rev. 1912; compressed edition 1880

R. Mann, *A Manual of Singing* [1866], edited and revised by Stainer (*c*.1876)

Daily Exercises for the Voice (London and Oxford: A. R. Mowbray & Co., 1876)

The Music of the Bible (1879); rev. F. W. Galpin, 1914

Tutor for the American Organ (Metzler, 1883)

Catalogue of English Books, forming a portion of the Library of Sir John Stainer, with Appendices of Foreign Song Books, Collections of Carols, Books on Bells, etc. (London: Novello & Co., 1891)

Articles, Lectures, Papers and Addresses

'Church Music', *Proceedings of the Church Congress* (Leeds, 1872), 334–9

'On the Progressive Character of Church Music', *Proceedings of the Church Congress* (Brighton, 1874), 530–8

'On the Principles of Musical Notation' [5 April 1875], *Proceedings of the Musical Association* 1 (1874–5), 88–111

Aids to the Student of the Holy Bible (see *Bible Educator* series; Part II, *Music of the Bible*) (*c*.1875–8)

'How Can Cathedrals Best Further the Culture of Church Music?', *Quarterly Church Review* (January 1879)

'On the Rhythmical Form of the Anglican Chant', *Musical Times* 13 (January 1872)

'Sir John Goss' [obituary], *Musical Times* 21 (June 1880)

'An Address to the Scholars of the National Training School for Music' [27 September 1881] (London: Novello & Co., 1881)

'The Principles of Musical Criticism' [3 January 1881], *Proceedings of the Musical Association* 7 (1880–1), 35–52

[with G. Phillips Bevan] *Handbook to the Cathedral of St Paul* London: W. Swan Sonnenschein & Co., 1882); copy with Stainer's annotations *GB-Bru*

Preface to S. J. Mackie, *Great Paul* (London: Griffith & Farran, 1882)

'Musical Education in Elementary Schools', *Health Exhibition Literature*, vol. 13 (London: William Clowes, 1884), 394–9

'The Present State of Music in England' [inaugural lecture, University of Oxford, 1889] (Oxford: Horace Hart, 1889)

'The Character and Influence of the Late Sir Frederick Ouseley' [2 December 1889], *Proceedings of the Musical Association* 16 (1889–90), 25–39

'Music in its Relation to the Intellect and the Emotions' [1892] (London: Novello & Co., 1892)

'Julian's "Dictionary of Hymnology" ' [review article], *Musical Times* (April 1892)

'Technique and Sentiment' [Eighth Annual Conference of the Incorporated Society of Musicians, London, January 1893], *Monthly Journal of the Incorporated Society of Musicians* (February 1893)

'Inaugural Address to the Twenty-First Session [of the Musical Association]', *Proceedings of the Musical Association* 21 (1894–5), xiii–xvi

'Music Considered in its Effect upon, and Connexion with, the Worship of the Church', *Proceedings of the Church Congress* (Exeter, 1894), 531–5

'Does Music Train the Mind?' [Tenth Annual Conference of the Incorporated Society of Musicians, Dublin, January 1895]

'Address of Welcome [to visiting American musicians]' [16 July 1895], *Proceedings of the Musical Association* 21 (1894–5), 149–52

'A Fifteenth Century MS. Book of Vocal Music in the Bodleian Library, Oxford' [12 November 1895], *Proceedings of the Musical Association* 22 (1895–6), 1–22

'On the Musical Introductions Found in Certain Metrical Psalters' [13 November 1900], *Proceedings of the Musical Association* 27 (1900–1), 1–50

Lectures given at the University of Oxford, 1889–99

1889–90

'The Present State of Music in England'. Published: see above.
'The Characteristics of Schumann's Songs'
'Mendelssohn's Oratorio *Elijah*'

1890–1

'Carols, English and Foreign'
'Origin and Development of the Ground-Bass'
'The Styles of Composers as Exhibited by Various Settings of the Same Lyric'

1891–2

'Mozart's Requiem'
'Canons as a form of composition'
'Music in its Relation to the Intellect and Emotions'. Published: see above.

1892–3

'Lute, Viol and Voice'
'Palestrina's Mass, "Aeterna Christi Munera" '
'Composer and Performer'

1893–4

'Song and Dance – Some Old Tunes'
'Mendelssohn's Oratorio *St Paul*'
'Composer and Hearer – A Sequel to Composer and Performer'

1894–5

'The Choral Responses of the English Liturgy'
'Handel's Oratorio *Messiah*'
'Influences which Affect Melodic Form'

1895–6

'Purcell, including the Te Deum'
'Tye's Mass "Euge bone" '
'The Secular Compositions of Dufay'

1896–7

'Song-writers of the Classical Period'
'Early Harmonisations of Psalm-tunes and their Treatment in Motet Form'
'Music as a Branch of Education'

1897–8

'Morley's "Plaine and Easie Introduction to Practicall Musicke" (1597)'
'Hans Leo Hassler (b. 1564)'

1898–9

'Psalm and Hymn-tunes' (continued)
'Madrigalian Composers of the Gallo-Belgian School'
'The Influence of Fashion on the Art of Music'

1 John Stainer, *c.* 1860

2 Lewis Tuckwell, *c.* 1860

3 The Choir of Magdalen College, Oxford, 1865. *Back row*: F. Cosser, G. Tylee, H. Bennet, H. Faber, J. T. M. Rumsey, H. W. Edwards. *Middle row*: A. E. Cooper, J. Stainer, J. Dyndham, C. Kitcart, Rev. C. Reade, Rev. L. Tuckwell, W. Pye, C. P. Billing, F. Bulley (son of President Bulley), Rev. W. Sawell. *Front row*: S. Swire, W. Philpott, J. R. G. Taylor, T. M. Everett, C. Couchman, J. C. Ford.

4 Magdalen College, *c.* 1860

5 The Magdalen Vagabonds, photographed at the Rufus Stone in the New Forest, 1863

6 John Stainer and family, *c.* 1873: John Stainer with Charles Lewis, John Frederick Randall, Cecie, Ellie (in front), Elizabeth Stainer with Frederick Henry, Edward (in front)

7 John Stainer, *c.* 1872

8 Portrait of Sir John Stainer by G. E. Moira (*c.* 1892)

9 *May Morning on Magdalen Tower* (1891) by Holman Hunt. Stainer is the sixth figure from the right.

10 Stainer and the men of St Paul's Cathedral Choir, 1888

11 Facsimile of 'God so loved the world' from *The Crucifixion* (1887)

12 *(above)* Performers for the 'Toy Symphony', 14 May 1880; Stainer can be seen at the back, one from the left

13 *(left)* Signatures of the 'Toy Symphony' performers

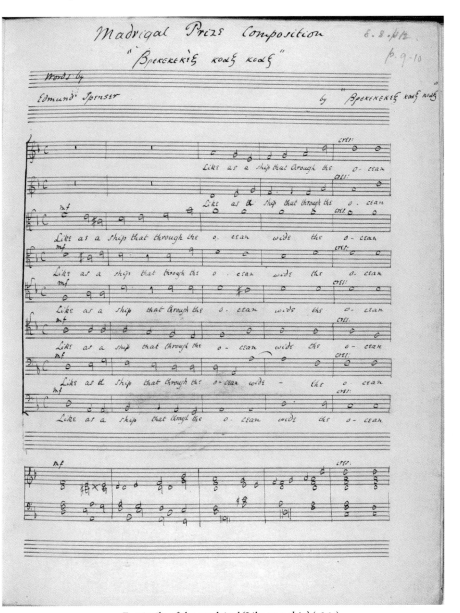

14 Facsimile of the madrigal 'Like as a ship' (1865)

15 Facsimile of the hymn 'Cross of Jesus' from *The Crucifixion* (1887)

16 Stainer in Egypt (in front of one the great pyramids), 1895

Bibliography

For all writings by Stainer referred to in this work, see the List of Works.

Alcock, W., 'Sir John Stainer and Church Music', *English Church Music* 5 (October, 1935)

Barrett, P., *Barchester: English Cathedral Life in the Nineteenth Century* (London: SPCK, 1993)

Barrett, W. A., & G. H. Beard, *English Church Composers* (London: Low, Marston & Co., 1925)

Bashford, C., & L. Langley, *Music and British Culture, 1785–1914* (Oxford: Oxford University Press, 2000)

Bates, F., *Reminiscences and Autobiography of a Musician in Retirement* (Norwich: Jarrold & Sons, 1930)

Bateson, J., *Alcock of Salisbury* (Salisbury, 1949)

Benecke, P. V. M., 'Some Remarks Suggested by Laurie Magnus's Book "Herbert Warren at Magdalen" ' (unpublished typescript, c. 1941–4)

Best, H., *Four Years in France* (London, 1826)

Bevan, G. P., & J. Stainer, *Handbook to the Cathedral of St Paul* (London: W. Swan Sonnenschein & Co., 1882)

Bland, D., *Ouseley and his Angels: The Life of St Michael's College, Tenbury and its Founder* (Windsor: private publication, 2000)

Boden, A., *Three Choirs: A History of the Festival* (Stroud: Alan Sutton, 1992)

Bradley, I., *Abide with Me: The World of Victorian Hymns* (London: SCM Press, 1997)

Bridge, [J.] F., *A Westminster Pilgrim* (London: Novello & Co., Hutchinson & Co., 1918)

Brightwell, G. W. E., 'The National Training School for Music, 1873–1882: Catalyst or Cul-de-Sac? ' (MA diss., Durham University, 1998)

Brock, M. G., & M. C. Curthoys (eds.), *The History of the University of Oxford*, vols. 6–7: *Nineteenth-Century Oxford* [Parts 1 & 2] (Oxford: Clarendon Press, 1997, 2000)

Bumpus, J. S., *The Organists and Composers of St Paul's Cathedral* (London: Bowen, Hudson & Co., 1891)

—— *A History of English Cathedral Music, 1549–1889* (London: T. Werner Laurie, 1908)

Caldwell, J., *The Oxford History of English Music*, vol. 2: *From 1715 to the Present Day* (Oxford: Oxford University Press, 1999)

Charlton, P., *John Stainer and the Musical Life of Victorian Britain* (Newton Abbot: David & Charles, 1984)

Church, M. C., *Life and Letters of Dean Church* (London: Macmillan & Co., 1895)

Cook, William T., *The Bells of St Paul's: An Account of the Bells of St Paul's Cathedral, London* (London, 1978)

Cooper, V., *The House of Novello: Practice and Policy of a Victorian Music Publisher, 1829–1866* (Aldershot: Ashgate, 2003)

Cox, G., *A History of Music Education in England, 1872–1928* (Aldershot: Scolar Press, 1993)

—— 'Inspecting the Teaching of Singing in the Teacher Training Colleges of England, Wales and Scotland, 1883–1899', *Research Studies in Music Education* 24 (June 2005), 17–27

Curwen, J. S., *Replies to Recent Attacks on the Tonic Sol-fa System* (London: Tonic Sol-fa Agency, 1882)

Darwall-Smith, R., 'Magdalen and the Rediscovery of Christmas', *Magdalen College Record* (2001), 92–102

Deneke, M., *Ernest Walker* (London: Oxford University Press, 1951)

Dibble, J., *C. Hubert H. Parry: His Life and Music* (Oxford: Clarendon Press, 1992; rev. 1998)

—— 'Stanford's Service in B flat Op. 10 and the Choir of Trinity College, Cambridge', in *Irish Musical Studies*, vol. 2: *Music and the Church*, ed. G. Gillen & H. White (Dublin: Irish Academic Press, 1993), 129–48

—— 'Parry as Historiographer', in *Nineteenth-Century British Music Studies*, vol. 1, ed. B. Zon (Aldershot: Ashgate, 1999), 37–51

—— *Charles Villiers Stanford: Man and Musician* (Oxford: Oxford University Press, 2002)

—— 'Musical Trends and the Western Church: A Collision of the "Ancient" and "Modern"', in *World Christianities, c.1815 – c.1914*, ed. S. Gilley & B. Stanley, The Cambridge History of Christianity 8 (Cambridge: Cambridge University Press, 2006), 121–35

Einstein, A., *Music in the Romantic Era* (London: J. M. Dent & Sons, 1947)

Engel, A. J., *From Clergyman to Don: The Rise of the Academic Profession in Nineteenth-Century Oxford* (Oxford: Clarendon Press, 1983)

Fallows, D., *Oxford, Bodleian Library MS. Canon. Misc. 213* (Chicago: University of Chicago Press, 1995)

Fellowes, E. H., *English Cathedral Music from Edward VI to Edward VII*, 3rd edn (London: Methuen & Co., 1946)

—— *Memoirs of an Amateur Musician* (London: Methuen & Co., 1946)

—— 'Sir John Stainer', *English Church Music* 21/1 (January, 1951)

Fifield, C., *True Artist and True Friend: A Biography of Hans Richter* (Oxford: Oxford University Press, 1993)

Forbes, D., *The Liberal Anglican Idea of History* (Cambridge: Cambridge University Press, 1952)

Frost, W. A., *Early Recollections of St Paul's Cathedral: A Piece of Autobiography* (London: Simpkin, Marshall, Hamilton, Kent & Co., 1925)

Fowler, J. T. (ed.), *Life and Letters of John Bacchus Dykes* (London: John Murray, 1897)

Gatens, W. J., *Victorian Cathedral Music in Theory and Practice* (Cambridge: Cambridge University Press, 1986)

Gilley, S., & B. Stanley (eds.), *World Christianities, c.1815 – c.1914*, The Cambridge History of Christianity 8 (Cambridge: Cambridge University Press, 2006)

Graves, C. L., *The Life and Letters of Sir George Grove* (London: Macmillan & Co., 1903)

—— *Hubert Parry: His Life and Works*, 2 vols. (London: Macmillan & Co., 1926)

Gregory, R., *Robert Gregory, 1819–1911: being the autobiography of Robert Gregory DD Dean of St Paul's*, ed. W. H. Hutton (London: Longmans, Green & Co., 1912)

Grimley, D., & J. Rushton (eds.), *The Cambridge Companion to Elgar* (Cambridge: Cambridge University Press, 2004)

Gurney, E., *The Power of Sound* (London: Smith, Elder & Co., 1880)

Havergal, Rev. F. T., *Memorials of Frederick Arthur Gore Ouseley* (London: Ellis & Elvey, 1889)

Holland, H. S., *A Bundle of Memories* (London: Wells Gardner, Darton & Co., 1915)

Hollins, A., *A Blind Musician Looks Back: An Autobiography* (Edinburgh: William Blackwood & Sons, 1936)

Horton, P., *Samuel Sebastian Wesley: A Life* (Oxford: Oxford University Press, 2004)

—— & B. Zon (eds.), *Nineteenth-Century British Music Studies*, vol. 3 (Aldershot: Ashgate, 2003)

Howes, F., *The English Musical Renaissance* (London: Secker & Warburg, 1966)

Hueffer, F., *Richard Wagner, 1813–1883* (London: Sampson, Low, Marston & Co., n.d.)

Hullah, F., *Life of John Hullah* (London: Longmans, Green & Co., 1886)

Husk, W. H., *Songs of the Nativity: being Christmas Carols Ancient and Modern* (London: John Camden Hotten, 1864)

Hutchings, A., *Church Music in the Nineteenth Century* (London: Herbert Jenkins, 1949)

Irving, H., *Ancients and Moderns: William Crotch and the Development of Classical Music* (Aldershot: Ashgate, 1999)

Jacobs, A., *Arthur Sullivan: A Victorian Musician* (Oxford: Oxford University Press, 1984)

Johnston, J. O., *Life and Letters of Henry Parry Liddon* (London: Longmans, Green & Co., 1904)

Joyce, F. W., *The Life of Rev. Sir F. A. G. Ouseley, Bart.* (London: Methuen & Co., 1896)

Keene, D., A. Burns, & A. Saint (eds.), *St Paul's: The Cathedral Church of London, 604–2004* (New Haven: Yale University Press, 2004)

Kennedy, M., *Portrait of Elgar*, rev. and enlarged edn (London: Oxford University Press, 1982)

Keyte, H., & A. Parrott (eds.) with C. Bartlett (associate ed.), *The New Oxford Book of Carols* (Oxford: Oxford University Press, 1992)

Klein, H., *Musicians and Mummers* (London: Cassell & Co., 1925)

Lathbury, D. C., *Correspondence on Church and Religion of William Ewart Gladstone* (London: John Murray, 1910)

Laurence, D. H. (ed.), *Shaw's Music: The Complete Musical Criticism of Bernard Shaw*, 3 vols. (London: The Bodley Head, 1981)

Levien, J. M., *Impressions of W. T. Best* (London: Novello & Co., 1942)

Long, K. R., *The Music of the English Church* (London: Hodder & Stoughton, 1971)

Mackie, S. J., *Great Paul: from its Casting to its Dedication*, with a preface on bells by John Stainer (London: Griffith & Farran, 1882)

McVeagh, D. A., *Edward Elgar: His Life and Music* (London: J. M. Dent & Sons, 1955)

Magnus, L., *Herbert Warren of Magdalen: President and Friend, 1853–1930* (London: John Murray, 1932)

Matthews, W. R., & W. M. Atkins (eds.), *A History of St Pauls Cathedral and the Men Associated with it* (London: Phoenix House, 1957)

Middleton, R. D., *Dr Routh* (London: Oxford University Press, 1938)

Newmarch, R., *Mary Wakefield: A Memoir* (Kendal: Atkinson & Pollitt, 1912)

Nockles, P. B., *The Oxford Movement in Context: Anglican High Churchmanship, 1760–1857* (Cambridge: Cambridge University Press, 1994)

Northrop Moore, J., *Edward Elgar: A Creative Life* (Oxford: Oxford University Press, 1980)

Oakeley, E. M. O., *The Life of Sir Herbert Stanley Oakeley* (London: George Allen, 1904)

Parry, C. H. H., *The Art of Music* (London: Kegan Paul, Trench, Trübner & Co., 1893)

Pearce, C. W., *A Biographical Sketch of Edmund Hart Turpin* (London: The Vincent Music Company, [1911])

Pemble, J., *The Mediterranean Passion: Victorians and Edwardians in the South* (Oxford: Clarendon Press, 1987)

Pennant, D. (ed.), *Surge on!: Stainer Centenary Snapshot* (Woking: Pennant Publishing, 2001)

Plumley, N., & A. Niland, *A History of the Organs in St Paul's Cathedral* (Oxford: Positif Press, 2001)

Pole, W., *Some Short Reminiscences of Events in my Life and Work* (London: private publication, 1898)

Prestige, G. L., *St Paul's in its Glory, 1831–1911* (London: SPCK, 1955)

Pugin, A. W. N., *The Collected Letters of A. W. N. Pugin*, vol. 1: *1830–1842*, ed. M. Belcher (Oxford: Oxford University Press, 2001)

Rainbow, B., *The Choral Revival in the Anglican Church, 1839–1872* (London: Barrie & Jenkins, 1970)

Russell, W., *St Paul's under Dean Church and his Associates* (London: Francis Griffiths, 1922)

Scholes, P., *The Mirror of Music, 1844–1944: A Century of Musical Life in Britain as Reflected in the Pages of the Musical Times* (London: Novello & Co., 1947)

Shaw, W., *The Succession of Organists* (Oxford: Clarendon Press, 1994)

Somervell, A., *Sir Arthur Somervell on Music Education: His Writings, Speeches and Letters*, ed. G. Cox (Woodbridge: The Boydell Press, 2003)

Sparrow Simpson, W. J., *Memoir of the Reverend W. Sparrow Simpson* (London: Longmans, Green & Co., 1899)

—— *The History of the Anglo-Catholic Revival from 1845* (London: George Allen & Unwin, 1932)

Stanford, C. V., *Studies and Memories* (London: Archibald Constable & Co., 1908)

—— *Pages from an Unwritten Diary* (London: Edward Arnold, 1914)

Stanier, R. S., *Magdalen School: A History of Magdalen College School, Oxford* (Oxford: Basil Blackwell, 1958)

Storey, T., 'The Music of St Paul's Cathedral, 1872–1972: The Origins and Development of the Modern Cathedral Choir', 2 vols. (MMus diss., Durham University, 1998)

Sumner, W. L., *A History and Account of the Organs of St Paul's Cathedral, London* (London: Musical Opinion, 1931)

Symonds, J. A., *The Memoirs of John Addington Symonds*, ed. P. G. Kurth (London: Hutchinson, 1984)

Temperley, N., *The Music of the English Parish Church*, 2 vols. (Cambridge: Cambridge University Press, 1979)

—— (ed.), *The Blackwell History of Music in Britain*, vol. 5: *The Romantic Age, 1800–1914* (Oxford: Blackwell Reference, 1988)

Thibaut, A. F. J., *Über Reinheit der Tonkunst* (Heidelberg, 1825), trans. W. H. Gladstone as *On Purity in Musical Art* (London, John Murray, 1877)

Thistlethwaite, N., *The Making of the Victorian Organ* (Cambridge: Cambridge University Press, 1990)

Tovey, D., & G. Parratt, *Walter Parratt: Master of the Music* (London: Oxford University Press, 1941)

Tuckwell, L., *Old Magdalen Days, 1847–1877, by a Former Chorister* (Oxford: B. H. Blackwell, 1913) (with an appendix by F. M. Millward)

Tuckwell, W., *Reminiscences of Oxford* (London: Smith, Elder & Co., 1907)

Walker, E., *A History of Music in England* (Oxford: Clarendon Press, 1907), 3rd edn rev. and enlarged J. A. Westrup (Oxford: Clarendon Press, 1952)

—— *Free Thought and the Musician and Other Essays* (London: Oxford University Press, 1946)

Ward, W. R., *Victorian Oxford* (London: Frank Cass & Co., 1965)

Watson, J. R., *The English Hymn: A Critical and Historical Study* (Oxford: Oxford University Press, 1999)

West, J. E., *Cathedral Organists Past and Present* (London: Novello & Co., 1899)

Wilson, H. A.: *Magdalen College* (Chippenham: Antony Rowe, 1899; repr. London: Routledge/Thoemmes Press, 1998).

Wilson, R. M., *Anglican Chant and Chanting in England, Scotland, and America, 1660–1820* (Oxford: Oxford University Press, 1996)

Winkworth, C., *Christian Singers of Germany* (London: Macmillan & Co., 1870)

Wollenberg, S., 'Music in Nineteenth-Century Oxford', in *Nineteenth-Century British Music Studies*, vol. 1, ed. B. Zon (Aldershot: Ashgate, 1999), 201–8

—— *Music at Oxford in the Eighteenth and Nineteenth Centuries* (Oxford: Oxford University Press, 2001)

Wood, H., *My Life of Music* (London: Victor Gollancz, 1938)

Young, P., *George Grove, 1820–1900* (London: Macmillan, 1980)

Zon, B., *The English Plainchant Revival* (Oxford: Oxford University Press, 1999)

Index

Bold type indicates pages including musical examples